WHEN AMERICA TURNED

D1605884

WHEN AMERICA TURNED

RECKONING WITH
1968

DAVID WYATT

UNIVERSITY OF MASSACHUSETTS PRESS
Amherst and Boston

Copyright © 2014 by University of Massachusetts Press
All rights reserved
Printed in the United States of America

ISBN 978-1-62534-061-0 (paper); 060-3 (hardcover)

Designed by Sally Nichols
Set in Berkeley Oldstyle
Printed and bound by IBT / Hamilton, Inc.

Library of Congress Cataloging-in-Publication Data

Wyatt, David, 1948–
When America turned : reckoning with 1968 / David Wyatt.
pages cm
Includes bibliographical references and index.
ISBN 978-1-62534-061-0 (pbk. : alk. paper) — ISBN 978-1-62534-060-3
(hardcover : alk. paper) 1. United States—History—1961–1969. 2. United States—
Politics and government—1963–1969. 3. Vietnam War, 1961–1975—Influence.
4. United States—Civilization—1945– 5. Nineteen sixty-eight, A.D. I. Title.
E846.W93 2014
973.922—dc23
2013035136

British Library Cataloguing-in-Publication Data
A catalogue record for this book is available from the British Library.

To Ann and to Luke,
for bravery

Contents

Acknowledgments

In the writing of this book two friends gave me essential support. Howard Norman cheered me on at every turn and urged me gently but firmly to revisit many missed opportunities. I will always remember with a smile his morning greeting, on those days when I stayed over at his home in Chevy Chase, as he met me at the stairs waving pages of manuscript and saying, "Wyatt, just one more thing . . ." What he wanted me to add, in almost every case, was more heart.

Bob Schultz, the most thoughtful and considerate of readers, once again found a way to unpack my condensations into followable prose. He deserves credit for my not having more often fallen for the usual mistake of claiming too little or claiming too much.

My sister Meleesa Wyatt gave my pages her usual warm response as well as the benefit of her copy editor's eye. She remains for me an inspiring example of the committed and lifelong reader.

Jay and Ann Hill, the most pleasant of traveling companions, deserve thanks for insisting on a trip to Southeast Asia that was to provide me with an epilogue.

I am grateful to Bob Brugger at Johns Hopkins University Press for sending my manuscript to University of Massachusetts Press. It was a fortunate day when I reached out to this old friend.

It has been a great pleasure to work with the crew at East Experiment Station, and my thanks go out to Bruce Wilcox, for running such a smooth operation, to Sally Nichols, for her lovely book design, to Mary Bellino, for her superb copyediting, to Carol Betsch, for help with last things, and above all to Clark Dougan, who, as a fellow student of 1968, proved the ideal editor.

Permission to quote from "The Last Spring at Yale," originally published in *The Virginia Quarterly Review,* and from "Living out the Sixties," originally published in *The Hopkins Review,* is gratefully acknowledged.

My home institution, the University of Maryland, generously supported this project with a RASA award.

Finally, I am happy to dedicate my book to my wife and to my son.

Preface
Two Speeches

This is a book bracketed by two speeches, one given by Lyndon Johnson in 1968 and one not given by John Kerry in 2004. Each of these will be discussed in the pages that follow. I want to begin, however, with another pair of speeches, one given and one not given. In the yet-to-be-given speech, an American president refuses to enter a land war in Asia *because* of "the hard lessons of Vietnam." The president would not claim that the country had moved beyond Vietnam. Instead, he would issue a call for an understanding of the complex causes and legacies of that war. He might speak of this effort as "the work we are in," to use Lincoln's phrase, a work as consequential for the future health of the nation as are our continuing and agonizing reappraisals of the meaning and consequences of the Civil War. And he would acknowledge that the division in the American house caused by that war involved another house as well, one inhabited by the people of Vietnam.

This once and future speech will in no way resemble the one given by Barack Obama on Memorial Day, 2012. Standing before the Vietnam Veterans Memorial and speaking to an audience consisting largely of veterans of that war, he took the occasion to applaud them for their service and to make certain promises. Never again, he said, will we send our soldiers into combat without giving them "a clear mission," "a sound strategy," and "the equipment they need to get the job done." (Ronald Reagan had made a similar claim in the 1980 speech in which he coined the phrase "Vietnam syndrome": "We will never again ask young men to fight and possibly die in a war our government is afraid to let them win.") Obama went so far as to tell his audience, "You won every major battle you fought in." In speaking about "how we treated our troops who served there," the president claimed that "you came home and sometimes were denigrated, when you should have been celebrated."

Such claims gave prevailing myths about the war the status of fact. Moreover, "the hard lessons of Vietnam," as the president called them, were treated as instrumental, as if adopting a set of best practices would somehow have altered the outcome. The question of whether the war should have been fought at all was once again obscured by diverting attention to how it might have been more effectively prosecuted.

As with the Civil War, serious minds are still debating the causes, meanings, and outcomes of the Vietnam War. While I held then—in the 1960s—and hold now strong views on the war, I also understand that people of good will sought to prosecute it for reasons they deemed honorable. What made the war so painful at the time and has made the subsequent fighting about it so impossible to stop is the profound division among Americans it created and continues to sustain. It may be most useful to look on the war as the story of two conflicting goods. There were the demands of the nation-state and its dedicated leader, Creon, and the demands of the aggrieved and resisting individual, Antigone. The conflicting demands were felt on one's pulses; in living through the Vietnam years, it was all too possible to feel torn between a searing love for one's country and the sense—one needing to be acted on—that she had also lost her way.

Let me say this at the outset: I do not believe that Vietnam was a war the United States could or should have won. But I do attempt in the pages that follow to enter into the thoughts and feelings and above all the *words* of those who thought of the war as a good fight. If I seem at times to take the side of those who believed in the domino theory or in a U.S.-driven world order, it is because I believe empathy has proven a capacity in short supply in the side-taking over Vietnam. "Empathy," a quality put forward by Robert McNamara as crucially lacking in the American experience of Vietnam, is also the capacity essential to the writing of an answerable history of those burning days.

To return to my two speeches: On March 31, 1968, Lyndon Johnson announced to the country that he would not seek nor would he accept his party's nomination for another term as president. "There is division in the American house now," he declared. He was therefore setting ambition aside in order to avoid becoming "involved in the partisan divisions that are developing in this political year." When Barack Obama spoke of "division among Americans" forty-four years later, he was echoing Johnson's words, words harking back to Abraham Lincoln's 1858 speech about "a house divided." The force and meaning of such refigurations across time are central to the argument of my book.

Johnson made his announcement at the end of a speech about Vietnam. The speech came as his response to the humiliations of the January Tet Offensive, to Senator Eugene McCarthy's strong showing as a Democratic candidate in the New Hampshire primary, and to Robert Kennedy's having entered the presidential race two weeks earlier. Johnson's speech marked, in fact, the beginning of the end; while U.S. troop levels in Vietnam would continue to climb in the ensuing months, and while 1968 would prove the bloodiest year of the war, it was clear after March 1968 that the war was one from which the country was trying to extricate itself rather than one it was trying to win.

In the fall of 2004, during his campaign for the presidency, Senator John Kerry was attacked by a group calling itself Swift Boat Veterans for Truth. Advertisements sponsored by the group claimed that Kerry had falsified his service record while commanding a patrol boat in Vietnam. They also maintained that on returning from the war he had betrayed his fellow service members by joining with other veterans to protest the conduct of the war. Given the threat to his candidacy represented by these attacks, as well as the importance to the national narrative of a story about a man who had both fought in the war and then fought against it, Kerry was called on to give a speech standing by what he had done. In the speech, and using his own experience as a template, the American experience in Vietnam was to be acknowledged as a tragedy rather than as a lost cause, or a *trahison des clercs,* or "a mistake."

Of course Kerry never gave such a speech. How he might have done so, along with all that stood in the way of such a reckoning, is the story of this book.

WHEN AMERICA TURNED

INTRODUCTION
The Turning

I turned twenty in 1968, the year in which the country, perhaps once and for all, broke its own heart. In reflecting back on that gone time at the age of sixty-three, it is now clear that a great divide then began to open up in American life, one that seems to grow deeper with every passing day. What came to feel like a long, complicated, and bitter divorce has left our children looking on at our public life with baffled wonder. Norman Mailer, ever alert to the convergence of the personal and the political, deploys just such a metaphor in *The Armies of the Night* (1968). He is marching arm and arm with Robert Lowell toward the "heart" of the nation's power when "the sense of America divided on this day now liberated some undiscovered patriotism in Mailer so that he felt a sharp searing love for his country in this moment and on this day, crossing some divide in his own mind wider than the Potomac, a love so lacerated he felt as if a marriage were being torn and children lost." Feeling as though he has stepped through some crossing in the reaches of space between this moment "and the Civil War," Mailer honors the rhyme across centuries, one in which the seventh decade is destined to mark an intense time of ideological, intergenerational, and interracial conflict. It is a family fight, as wrenching as a divorce. Mailer thus understands his suddenly recognized love as also bound up with an imminent sense of loss: "Never does one love so much as then, obviously then."

I have spent a fair amount of my adult life pondering my own conflicted love for my country, and attempted, in 1993, to put my thoughts into print in *Out of the Sixties: Storytelling and the Vietnam Generation.* There I tried to answer a simple question: What have we—Americans born between Pearl Harbor and Ike's election—given to the culture? My answer took the form of close readings of ten literary careers. But the answer provided now appears to me to have been insufficiently historical, failing to supply the context out of which these artistic performances arose. I treated art as belonging to a world apart.

Then came John Kerry's defeat in the presidential election of 2004. How was it that a decorated hero of an earlier Asian war proved unable to attract more votes than a man who had dealt with the most agonizing choice of his youth by finding himself a stateside sinecure? From where I stood, it looked as if Kerry had done two honorable things: he had fought in the Vietnam War, and then he had fought against it. It was brave to go, and it was brave to reconceive his action as contributing to a terrible and ongoing "mistake." His behavior—then, in the late sixties and early seventies—modeled a capacity for self-critique largely absent in our public life. It also embodied the power of the concerned young to change the course of American history. Yet when Kerry came to run for the presidency, and against a man who had neither fought in the war nor fought against it, he was unable to find the words to express the meaning and value of his and his generation's complex fate. This act of self-silencing, along with the ongoing influences of the old debates in a new wartime, made clear to me the need to find adequate words—and occasioned my second attempt to do so.

I wanted to see whether my reading and writing could somehow yield a narrative capable of building a bridge—Mailer himself is crossing the Memorial Bridge when he makes his discovery of an America divided—between our dispirited national moment and the richly confused year in which Mailer published his book. I knew, above all, that I had to deal with the iceberg still cruising through our dreams, with the Vietnam War. "I had to explore the ground again," as John Laurence writes in *The Cat from Hué* (2002). "Part of the process was to figure out what could not be understood while the war was being fought: the secret history of the war, the hidden agendas of the participants, the truth behind the lies and propaganda."

Standing in the way of any serious answer were forty years of "polemical cartoonization of the era," a process carefully detailed in Bernard von Bothmer's *Framing the Sixties* (2010). As early as 1980 Harris Wofford could write, in *Of Kennedys and Kings,* that "revisionist historians and ideologues" had already managed to install in the popular mind a "widespread misreading of that curious and critical decade." In a recent attempt at debunking, *The Sixties Unplugged* (2008), the historian Gerard J. DeGroot dismisses the sixties as "an era of magnificent futility." In her 1996 Jefferson Lecture, Toni Morrison issued an eloquent plea against this continuing assault: "Killing the Sixties, turning that decade into an aberration, an exotic malady ripe with excess, drugs and disobedience is designed to bury its central features—emancipation, generosity, acute political awareness and a sense of shared and mutually responsible society." For those who find Morrison's plea compelling—*Yes, surely, this is the case*—assent then gives way to a further question: But where to find out what had really happened?

One place to explore is the play of the competing discourses, the immense outpouring of imaginative literature, historical scholarship, new and old journalism, and personal reflection that has further complicated—as it has constructed—our sense of those burning days. In other words, *in words*. If willfully falsifying and reductive words have converted one of the most intense years in American history into a cartoon of itself, only more answerable and accurate words can recover a usable past.

It was Richard Nixon, in his first inaugural address, who referred to 1968 as "a fever of words," just as it was Nixon who maintained in a 1977 interview that "what history says about this administration will depend upon who writes history." It is unlikely that Nixon meant to make a case for written histories as a set of vying mediations; no doubt he hoped that his versions of the past, articulated in the seven books he published after resigning the presidency, would someday "win" and be accepted as fact. But Nixon's observation does comprise one more instance of the ways in which the word "history" became during this period a noun of charged and mounting significance. Mailer was to give *The Armies of the Night* the subtitle "History as a Novel/The Novel as History," as if to conflate two distinct modes of prose. In 1973, Robert Lowell brought out *History,* a gathering of unrhymed sonnets seeking to capture in poetry everything from "The Pacification of Columbia" to "Election Night." Michael Herr was to draw a crucial distinction between "straight" and "secret history" in *Dispatches* (1977), his anguished and passionate memoir about living through 1968 in Vietnam. Each of these writers produced what we call "literature," and each also made a claim for the power of literature to tell "history" in a unique and authoritative way.

The nation's imaginative writers have provided its citizens with many of the most moving and enduring histories of 1968, a history still being written. Three examples may suffice. The "grief" Robert Kennedy spoke about so publicly during his campaign, and that gave him the power to deliver his great impromptu elegy for Martin Luther King Jr. on the evening of April 4, 1968, is fully fathomed in a novel, Don DeLillo's *Libra* (1988). The cost of the cover-up of the My Lai massacre (it occurred on March 16, 1968), an act that multiplied the pain and guilt caused by the actual event, is powerfully summoned in another novel, Tim O'Brien's *In the Lake of the Woods* (1994). And the racial subtext of the August 1968 police riot in Chicago is painfully evoked in a third novel, Saul Bellow's *The Dean's December* (1982). Each of these writers makes a profound study of the American past, and each asks his reader to confront truths about the nation a work of the imagination can best compel.

These three novels focus on a moment of turning occurring in 1968. The word "turning" is John Kerry's, and comes from his 1971 statement before the Senate Committee on Foreign Relations. Kerry ended his remarks with a wish that

> when 30 years from now our brothers go down the street without a leg, without an arm, or a face, and small boys ask why, we will be able to say "Vietnam" and not mean a desert, not a filthy obscene memory, but mean instead the place where America finally turned and where soldiers like us helped it in the turning.

The turning Kerry imagines also has a second coming, a future moment decades down the road in which a rearticulation might occur. In that future, he hopes, "we will be able to say" something. Kerry imagines an ongoing national project of self-definition, one requiring us to assign new meanings to big words. "Vietnam" is the keyword for Kerry. But he could as easily have said "New Hampshire," or "Memphis," or "Chicago," words which, since 1968, have acquired a haunted and contested place in American memory. And Kerry's failure to say *Vietnam* in the way he had hoped—his inability to speak back to the Swift-Boaters in effective and eloquent words during his 2004 presidential campaign—marks a crucial recent instance of how successfully one set of narrators has come to control, for many Americans, a sense of that time and place.

Of course the turbulent events occurring in the United States in 1968 did not happen in isolation. As Tariq Ali and Susan Watkins write, "It was a year that marked an entire generation." Soviet tanks invaded Prague in the week before the Democratic convention began in Chicago, bringing an end to socialism with a human face; in Mexico, ten days before the opening of the Summer Olympics, government troops shot into a crowd of unarmed students, killing over fifty; in France, the student protests beginning in May sparked wildcat strikes throughout the country; in Pakistan, a student move-ment helped overthrow a military dictator and led to the establishment of Bangladesh; and in China, the Cultural Revolution ended in a retrenchment as

Mao Zedong set out to dismantle the Red Guards. Jeremi Suri, Jeremy Varon, Samantha Christiansen, and Zachary Scarlett have each produced compelling accounts of this global upheaval. While my focus falls on events occurring in the United States and in Southeast Asia, the work of these scholars and many others reminds us that for anyone seeking an understanding of an unprecedented year, "relations stop nowhere."

While for those of us who lived through 1968 in the United States the great public events arrived as a series of shocks, they can be made to take on, in retrospect, a pattern of linked and successive consequence. This apparent pattern of determining linkage can work to obscure the fact that any account of the past is a rearrangement of it. In order therefore to leave the question of act and consequence as open as possible, I have chosen to adopt a chronological approach to the story and to deploy the political events of 1968 as the spine of my narrative. In doing so, was I not simply following the lead of Henry Adams? "Historians," as he argues in *The Education* (1907), "undertake to arrange sequences,—called stories, or histories,—assuming in silence a relation of cause and effect." The result, in the case of my arrangement, may appear to be a sequence of overdetermined outcomes.

The scandal of the Tet Offensive in January led directly to Robert McNamara's February reassessment of the U.S. bombing campaign in Vietnam and to Eugene McCarthy's "moral victory" in New Hampshire. The Democratic primary was then followed by Robert Kennedy's decision to declare for the presidency and Lyndon Johnson's March 31 speech in which he announced his decision not to seek another term. On the very day of Kennedy's announcement, Lieutenant William Calley took his platoon into a village called My Lai. Martin Luther King Jr. was shot in Memphis on April 4, and riots followed in Washington, D.C., and cities throughout the country. The gathering storm included a student strike at Columbia; Kennedy was assassinated a month later. The disarray of the Democratic Party culminated in the police riots in Chicago and ensured the election of Richard Nixon, a candidate who had meanwhile consented to the manipulation of the outcome by having his people, working through Henry Kissinger and Anna Chennault, convince the president of South Vietnam to boycott the Paris peace talks. Two weeks after Nixon was elected, Lieutenant John Kerry arrived in Vietnam.

The sequence I have just arranged seems to point to an inevitable outcome—the election of Richard Nixon. A closer look at the evidence reveals this outcome to be contingent, not fated, one subject to all the vagaries of human action and intention. "It was a year," write Nancy Zaroulis and Gerald Sullivan about

1968, "in which events cropped up so quickly, hammer blow after hammer blow, that in retrospect it seems astonishing that the national psyche survived intact." A more useful word than *causality*, then, and one that reveals my focal year as exemplary rather than unique, is the word *compression*. Writing for the *New York Review of Books* in April 1968, Andrew Kopkind maintained that "these weeks" since the shock of the January Tet Offensive seem "a revolutionary time in which things fall rapidly out of place and historical space is compressed." My task has been to rearticulate this felt sense of compression and to work within the knowledge that any attempt at recovery can only be accomplished, as Kerry suggests, by way of what we find ourselves "able to say" about it.

In a lecture we have come to know as "On Poesy or Art," Coleridge makes a distinction between "form as proceeding and shape as superinduced." There is a kind of writing that moves forward as a discovery process, and a kind that is governed by conclusions already reached. While I have aimed to create a "form as proceeding" in the pages that follow, and therefore to allow pattern and meaning to emerge, it may nevertheless be useful at this point to describe the method governing my attempt to "re-say" the past.

To take the case of the opening chapter on the Tet Offensive: this is a well-known story, or at least a story many readers will think they know. I begin by recapitulating it and rely for my account on Don Oberdorfer's *Tet!* (1971). Oberdorfer "owns" the Tet story, and I quote heavily from him. Generous quotation is central to my method: I quote in order to forward the narrative, to acknowledge the most reliable sources, and also to foreground the style and stance of the writer being quoted. In doing so, and in interweaving so many different voices, my book achieves a critical distance from the sheer question of "what happened" and becomes a study of *how* history gets told.

The voice I choose to lay alongside Oberdorfer's is Michael Herr's. The turn toward *Dispatches* at the end of chapter 1 is the key move: it is meant to argue that once the analysis is over, the therapy can begin. What does this mean? That acknowledgment of the burden and meaning of the past can best be completed by moving beyond "straight history" to the imaginative embodiment of it in literature, in words that enact as well as tell. Herr puts us in Tet in a way that Oberdorfer does not. He gets us to feel it, to go through it, in part because he is on the ground ("ground" is a key word for Herr) in an immersed and responsive way. The most important result of our moving through Herr's form as proceeding is to develop empathy. And this process—my book is all about how reading changes us—is thereafter repeatedly enacted in the chapters that follow.

Why empathy? Because the lack of it was central to our prosecution of the war in Vietnam. This is the point made by Robert McNamara in the documentary *The Fog of War* (2003). There, in his onscreen struggle to articulate why the United States lost the war, McNamara comes up with a number of answers. But the primary answer—the first one given in his list of thirteen—is that we did not do what must be done if a nation truly wishes to win a war: in order to win, you must "empathize with your enemy." Despite having already published an apologetic memoir, McNamara is still, in 2003, conceiving of the war as something that could have been won, with "empathy" as the key component of a winning strategy. His more profound and unintended point is that our lack of empathy for the Vietnamese was itself the cause of a unnecessary war that our continuing lack of empathy also made it impossible to win. In Michael Herr's words, we never took the trouble to learn *"to read"* the Vietnamese. Learning to read, to empathize with the Vietnamese other, is precisely what Herr offers us in the scene I bring forward near the end of chapter 1, the scene between Herr, the doctor, and the little girl.

My book has a gathering momentum; the chapters build on each other. By following a month-by-month sequence, I may seem to be letting chronology have its way. But something more is at work: as the various destinies and voices become intertwined, the emerging story takes on the shape and force of a tragic political novel, one with something of a surprise or at least an unlooked-for ending. In the final two chapters, as I move beyond 1968 to Watergate and the intrigues of the Nixon administration, the story begins to echo forward all the way to the 2004 presidential campaign and to the strange fate of John Kerry. His story, one both exemplary and unique, thus concludes with a piece of counterfactual history, as I enter the narrative and write a speech that would have brought Vietnam forward into the present moment of the campaign, a speech of course Kerry did not give.

As a historical actor I will already have entered the narrative a number of times along the way: when remembering the night of the first draft lottery in 1969; at the beginning of the chapter on Johnson's "I will not accept" speech; in the opening and closing pages of the chapter on the assassination of Martin Luther King Jr.; in the paragraphs in chapter 9 on Nixon and growing up in California. The point of doing so is to reinforce what is I hope evident in every sentence of my book: that *I stand in* what I write. As Nick Carraway says near the end of *The Great Gatsby,* "I am part of that." I am part of the story I am telling, not a disinterested observer but an impassioned participant. In acknowledging this, I declare my allegiance to the engaged and implicated stance taken up by writers like Norman Mailer, Michael Herr, Joan Didion, and Richard Rodriguez, rather than to some notion of an "objective" standpoint. One of the running arguments of my book holds that no such standpoint exists and that even the most carefully researched history originates in and is governed by, in Hayden White's words, "the form which is its fiction."

To acknowledge this is not to say that all accounts of the past have equal authority. One of the major offerings made in *When America Turned* is the "Works Cited" list. In choosing to quote a book, I am also saying, "Read this." The books that have made the list have been selected according to their concern for accuracy. Accuracy to what, one might ask, since I have just ceded away the notion of objectivity? To two kinds of truth: scholarly truth, to the most that can be learned from researching the surviving documents; and to imaginative truth, to the honest and self-interrogating recordings, as Joan Didion writes, of *"How it felt to me."*

For the most part, I admit into my narrative only those voices that aim at such accuracy. But of course the story would not be complete without attending to writing by public figures "too big to fail" of being included, figures like Johnson, McCarthy, McNamara, Nixon, Kissinger. These men are skillful writers indeed, and my approach in each case has been to unpack the ways in which their self-defensive accounts of the past also succeed in being self-revealing. In their attempts to rationalize what can only be described, and in terms they themselves might employ, as a massive case of mismanagement, the memoirs these historical actors have left behind only render more urgent Robert Lowell's call, one made in "Epilogue": "Why not say what happened?"

In order to answer Lowell's call, I have created a kind of call-and-response between the voices of the usual suspects and those that have for too long gone unattended. To do this is to engage in an act of canon (re)formation, not a replacing of one set of testimonies with another, but a setting of the familiar alongside the heretofore unknown or underread text. In the pages that follow, I attend to the voices of professional historians like George Herring and Becky Nicolaides, speechmakers and speechwriters like Martin Luther King Jr. and Raymond Price, journalists like Jonathan Schell and Jules Witcover, new journalists like Joan Didion and John Hersey, memoirists like Le Ly Hayslip, Eldridge Cleaver, and Richard Rodriguez, and articulate activists like David Harris and Mark Naison.

The category of articulate activism deserves special comment. A significant number of young Americans seeking to bring about change through direct action during the 1960s also chose to write about the experience. These figures typically occupy a middle ground between the extremes—between the Reaction and the New Left—that have dominated the discourse about the sixties into our own day. In choosing to give their stories and their words a central role in my narrative, I distinguish my book from other accounts of that time and place and also demonstrate that the productive lives many of these articulate activists went on to live were the deserved harvest of a difficult seed-time. What they had been was integrated into what they went on to become.

In Edward P. Morgan's terms, the articulate activist was at once "instrumental" and "expressive." He or she acted, and he or she also wrote. These attempts to say what happened each repay the kind of attention I give to Herr's *Dispatches* or to Karnow's *Vietnam* (1983), and the best among them seek out a unique "form as proceeding." As Hayden White argues, "there is something in" any serious work of history "that cannot be negated, and this nonnegatable element is its form, the form which is its fiction."

Of course my history has a form which is its fiction as well. I departed from the conviction, one sustained by fifty years of studying literature, that thinking involves thinking against oneself and standing back from what one has come to know. The workers with words I have come to trust and to admire all answer to Thoreau's difficult call: "With thinking we may be beside ourselves in a sane sense." In the four years it took me to write this book, I appear to have converted this conviction into its most urgent subject.

Near the end of *A Tale of Two Utopias* (1996), Paul Berman invokes a "strange wavering" in the thought of his subjects, thinkers who can never settle on "history's final destination." In this wavering Berman discerns "a kind of poetry," the expression of "an impossible mix of hope and dismay." While for some, like Hans Koning, "the essence of 1968 was a clarity of perception," that year also confronted and still confronts many thinking Americans with an array of difficult if not insoluble conflicts, so much so that to think and to write about it can lead to a kind of wavering. To stand on both sides of a question, to find oneself caught between irreconcilable imperatives, to feel "lacerated" as Mailer does in attempting to bridge inner and outer divides—was not this the human stance the times so clearly called for?

Thinking-as-wavering is inherently self-challenging and self-critical. The criticism begins at home, and then extends itself out to the body politic. "Some damn mistake had been made," Mailer admits in *The Armies of the Night,* and the word "mistake" is repeated in writings by Michael Herr, and

Ben Stavis, and John Kerry. The capacity to admit error—to move the admission out of the passive voice, as Mailer so quickly does, in the scene in the Ambassador Theater's men's room—and then to change course becomes the best evidence, among the characters I summon, that they are thinking. It also models on the level of the individual soul what a citizenry might attempt.

The downside of thinking-as-wavering is to appear to produce a country in which the best lack all conviction while the worst are full of passionate intensity. The words are from Yeats's "The Second Coming," the poem from which Joan Didion quarried the title of *Slouching Towards Bethlehem* (1968), her brooding meditation on the atomization of the late sixties. But as Didion knew then, and as our strongest writers have continued to know ever since, such a mordant view only appears to be the case if one consents to the view that life is all about winning.

Most of the stories told in the following chapters are about defeat. Even those who "win"—Nixon and Agnew, for instance—eventually fall, and are consigned to an obloquy far worse than losing an election. Above all, the nation loses a war. Why and how it was lost remain a subject of debate, but that it was lost cannot be denied. Living out that defeat has proven a grave moral and political challenge, one the country has struggled to meet. A good deal of this continuing reluctance *to accept failure* derives from our refusal to surrender our innocence. As long as we turn away from a knowing rather than an opinionated take on our past, we will remain imprisoned by a self-defeating belief in our own and our nation's purity of intent. We meant well; we therefore deserved to win; we therefore cannot have lost. But the thinking writers summoned in this book know better. With Didion, they know that "the ability to think for one's self depends upon one's mastery of the language," and that such mastery is inherently self-critical. For the worker in words, the ongoing work of the imagination is to aspire to the rejection of error and the embrace of truth by way of which, as William Blake claims, "a Last Judgment passes" upon an individual. Thinking as Blake and as Thoreau and the courageous imaginations assembled here come to engage in it thus involves an experience of continual self-reckoning, a seeking and a finding of the wished-for words.

CHAPTER

1

Tet

In Vietnam, before the American War changed everything, Tet was the biggest holiday of the year. From all over the country, as the twelfth lunar month neared its close, people returned to their home villages to honor the family tombs and to feast on rice cakes and soybean soup. As a defense against ill fortune, some families erected a tree made from bamboo branches. At the end of a week, as the first day of Tet—the new year—approached, fireworks were set off to drive away evil spirits. Once the year turned, another round of celebrations began, some involving the veneration of Vietnamese military heroes. Combining elements of Thanksgiving, Christmas, New Year, and the Fourth of July, the full span of Tet could consume two weeks of Vietnamese life. In 1968, Lunar New Year's Day fell on January 30.

On January 31, at 2:47 a.m. Vietnamese time, a Peugeot truck and a taxicab approached the United States Embassy in Saigon. Enclosed by a masonry rocket shield, the embassy had opened in 1967. The compound contained lawns, gardens, a parking lot, a villa, small outbuildings, and the six-story Chancery building. Members of the C-10 Battalion of the National Liberation Front (NLF) began firing from the taxicab at the two MPs guarding the embassy's night gate, while those in the truck began unloading explosive materials. After blowing a three-foot hole in the compound wall, the invaders quickly entered the embassy grounds. Four American defenders died within five minutes, while the Vietnamese policemen assigned to guard duty either hid or ran away.

The Chancery building itself was defended by three U.S. Marines. The most powerful weapon in their possession was an Italian submachine gun. The NLF attacked with rifle fire, antitank guns, and fragmentation grenades. The first AP bulletin about the firefight went out at 3:15 a.m., at about the time twenty Marines arrived to retake the embassy.

With fire now coming largely from outside the compound, the Americans inside the Chancery building found themselves cut off from the fighting, while being kept busy fielding phone calls from the White House, the State Department, and bases around Vietnam. Around 5 a.m., a helicopter carrying men from the 101st Airborne tried and failed to land on the Chancery roof. A second chopper brought in ammunition and carried off three men. The ammunition was for an M-16, although none of the Americans inside possessed such a weapon.

When NBC news picked up the story, it mistakenly reported NLF fighters as having taken the Chancery building. As the sun began to come up, U.S. military police used a jeep to ram through the still-locked front gate. Soon after an Airborne helicopter succeeded in landing on the Chancery roof, UPI repeated and expanded on NBC's mistaken report, claiming that the attackers had penetrated the five first floors of the building.

So what we had, by dawn's early light, was a failure not only of American power but of American knowledge. As Michael Herr was to write, in *Dispatches*, "Conventional journalism could no more reveal this war than conventional firepower could win it, all it could do was take the most profound event of the American decade and turn it into a communications pudding." Given the shock and chaos of those early hours, it was perhaps expecting too much to have asked for more. As the Tet Offensive unfolded, over the next twenty-five days, the press would go on, at times, to distinguish itself, as in Edie Adams's photograph of Brigadier General Nguyen Ngoc Loan shooting a prisoner in the head at point blank range, or in CBS news anchor Walter Cronkite's painfully reluctant claim, made on the evening news two days after the retaking of Hué, Vietnam's old imperial capital, that the only rational way out of the war was "to negotiate, not as victors, but as an honorable people who lived up to their pledge to defend democracy, and did the best they could."

The U.S. embassy was held by the NLF for a little over six hours. A UPI reporter, finding the adequate words, called it "a butcher shop in Eden."

General William Westmoreland, commander of U.S. forces in Vietnam from 1965 to 1968, toured the compound and reported nineteen enemy dead. The figure was later revised downward to fifteen. When Ambassador Ellsworth Bunker arrived, he declared the attack unsuccessful because the NLF were "never able to enter the Chancery building." On February 2, twenty-three days before the last enemy forces were cleared from Hué, President Johnson declared that the Tet incursions had been, militarily at least, a "complete failure."

It is true that the general uprising envisioned by Hanoi as a response to Tet did not materialize. The NLF officer who could have coordinated the attack on Saigon managed to absent himself from the city. The assault on Independence Palace (headquarters of South Vietnam's president, Nguyen Van Thieu) was repulsed, while a lieutenant colonel in the Army of the Republic of Vietnam (ARVN) managed to cut off the audio feed after the NLF captured the city's radio station. The big attack on the Joint General Staff complex, home to Air Marshal Nguyen Cao Ky, was beaten back.

Ngo Vinh Long has written the seminal article on the NLF's experience of 1968. After extensive interviewing of guerrilla participants, Long concluded that NLF fighters "achieved dramatic gains while receiving relatively light casualties" during the first phase of Tet—the phase that has come to be known as the Tet Offensive. The planned offensive was, however, "composed of three phases, lasting until October of that year." In the second and third of these phases the Politburo made the mistake of leaving revolutionary units "too long in forward positions and urban areas, where they were subjugated to horrendous air and artillery strikes." In addition, "the Vietnamese leadership in Hanoi made one of the biggest errors in the war by ordering the remnants of the revolutionary units to retreat to the border areas of Cambodia and Laos to regroup." An entire grassroots infrastructure in the South was thereby abandoned, and, as a consequence, for the NLF "1969 and 1970 were the two most difficult years in the entire war." Only by returning to the strategy of "clinging to the post (remaining close to the people)" was the NLF eventually able to rebuild connections between villagers and its members and so to return to effective fighting strength by 1971.

To call Tet a "failure" is, however, not only to bracket out the obvious victory it achieved in the realm of public opinion, but also the arresting scale of the undertaking, one that bespoke a will to risk and to sacrifice. The Tet Offensive involved coordinated attacks by the People's Army of Vietnam (PAVN) and the NLF along an eight-hundred-mile front. The attackers invaded thirteen provincial capitals in the Mekong Delta. They deployed some four thousand men in Saigon, not only overrunning the embassy but burning down the radio station and conducting firefights in the city for two weeks. Having surrounded the U.S. Marine outpost at Khe Sanh in mid-January, the North Vietnamese sat tight while Westmoreland airlifted in six thousand Marines and increased the supporting troops between Hué and Khe Sanh to forty thousand. As American energies in the north were diverted by the siege of Khe Sanh, the enemy then struck at the old imperial capital.

The battle for Hué was to become, as Don Oberdorfer writes in *Tet!* (1971), the "bloodiest ground action of the Tet Offensive." Rebuilt in the nineteenth century to replicate Peking, Hué was a lovely town of gardens and palaces lying along the Perfume River. Of all the targets hit during the offensive, as Westmoreland was to admit, Hué "may well have been the least prepared for what lay in store."

Infiltrated by at least eight NLF and PAVN battalions on the night of January 30, most of the city lay in enemy hands by daylight. A small band of Marines still held the U.S. command compound. Retaking Hué would involve house-to-house fighting in chilly rain. Only on February 24 did the Black Panther Company of the ARVN rip down the NLF flag that had flown for almost a month over the wall of the old imperial citadel.

Near the end of World War II, as U.S. bombers pounded Japan, Secretary of War Henry Stimson intervened to insure that Kyoto, Japan's old imperial capital, would be spared. In "saving" Hué, U.S. forces showed no such restraint. The combat photographer David Douglas Duncan was to write that "the Americans pounded the citadel and surrounding city almost to dust with air strikes, napalm runs, artillery and naval gunfire, and the direct cannon fire from tanks and recoilless rifles." As Michael Herr saw it, "We took space back quickly, expensively, with total panic and close to maximum brutality. Our machine was devastating. And versatile. It could do everything but stop." When the Marines finally recaptured the city, 80 percent of its buildings were destroyed, and three-quarters of its inhabitants were homeless.

The United States went to the war in the service of a metaphor, what came to be known as "the domino theory." The theory received one of its early formulations by Dean Acheson, then serving as under secretary of state. In *Present at the Creation* (1969), Acheson recalls words spoken before Congress in response to the "crisis" of 1947, when Soviet pressure was seen to be bearing down on Greece: "Like apples in a barrel infected by one rotten one, the corruption of Greece would infect Iran and all to the east. It would also carry infection to Africa through Asia Minor and Egypt, and to Europe through Italy and France." One of the most striking things about Acheson's metaphor, where apples have not yet been replaced by dominos, is its implied sense of momentum. Given the logic of the domino metaphor, where does it stop? And once a mind had submitted to this logic, how would it be able to step aside from the implicit call to stand firm in the face of an inevitable fall?

In 1954, President Eisenhower invoked the "falling domino principle" in some comments on Southeast Asia. By the same year, the United States was paying 75 percent of the costs incurred by the French military in its war against the Viet Minh. With the French surrounded at Dien Bien Phu, Eisenhower resorted again to the metaphor: "You have a row of dominos set up. You knock over the first one, and what will happen to the last one is a certainty." Dien Bien Phu fell a month later, and the French sued for terms.

At the peace conference in Geneva, Vietnam was divided at the 17th parallel into two separate and provisional governments, the Democratic Republic of Vietnam (DRV) in the north under Ho Chi Minh, the south under Bao Dai, who had been installed by the French as chief of state in 1949. The Geneva Agreements envisioned South and North Vietnam as regroupment zones; as John Prados argues, "National status was explicitly *denied* them. They were to be reunited by a political process and *then* become a nation." The political process envisioned was a unifying election to be held in 1956. Ho Chi Minh looked likely to win any election, and Ngo Dien Diem, who became president of the new Republic of Vietnam (RVN) in 1955, rejected the plan. In *Mandate for Change* (1963), Eisenhower was to write that "had elections been held . . . possibly 80 percent of the population would have voted for the Communist Ho Chi Minh."

Townsend Hoopes served as under secretary of the Air Force from 1967 to 1969. In *The Limits of Intervention* (1969), Hoopes writes of a Washington "predisposed to view an effort to overthrow the existing order *anywhere* as a national-liberation war fomented by and for the benefit of Russia or China." The key word here is *predisposed.* By the years of the Johnson presidency, the domino metaphor had taken on a life of its own. In *Counsel to the President* (1991), Clark Clifford recalls a July 1965 meeting in which Secretary of Defense Robert McNamara, as if channeling Dean Acheson, replied to a comment about Vietnam "with the most extreme version of the domino theory that I had ever heard: 'Laos, Cambodia, Thailand, Burma, Malaysia are all at immediate risk. For two or three years, communist domination would stop there, but the ripple effect would be great—in Japan, and India. . . . Ayub Khan would move closer to China. . . . Communist agitation would increase in Africa.'"

Metaphors like the domino theory acquire the status of complex arguments; they become tools to think with. This is why the American poet Hart Crane can write about "the logic of metaphor." In their attempts to compare one thing to another, metaphors also call on the mind to consider how two things are alike—and different. Above all, they must stand the test of experience; metaphors are trials, essays, attempts, and when the approximations they assert no longer comport with the evidence, they must be discarded. As T. S. Eliot writes, "last year's words belong to last year's language / And next year's words await another voice." Poetry—all literary language—remains useful not only because it provides a store of living metaphors, but because it helps us clear away the dead ones, encouraging in its continual refigurings a critical attitude toward the act of the mind that generates our necessary and determining figures of speech.

By 1965, the domino theory had become a dead metaphor, preempting rather than inciting thought. (Reflecting back in 1995, former national security adviser McGeorge Bundy would call the domino theory "an extraordinarily unfitting simile.") It "predisposed" someone using it toward certain conclusions about geopolitics. The theory rested on an image of toppling tiles beginning in the Soviet Union, which knocked down China, then Vietnam, then Cambodia and Laos, then Thailand, then Malaysia, and on to Indonesia and beyond. The theory assumed a concerted motion running from north to south. But how many Americans in 1968 knew of the flaw in the theory, the fact that China and Vietnam had rarely acted in concert, and were in fact historical enemies? Robert Schulzinger begins his *A Time for War* (1997) by noting that for the Vietnamese, the fight against the Americans "represented the latest phase of a centuries-long, even millennial, effort to define themselves and cast out invaders."

The Chinese first entered the Red River Delta in 207 B.C. The mix of tribes occupying the future country of Vietnam eventually adopted Chinese religions, technology, and writing. It is difficult to fix the date at which the Vietnamese began thinking of themselves as distinct and also independent from the empire to the north, but a conservative guess would place the date near the beginning of the second millennium. The Trung sisters had risen against the Chinese as early as 40 A.D. While over the centuries the Vietnamese did absorb much of Chinese culture, having to face its military incursions also bred in them a fierce sense of political solidarity. So deep was Ho Chi Minh's mistrust of China that in 1945 he accepted a plan to allow the French to reoccupy the north, in order to drive out the occupying Chinese. "The white man is finished in Asia," he told his critics. "But if the Chinese stay now, they will never go. As for me, I prefer to sniff French shit for five years than eat Chinese shit for the rest of my life."

On a spring day in 1966, Daniel Ellsberg, then apprenticing in political warfare under General Edward Lansdale, found himself driving from Da Nang to Hoi An. "Along the road was an unusual succession of abandoned fortifications." First he saw Popular Front outposts, mud forts built to protect local hamlets from the NLF. They had been recently abandoned. Then he came to pillboxes of "another kind, better constructed and made out of concrete." These had been built by the French during their attempt to regain the colony of Vietnam during the 1946–54 war. Ellsberg then discerned a "different sort" of pillbox, also concrete but rounded, like outdoor ovens. "They were Japanese, built when the Japanese had pacified the area" in World War II. Finally, he came to a massive knoll. It was an ancient Chinese fort, constructed when the Chinese "had pacified Vietnam . . . over a period of a thousand years."

Ellsberg likens his experience to visiting "a kind of open-air museum of successive efforts by foreigners to establish their authority and control over Vietnamese." The "unusual succession" here uncovered takes on the status of a metaphor, one to set against the domino theory. It might be called "the abandoned fort theory." Rooted in Vietnam's material conditions, in the very earth of the country itself, the four fortifications are a string of historical facts that testify to the Vietnamese refusal to fall—to be anyone's domino— even China's. Able to make the clear connection, to read the terrain giving rise to the metaphor, Ellsberg at this point remembers something said to him by a Vietnamese friend. "You must understand that we are a people who think of ourselves as having defeated the Chinese, though it took us a thousand years."

To the question "Why are we in Vietnam," one answer often given was: to prevent its falling to China. Or, more narrowly, to prevent the South from falling to the North. But could the two areas above and below the 17th parallel reasonably be described as separate, sovereign countries? Neither had existed before the 1954 Geneva Agreement, when the line was drawn. And the agreement itself was premised on the expectation of future and more-or-less immediate union of the two areas through elections that, in accord with U.S. wishes, were never held. While northern and southern Vietnam did share a long history of reciprocal tensions, they also experienced a continual circulation of peoples. In 1954, as Communist elements asserted control over the North, close to one million people, many of them Catholics, fled to the South: did these people suddenly become "South" Vietnamese? North Vietnamese regulars often spent years fighting in the South. After 1954, between 50,000 and 100,000 of the party's "most loyal followers" were sent

north. In 1959, after the formation of the National Liberation Front, many
of these "regroupees" were then reinfiltrated into the South.

With so much movement of population, and with such a short and arbitrary history of division, it becomes less than plausible to think of North and
South Vietnam, in Dean Rusk's words, as "two distinct countries." George
Ball, Rusk's under secretary of state, came to believe that South Vietnam
"was never a country—merely an artificial slice of territory created by an
improvised dividing line as a diplomatic convenience to obtain the 1954
settlement." South Vietnam thus becomes "an American invention," Loren
Baritz argues, "conceived by Dwight Eisenhower but delivered by John
Kennedy." Or, as Senator William Fulbright said, in response to Rusk: "It
used to be one country."

Why Are We in Vietnam? is the title of a novel published by Norman Mailer
in 1967. In answer to the question posed in his title, Mailer comes up with
a theory as ingenious as the domino.

The story follows two pairs of fathers and sons from Texas on a bear
hunt in Alaska. They have gone north to kill some animals. At the heart of
the enterprise, Mailer speculates, may also lie powerful surgings of unacted
desire. As the sons, Tex and D.J., huddle under the blankets on their last
morning out in the wilderness, they find they cannot sleep. Breathing hard,
and "lying next to each other like two rods getting charged with magne-
tism," and then *not* acting on the "unknown panic" of the moment, they
transmute the energy of this encounter into the will to "go forth and kill."
And the best place to take this unspent energy and unplumbed dread is the
place where Mailer sends his two "hard as a hammer" young men on the
last page of his novel. As D.J. tells us: "Tomorrow Tex and me, we're off to
see the wizard in Vietnam."

"What I was saying," Mailer later concluded about his novel, "is that the
fevered egos of the men were the explanations for why we are in Vietnam."
In understanding the complex relationship of the United States and Vietnam,
ego seems a term of understanding as useful as *domino*. As fragile as it was
fevered, a number of accounts agree, this ego experienced a preoccupation
with what it means, in America, to be "men." Little sense of this burden
entered the official responses to the moment, although as early as 1958
establishment figure Arthur Schlesinger Jr. published an article in *Esquire*
titled "The Crisis of American Masculinity." Anticipating the culture of self-
help, he offered up an increase in "individual spontaneity" as a cure for the
male malaise. For the most part, however, in "conventional journalism," as

in "straight history," Herr maintains, "something wasn't answered, it wasn't even asked." The accounts willing to ask the relevant questions often lay at the extreme edge of the culture, in sites like Mailer's somewhat overheated novel.

A few weeks after the Democratic convention in Chicago, held in August 1968, Todd Gitlin wrote that "we are living through some profound crisis of masculinity." He made the claim while trying to take in the reaction of the Chicago police to the demonstrators in the streets. To use a phrase from Mailer's novel, the police had gone "insane with force." But so had some of the demonstrators, as Gitlin acknowledges: "The guy who hits hardest and moves fastest begins to look like the biggest revolutionary cock; it doesn't seem to matter whom he hits; where he runs." An excess was being expressed, on both sides, something powerful because unadmitted. The issue had surfaced as early as 1965, when Alfred Friendly of the *Washington Post* compared a SANE antiwar demonstration to the 1963 civil rights march: "The difference was a certain virility: that one had it—this one didn't."

It was also "a nation in which assertive 'New Women' were encroaching on men's traditional prerogatives." While these words certainly describe the United States in the late 1960s, they were written by Kristen Hoganson, in *Fighting for American Manhood* (1998), about the 1890s, another decade in which the country found itself in a land war in Asia. One year before Admiral Dewey steamed into Manila Bay, Alfred T. Mahan, the author of *The Interest of America in Sea Power* (1898), had urged on him and his countrymen a "manly resolve."

The crisis of masculinity extended to the highest reaches of power; when Johnson and Nixon articulated a stance toward the war, they often used words like "weak" and "pitiful" and "strong," as if it were a matter of physical measure. In 1965, as the first ground troops were being deployed, McNamara's assistant John McNaughton produced a memo on U.S. aims in Vietnam. Each objective was assigned a percentage, and the first one in the list is oddly self-regarding: "U.S. aims: 70%—To avoid a humiliating U.S. defeat (to our reputation as a guarantor)." Lyndon Johnson gave this aim perhaps its most pointed expression in a conversation with Doris Kearns Goodwin. If I had "lost" Vietnam, he asserted, Robert Kennedy would say "that I was a coward. An unmanly man. A man without a spine . . . 'Coward! Traitor! Weakling!'" "During a private conversation with some reporters who pressed him to explain why we were in Vietnam," Robert Dallek reports, "Johnson lost his patience. According to Arthur Goldberg, 'LBJ unzipped his fly, drew out his substantial organ, and declared, "This is why!"'"

Johnson and Nixon appeared to live out a disturbing competition with the physically smaller men they fought abroad, as well as the nonviolent men who marched against them in the streets at home. Did they have . . . spine? The "one full example of the masculine principle" Mailer meets on the March to the Pentagon is William Sloane Coffin, the Yale chaplain who publicly counsels the young men handing in draft cards. Coffin, at first unknown to Mailer, enters his prose as a physical presence, "a well-knit man" with a "well-dimpled chin" and a "well-balanced grin" and a "tough reedy almost barking" voice. On the steps of the Justice Department, as he begins to speak, Coffin's "sentences had a nonpoetic bony statement of meaning." James Carroll, arrested with Coffin during a later antiwar action, shared similar impressions. As Coffin began to sing, in the absolute middle of the night in a fetid D.C. jail, what Carroll heard was "an epiphany of manliness."

The solution to this widespread cultural anxiety, then as now, was not to attempt to deny it or transcend it, but to acknowledge it, to play with it and to take it in. Which is what Mailer does in his next book, *The Armies of the Night* (1968), the one in which he pursues his recognitions all the way. Mailer has come to Washington "to protest the war in Vietnam." *Why Are We in Vietnam?* is the book Mailer holds in his hand when he suddenly feels the urge "to micturate," as he arcanely puts it, and so seeks out the unlit men's room at the Ambassador Theater,

> and taking a sip of bourbon from the mug he kept to keep all fires idling right, stepped off into the darkness of the top balcony floor, went through a door into a pitch black men's room, and was alone with his need. No chance to find the light switch for he had no matches, he did not smoke. It was therefore a matter of locating what's what with the probing of his toes. He found something finally which seemed appropriate, and pleased with the precision of these generally unused senses in his feet, took aim between them at a point twelve inches ahead, and heard in the darkness the sound of his water striking the floor. Some damn mistake had been made, an assault from the side doubtless instead of the front, the bowl was relocated now, and Master of Ceremonies breathed deep of the great revelries of this utterly non-Sisyphian release—at last!!—and thoroughly enjoyed the next forty-five seconds, being left on the aftermath not a note depressed by the condition of the premises. No, he was off on the Romantic's great military dream, which is: seize defeat, convert it to triumph. Of course, pissing on the floor was bad, very bad. . . .

A man trying to relieve himself in the dark misses his aim and instead hits the floor. Out of this candid and funny embrace of awkwardness, Mailer discovers a fearful symmetry between the sole self and the body politic. In an uncanny replay of Johnson's parading of his "substantial organ," he thereby blunders carefully upon a conceit that answers the question not *why*—but the even more urgent question of *how*—we are in Vietnam.

The pissing scene is an allegory, of course, one riding on specific and detailed parallels between Mailer's performance in the men's room and his country's performance in the war: he is operating in ignorance, in the dark; he cannot locate his objective; he resorts to the Romantic's conversion of "defeat" into "triumph"; he relies on fancy words—euphemisms, really, like "micturate," when the honest verb "piss" will serve. And, once he starts, he cannot stop.

The scene in the men's room is not put forward as mere satire. It at once models a liability toward error and a corrective response to it. The passive construction "Some damn mistake had been made" mimics the decision of those who conducted the war to mystify the issue of responsibility. But when Mailer makes a mistake, he also admits it to be one.

Mailer here stakes a claim to being the essential writer of the stateside moment because in the pissing scene he makes his "manhood," however misguided, the vehicle of his ironic insight. He bravely exposes and risks the fear of abjection that participates in sending up the war. In so openly mobilizing this abjection, Mailer reminds us that education can only occur if one is willing to submit to embarrassment. The very bravado propelling the imperial self into the "pitch-black" place can be matched by having the courage of one's mistakes. Of course there has to be a willingness to "confess straight out to all aloud," a willingness Mailer repeatedly demonstrates in *The Armies of the Night*. Strength arises only from the acknowledgment of vulnerability. "From gap to gain is very American," Mailer goes on to write, and yet this is not a recognition guiding his country's foreign policy in 1968.

An anxious manliness might have given Vietnam one of its subtexts, but only an agreed-upon beginning and end could confer on the war a significant story-shape. By the time most Americans became aware of the war, it had become all middle, soliciting words like "endless," "quagmire," and "interminable." Yet to make any judgment on it, one needed some working sense of when it had started and how it might acceptably stop. As Herr asked, how was one to "date the doom"?

In 1967, at the height of administration anguish over the war, Frank Kermode published *The Sense of an Ending*. Kermode's book is a study of "fictions," of the value and power of the shape of story. "Fictions, whose ends are consonant with origins, and in concord, however unexpected, with their precedents, satisfy our needs." Admitting that we live always "in the middest," in the overcoming confusions of the present, Kermode also argues for the recognitions arising from the self-aware makings of story. All stories are constructs, things made. They can best work to our good if they include this knowledge, Kermode argues, if they present themselves as fictions rather than as myths. A myth is a construct that believes itself to be true; a fiction is a construct frankly presented as such, and offered up for our provisional use. Fictions arise from and depend on what Wallace Stevens calls "the nicer knowledge of/Belief, that what it believes in is not true." In the terms provided by Kermode, the domino theory was a fiction passing itself off as a truth-revealing myth.

American strategy in Vietnam lacked a coherent sense of an ending, a defined goal that would signal victory, because, in part, it lacked a critical awareness of the war's beginnings. The American imagination was just not prepared to look that far back. Moreover, there was a sort of terror involved in the picking of a start date, since any year chosen gave the war a different story. The year 1965 appealed to some, since it was the one in which American combat troops were first sent to Vietnam. Choosing this date as a beginning converted the war into a story about American soldiers fighting and dying on Southeast Asian ground. "The common run of Mission flak insisted on 1965," Herr writes, "post–Tonkin Resolution, as though all the killing that had gone before wasn't really war." The historian George Herring, on the other hand, dates what he calls "America's longest war" from 1950, the year in which the Truman administration formally recognized the Bao Dai government in the south and began to supply the French with direct military aid.

The more one reads about Vietnam, the more a sense of beginning is borne back ceaselessly into the past. One strength of Stanley Karnow's *Vietnam: A History* (1983) is in its running start: Karnow devotes two opening chapters to the history of French imperialism and Vietnamese nationalism. It is a history of outside intervention and intermittent civil war between the northern and southern regions of Vietnam. "The war between North and South Vietnam after 1954," he argues, "largely expressed ancient regional animosities only newly overlaid with an ideological veneer." On the other hand, the thousands of years of incursions by the Chinese had aroused in all the regions of the country "a sense of Vietnamese national identity."

For Karnow, the war after 1954 is the second act in an ongoing struggle. "If any one date marks the start of the first Indochina war," he argues, it is the general strike launched by the Vietnamese on September 24, 1945, an action taken in response to the release by the occupying British forces of fourteen hundred French army troops who had been interned by the recently defeated Japanese. The strike was called after the French troops went on a rampage in Saigon, taking over the city hall and breaking into Vietnamese homes and shops. As Karnow structures his story—posits various beginnings—the two Indochina wars then become to double business bound, a nationalistic struggle also involving elements of a civil war. In such a narrative, Americans can only be latecomers.

Of course, for most Americans the question of when the war began held only "historical" interest. "Isn't it after all only history?" a man as cultivated as William Fulbright could say, in 1970, when dodging an inconvenient proposal to make public the Pentagon Papers. The more pressing challenge was to come up with an acceptable ending. As Kermode points out, an ending can only work—feel earned and appropriate—if it grows out of and takes account of the tensions and complexities of a story's beginning and middle. But American officials, although privately well-aware of the war's varying fortunes, were, in public, remarkably sanguine about outcomes. The result of this disjunction between words and deeds was the growing problem of "credibility." And for no event of the war was the public less prepared than the Tet Offensive.

Samuel Coleridge once maintained that the genius of Shakespeare lies in "expectation in preference to surprise." By this he means that Shakespeare prepares us for his endings through a careful foreshadowing of them. An end in a Shakespeare play is a "promis'd end." Strong stories—stories of genius—Coleridge is arguing, raise and fulfill expectation; weak and sentimental ones go for unlooked-for surprise. In *A Soldier Reports* (1976), Westmoreland's key rhetorical move in his chapter "The Tet Offensive" is to insist that he "knew that a major enemy offensive was coming." He consequently expends more pages on the lead-up to the offensive than on the offensive itself. Yet the power of the event had everything to do with its arriving, for the American public, as a surprise. How was the public to feel prepared for Tet when in November 1967 Westmoreland had told Neil Sheehan of the *New York Times* that the enemy stood at the "beginning of a great defeat"? In after years, Westmoreland would persist in calling Tet a "defeat," but it remains difficult to reconcile the claim that the enemy had "suffered great casualties," made by Westmoreland on the first day of the offensive, with his subsequent call for over 200,000 new combat troops. A West Point textbook was later to designate the surprise of Tet as an "intelligence failure ranking with Pearl Harbor."

It turned out that there was a gap between knowing that something was coming and knowing what it might be. "It finally became clear that General Westmoreland did not understand this war," Michael Herr was to write in his first *Esquire* article, "and he was asked to leave it." Soon after Tet the general was reassigned to Washington, where he became Army chief of staff. What continued, however, was the attempt to rewrite Tet so as to have the outcome conform to administration predispositions. There is Lyndon Johnson's claim, made in *The Vantage Point* (1971), that Tet was "a military defeat of massive proportions for the North Vietnamese and the Viet Cong." *Defeat* is of course Westmoreland's word, one he applied to Tet three months before it began and, again, on the day after it began. Johnson borrows more than one word from his general. In summing up enemy goals and intentions, he adopts a mantra-like repetition: "They failed . . . They failed . . . the enemy failed." The claim has the force of a strong rhyme. Two pages further on in Johnson's memoir, the claim loses a little of its force when the reader comes upon the template for it, Westmoreland's February 21 assessment of Tet: "His first phase . . . has failed"; "the second phase . . . has also failed."

Walt Rostow, who served during Tet as special assistant to the president, would prove an even more stubborn dreamer. In *The Diffusion of Power* (1971), published as Nixon's Vietnamization proceeded apace, Rostow is still maintaining that "the Tet Offensive was a military disaster for Hanoi." He goes on to say that "the heart of Hanoi's failure in South Vietnam at Tet was political"; the great uprising in which the Communists imagined the populace joining them in a spontaneous overthrow of the Saigon regime "did not occur." The uprising occurred, instead, in the United States, where the surprise generated by the offensive led to a sudden increase in public doubt about the war. In a Gallup poll taken in November 1967, 41 percent of respondents judged the U.S. to be "Losing" or "Standing Still." By February 1968, that figure had risen to 61 percent. Trying to win a PR victory of its own, the administration got itself into a language trap. Then when the enemy won the PR victory instead, the administration complained that the victory was somehow invalid, since, in failing to hold any of the ground gained in Tet, the enemy won in spite of experiencing a "military" defeat.

As late as 1971, Rostow can persist in this reading of the Tet Offensive and, without any qualification, proceed to quote from a speech given on February 18, 1968, in which he said that the attacks "have left the ARVN and the government stronger institutions than before they were attacked." He continues to judge Tet a "failure" and recommends "forcing the end of the war" with an invasion of North Vietnam.

Rostow can deploy such sentiments because he is still writing out of the middle of the conflict. He can even include in his text a graph showing the war as two curves representing the working capital of the two sides, with the curve for the Allies rising and moving off the top of the page, while the Communists enjoy a dramatic spike upward and then a rapid decline down the page. Graphs of course reach into the future; they forecast ends. Three months before the Tet Offensive, Westmoreland had even ventured to say of the war that "the end begins to come into view." But it was for Westmoreland, as for Rostow, an end unlinked to any accurate sense of the war's unfolding middle. The two men, and the president they served, were unable or unwilling to attend to the actual shape of the story they were helping to author. And so the end came in a form that had been deemed unimaginable, a compromise solution in January 1973 described as "peace with honor," an agreement allowing North Vietnamese forces to remain in South Vietnam. This false or premature ending made inevitable the much more arresting one occurring in April 1975, when the last Americans left Saigon, with their Vietnamese allies clinging to the runners of the helicopters as they lifted off from the Chancery roof. At that moment, for the United States, at least, the story of the American War could be said to have ended.

Twenty-seven years after the fall of Saigon, in Errol Morris's film *The Fog of War*, Robert McNamara traced the outcome of the war to a failure to "empathize with your enemy." But empathy could only have been based on knowledge of the Vietnamese other, a commodity too often in short supply in the Washington of the 1960s. As McNamara admits, "we didn't know them well enough to empathize." Most of the China Hands had been driven out of the State Department by Senator Joseph McCarthy in the early 1950s. Scholars of Southeast Asia were denied access to Lyndon Johnson; the insights of a book like Frances Fitzgerald's *Fire in the Lake* (1972), which attempted to explore a Vietnamese worldview, were unlikely to surface in the president's daily briefing. McNamara's conclusion, however belated, was nevertheless profound, and the cultivation of empathy determines now, as it determined then, the outcome of any foreign adventure.

In making his point, McNamara may seem to be saying, "If only we had had empathy, we would have won." The value of his claim, as I have argued earlier, yields up a different conclusion: "If only we had had empathy, we would not have entered the war in the first place." Empathy means to "feel with." To feel with the Vietnamese would have been to acknowledge their millennia-long struggles against invading powers and their recent defeat of the French. It would have been to acknowledge that while Ho Chi Minh had aligned himself with a Communist agenda he had also based his founding documents for a free Vietnam on the Declaration of Independence. And it would have been to acknowledge that Vietnam had a history and a set of factions far too complex for any outside power to hope to mediate.

Empathy, in a word, is historical imagination. If my book makes one call, it is that the United States needs to develop one. Whether or not history can be mined for "lessons" on how to conduct ourselves in the present is an open question; the search for analogies between wars has often led to profound miscalculations. When it comes to war, the historical imagination creates a usable past by restoring a sense of the complexities and ambiguities that wartime rhetoric is required to kill off. The enemy becomes "known" after the fact, but what comes to be known is the difficulty of "*reading*" that enemy. This is a humbling discovery, one that might lead even a superpower to question whether one country can hope to fix or save another country by invading it.

Empathy is a good part of what Michael Herr's "dispatches" from Vietnam have to offer. By attending so closely to "*How it felt to me*"—Joan Didion's formula for the subject of her art—Herr learns how to be honest about the complexities of human action and emotion and can then extend his imagination outward, toward how the war felt to us, and, even, to them—to the Vietnamese. To turn away from the officials and experts and toward Herr, then, is not to digress from hard facts into mere storytelling. It is to open ourselves to words that teach us how to interpret, manage, and distance ourselves from dead or self-deceived language. The point is not that if Johnson had read Herr we might have won the war, but rather, in our encounter with his book, to find ourselves drawn into a more complex stance toward the war than is afforded by metaphors of winning, losing, honor, and manhood.

As a paid observer, Herr takes pride in his ability to see Vietnam steadily, if not whole. His book is meant to model an ongoing act of honest clear-seeing. The moments of greatest dramatic interest are therefore those in which "the war still offered at least one thing that I had to turn my eyes from." In this case, the thing is a look itself, a glaring gaze from a Marine, "the look that made you look away." This is the look of the combatant who has no use for the mere and voluntary onlooker.

"Their story was always there and it was always the same," Herr writes; "it went, 'Put yourself in my place.'" Herr remains aware, however, that he cannot fully occupy the place of a Marine and that his readers operate at a double remove: our task is to watch Herr watch another's pain. Herr's prose consistently strives to overcome and to acknowledge these limits, as when a Marine walks out of a triage tent at Khe Sanh: "A Marine came out and stood by the flap for a moment, an unlighted cigarette hanging from his mouth. He had neither a flak jacket nor a helmet. He let the cigarette drop from his lips, walked a few steps to the sandbags and sat down with his legs drawn up and his head hanging down between his knees. He threw one limp arm over his head and began stroking the back of his neck, shaking his head from side to side violently, as though in agony. He wasn't wounded." As we read into these sentences, we prepare ourselves for the uncovering of a wound. But the kind of pain we understand the Marine to be suffering from is not a physical pain. He is feeling for another, someone back inside the tent. In this chain of imaginings, the reader watches Michael Herr watch a Marine who in turn shares the "agony" of someone we cannot see. The effect is anything but distancing. Instead, the deliberate, attentive prose, which builds toward a tension that is never released, leaves us caught up in an unspecified anguish, all the more real for going unseen. In moments like this, Herr connects with the possibilities of witness and reveals that the respective distance from the point of impact does not prevent hurts from being felt.

One of the most moving scenes in *Dispatches* dramatizes a loss of Herr's ability to look, and comes near the end of "Illumination Rounds," as Herr visits the provincial hospital at Can Tho:

> One of the Vietnamese nurses handed me a cold can of beer and asked me to take it down the hall where one of the Army surgeons was operating. The door of the room was ajar, and I walked right in. I probably should have looked first. A little girl was lying on the table, looking with wide dry eyes at the wall. Her left leg was gone, and a sharp piece of bone about six inches long extended from the exposed stump. The leg itself was on the floor, half wrapped in a piece of paper. The doctor was a major, and he'd been working alone. He could have not looked worse if he'd lain all night in a trough of blood. His hands were so slippery that I had to hold the can to his mouth and tip it up as his head went back. I couldn't look at the girl.
> "Is it all right?" he said quietly.
> "It's okay now. I expect I'll be sick as hell later on."
> He placed his hand on the girl's forehead and said, "Hello, little darling." He thanked me for bringing the beer. He probably thought that he was smiling, but nothing changed anywhere in his face. He'd been working this way for nearly twenty hours.

"Is it all right?" the doctor asks. He speaks out of the middle of this scene to an unwounded journalist, asks him about his pain. He takes time out to imagine what Michael Herr might be feeling. As if it mattered. As if, compared with what the girl below him must be feeling, it mattered. He turns aside from one act of pity to another, and then turns back to the girl.

The brilliance of this scene is that Herr is able to notice this story *as a story* and to elevate a casual aside into one of the most moving examples of the capacity for pity in the literature of war, a pity so far beyond the call of duty that if feels terrifyingly, limitlessly sublime. Meanwhile, the girl's eyes are dry. They have been permanently opened. Meanwhile, Herr looks away. "I couldn't look at the girl." But not before he has looked and made us look as well. After all, we were just carrying a beer down a hall. Two kinds of vision collide here—one beyond and the other still burdened by feeling—and they are mediated by the doctor's two sayings, his attempts at comfort, his seemingly endless love.

In using the word "pity" here, I follow Wilfred Owen's claim that when it comes to war, the poetry is in the pity. The emotion of pity has nothing to do with feeling "sorry." By "pity," Owen seems to mean something like the all-including emotion of the scene with the doctor and the girl, a feeling originating in self-compassion and then moving out from it toward *com*-passion with others. On this circuit of emotion, pity leads to, and is instructed by, empathy. But the motion has its limits, as Herr acknowledges in his handling of the scene. He will make no claims about what the girl may be feeling. There must be pain, we imagine, and yet her eyes are dry. Our empathy does not stop at this point, but it does pause to acknowledge all that is not known and so refrains from merely projecting the self onto the other. Herr's delicate handling of the balance between knowing and feeling in the scene allows a reader to approach a subject largely missing from American accounts of the war, the subject of the pain we were inflicting on the Vietnamese.

The scene also confronts the reader with the vexed question of "sides." When it comes to the little girl, we do not know, as we so often did not know in Vietnam, whether she is an enemy or a friend. There is certainly no way to tell by looking. For many South Vietnamese, simple side-taking was not an option, caught up as they were between the ARVN by day and the NLF by night. "We were people in the middle," Le Ly Hayslip concludes. Being so caught up often became for a Vietnamese less a matter of political conviction than of personal survival, one that could lead to shifting commitments and alliances. For the onlooking or "helping" American, the challenge was less existential than epistemological, part of an ongoing and ultimately inconclusive work of knowing. Herr came to accept and even to love this work as he wrote his book, which is why, somewhere along the way, he decided to open it with a scene about trying "to read" the Vietnamese.

Michael Herr arrived in Vietnam in December 1967. He had been sent by *Esquire* magazine to cover the war. "Talk about impersonating an identity, about locking into a role, about irony: I went to cover the war and the war covered me; an old story, unless of course you've never heard it." Herr had never heard the story because he had no experience as a war correspondent; he was twenty-seven years old, and his journalistic career consisted of having worked as a film critic for the *New Leader* and writing a few travel pieces for *Holiday* magazine.

Herr had been assigned to cover the war by *Esquire* editor Harold Hayes. When Herr approached Hayes about going to the war, all he had was a plane ticket from *Holiday* and the belief that Vietnam "was the time and the place and the subject." Hayes agreed to provide Herr with $500, a travel visa, and press credentials. The credentials brought Herr the honorary rank of lieutenant colonel and access to military transport. In return, Herr was to send *Esquire* a monthly column from Vietnam.

Soon after his arrival, Herr began accompanying Marines and Army Special Forces units on field patrols. He entered Hué in early February with the Marine 1st and 2nd Battalions. As the Marines attempted to retake the citadel, experiencing "roughly one casualty for every meter taken," Herr quickly reassessed his mission. On February 5 he contacted Hayes, asking to scrap the two columns he had already written about the war. "Before the Tet Offensive, the war had a kind of easy sameness to it," he was to write. After Tet, "all the terms had changed." Herr decided he wanted to write a book. "Well, you're there," Hayes responded. "Do what you want to do."

After Hué, Herr headed for the Marine firebase at Khe Sanh. Herr calls Khe Sanh "the false love object," false because it was where Westmoreland had mistakenly expected the big attack at Tet, and loved because the general preferred fighting near the northern border of South Vietnam. Khe Sanh also appealed as the repetition of a script; as Herr writes, the parallels with Dien Bien Phu "were irresistible." Deciding to hold that ground at all costs, Westmoreland hoped to revise the French script of defeat into a dramatic American victory.

The airstrip at Khe Sanh "was the worst place in the world," and Herr landed there in a C-10 transport plane. He spent a lot of time waiting with the Marines for an attack that never came. By early April, the enemy had simply melted away. Westmoreland may have read Khe Sanh as "a Dien Bien Phu in reverse," but the story of that spring refused to deliver up this sense of an ending. "A great many people wanted to know how the Khe Sanh Combat Base could have been the Western Anchor of our Defense one month and a worthless piece of ground the next, and they were simply told that the situation had changed." Long before the engineers rolled up the air strip at Khe Sanh, Herr was back in Saigon, holed up at the Continental Palace. In *The Cat from Hué,* John Laurence remembers the hotel and "Mike Herr, who kept a room upstairs while he worked on his first article for *Esquire* and also took notes for his book."

The book took almost ten years to write. Herr would send *Esquire* only two dispatches from Vietnam. The first, "Hell Sucks," was published in August 1968; the second, "Khe Sanh," appeared in October 1969. These two pieces would become, in altered form, the second and third chapters of *Dispatches.* Herr spent a little over a year in Vietnam and wrote two-thirds of the book in the eighteen months after he returned to the United States. Then he suffered "some kind of massive collapse," only finishing the book in 1976.

"Hell Sucks" deals with the Tet Offensive and focuses on the relief of Hué. For the Marines, the tactical problem involved driving the enemy forces out of the city. For the writer, the narrative issue was, in Tim O'Brien's phrase, "how to tell a true war story." Deeply embedded with the soldiers, Herr could have chosen to limit his view to the moment-by-moment action on the ground, and on the slow gaining of it. For the most part, this is what he does. But in a key formal decision, he begins by calling attention to the overall strategic implications of Tet rather than to immediate tactical gains. In doing so, he supplies a perspective on Tet noticeably absent from official briefings on the war.

In the original version of "Hell Sucks" published in *Esquire,* Herr makes only a limited claim to a strategic overview: "It has finally become that kind of conventional war that the Command so longed for, and it is not going well." He drops this sentence from the "Hell Sucks" chapter in *Dispatches,* and leads off with this instead: "Vietnam was a dark room full of deadly objects, the VC were everywhere all at once like spider cancer, and instead of losing the war in little pieces over years we lost it fast in under a week." This will become Herr's summary judgment on the Tet Offensive, one reserved for the reconsiderations of his 1977 book. *We lost it.* Like so many of the stories Herr will tell about Vietnam, this one kills off hope at the start. With the war effectively over, Herr sees no point in trying to create narrative suspense. He will instead try to go through the experience of war with the Marines, to be "with" them, as McNamara has it, and even to be with the enemy.

Herr rides into Hué with sixty men packed into "a deuce-and-a-half, one of eight trucks moving in a convoy." They are bringing in replacements for the casualties taken in the earliest fighting south of the Perfume River. On the road going in, he sees that not a single building has been left without pitting from shell fragments. Among the refugees they pass along the way, the kids laugh and shout, the old look on in silent tolerance or misery, while the younger men and women show unmistakable contempt.

They bivouac in An Cho, a village south of the city. Camp is set up, and then two Marine gunships come down and begin strafing them. " 'Way to pinpoint the fuckin' enemy,' one of the grunts said." In the morning they cross the canal on a two-by-four and begin walking into Hué. Herr will be there for ten days. Civilians keep appearing, trying to get back into their homes. Herr catches a helicopter ride back to Phu Bai and then makes his way to the press center at Da Nang, where he finds himself in a dining room with freezing air-conditioning. He orders four hamburgers and a dozen brandies. He takes a hot shower, and then returns to the dining room for a steak and another string of brandies.

On returning to Hué, Herr notices that morale has become "snappish." A Marine, injured in the knee, is told he is going home and cries enormous tears. Herr choppers out a second time, riding with a lieutenant whose ears and eyes are full of caked blood. "But by then," he writes, "the battle for Hue was almost over." Herr then fills in the tactical details, the Cav working the northwest corner of the citadel, the 101st coming in through a former North Vietnamese Army (NVA) resupply route. Vietnamese Marines and the 1st ARVN Division move the "remaining NVA down toward the wall." The NVA flag over the citadel is torn down. When Vietnamese Rangers storm the Imperial Palace, there is no one left inside. "Before they left," so desperate had become their hunger, "they'd skimmed all the edible vegetation from the surface of the moat." By the time he returns to Saigon, he has also picked up on a rumor about "thousands of NVA executions in Hue and the 'shallow graves' in the flats outside the city . . . which proved to be true."

Herr alludes to the rumor about executions once again in the closing paragraph of "Hell Sucks" and again calls the rumor "true." In assenting to the truth of the rumor, he thus promulgates the myth of the "Hué Massacre." It is one I myself believed for many years until belatedly coming across the pioneering work of D. Gareth Porter. Porter's 1974 article in the *Indochina Chronicle* traces the origin of the myth to the ARVN's Tenth Political Warfare Battalion and to a 1970 document authored by Douglas Pike, an employee of the U.S. Information Agency. Pike's story was given wide circulation when excerpted in the September 1970 issue of *Reader's Digest*.

Porter reports that initial estimates of those executed at Hué were "over one thousand." By the time Pike published his article, the estimate of the number of "civilians killed by the NLF in and around Hue" had risen to 4,756. Later scholarship would adjust the number downward to 700. While Porter allows that the execution of civilians did occur, just who did what to whom—and why—remains a matter of "academic dispute."

The numbers in any case reveal very little, since the bodies disinterred near Hué came from the sites of recent fighting and bombardment. According to Porter, many of those killed "were in fact victims of American air power or ground fighting that raged in the hamlets." As Scott Laderman has shown in *Tours of Vietnam* (2009), tourist guidebooks to Vietnam—by Fodors, Lonely Planet, and Moon—have helped to promote the myth of the massacre and even to inflate the estimate of those executed to a number as high as fourteen thousand. "What happened in 1968 remains uncertain," Laderman writes. "However, uncertainty about precise details should not be confused with affirmation of the claim, represented uncritically in most Western guide-books, that thousands of civilians were methodically executed by the Vietnamese insurgents." Even a writer as committed to uncertainty and as skeptical of the claims of conventional journalism as Michael Herr could nevertheless be drawn into the communications pudding that produced the myth of the Hué Massacre.

Throughout *Dispatches,* Herr will live out a complex stance of complicity and distance: One minute he rides with the wounded, and in the next he is eating hamburgers and drinking brandy. He is at once in Vietnam and not of it, part of the passionate anguish and also afforded, by dint of his salaried role, a capacity for spatial and temporal remove. "I went there behind the crude but serious belief that you had to be able to look at anything, serious because I acted on it and went, crude because I didn't know, it took the war to teach it, that you were as responsible for everything you saw as you were for everything you did." Where the distinction between seeing and doing collapses, the journalist's detached stance vanishes. " 'Must be pretty hard to stay detached,' a man on the plane to San Francisco said, and I said, 'Impossible.' " Herr's text finds no stance free from responsibility and so delivers not only a timeless treatise on the ethics of journalism but also a historically specific analysis of the implication of any onlooking American in the war in Vietnam.

So *Dispatches* asks us "to perform a witness act." But it does not indulge in "the mistake of thinking that all you needed to perform a witness act were your eyes." Feeling is the thing, and if we do not move from looking to feeling, then we have refused to go to Herr's war; we have stayed home.

We can see this insight at work in the opening of Herr's first *Esquire* article, a passage Herr eventually moved out of the "Hell Sucks" chapter and converted into the opening paragraph of the published book:

> There is a map of Vietnam on the wall of my apartment in Saigon and some nights, coming back late to the city, I'd lie out on my bed and look at it, too tired to do anything more than just get my boots off. The map is a marvel, especially absorbing because it is not real. For one thing, it is very old. It was left here years ago by a previous tenant, probably a Frenchman since the map was made in Paris. The paper has buckled, and much of the color has gone out of it, laying a kind of veil over the countries it depicts. Vietnam is divided into its older territories of Tonkin, Annam and Cochin China, and to the west, past Laos and Cambodge, sits Siam, a kingdom. That's old, I told the General. That's a really old map.

When Herr repositions this paragraph in *Dispatches,* he shifts it out of the present and into the past tense: "*There was a map on the wall of my apartment in Saigon. . . .*" He is no longer writing out of the middle of the conflict; there is time now for considered revision. So he corrects the tenses, in order to indicate the ever-increasing distance from the war brought with the years. In doing this, Herr reminds those of us who were young with him, in 1968, of how long it has taken to begin to understand our past, and of all we have had to live through in order to learn something about ourselves.

By positioning this paragraph at the beginning of his book, Herr decided to open *Dispatches* with the act of looking at a map. He also made a second crucial decision: to add a new and a further paragraph about the map, one not found in the original *Esquire* article. Here is the second paragraph of *Dispatches:*

> *If dead ground could come back and haunt you the way dead people do, they'd have been able to mark my map CURRENT and burn the ones they'd been using since '64, but count on it, nothing like that was going to happen. It was late '67 now, even the most detailed maps didn't reveal much anymore; reading them was like trying to read the faces of the Vietnamese, and that was like trying to read the wind. We knew the uses of most information were flexible, different pieces of ground told different stories to different people. We also knew that for years now there had been no country here but the war.*

So Herr begins his book by acknowledging that in Vietnam we were fighting over a map. Maps are not only abstractions—lines on paper trying to capture the boundaries imposed by governments on the face of the earth—but they are also palimpsests, a sort of freeze-frame of temporary geopolitical forces behind which earlier and different lines recede in an endless dissolve.

But the key move made here, the one most crucial to an appreciation of *Dispatches* and of the war it so tenderly chronicles, has to do with the controlling verbs in Herr's two paragraphs. "Look," he writes in the first paragraph; "*read,*" he writes, in the second, the added one. To move from looking to reading: this is the act of the mind enjoined by the experience of Vietnam. It carries with it the awareness that even the most casual glance entails interpretation. Looking without "reading" is impossible, Herr urges, and learning how to read also involves acknowledging the limits and difficulties of the process: "*reading them was like trying to read the faces of the Vietnamese, and that was like trying to read the wind.*" There is no empathy for the enemy here. Not yet—because we have not yet gone through the experience of the book that would make such a feeling possible. All this map presents to our eyes is "information." Throughout *Dispatches,* Herr deploys the word *information* as the product of a convenient and premature stopping along the way toward something much more to be desired, and dearly bought: historical knowledge.

Herr's willingness to revise his own prose stands as evidence of his willingness and ability to convert information into knowledge. "Straight history, auto-revised history, history without handles, for all the books and articles and white papers, all the talk and the miles of film, something wasn't answered, it wasn't even asked. We were backgrounded, deep, but when the background started sliding forward not a single life was saved by the information. The thing had transmitted too much energy, it heated up too hot, hiding low under the fact-figure crossfire there was a secret history, and not a lot of people felt like running in there to bring it out." Herr's performance reveals that information can only be converted into knowledge by way of a resolutely self-aware and self-interrogating language, one beholden to and willing to be corrected by experience, since Herr is always "going out after one kind of information and getting another."

Near the beginning of his book, Herr recalls that the burden of living with unconverted information began for him as a boy, when looking at war photographs in *Life* magazine. "Even when the picture was sharp and cleanly defined, something wasn't clear at all, something repressed that monitored the images and withheld their essential information." He "didn't have a language for it then," Herr continues, and the best word he can come up with now is "something." *Dispatches* records its author's painful acquisition of this language, an always embattled achievement since, even after Herr begins "seeing" a war "on real ground," the mind still "tended to manufacture" a "kind of obscuration" so as to afford "protection from what you were seeing." Any claim to authority as an artist depends on this continual acknowledgment of all that stands in the way of clear seeing, the "something" within that resists opening the self to pain and the attendant knowledge to be gained from it. The threat of failure lingers, still with Herr in his closing paragraphs, where he finds himself beset by "another" piece of information, as if, for all the struggle to articulate a "personal style" aimed against the obscuring and official jargons, something still hasn't been answered, it hasn't even been asked. All Herr can do, as he ceases trying to ask and to answer, is to offer up a dispersion, concluding his book with the sort of Amen one makes at the end of a desperate prayer: "Vietnam Vietnam Vietnam, we've all been there."

CHAPTER

2

The Movement and McCarthy

In 1987, Eugene McCarthy wrote that his 1968 run for the presidency "probably had little or no effect on how the Vietnam War was conducted and how
it finally ended." To those who worked for McCarthy in the snows of New
Hampshire and the suburbs of Oregon, the claim may come as a surprise.
After studying the histories of the campaign, however, the comment registers
less as something new than as the expression of an incertitude present in
the candidate from the very start. One of 1968's more salient ironies is an
antiwar movement that came to invest much of its energy in a man with a
serious case of "Yes-No." Accepting the call of the movement in November
1967, by the next summer the fight had gone out of him. Perhaps this was
a predictable behavior in a mind so fine no one commitment could long
command it. If his "moral seriousness" compelled him to run, as Thomas
Powers writes, his "spiritual pride" prevented him from trying too hard to
win. There was a vanity in McCarthy, a vanity inseparable from what Ezra
Pound calls "the diffidence that faltered," and yet something marvelous was
also accomplished, an upspringing of hope made possible by the courage
of a single man.

When did he decide to run? McCarthy himself gave one kind of answer:
"It was nothing like Saint Paul being knocked off his horse, I assure you. I

don't think I had any kind of a special light. I think that it is very hard to fix the exact moment of something of this kind—it's a little too soon and a little bit too late. Somewhere between those two points you pass the point of no return." In refraining from fixing the moment of beginning, McCarthy renounces the consolations of dramatic narrative. His story is to remain . . . underdetermined. A moment proving so fugitive merges in any case with a much larger story, with two decades of antinuclear agitation in America, and with an indigenous peace movement that, by 1967, had whittled itself down to two words: "Dump Johnson."

Allard Lowenstein was the man who finally convinced McCarthy to run. President of the National Student Association during the 1950s, Lowenstein had worked as well for the Student Nonviolent Coordinating Committee (SNCC) in the South. He was a liberal organizer rather than an antiestablishment radical. By early 1967 he had decided to build a movement to stop the Vietnam War. Meanwhile, wealthy veterans of the Adlai Stevenson campaigns approached McCarthy in January of that year with an offer of $50,000 in campaign funds if he would agree to challenge Johnson on the issue of Vietnam. "Although McCarthy was initially enthusiastic," his biographer Dominic Sandbrook writes, "he never wholeheartedly endorsed their plan, and very little came of it."

McCarthy's doubts about the war had surfaced publicly a year earlier. In January 1966 he was one of fifteen senators urging President Johnson to declare a bombing halt. On the Senate floor, the day the letter to Johnson was delivered, McCarthy spoke out against being "called upon to make a kind of moral commitment to an objective or to a set of purposes which we do not clearly understand." By early 1967, he was seeking a "severe judgment" on the conduct of the war. A month later, under serious pressure from his daughter Mary, a Radcliffe undergraduate, he declared the war "morally unjustifiable."

Lowenstein and fellow National Student Association veteran Curtis Gans founded the "Dump Johnson" movement in August 1967 and then spent the fall asking liberal senators, including Robert Kennedy, to run against Johnson. When George McGovern turned them down, he said, "Have you talked to Gene yet? I know he's feeling very frustrated by the war." McCarthy then surprised Gans and Lowenstein "by readily agreeing" to run. But, in a pattern repeated throughout the campaign, he "continued to waver both in public and in private for at least another month."

The formal announcement came on November 30, 1967, when McCarthy said he intended to enter four primaries. He hoped his candidacy would

"alleviate the sense of political helplessness" and a "growing sense of alienation from politics." He was running in order to shape policy—to obtain
an antiwar plank in the party platform—rather than to "dump Johnson,"
a phrase he abhorred. At the same time, he began to criticize a "personalized presidency" and was steadily drawn into the momentum of running
against LBJ.

A practicing poet, McCarthy often mused on the power of figuration
to misrepresent and therefore to mislead. On December 2, in Chicago, he
gave an eloquent formulation of a running theme, the corruption of public
policy resulting from inattention to the logic of metaphor: "Instead of the
language of promise and of hope, we have in politics today a new vocabulary
in which the critical word is *war*: war on poverty, war on ignorance, war
on crime, war on pollution. None of these problems can be solved by war
but only by persistent, dedicated, and thoughtful attention." As prophecy,
this was to prove unerring. In the decades to come, the United States was
to militarize its response to foreign and domestic crises, proceeding as if
the best way to fix a thing was to make war on it. So McCarthy set out to
campaign not only against a specific war but against the growing place of
war and its metaphors as a sufficient response to trouble in every corner
of American life.

"The anti–Vietnam War movement did not start in a vacuum," writes David
Dellinger, in *From Yale to Jail* (1993). "It was the offspring of previous movements for justice and peace." The string of historical facts supporting this
claim could be traced at least as far back as Congressman Lincoln's vote against
the Mexican War, or Thoreau's jailing for refusing to pay a tax supporting it,
an experience that resulted in the writing of "Civil Disobedience." H. Bruce
Franklin dates American resistance to intervention in Vietnam as early as
1945. In that year, U.S. troopships were diverted from bringing American
soldiers home from World War II and were used to transport "U.S.-armed
French troops and Foreign Legionnaires from France to recolonize Vietnam.
The enlisted crewmen of these ships, all members of the U.S. Merchant Marine,
immediately began organized protests. On November 2, all eighty-eight non-
commissioned crew members of the *Pachaug Victory* drew up a protest letter
they sent to the War Shipping Administration in Washington." Once in Saigon,
crew members signed a resolution condemning the use of American ships
" 'to subjugate the native population' of Vietnam."

As the anti–Vietnam War movement took shape, Old Left groups saw the
issue as providing a chance to remake the country from the ground up, while

traditional peace organizations like the one headed by A. J. Muste framed resistance as part of a long history of opposition to state-sponsored violence. Students for a Democratic Society (SDS) remained torn between opposing the war and community organizing projects, like Tom Hayden's work in the streets of Newark. The Weathermen finally turned to bombs. No one tent ever did or ever could include the disparate interests of those who sought to stop the war; the National Coordinating Committee to End the War in Vietnam, meeting in August 1965, was made up of thirty-three separate member groups. In *Antiwarriors* (2002), Melvin Small estimates that by 1969 the movement included as many as seventeen thousand national, regional, and local organizations, involving some six million active participants.

Large, publicized gatherings protesting the war lasted some six years, from an SDS-sponsored Washington, D.C., demonstration on April 17, 1965, to a final wave of protest in late April and early May 1971, again in Washington, one involving perhaps the largest single rally in the history of the antiwar movement. American universities would become and remain the seedbed of antiwar activity. SDS had been founded at Michigan in 1962, with its call for "participatory democracy." Michigan led the way again, with the first teach-in against the war on March 24, 1965. A bomb threat interrupted the proceedings and the main speaker was forced to finish his address outside, in the snow. By the fall of 1967, sit-ins and demonstrations against the war had taken place at Wisconsin, Brooklyn College, Princeton, Harvard, Colorado, Stanford, Iowa, and Rochester. In 1970, 20 percent of college students polled claimed to have attended at least one antiwar demonstration.

For young men, the draft became the catalyzing issue, especially after February 1966, when Johnson approved "Program 2," a major build-up in Vietnam. Draft calls soon jumped from ten thousand to thirty thousand men a month. By 1967, one-third of all combat deaths in Vietnam were incurred by draftees.

But resistance had begun long before that. In May 1964, twelve men burned their draft cards in New York City. On October 15 of the next year, David J. Miller, a member of the Catholic Worker Movement, burned his card before television cameras outside an induction center, again in New York City. The action violated a newly passed act of Congress making the "willful destruction" of a draft card punishable by a five-year jail term and a fine of $10,000. The first draft-card burner to be prosecuted, Miller was given a suspended sentence in March 1966, on condition that he accept a new draft card. Miller refused, and spent two and a half years in a federal penitentiary. Out of the 27 million young men eligible for the draft during the Vietnam years, Miller became one of the 570,000 who would be classified as "Draft Evaders."

But David Miller had evaded nothing. He had issued his protest and made himself available to punishment by the state. Figures like David Miller and David Harris occupy a unique place in the experience of the Vietnam generation, since they neither went to the war nor managed to "evade it." They chose jail. In Patrick Hagopian's words, such men were able to live out their lives "neither consumed by misgivings about their service in Vietnam nor ashamed that they had evaded the war and let others serve in their place." "They seem," as Myra MacPherson was to observe, "the most guilt-free of their generation."

The war first came home to David Harris shortly after his graduation from a California high school in 1963, when he saw the photograph in *Time* of Buddhist monk Thich Quang Duc immolating himself on a Saigon street. Harris went on to become student body president at Stanford. After four arrests and nearly one thousand speeches against the war, he was imprisoned for twenty months for "refusing to go to the war when my name was called." "None of us should have had to make such choices when we did," Harris writes, in *Our War* (1996). "We were too young, and the choices were too hard. But we made them anyway." When he announced his intention to refuse an order for service, his father begged him in tears not to ruin his life. Harris might have responded that he had to fight with what he had, and what he had was "the tool of a life."

In 1982, Harris published a sort of involuntary autobiography: "I would have left this story alone," *Dreams Die Hard* begins, "if it weren't for the ending Dennis wrote to it all so much later in our lives. What he finally did to Allard finished off a decade long gone but still much too important to ignore." Harris here refers to the March 14, 1980, shooting and murder of Allard Lowenstein by Dennis Sweeney. The end of Harris's chosen story is known, and has been written by someone else. His task is therefore not to worry what happened, but rather the larger question, one posed to him by a friend on the phone, "So how did it all end up like this?"

Harris stands before his tale the way Quentin Compson does before the story of Henry Sutpen, or Nick Carraway before the life of Jay Gatsby, stunned into narrative by an act that generates speculation. And, like Faulkner and Fitzgerald, he adopts the time-honored structure of the Interpreted Design. Harris moves beyond the narrator-hero dynamic, however, by taking on the story of not one but two silent centers. In the course of the telling, he becomes the third point of an uncanny triangle and the maker of a story in which the narrator, above all, stands revealed.

Dennis Sweeney met Allard Lowenstein at Stanford in the fall of 1961. The eighteen-year-old freshman quickly became a protégé of the thirty-two-year-old dean of men, who habitually "sought out and attracted bright young men who cared about making the world better." In exchange for becoming a protégé, a young man was "given a safe pass to pursue his developing urge for commitment and clarity." When Lowenstein went to Mississippi in 1963, Sweeney followed him, and the two became caught up in the voter registration work originated by Robert Moses. Lowenstein saw himself as a "bridge" between white and black activists, and would later claim credit for thinking up the 1964 Mississippi Summer Project. During one of their recruiting junkets together, Allard and Dennis shared a motel room with only one bed. "Lowenstein left his side of the mattress for Dennis's," Harris writes, "and began to embrace his protégé, offering no explanation of his intentions." When Dennis said he was "uncomfortable," Lowenstein stopped immediately, and nothing was ever again said between them about it.

At this point in his narrative, Harris pulls back to comment on Dennis and the motel room scene, asserting that "any explanation of him or Allard or their relationship would be flawed without an account of it." Harris has little doubt that the incident occurred, having located five other people besides himself to whom Dennis was to tell the story, and having himself later been the object of a similar motel-room embrace. The question is not one of fact, but feeling: What did it mean for Dennis? Harris sees him as torn between a role model and an incestuous father-figure; Lowenstein would increasingly be seen by Dennis as possessing a "hidden agenda." Harris qualifies his reading of the scene, however, adding that when the rift between the two men occurred, "politics was the most immediate reason."

That reason had to do with Lowenstein's sudden withdrawal from the Summer Project in the spring of 1964 and his insistence that Dennis do so as well. Under what he called "tremendous pressure" from Lowenstein, Dennis finally said "No." The break became final in August, when Lowenstein sided against seating the Mississippi Freedom Democratic Party, a delegation of which Dennis was a member. Dennis was to feel "betrayed" by Lowenstein and by the Democratic party's refusal to seat the delegation at the Atlantic City convention. For "Dennis and Allard, it would also be their last joint political endeavor." "Al has his way . . ." Dennis was to say. Over the next fifteen years, as Dennis's mind became increasingly troubled, he came to believe that Lowenstein had links with the CIA. "Call off your dogs," he warned

Lowenstein in a 1975 phone call. The next time he talked to Lowenstein was on the day that he shot him.

The path of Dennis Sweeney's disillusionment "was difficult for me to reconstruct," Harris admits, just as it "was obscured by his own close-mouthed style." Such admissions are characteristic of Harris throughout. He enters the book as a narrator well before he becomes a character in it, and, as a narrator, he chooses to distance himself from his youthful quest for certainty. Then, he had been "comfortable making definitive statements about important subjects." Now, he feels differently, and wants only "to backtrack and string it all together piece by piece." It turns out that there is no way to date the doom. "What Dennis Sweeney eventually did to his former mentor would make many look back and try to locate a time and place when some kind of definitive 'break' happened between them, but 'break' is much too clean and quick to what happened." Harris's narrative traces a movement away from the definitive and toward a kind of suspended judgment on why, and how, it all ended.

Harris's career as an activist began in the fall of 1964, when, on the spur of the moment, he joined a carload of Stanford volunteers driving to Jackson to assist in the Freedom Vote being organized by SNCC. "I still don't understand why, out of nowhere," he writes, "I jumped at that opportunity. Part of it must have been an urge to adventure, to be tested." Harris was menaced with a shotgun in the town of Lambert, and a senior working with him was forced off the road, beaten, kicked, and urinated on. After a visit from the FBI, during which Harris was addressed as "nigger lover," he and two other sophomores fled the state and headed back to school.

Harris took part in his first antiwar demonstration in the fall of 1965, standing in the crowd but imagining himself on stage, behind the microphone. "As yet," he was to admit, "I had no words for what I felt." Elected student body president in the following fall, he was to meet Dennis Sweeney during a protest against the Selective Service in front of the university vice president's office.

As a character in the story told in *Dreams Die Hard*, Harris enters it relatively late. "David Harris is the third character in this story," he writes, early on. But he does not meet Lowenstein until 1965, about one hundred pages in, and first runs into Dennis Sweeney in the spring of 1966, on page 137. At a "bull session" in Palo Alto, Harris finds himself drawn to Lowenstein's argument "that one person can make an immense difference and that the course of history itself could be shaped by a single decision." He becomes Lowenstein's driver and "gofer," and attends Lowenstein's Encampment for

Citizenship in the summer of 1965. "At the Encampment's discussion of Vietnam, I maintained that the most important question was whether the war was wrong. If it was, it had to be denounced, pure and simple." Sweeney and Harris became friends the following summer, got high together, and began talking about resisting the draft. Sweeney moved in with Harris after his marriage broke up. In March of the next year, Harris, Sweeney, and two Berkeley students founded The Resistance. The relationship with Dennis "peaked on October 16," 1967, at a Kezar Stadium rally. Dennis then turned briefly to sabotage, burning down the Stanford ROTC building, and within nine months of the rally, "we would have stopped talking to each other."

Harris's own story centers around ends known and unknown. Once he made the decision to work against the war in so public a way, he became a condemned man. Each time he gave a speech advocating draft resistance, he knew he was violating the conspiracy provisions of the Selective Service Act. "I was drawn to the exemplary existential act," Harris says of his youthful self, "as a means of transforming both myself and the world around me." For Harris, the word *act* becomes a sort of god-term, and he understands action as existential, a sally into the unknown. So when, in the summer of 1966, he returned his draft card to the Fresno draft board and declined to accept the student deferment it signified, he performed "an act of wonderment and impulse, taken in the calmest and most practical frame of mind." Yet the act was and was not existential—and therefore even more demanding of courage—since while the timing of the event might be up in the air, Harris was more or less certain that he would, one day, be arrested. When that day came, and he was sent to the San Francisco City Jail, on July 12, 1969, he felt relief, having "spent the last three years knowing prison was coming." Sweeney saw going to jail as an unnecessary martyrdom, and tried to talk Harris out of his resolve. But Harris stood firm, inspiring in the judge who sentenced him a backhanded compliment about his three-year sentence: "It has to be as stark and real and just as hard and tough as you are."

Of the many actors on the sixties stage, Harris was perhaps burdened with the most acute sense of an ending. His existential act could lead to only one thing. Between the day in January 1968, when he formally refused induction and the July morning eighteen months later when the federal marshals came for him, he lived, as he says, "no more than a momentary pause before incarceration."

But what an eighteen months they were! Harris had fallen in love with Joan Baez in the fall of 1967. "She got out of jail several days after my induction refusal, and we spent the next few weeks largely together. Within ten days, we had announced that we would undertake a month-and-a-half-long speaking tour of college campuses in March." Baez thought Harris "the best speaker she had ever heard."

And so David Harris took to the road with the girl on the half shell and her anthemic melancholy. On March 26, 1968, the day the new F-111 was unleashed on Vietnam, they were married. As they careened through the heartland, their deeply serious, non-Keseyan road trip projected an unassailable air of romance, a feeling intensified by its being so temporary. While they traveled always within the knowledge of how it was going to end, the sense of dread gathering about them had to do with more than a looming date with the penitentiary. Howard Norman, who joined the tour in Grand Rapids, remembers that

> Baez could barely get through a song. She would get up there and start to sing, and the "boos" would well up. Then David would talk about resisting the draft. Things were really tense in Ann Arbor, with the ROTC guys in the back of the auditorium, interrupting. Jeff Shertliff was accompanying Joan on the songs, and a bottle flew out of the crowd and hit him in the head. He would have to have stitches at the emergency room. After that the longhairs turned on the guys in the back. Joan and David just stood there, and went on with their little program. I began to have this sinking feeling: I wondered if they comprehended their own vulnerability—if they were going to make it out of there alive.

The tour is the height and plateau of Harris's public life, and in *Dreams Die Hard* he gives it only one page. Harris's interpreted design allows him to allude to his heroic winter and spring without detailing it. He will not recycle a twice-told tale, one that belongs largely to the culture of celebrity. Better to leave that to *Look* magazine, a copy of which he receives while in prison, and one featuring on its cover a photograph of Harris, Baez, and their newborn son. "Joan Baez and David Harris," the tagline went. "A family kept apart by conscience." Harris reads the magazine, thinks about "Joan for a while," and then remembers talking with Dennis Sweeney about "doing time." "That I was the only one of us who actually had been locked up lent an ambivalence to my memories."

Sweeney eclipses Baez, to be eclipsed in turn a few pages later, in Harris's memory, by Lowenstein visiting him in prison. They find little to talk about; Allard tells David that he had not wanted to "abandon" him. "Everyone involved in the decade would have their own date for when the Sixties ended, and that cell time with Allard Lowenstein would be mine."

"The rest amounted to aftermath," Harris maintains, in the chapter that follows. He then supplies a brutal summary of where everybody in his story ended up. There is something deeply unsatisfying about the list, and it is meant to be. Writing in the early 1980s, Harris knows that the sixties have not ended and that there will be many more decades of living them out. And the fact that his 1960s "ended" in prison and in apparent political defeat is no less beside the point. "The ending Dennis wrote" cannot define the meaning and value of Allard Lowenstein's life, just as a reader's knowing how Harris's story will end, and from the beginning of the book, can in no way substitute for the experience of going through it. Harris and those who stood with him had tapped into something permanently ongoing in American life, an unending struggle having no part in the finalities—the winnings and losings—of a game. The existential act, he came to know, had meaning and value regardless of whether it achieved a desired outcome. To be a citizen was to take up "the work we are in," as Lincoln names it, and to accept that in this work we are always in the middle of the way.

Harris and Sweeney founded The Resistance in 1967, a year that would see the first big wave of antiwar activism: the founding of Another Mother for Peace, the organizing of Vietnam Veterans Against the War, and the publication of *Handbook for Conscientious Objectors*, a modest blue-covered volume that sold eleven thousand copies in five months. The summer before my senior year at Yale I bought the handbook and joined a study group taught by a Quaker under the Old Campus elms. I decided to apply for I-O status, which meant exemption from "both combatant and noncombatant training." The form consisted of four questions centered around my "religious training and belief." I began the application with these sentences: "I object to warfare, and to my personal participation in it, because it involves a system of institutionalized killing in which one must surrender personal responsibility for his actions to the state. I also object to warfare because it destroys environment that sustains life and shatters my solidarity with all men. The first objection is a personal concern, the second a social one." In proceeding to describe the connection between my upbringing and my present beliefs, I fleshed out my case with quotations from Sartre, Camus, and Dostoevsky. On September 15, 1969, Local Board No. 132 wrote back to say that "at the expiration of your present deferment, your complete file, including your SS Form 150, will be reviewed by your local board."

Later that fall the first draft lottery rendered my C.O. application moot. On the evening of December 1 my roommates and I bent toward a radio and heard the birth dates being read out; few of us went down to the TV room to actually witness the spectacle. But the evening was spent within shouting distance of one hundred Davenport seniors, and, as the first dates were announced, we learned to wait in silence for the screams echoing through the entryways. "They're bombing the courtyard," my bunkmate Barney O'Meara muttered, as the second couch fell past our window. Small fires broke out; glass could be heard breaking; we huddled in our cell-like rooms and endured the mass sentencing.

It divided us, that evening; there was no forgetting the noises we had made. As it turned out, only men with the first 195 birthdates drawn would eventually be called to report for possible induction. I had pulled number 235, and so was free to move on to marriage and graduate school. Barney did not need to listen; as a member of Naval ROTC, he was headed for a minesweeper in the Mekong Delta. A separated shoulder won him a discharge from the Navy in the spring, and a few months later he was working with Ralph Nader on auto safety in Washington, D.C.

The most dramatic event of 1967 was the October March on the Pentagon. On the steps of the Justice Department, on a sunny fall day, Norman Mailer found himself standing in stunned tribute before a line of young men, a procession that "soon became a ceremony. Each man came up, gave his name, and the state or area or college he represented, and then proceeded to name the number of draft cards he had been entrusted to turn in." Two hundred from New York, more than that from Boston, a good number from Yale. "By handing in draft cards, these young men were committing their future either to prison, emigration, frustration, or at best, years where everything must be unknown." That night, at the Ambassador Theater, Mailer owned up to his fear of that unknown: "We are up, face this, all of you, against an existential situation—we do not know how it is going to turn out, and what is even more inspiring of dread is that the government doesn't know either." On behalf of their country, as Mailer saw it, the young men at the Justice Department were performing, like David Harris, a self-sacrificing existential act, risking into an unforeseeable future the most precious thing they had—"the tool of a life."

Mailer cannot display the kind of courage shown by the young men gathered at the Justice Department; he is not a member of the generation called upon to show it. But he can offer up his artistic performance as exemplifying another kind of courage and as also committed to existential risk. In an "activity like writing," "one had to trick or seize or submit to the grace of each moment," and in doing so the risks are considerable, liable to result as much in embarrassment as achievement. Writers, like draft resisters, have to "ride the beast" of uncertainty, and in each endeavor the challenge is to attend to "the intimate truth of the way it presented itself to your experience." Truth can only result from a probing forward, from experiment. "The clue to discovery was not in the substance of one's idea, but in what was learned from the style of one's attack." Style is something one learns from because it emerges as one moves forward; it is not imposed, but discovered. The mock-heroic and speculative and sometimes obscene style Mailer finds himself deploying in *The Armies of the Night* arises, then, from a national crisis that becomes, for him, as for the young, a test of existential readiness. And his chance to perform in the street without being killed becomes the measure of a working culture, one willing to honor its promise of the right of free speech and public assembly. The point of such endeavor is less to win or to overcome than to share the experience of what it feels like to attempt, to essay, to fare forward, to resist.

The Armies of the Night opens with an article from *Time* magazine, one which mocks Mailer's performance on the stage of the Ambassador Theater. Mailer quotes the bulk of the article, and then writes: "Now we may leave *Time* in order to find out what happened." It was to prove an inspired opening, since the media coverage of the March on the Pentagon, as with most antiwar actions, was to provide it with its political force and much of its publicly agreed-upon meaning. Those who were to read Mailer's "History as a Novel" had a chance, on the other hand, to dig out from under the fact-figure media crossfire and to discover the secret history of the event.

Legend has it that the American media teamed up with the antiwar movement to help defeat the American war effort in Vietnam. But the press coverage of the March on the Pentagon was anything but reinforcing or sympathetic. And it missed the core story. The real story had to do with the enduring power and dignity of a homegrown American tradition of civil disobedience, one given its most eloquent formulation by Thoreau. According to Thoreau, American civil disobedience depends for its efficacy on an implicit contract between the "authority of the state" and the "individual," an agreement to refrain from violence on the one side and to submit to arrest on the other. When Mailer finds in himself "a sharp searing love for his country" as he crosses Memorial Bridge, he traces his love back to his gratitude for our "liberties to dissent." And he is walking beside a man, Robert Lowell, who had a year earlier predicted that "we will look back upon this troubled moment as a golden time of freedom and license to act and speculate." Over 35,000 people would march peacefully across the Potomac and gather themselves around the Pentagon. This action perhaps fell short of true civil disobedience, since a permit for the march had been granted, and the marchers had therefore broken no law. This respectful display of dissent was nevertheless the true story, much more indicative of a shift in the American soul than the action taken by some one thousand marchers who chose to become violent.

And yet the one thousand became the story. On Sunday, October 22, the *New York Times* reported that "thousands of demonstrators stormed the Pentagon today." This was the newspaper edited by A. M. Rosenthal, a hawk who "sometimes altered or refused to run stories at variance with his views of the war." *Times* columnist Tom Wicker routinely cut in half crowd estimates coming from organizers of antiwar rallies. So we must leave the *Times,* in order to find out what happened.

Almost four hundred draft cards and enlistment notices were gathered from young men on Friday, October 20. On Saturday, a rally was held at the Lincoln Memorial. After the rally, the crowd marched across Memorial Bridge. "As many as 1,000 radicals," writes Melvin Small, "ignored the ground rules and left a rally in a Pentagon parking lot in order to break into the building itself." They were met by over 8,000 members of the 82nd Airborne; for the first time since 1932, federal troops had been called out to protect the capital. Small estimates that twenty-five radicals made it past the Airborne, and the marshals and the police, and into the Pentagon, before being arrested. All this made very good copy, but "the real climax on the steps of the Pentagon," as Mailer claims, "was yet to occur."

Verbal confrontations between marchers and the uniformed went on throughout the day; Abbie Hoffman tried to levitate the Pentagon. Flowers were stuck in gunbarrels. By midnight, most of the demonstrators had dispersed. Soldiers and marshals then swept through the crowd, "using excessive force," Small writes, "against the remaining several hundred demonstrators. Several observers reported that some soldiers seemed to have singled out the women for special physical punishment." Mailer also notices that "a startling disproportion of women were arrested." He also quotes Margie Stamberg of the *Washington Free Press* on what became known as the Battle of the Wedge: "Slowly the wedge began to move in on people. With bayonets and rifle butts, they moved first on the girls in the front line, kicking them, jabbing at them again and again with the guns, busting their heads and arms to break the chain of locked arms." Thomas Powers writes of "women beaten senseless and then dragged off into the dark with bloody, broken faces." Mailer goes on to speculate that "they beat the women for another reason. To

THE MOVEMENT AND MCCARTHY

humiliate the demonstrators, to break them from their new resistance down to the old passive disobedience of the helpless sit-in waiting one's turn to be clubbed. . . . It is the worst hour at the Pentagon for the demonstrators. . . . [T]he working class had plucked all stolen balls back."

None of this—neither Stamberg nor Mailer—was to make the front pages of the newspapers of record or the evening news. According to Melvin Small's definitive *Covering Dissent* (1994), "those who reported major antiwar demonstrations concentrated on violent and radical—albeit colorful—behavior on the fringes of the activity, undercounted the crowds, and ignored political arguments the protestor's leadership presented." Such coverage was to have serious consequences for the writing of history, since as Terry Anderson demonstrates in *The Movement and the Sixties* (1995), authors who "relied on the mainstream press" were likely to have "misunderstood or distorted the movement."

Daniel Berrigan was to maintain that the media's "addiction to violence is matched only by its contemptuous indifference to non-violence." Sensing this—that only a violent act, however small, can somehow command the attention of the powers that be—Mailer has physically to force the issue of his own arrest by "stepping neatly and decisively over" a low rope. He then begins running, "as if he were a back cutting around the nearest man in the secondary," and runs until he forces two marshals to leap on him "at once."

What made the news were comments like David Brinkley's on NBC, who reduced the March on the Pentagon to "a coarse, vulgar episode by people who seemed more interested in exhibitionistic displays than any redress of grievances." *Time* called David Dellinger a "mob leader." James Reston titled his report "Everyone Is a Loser." From Jimmy Breslin came the headline "Quiet Rally Turns Vicious." The viciousness invoked had nothing to do, for Breslin, with the late-night sweep at the Pentagon; instead, emphasis fell on the violence of the protestors, as in the *Post* headline: "GI's Repel Pentagon Charge: 55,000 Rally against War." No wonder that at the Justice Department, when invited to speak, Mailer "scolded the press for their lies, and their misrepresentation, for their guilt in creating a psychology over the last twenty years in the average American which made wars like Vietnam possible."

The best that can be said of the mainstream press, in its coverage of the antiwar movement, is that even while mocking and misrepresenting, it succeeded in conveying a sense of appalling domestic disarray. It conveyed the force of the movement while missing its spirit, that of "a typically American reform movement," in the words of Charles Chatfield, "a voluntary crusade attracting adherents and impelling them to act out of a felt personal responsibility for social wrongs."

Meanwhile, LBJ was watching. And despite the reductions and distortions of the media coverage, it got to him. One of the larger ironies of the period is that even in the highly unsympathetic press coverage of the antiwar movement, Johnson heard in it a bell that tolled for him. A 1967 Pentagon memo was to reveal that Johnson "had been obsessed with the protest for most of the month" of October. His night reading included information about antiwar activists. He even read a list of "antiwar leaders and their communist connections" while having a haircut. When the wire service ticker brought him news of William Sloane Coffin attempting to return draft cards to the Justice Department, he jabbed his finger at the report and ordered his chief domestic aide, Joseph Califano, to have the FBI investigate. Johnson's press secretary later said that despite the White House business-as-usual pose over the October weekend, there was "the feeling of siege." Melvin Small consequently judges the March on the Pentagon as "the first in a chain of events that led to Lyndon Johnson's decision on March 31, 1968 to deescalate in Vietnam and to drop out of the presidential race." In *The War Within* (1994), Tom Wells uses the same verb: "The movement played a major role in constraining, de-escalating, and ending the war." Edward P. Morgan seconds these emotions in *The 60s Experience: Hard Lessons about Modern America* (1991): "The antiwar movement so effectively charged the domestic political atmosphere that it became the problem for the Johnson and Nixon administrations bent on carrying out their policies."

Each morning Johnson read the *New York Times*, the *Baltimore Sun*, the *Christian Science Monitor*, and the *Wall Street Journal*. He read the 11 p.m. edition of the *Post* and the *Star*, and watched the three early evening news programs. The Oval Office was equipped with a wire ticker from AP, UPI, and Reuters. Johnson was a "news junkie," and he saw the news as against him. The *Times* was "prejudicing people." NBC was "committed to an editorial policy of making us surrender." McGeorge Bundy, Johnson's national security adviser, saw *Newsweek* as having "a vested interest in defeat." *Defeat*. William Westmoreland also deploys the word, at the end of *A Soldier Reports*. Had Johnson "changed our strategy" after Tet, he argues, "the North Vietnamese doubtlessly would have broken. But that was not to be. Press and television had created an aura not of victory but of defeat, which, coupled with the vocal antiwar elements, profoundly influenced timid officials in Washington."

Defeat was precisely what the antiwar movement had to offer the United States. It prepared the nation for what eventually happened. We lost the war.

Charles Chatfield is eloquent on this point. The antiwar movement played "its major role" in that "it kept open the prospect of an American defeat as a national option." Only an acknowledgment of the failure could transform it into a "failure with dignity." As Thomas Powers concludes, in *The War at Home* (1973), "the opposition to the war did not *cause* the failure; it forced the government to *recognize* the failure."

In his chapter "A Palette of Tactics," Mailer has an imagined demonstrator say to a soldier at the Pentagon, "Why am I against the war in Vietnam? Cause it's wrong." Before returning to the story of Eugene McCarthy and his antiwar candidacy, it is important to tackle a question, one often lost in the arguments over whether the antiwar movement failed or succeeded: Just what was "wrong" with the war?

Mailer takes a stab at the question in the pissing scene in *Armies,* as discussed in the previous chapter. He comes up with something like: We are operating in the dark. Changing circumstances could eclipse any one answer to the question, as Michael Herr acknowledges near the end of his "Hell Sucks" article, when he and the General, talking in the wake of the Tet Offensive, downgrade the question from whether the war is "morally" to "militarily" defensible. The danger in the slippage from *should* to *could* lies in the contraction of the debate. Once you have started talking about whether a war is winnable, you have put aside the question of whether it should ever have been fought in the first place.

One could argue, as Senator Wayne Morse did, that the war was *illegal.* Congress had never formally declared war and had given the president the power to conduct it based on dubious reports of enemy attacks in the Tonkin Gulf. In *For Reasons of State* (1973), Noam Chomsky sees the war as *misdirected,* a campaign of destruction waged largely against the rural population of South Vietnam. Perhaps our military strategy itself was the problem, a point oddly reinforced by a reading of Westmoreland's memoir, in which his complaints about "graduated response," an approach he enforced but in which he did not believe, leave him judging our behavior as *incompetent.* Harry McPherson, Johnson's top speechwriter, invokes "the disparity between America's expressed war aims, and the means we were employing to achieve them." Massive bombing of both the North and the South was the most vivid example of this. There was something cruel and bullying in the spectacle; our behavior was *disproportionate.*

What was wrong with the war? The question takes us back to McNamara, and to Herr. In order to win a war, McNamara argues, there must be empathy for your enemy. Empathy can only occur where the enemy is, in a sufficient number of ways, scrutable, readable. We were able to avert disaster in the Cuban missile crisis, McNamara argues, because we had spent decades learning to read the Russians and because people who knew Nikita Khrushchev sat in the room with President Kennedy when the decisions were made. But trying to "*read*" the Vietnamese, Herr maintains on the first page of *Dispatches,* "*was like trying to read the wind.*" Not because they were the inscrutable Oriental. Vietnamese culture is presumably as accessible to study as any other. But we had not done our homework with them; we had not cultivated the experts who might have been able to read and therefore to know and then be able to empathize with our Vietnamese enemy.

Vietnam therefore became for the United States a Heart of Darkness situation. This is one of the reasons why, forty years after movies about Vietnam started being made, Francis Ford Coppola's *Apocalypse Now* (1979) has risen to the top of the list. Herr's script for the movie, with its Marlowe and Kurtz figures, and the long trip upriver, makes the recurrence plain. The movie, like Conrad's book, calls upon the imperial reader to acknowledge his "dark patches," as Whitman calls them. "It is not upon you alone the dark patches fall," he writes in "Crossing Brooklyn Ferry." The gesture is inclusive, meant to affirm a shared complicity. "This also . . . has been one of the dark places of the earth," Conrad has Marlowe say, at the beginning of *Heart of Darkness,* and his narrator is talking about London, not the Belgian Congo. It is a dark place because, like all imperial capitals, it is where the war against a place beyond the "known" world is conceived, a war which creates a dark patch in the soul of all who profit from it.

Conrad invokes in Africa an "inscrutable intention" and converts Marlowe's inability to decipher the Congo into the story's major subject. Marlowe keeps coming across texts he cannot read, like the marginalia in Towson's manuscript, jottings he assumes to be written "in cipher," but which turn out to be Russian, or like Kurtz's final note, dashed across the bottom of his report, "Exterminate all the brutes!" Nothing is learned on Marlowe's journey in and out of Africa, except perhaps the necessity of lying, which is what he does in the final scene with Kurtz's Intended. The moral to be drawn from such situations is this: Don't go in there. Don't go in there until you have learned how to read.

The problem, then, had to do with insufficient knowledge. For Kurtz, and for Marlowe, the Congo "had whispered to him things about himself which he did not know." But of course for ignorance to be useful, you have to know that you do not know. In its foreign relations, the United States has a habit of assuming an expertise it does not possess, or, on the other hand, of dismissing such knowledge as unimportant. Both stances betray an anxiety about the work of knowing itself, a fear of where it might lead. Because all true knowing leads within, into the heart of darkness in the nation, and in the self.

Marlowe will assert that "the most you can hope from" life "is some knowledge of yourself." Gaining it involves a reclaiming of projections outward as well as a relinquishing of the more seductive self-idealizations. A *New Yorker* column, published in the month after Saigon fell, recurs to the question of knowing. Suddenly the blame is flying everywhere, "the longest war in our history was at last coming to an end, and we did not know who the enemy had been."

We did not know, even at the end, who the enemy had been because we never knew what the war had been about, and that was because we were uneasy about knowing ourselves. Ideas, like the domino theory, were allowed to displace an honest scrutiny and admission of what people always fight for—their interests. "All knew that this interest was, somehow, the cause of the war." This is not someone invoking oil in Iraq or markets in the Pacific, but Lincoln, in his Second Inaugural Address, talking about slavery. Lincoln's sentence makes two important points. The phrase "all knew" is key. Lincoln is arguing that even then—in 1865—all Americans knew what the war had been about. What is being fought over is something "all knew"; like the founding truths, it is self-evident—even to those who would most passionately deny it.

The second point has to do with the nature of what is being fought about. Slavery is an "interest," not a principle or an ideal or a value. Both sides have chosen to go to war over this interest, rather than for the sake of something ineffably higher. A fight about interests can end, while one about ideas—a religious or ideological struggle—has a way of continuing. By reducing the cause of the war to an interest, and by insisting that all know it to be the cause, Lincoln dignifies and contains the meaning of the struggle, while implying that to reject this reading of the conflict is to go against what everybody already knows. That fourteen decades later the Civil War is still spoken of in some quarters as having been about "states' rights" only testifies to the stubbornness of the American habit of wanting not to know what we know.

What is the word for such persistence in wanting not to know what we know? When Faulkner came to take up Lincoln's question, and to give it the same answer through the story of Thomas Sutpen in *Absalom, Absalom!* (1936), he came up with the word Graham Greene was later to apply to the Quiet American: "His trouble was innocence." *Innocence*? The seemingly benign term can cover such a complex case because it is exactly right. Americans commit error in the world less in the service of cynicism and greed than out of a conviction that they are exceptional, well-meaning, right—and are therefore not required to know much more. This is the essence of innocence, a refusal to see oneself as caught up in the same motives and drives and imperfections—the same stories, really—as those that move other people. Mailer detects this "infernal American innocence," a way of mind "which could not question one's leaders," in the turnkey who hurries him from the phone. As Patrick Hagopian argues, the price of unknowing is high: "The unquestioning conviction that the nation is virtuous allows, indeed *requires*, state crimes to go unjudged, because accountability for past crimes would tarnish the nation's image of innocence."

To quote Eugene McCarthy: we were not "willing to open the box and see what America was." Sutpen thinks he can take revenge on the past without paying any corresponding price, and the price he will pay, as with America in Vietnam, is the self-created destruction of his own design. At every point where he is offered evidence or a chastening glimpse into the workings of his culture, Sutpen turns away. Chang-rae Lee gives this deeply ingrained American behavior—is it not the American ideology itself?—an eloquent formulation in his novel *A Gesture Life* (1999), where another character gifted at looking away speaks of "innocence, wanting not to know what I know." So the question may then be not "What was wrong with the war?" but "What was wrong with us?" And the answer would be: We were *innocent.*

By the fall of 1967, Richard Goodwin was looking for an antiwar candidate. A speechwriter and an old Kennedy hand, he was summoned to Hickory Hill, Robert Kennedy's Virginia estate, in January 1968. "I guess I'm not going to do it," Bobby said. On the ride back to Dulles Airport, Goodwin made his reply. "I guess if you're not going, that I'll go up to New Hampshire and see if I can help McCarthy."

Goodwin headed north in late February. He drove to Berlin, New Hampshire, listening to Bob Dylan all the way. Arriving at midnight, he was greeted by McCarthy's press secretary, Seymour Hersh. Goodwin asked how many reporters were covering the campaign. "None," Hersh replied. However quixotic the effort—Goodwin is later reminded of the gentle Don and Sancho Panza—he decided to put "aside the secret enemies of hope." And so he said: "You, me, and this typewriter, Sy; together we're going to overthrow the president of the United States."

Goodwin is one of the great waverers of 1968. He had come to Washington as a speechwriter for John Kennedy, and stayed on, until 1965, to do the same for Lyndon Johnson. He was to stick with the McCarthy campaign until Kennedy declared for the presidency, when he switched his support back to his old friend. After Kennedy's assassination, Goodwin rejoined the McCarthy campaign. Abigail McCarthy's memoir, *Private Faces/Public Places* (1972), captures the lingering ambivalence the McCarthys must have felt for Goodwin. "There is no denying that Dick Goodwin with his ugly, compelling face, his direct, black eyes, and his cheerful, permanent half-grin brought a lift to the campaign." Her husband saw Goodwin as certifying him. But she had no doubt that Goodwin "came to New Hampshire in the first place to prove to Bobby Kennedy that he should run." Mary McGrory was to call Goodwin "a Trojan horse."

According to Jules Witcover, McCarthy had "at first seemed persuaded to duck New Hampshire." He deemed it "not a particularly significant test." Deciding to run there only on January 2, he showed small commitment to organization. We will "live off the land," he declared.

Despite making it sound as if he and Sy Hersh were to create a campaign *ex nihilo,* Goodwin was a latecomer. Looking back, in *Remembering America* (1988), he would come to conclude that McCarthy had somehow managed to surround himself with "the biggest and best field organization ever assembled for any political campaign, before or since." No one better captures the grass roots energy of the New Hampshire effort than Ben Stavis, in *We Were the Campaign* (1969).

In the winter of 1968, Stavis was a graduate student studying Chinese politics at Columbia. On February 15, he and his wife, Rosann, took a bus to Concord. Arriving at 10:30 a.m., they found a headquarters located in an old electrical appliance store. They immediately started to clean up the place, shoveling out rubbish and stationing pails of water in the basement to serve as fire extinguishers. They soon met Sam Brown, a Harvard graduate student in charge of mobilizing student volunteers, and Curt Gans, the newly appointed campaign director. "There was plenty to do," another memoirist writes, "only you had to figure out a job description, and fill it, yourself."

New Hampshire was unpromising ground for an insurgent campaign. Home to a number of defense industries, the state collected no income tax. The *Manchester Union-Leader,* the state's biggest newspaper, was ultra-conservative. In early canvassing, Ben and Rosann found that people wanted, above all, an end to the war, either "immediate withdrawal or military victory. The means did not matter as much as the immediacy of the exit. Thus several voters were carefully weighing McCarthy and Wallace, considering them to be similar, not at opposite ends of a political spectrum." This convergence of apparent extremes would be uncovered later by post-election polling, when it was revealed that a good percentage of those voting for McCarthy were hawks unhappy with Johnson's strategy of graduated response.

Ben quickly became known as the "map man" because of his skill at cutting up state highway maps and marking out canvassing routes. Rosann became the office manager out of "her simple habit of putting things away." When Gans showed up, the Lowenstein ally tried to keep his existence from the press, hoping to project the image of a movement run by "innocent students." On the other hand, he discouraged those with beards from working the streets. It was important to be Clean for Gene; the campaign should be "dignified and polite." Mini-skirts were phased out. By election day, the original small cadre of workers had grown to where it could deploy one volunteer for every twenty-five voters, and was to reach almost all of the 89,000 registered Democrats in the state. Despite a number of high-profile departures along the way—Hersh was to resign in Wisconsin—the staff assembled in New Hampshire became the "core" of the McCarthy campaign.

The high moment in Stavis's narrative is when he confesses to error, a miscalculation "which in a strange way taught me a little bit about the Vietnamese war." He has been given the task of distributing sample ballots to every doorstep in the state. At first, he approaches the task in an "academic way," consulting census figures and dispatching people to the local library to analyze town registers. It is a model of centralized, "elegant planning." Then he realizes it would be easier and more efficient to give each town ballots of its own and to let it decide how to distribute them. "As I thought of that, I thought too of Lyndon Johnson. Through a mistake I had wasted only time. Through a mistake he had wasted tens of thousands of Americans and hundreds of thousands of Vietnamese lives. How much more difficult for him to admit error than for me!" "Some damn mistake had been made," as Mailer puts it, and realizing it, Stavis changes his strategy. Stavis here comes upon one of the profound and enduring themes of words written in and about 1968: the adaptive value of the capacity to admit error.

Stavis saw McCarthy campaigning only once. The candidate "would not push himself beyond endurance," Arthur Herzog maintains. "He had his own campaign chemistry—strong in the morning, progressively weaker in the afternoon, good again in the evening. He wanted his rest periods and his martini." He sometimes ate breakfast alone. McCarthy was eventually to employ a valet to walk behind him, to keep well-wishers away. Despite the intermittency of the effort, and a big snowstorm on March 12, when the votes came in McCarthy had won 42.2 to Johnson's 49.4 percent. Once Republican write-ins were counted, he trailed Johnson by only 230 votes. This marked the "turnaround," as Don Oberdorfer calls it. "The President and his circle were confronted with something akin to a national veto on the indefinite continuation or further enlargement of the United States involvement in the war in Vietnam." As Stavis argues, "our campaign was an unusually successful mass movement," one that succeeded in "shortening the war."

On election night, McCarthy said something wonderful: "People have remarked that this campaign has brought young people back into the system. But it's the other way around. The young people have brought the country back into the system." The compliment to young people is generous, and lovely. Young people *are* the country, and whither they goest, it will go. But a "country" can become entirely alienated from the "system" that governs it; by driving a wedge between the two words, McCarthy implies that for too long we have had, in the United States, a system without a country.

In Wisconsin, in April, McCarthy was to beat Johnson by twenty percentage points. In Indiana, he lost to Kennedy. He won again, in Oregon, and lost to Kennedy again, in California. Then Kennedy was shot. On the plane back to Washington, in the hours after the assassination, McCarthy turned to an aide and said, "It's all over." After that, as Albert Eisele was later to say, "He just kind of gave up." On November 6, after Nixon was elected, McCarthy called for "a day of visiting the sick and burying the dead. It's gray everywhere, all over the land."

From the start, the campaign gave off a sense of the already-over. The candidate refrained from asserting himself. When Hubert Humphrey trumpeted a "politics of happiness," McCarthy urged settling for mere "satisfaction." He betrayed a habit of disdaining the very thing he had set out to achieve, as in his first loss to Kennedy, when he said, "I'd rather win the college primary than the Indiana primary." His run for the nomination had about it something of the fortuitous; as he said in Wisconsin: "The seeking of me as a candidate came like the dew in the night. It was rather gentle, I must say, soft, but there were signs in the morning that something had happened during the night, and so here I am." The metaphor of the dew argues for his presence on the scene as the result of a natural process, rather than from the agency of committed supporters. Ben Stavis came to believe that McCarthy viewed the enterprise "as a spontaneous happening." This tendency to discount or mystify the efforts of others culminates in *The Year of the People* (1969), McCarthy's benumbing look back, where he allows that "one cannot overrate the contribution of the new people." No "I" here expresses gratitude to the faithful or takes responsibility for success or failure. And the double negative in "cannot overrate" offers toward all those who worked so hard for him only a grudging gesture of thanks. As he said, watching the rioting in Chicago from above, "If I go down, I claim them, and they're not mine."

So, as the summer wore on, McCarthy stood "passive and self-absorbed in the winding down of his campaign," Jeremy Larner maintains, regressing "to his balanced presentation of self, to the sacred ceremony of his personality." McCarthy would label Larner's *Nobody Knows* (1969) "a political *Portnoy's Complaint,*" and the book does seem to issue from a deeply wounded sensibility. Yet Larner, who joined the campaign as a speechwriter after New Hampshire, is also well-positioned to unpack the spirit of "a presidential campaign that completely rejected," in Eisele's words, "the element of emotion."

After June 6, part of the blocked emotion was, surely, an expression of shock and grief. "In the days after the funeral," Abigail McCarthy remembers, "Gene seemed deeply depressed and almost unreachable. Night after night he lay beside me sleepless, staring at the ceiling." In this, McCarthy simply lived out the experience of many of his fellow citizens. But there was still a campaign to run, and, while he soldiered on with it, "it seemed to Gene all that summer that we were simply going through the motions." McCarthy had the tremendous fortune of living through and finding himself at the center of a season of high hope, one followed by a period of deep despair. It would perhaps be asking too much of any man to have ridden out the aftermath with good grace.

Still, Larner's account raises questions about McCarthy's interest in and capacity for "executive" office. After the win in Wisconsin, when Goodwin was still on the team, he turned to Lowenstein and said, "You and I can make McCarthy president. . . . The question is, do we want Eugene McCarthy to be our next president?" Larner saw McCarthy as running against the very thing he had set out to get: presidential power. "The concentration of power in the executive," McCarthy once said, was the "basic problem" in American government. He feared excess, preferring "balanced judgment." A Christian politician, as he deemed himself, "should shun the devices of the demagogue at all times." Arthur Schlesinger Jr. concluded that McCarthy was the first modern liberal "to run *against* the Presidency." McCarthy had begun running, after all, *against* the war; no one may have been more surprised, and then shocked, when Johnson's withdrawal, and then Kennedy's death, left him free to run *for* the White House.

McCarthy also appeared to be running against ego. Yet "again and again," Larner writes, "his conduct referred us back to the man's conception of himself." In this, McCarthy and Johnson were opposites: the one man calmly fighting to preserve an ego-ideal; the other trying, more and more desperately, to overcome the lack of one. "What reporters and others took as modesty or mystery or some form of concealment, or retreat from personality, was really personality itself." This well-disguised self-regard, a refusal to stoop to conquer, resulted in damaging hesitations, as when McCarthy refrained from visiting the Milwaukee ghetto and then consented so late to expose himself to the politics of "reaching out" that he arrived there on a cold day and found only a handful of people on the streets.

The pattern of Yes-No can be traced back as far as Eugene's courtship of Abigail. Her first impression of the man who became her husband was of "some sort of inaccessible saint with a mysterious purpose of his own." Over the subsequent memories there hovers a presentiment of loss. Looking at a photograph from the period of the courtship, she notices her hands "tightly clasped as if something precious might escape." Eugene asked Abigail to marry him in January 1938. On Good Friday, 1941, he told her that he felt called to be a priest and suggested she might enter a convent. On March 21, 1942, he became Brother Conan. McCarthy eventually fell out with the man in charge of his training and was effectively expelled from the novitiate, leaving it in May 1943. The complaint against him centered around intellectual pride. Reconnecting with Abigail, he married her in June 1945. The marriage would last twenty-four years, until he left their home in 1969. Abigail never granted a divorce, and they remained legally married for the remainder of her life.

As early as 1948, Abigail detected in her husband a horror of revealing anything personal in public life. He "refused to use the pronoun 'I' in his speeches, preferring the more generic and indefinite 'we,' a verbal habit which was to confuse some of his young followers in 1968." The habitual use of the first-person plural masked a felt "loftiness," as Larner has it, a sense of his own star "as distant and as solemn as an image."

While McCarthy's standoffishness expressed the depth of his own reserve, it also served as a mockery of the patriarchs. As Larner saw it, McCarthy's obvious self-possession pointed up the fact that "it was the great big people who lacked true personality." The government Wise Men "tried to cover up the horror of their deeds with giant masks of super-gravity," a performance of probity that would prove most enduring in the career of Henry Kissinger. This is why the accounts coming out of Washington or off the front pages of the *New York Times* had to be met with humor, self-deprecation, exaggeration, or even, as Herr and Mailer understood, with obscenity. Nothing a writer could conjure in his prose could come close to matching the profanity of the official horrors. McCarthy's wit stands closer to the work of these writers than to it does to the idiom of any politician on the scene in 1968. With them he shares a sense of the extremity of the moment and of "style as the chief sign of substance." This is Larner's claim, one McCarthy reframes in *Up 'Til Now* (1987): "Style can become substantive, or have substantial effects, if not watched." McCarthy's wit allowed him to brag, for instance, without seeming to. "Bobby's campaign is like a grass fire—it will just burn off the surface. Mine is like a fire in a peat bog. It will hold on for six months." In refiguring the parable of the tortoise and the hare, McCarthy finds a round-about and seemingly modest way of saying *I will win.*

There was one night when style and substance came fully together, in the May 22 Cow Palace speech on Vietnam. It was a speech about the determining and unacknowledged power of underlying assumptions. These assumptions give rise to systematic "misconceptions" about "America's moral mission in the world; the great threat from China; the theory of monolithic Communist conspiracy; the susceptibility of political problems to military solutions; the duty to impose American idealism on foreign cultures, especially Asian." It is difficult to imagine a more cogent summary of the stances informing American foreign policy after 1945. Under the pressure of McCarthy's discrimination, the war in Vietnam emerges as part of a larger mis-"conception," the Cold War consensus that now—in 1968—needs to be rethought. The misconceptions underlying this consensus are powerful because they are interlocking. And yet any one of them, alone, can also be summoned to justify an adventure like Vietnam. With its balanced series of phrases set off by of semicolons, the syntax of McCarthy's sentence enacts this point. Remarkable about his series is that as one of its elements—the *threat* of China or the domino *theory*—disappears, or is discredited, the *mission* and the *susceptibility* and the *duty* still abide, sufficient each unto themselves to drive and maintain the ongoing policy.

McCarthy was powerfully responsive to the ironies and histories hidden within single words, and Jeremy Larner noticed early on that his speeches were centered around "bits," "fixed phrases" or individual words suggested by an adviser or thought up by McCarthy himself. In the Cow Palace speech, he comes up with a sentence and a series of words that unpack the ideology of his moment. Like all ideologies, as McCarthy demonstrates, this one is able to survive questioning and disproof because its fundamental assump-tions, encoded in the five foregrounded words, are articles of faith rather than thought-out positions, jargon terms that inhabit a self-enclosed and self-reinforcing circularity. As McCarthy summed things up: "The process is wrong as well as what it produces." This is a substantive insight, won through style.

So, yes, McCarthy was cool to Kennedy's hot; he was ambivalent about power; he was perhaps too caught up in preserving a sense of his own disinterestedness. Yet he was what was needed. He represented seriousness, a move to the interior. It was time for the nation and its citizens to look within and to stop being afraid to think. It was this very thoughtfulness that impressed the young, in an adult who seemed scrupulous without also insisting on being parental. Larner writes eloquently about McCarthy's gift: "American optimists at heart, immune in the long run to ideology, they were terribly grateful to have the chance to do something real." It is such figures—the "A" students who abandoned their studies, and who may also have romanticized, as Larner argues, the NLF, Ché Guevara, and Malcolm X—that we need to find a way to honor. It was her energy, and his faith, that made the campaign.

On the afternoon of the June 1 debate with Robert Kennedy, McCarthy found himself singing songs and quoting poems with Robert Lowell. After the debate was over he said to his California front man, "I don't want to talk about politics. I want to talk about Dante's Sixth Canto." Which is what he proceeded to do, again with Lowell.

The Sixth Canto of the *Inferno* deals with the sorrows of a "divided state" and with the civil war in Florence that eventually sent Dante into exile from his beloved city. So talking about it was not an altogether extravagant gesture. McCarthy's country was divided, and he was, soon enough, to live out his days in a kind of internal exile. For McCarthy, the civil war had always been as much within as without. "Hardest to accept" about McCarthy, Larner would argue, "was a deep-seated bitterness . . . which made him down-rate individuals, even as he was calling for a national policy of generosity." The down-rating extended also to the man himself. Goodwin saw him as "compelled to battle with an inward self-hatred that would, much later, lead him to destroy the immense future possibilities that remained to him after the 1968 campaign was over." By 1970, McCarthy would write, in "Lament for an Aging Politician," that "my metaphors grow cold and old."

The antiwar movement had hitched its star to the soul of a poet, and it would reap the benefits of the choice as it would pay the price. And yet, as Lowell himself wonders, in his sonnet "For Eugene McCarthy," "Who will swear you wouldn't/have done good to the country—that fulfillment wouldn't/have done good to you." Lowell's question reminds us that 1968 was a year of emotional momentum continually being stopped. For those who loved King and Kennedy, it was stopped altogether. McCarthy survived, but just barely. He went on to live a kind of posthumous life, making occasional ghostly forays into the public realm from his remove in Rappahannock, Virginia. In passing so quickly across the scene, and in then continuing to haunt it, McCarthy left only the trace of a hope, a hope with which we did not get to live long enough.

When it comes to assessing the good McCarthy did for his country, it can be difficult to separate the hard fact of winning from the sheer experience of participating. He and the young who worked for him, had, truly, *brought the country back*. Ben Stavis believes that the movement shortened the war, a claim that will be endlessly debated. But he also recognizes that by way of it, Americans "learned how they might shape their political destinies." In a process so endless, and incremental, winning may be merely the happy and only occasional byproduct of the transforming experience of showing up for a fight.

Two days after formally announcing his candidacy, McCarthy invoked "the language of promise and of hope." When I first began writing this chapter, in the winter of 2008, another candidate was barnstorming the country, invoking the same word, stirring strong emotions. Some dismiss the word and call it mere rhetoric. But hope is what Lincoln brought, what Franklin Roosevelt brought, what John F. Kennedy brought. They brought it by speaking the wished-for words—they brought it, as McCarthy did, through a kind of poetry. And they brought it despite their political failures, and it mattered. Hope, like words, matters.

How do you measure the social value of hope? McCarthy afforded those who sought an end to the war a sense of power in relation to the world. What was given, and felt, could not be bound up solely within the terms of political victory. It was an access of energy and self-belief that passed into people's lives and offered itself, in the low, dishonest decades to come, as a resource of the spirit. For all that was not achieved, something had been changed in the political landscape, a generational "rite of passage" had been endured, as Mailer writes, and those who chose to take part in it "were forever different."

CHAPTER

3

McNamara, Bombing, and the Tuesday Lunch

On February 28, 1968, in the East Room of the White House, Lyndon Johnson presented Robert McNamara with the Medal of Freedom. McNamara was to retire as secretary of defense on the following day. Johnson makes no mention of these ceremonies in his memoir, *The Vantage Point;* the fact of Clark Clifford's succeeding McNamara as secretary of defense is consigned to a footnote. It was all he could muster for the man he had so highly praised in a 1965 interview. "He is the first at work and the last one to leave. When I wake up, the first one I call is McNamara. He is there at seven every morning, including Saturday. The only difference is that Saturday he wears a sport coat. He is the best utility man. I would make him Secretary of State or Secretary of Transportation tomorrow—he is that qualified. He is smart, patriotic, works hard. I never heard him say, 'I told you so.'" By the time Johnson retired him, McNamara had long since begun saying, "I told you so."

A man more in love with numbers than with words, McNamara was nevertheless highly articulate. George Ball found his verbal "performances formidable and scintillating." Yet on being presented with the medal, McNamara seemed suddenly struck dumb. Johnson had spoken warmly of him, despite the rift that had grown up between the two men over Vietnam. McNamara was clearly moved and attempted to respond. But he could only manage one halting sentence. "I cannot find words to express what lies in my heart today, and I think I'd better respond on another occasion." It was a curious moment of self-silencing.

Only the day before, however, McNamara had found the words, those he had perhaps been seeking to express over the painful months since he had come to doubt the nation's course in Vietnam. It happened at the Tuesday lunch, his last as a member of the Johnson administration. The Tuesday lunches had been initiated soon after Johnson became president; Walt Rostow called them the "heart" of the national security process. According to H. R. McMaster, Johnson "made his most important decisions at the Tuesday lunch meetings."

Johnson was in Texas during McNamara's last Tuesday lunch; the report of the meeting was sent to his ranch that evening. His account of the lunch in *The Vantage Point* is a reconstruction by an absentee, one innocent of the knowledge of the emotional intensity displayed that day in Dean Rusk's comfortable dining room at the Department of State.

"On February 27," Johnson writes, "some of my advisers met at lunch in Washington to discuss Vietnam." The specific purpose, as Johnson recalls it, was to review his upcoming speech on the war, a speech eventually merging with his announcement that he would not seek the presidency in 1968. Most of the time at the meeting was taken up not with the speech, however, but with the request from General Westmoreland, forwarded through the chairman of the Joint Chiefs of Staff, General Earle Wheeler, for 206,000 additional American troops to be sent to Vietnam.

Johnson summarizes the meeting as one in which his advisers put forth competing if reasonable proposals. McNamara presented "three options." Clark Clifford supported "a fourth." Rostow reported in summary that the "only firm agreement" among those present was that "the troop issue raised many questions."

Faced with the challenge of dramatizing a scene of which he had no direct knowledge, Johnson falls back on his chosen mode of deliberative and enumerative prose. The Olympian tone of his memoir is calculated to represent its speaker as a judicious overseer: one paragraph alone contains the phrases, "I discussed," "I listened," "I consulted." But the prose is utterly dead, lacking any of the color and force and inspired obscenity of Johnson's actual speaking voice, with its running jokes about "quivering" cows and the bull, or his vow to have every man's "pecker" in his drawer. As she helped put the memoir together, Doris Kearns Goodwin quickly became aware that Johnson did not want to write it and that when talking to the tape machine—the memoir was largely dictated—"his language became artificial." The very flatness of the prose is itself an expression not of the mature and rational self Johnson means to project, but of a disappointed and rejected soul. Daniel Patrick Moynihan would one day read the self-idealizing tactics of Johnson's memoir as "bitterness seeping through memory."

Had Johnson been present at the lunch, he might have reduced its essence to one word: bombing. The meeting turned on a prolonged outburst by the secretary of defense. In an interview with Paul Hendrickson, Johnson's speechwriter Harry McPherson recalled the scene eighteen years later: "McNamara, who hadn't been slumped in silence, who had been contributing to the discussion, got up—and with such fury and passion and tears he's lashing out at the whole war, his voice rising and cracking and the room swelling with all of it: the goddamned bombing campaign, it's been worth nothing, they've dropped more bombs than in all of Europe in all of World War Two and it hasn't done a fucking thing. . . ."

The words "just incredibly caught in" McNamara's throat, McPherson continues, "like somebody in the third week of laryngitis. . . . I was shaken, riveted, the room looking down at its shoetops. The most emotional moment I've ever seen."

As Johnson's point man on domestic policy, Joseph Califano had been invited to attend the lunch. "It was the most depressing three hours in my years of public service," he was to write. He drove back to the White House with McPherson:

> I was physically shaken. Both of us were completely drained.
> "This is crazy," I said.
> McPherson nodded.
> "It really is all over, isn't it? I said.
> "You bet it is," McPherson responded.

Born in San Francisco in 1916, Robert Strange McNamara entered UC Berkeley in the depths of the Depression, in 1933. After taking a course in logic he began to "talk and think in numbers." An MBA at Harvard was followed by a teaching post there until the war broke out, when he joined the Army Air Corps in Statistical Control, a vast tracking system that attempted to keep an inventory of the "objects, resources, and people" involved in the air war. He worked with the Eighth Air Force on the campaign against Germany, on the ill-fated airlift over the Hump to China, and most tellingly with General Curtis LeMay on the bombing of Japan. Asked by filmmaker Errol Morris about the firebombing of Tokyo, in which one hundred thousand Japanese perished in a single night, McNamara replied: "I was part of the mechanism that in a sense recommended it."

McNamara and bombs; the convergence of the twain. In 1937 he had watched from the *President Hoover* as the Japanese attacked Shanghai. He would thereafter keep on his desk a fragment of the bombshell that had landed that day on the ship's deck.

In 1946, McNamara and a group from Stat Control sold themselves to the Ford Motor Company as the Whiz Kids. McNamara would stay at Ford for fourteen years, rising to the presidency of the company only a month before he accepted John Kennedy's offer to become secretary of defense. At Ford, he had the chance to put his theories of management to the test.

When McNamara arrived in Detroit, he discovered that "no one knew what it cost to build a Ford car." Bookkeeping was so lax that accounts payable and receivable were sometimes determined by laying invoices and bills on benches and measuring which row was longer. McNamara's emerging field of "management control" set out to replace accrual accounting with "a new way of assigning costs that took account of the varied activities involved in making the product." Everything—car parts, workers, dealers, customer whims—was to be counted and tracked. Financial data became the key tool in the process, and "numbers became the common language." A corporation was a quantifiable thing, its numberless processes reducible to charts and graphs. "The monitoring of progress" became, for McNamara, the bedrock of good management, and progress was to be measured "against the plan." While this approach did temporarily restore Ford to profitability, it was a far cry from the engineering and entrepreneurship and the sheer love of making cars that had created the company, and as time passed it became clear that under McNamara's system innovation and feedback flowing upward from the men on the line had no part in the process. When Japanese carmakers began to surpass Detroit in the 1970s by making cars that were better and cheaper, they did so by encouraging every worker to become a partner in management.

When McNamara arrived at the Department of Defense, he found an organization in a disarray not unlike Ford's. He set out not only to modernize the armed forces but to replace a loyalty- and field-experience-based culture with a corporate one. "I had no patience with the myth that the Department of Defense could not be managed," he wrote in his memoir. "Control" became the byword, a goal to be realized by concentrating decision making in the hands of a select few. Once again, McNamara committed himself to a plan without real people in it: left out of Defense Department reckonings were the members of the Army, Navy, and Air Force themselves, since the express aim of his management revolution was to deny the Joint Chiefs direct access to the president and to provide, as H. R. McMaster writes, only a "facade of consultation."

In *Dereliction of Duty* (1997), McMaster tells the story of how the Kennedy administration shifted power away from the military men and toward the Pentagon's civilian leadership. Early on in his tenure at Defense, McNamara forged an alliance with the newly appointed head of the Joint Chiefs, Maxwell Taylor, a man who saw the president, rather than his fellow officers, as his constituency. By the time of the Cuban missile crisis, Taylor was "the only professional military officer" to attend the meetings of EXCOM, the group of advisers set up to deal in secret with weighty military and political options. McNamara came up with the idea of a blockade, against the recommendations of the chiefs, who favored bombing and invasion. When the blockade worked, McNamara set out to assume "the role of chief strategist in the Pentagon."

McNamara enjoyed immense early success, becoming a close confidant of Kennedy and, later, Johnson's most trusted cabinet member. He was the man who selected the Kennedy gravesite, at Arlington; he was the man Johnson seriously considered in 1964 as a running mate. An impressive briefer, he dominated any gathering with his command of figures, capacious memory, and rat-a-tat style of delivery. "No one ever held the capital in greater sway," Clark Clifford was to write, "than Robert S. McNamara did from 1961 until the end of 1967." When the sway ended, it did so as if part of a process of karmic return, with the middle-aged man taken down by the very thing that had made the young one, by the incalculable consequences of bombing.

By the summer of 1964, the Joint Chiefs were pressing for an air campaign against North Vietnam. The government of South Vietnam was in disarray, passing through a period of frequent coups, while the battle of Ap Bac, joined a year earlier, had shown the Army of the Republic of Vietnam (ARVN) as unprepared or unwilling to stand and fight. McNamara allowed the chiefs to begin planning air attacks. By August, they had located ninety-four targets in the North. Then came the Gulf of Tonkin incident, which opened the way for a wider war.

On the morning of August 2, 1964, the USS *Maddox,* pursued by North Vietnamese torpedo boats, was attacked on the high seas. The attack was not unprovoked, since the *Maddox* had just completed an operation in support of a bombardment by South Vietnamese fast boats of two islands off the North Vietnamese coast. The *Maddox* itself had been ordered to the Gulf of

Tonkin on a top-secret mission to intercept North Vietnamese radio and radar signals. "Johnson ruled out retaliation," Gareth Porter writes, "because he did not believe the incident was the result of a deliberate policy by Hanoi."

In response to the North Vietnamese attacks, President Johnson ordered the *Maddox* and a second destroyer, the USS *C. Turner Joy*, back into the Gulf of Tonkin. On the night of August 3–4, the two American ships "thought they were being attacked." This second reported attack on U.S. naval vessels became the basis for the Tonkin Gulf resolution, which gave Johnson the power to "prevent further aggression" in Southeast Asia. Congress passed the resolution in record speed, after being assured there had been no American provocation. By 2007, when the National Security Agency's history of Vietnam was declassified, even its official historians had come to "agree," as John Prados maintains, that the second "engagement was illusory."

Johnson used his expanded authority to authorize the first *official* bombing of the North—the U.S. had in fact been carrying out various kinds of sabotage in the region since the early 1950s. In the few hours allowed for the attacks, naval pilots flew sixty-four sorties against North Vietnamese vessels and an oil storage facility. Two American planes were shot down; one aviator was killed, and a second was captured and spent over eight years in captivity.

McNamara went out of his way to mislead Johnson about what happened after the *Turner Joy* joined the *Maddox* in the Tonkin Gulf. Looking to place increased military pressure on the North, and facing a reluctant president, McNamara called Johnson "well before the first report of an attack on U.S. naval vessels on August 4" in order "to alert him to the intercept of a North Vietnamese message indicating that some kind of naval action was imminent." The first report of torpedoes firing at the *Maddox* came at 11:18 p.m. In the face of these reports, Johnson agreed to two retaliatory air strikes. What McNamara did not tell Johnson was that John J. Herrick, the captain of the *Maddox,* had in the meantime alerted Admiral Sharp of "freak weather effects" on his ship's radar that made the reports of the "torpedo attacks questionable." Herrick suggested a "complete evaluation" before any action taken in response.

When McNamara called Admiral Sharp at 4:08 p.m., he made no mention of Herrick's concerns. Sharp however had independent word from Herrick indicating "a little doubt on just exactly what went on." As Porter reports, McNamara countered with "an obviously leading question: 'There isn't any possibility there was no attack, is there?'" Sharp's answer was to suggest that any strike order be postponed "until we have a definite indication that this happened." McNamara responded by insisting that pilots be briefed and planes armed. When McNamara called Johnson about an hour later and read him a statement about "two destroyers" being attacked, he made no "reference to the problem of uncertainty about the alleged attack on U.S. vessels."

Despite their agreeing to these "limited and fitting" air strikes, as the president called them, Johnson and McNamara still refrained from authorizing a sustained bombing campaign against the North. The turning point came on February 6, 1965, when eight Americans were blown up at a barracks in Pleiku. The subsequent strikes against North Vietnamese targets were described as a "reprisal." As national security adviser McGeorge Bundy saw it, air attacks on the North would "correspond" to "the level of outrages in the South." Johnson and McNamara, cautious about angering the Soviet Union and China, insisted that the bombing campaign, soon to be called Rolling Thunder, be limited. The president preferred "seduction, not rape," Doris Kearns Goodwin writes, and "a total assault on the North . . . would be rape rather than seduction."

Johnson's metaphor complements McNamara's view of bombing as a form of communication. According to McMaster, McNamara believed that "the aim of force was not to impose one's will on the enemy but to communicate with him." In William Bundy's words, we bombed "not so much for the sake of damage as to show how hopeless" was any resistance by the North. McNamara's view derived from the theories he had developed in the early 1960s about "signaling and bargaining among adversaries in nuclear war." A model applying with some efficacy to the Soviet Union would prove, however, inapplicable to Hanoi, an enemy apparently unmoved by "gradations of pain."

Troops were needed to guard planes and their crews, and so the bombing campaign against the North led, inexorably, to the introduction of U.S. combat ground troops into the South. In March 1965, the first Marines waded ashore near Da Nang, their mission again defined as a "limited" one of defending resources already in place. Johnson and McNamara thus initiated their policy of graduated response, imagining themselves as responsible reactors in a largely symbolic struggle—in an attempt to "communicate."

Bombing was of course also meant to have practical results, especially the interdiction of material flowing to the South. As Thomas Powers puts it, "Pressure for a bombing campaign was largely the result of the official explanation of the war. The administration's insistence that the war was led and supplied by the North supported the notion that bombing the 'supply lines' could have a decisive effect." Even had this model of the conflict been wholly accurate, bombing, Powers maintains, could have done little to alter it. The very word *trail* "allowed the notion to spread" that the Ho Chi Minh Trail was "a literal *line* . . . but the situation in Vietnam was like trying to stop someone from driving a pickup truck through Connecticut between April and October, by any of a thousand routes, at any hour of the day or night, in any kind of weather."

But they were of course very good bombs, and the United States had a lot of them. Over three million fixed-wing sorties were flown by U.S. and South Vietnamese forces over South Vietnam, North Vietnam, Laos, and Cambodia during the war. Insufficient outcry was directed against the damage to the South. It was the South that was showered with defoliants and the herbicide Agent Orange. It was the South that began receiving maximum loads from B-52s by June 1965. It was in the South that an observer like Frank Harvey could watch air power "cutting people down like little cloth dummies." Navy pilot Porter Halyburton recalls: "Flying in the North, we were very, very constrained. In the South, the B-52s would lay down a string of thousand pound bombs and just completely devastate an entire area." A rice exporter until 1964, South Vietnam became a heavy importer of rice after 1965. As Harrison Salisbury put it, "We bombed *our* Vietnam more than the North."

In the North, despite immense human suffering, aerial bombardment had the strategic effect predicted by the war games conducted by SIGMA II in September 1964: it "actually stiffened North Vietnamese determination." The games even forecast the American future, the introduction of at least ten ground combat divisions because once "your honor is at stake, now you've got to do something."

While the bombing technology of the 1960s was not always efficacious —432 American bombs hitting one key bridge in the North left it damaged, but no part of it knocked down—it nevertheless possessed the capacity to inflict significant if untargeted loss. David Dellinger visited the North in 1966, traveling east and south of the capital. He moved mostly at night in a jeep camouflaged with tree branches. "An hour or so out of Hanoi, we had just turned from a barely traversable byway onto a real road when we heard the roar of planes. The jeep stopped and we got out and lay in a shallow drainage ditch by the side of the road. Suddenly, the darkest of nights became like midday as the planes released flares that seemed to have the power of a dozen midnight suns." Sleeping in the daytime, he moved "hurriedly through devastated towns and villages." In a village thirty-five miles south of Hanoi, "not a building was standing." After the heaviest bombings, survivors told

him, low-flying planes came in at intervals to strafe the remains. Salisbury
would later augment such reports, his first dispatch from the North appearing
in the *New York Times* in 1966, on Christmas day.

The first American newsman admitted to North Vietnam during the war,
Salisbury surmises that he is granted entry largely on the recommendation
of Mrs. Norman Morrison, the widow of the man who had burned him-
self to death below McNamara's office window at the Pentagon. *Behind the
Lines—Hanoi* (1967) details Salisbury's travels throughout the country between
December 23, 1966, and January 7, 1967.

Once in, Salisbury is surprised by the "good coffee" but "not impressed"
by the bomb damage he sees on his first walk through Hanoi. An American
leaflet is found in a street after an attack, and a translator reads it to him:
"Don't live near a military target." South of Hanoi he sees a parallel rail and
road system "incredibly vulnerable" to attack, "a bombardier's dream," and
yet "the movement of men, materials, food and munitions" along it has not
been halted. Wherever he looks, he sees fifty-five-gallon drums in which the
North's petroleum supply is stored, since the bombing has eliminated "all
the consequential storage facilities in the country." In Namdinh, the bombing takes on "human dimensions" as Salisbury walks down the main street
past a textile factory that has been hit nineteen times. "The Americans think
they can touch our hearts," the mayor of the town tells him. In Phatdiem,
he finds "an astonishing amount of high explosives was falling on a simple,
quiet, rice-growing area." He remembers that Johnson "himself approved
every target and every operation in the vicinity of Hanoi and Haiphong."
He finds it difficult to reason from damage on the ground to intent in the
sky. And the conviction deepens that "American planes, particularly the
fighter-bombers, were subject to orders which lay on the far horizon of
their capability."

A year after Salisbury traveled to North Vietnam, Tom Wolfe found himself
in the Gulf of Tonkin aboard the USS *Coral Sea*. His deep identification with
Navy pilots who flew missions over the North led him to judge Salisbury's
reporting a "propaganda coup" for the enemy. "It seemed as if the North
Vietnamese were playing Mr. Harrison Salisbury of *The New York Times* like
an ocarina, as if they were blowing smoke up his pipe and the finger work
was just right and the song was coming forth better than they could have
played it themselves." Wolfe's pilots stick with a deflationary rhetoric and so
refer to a bombing run fifty feet above the Phun Cat ferry in a flak-ridden
sky as "a good hop." F-4 pilot John Dowd will allow himself the words
"skill & cunning" in a journal entry about evading three lethal SAM missiles

but will not venture the word "death." "Pilots never mentioned death in the abstract. In fact, the word itself was taboo in conversation. So were the words 'bravery' and 'fear' and their synonyms. Which is to say, pilots never mentioned the three questions that were uppermost in the minds of all of them: Will I live or die? Will I be brave, whatever happens? Will I show my fear?" Wolfe does not attempt to find words for, or to ask such questions on behalf of, the people being bombed.

In *Hiroshima* (1946) and in *Slaughterhouse-Five* (1969), John Hersey and Kurt Vonnegut invite readers to feel what it is like to be under American bombs. But *under* was not a place where U.S. policy planners attempted to place themselves; not until 2003 would McNamara counsel the need to "empathize with your enemy." The enemy as a set of human persons did not enter into the plan—no more than had the men on the assembly line at Ford, or the Joint Chiefs down the hall. Such imaginings remain implicit in the surviving numbers, as in David Harris's description of the pineapple bomb: "A yellow cylinder, it contained 250 steel ball-bearing pellets packed around an explosive charge. On impact, its pellets fired out horizontally. A batch of a thousand pineapples would cover an area the size of four football fields, leaving anything above ground level a casualty."

A weapon of such gratuitous ruthlessness argued for some immensity of enemy crime, with napalm providing the extreme instance. British photographer-writer Philip Jones Griffiths heard a story about the evolution of napalm from an American pilot in 1966:

> The original product was not so hot—if the gooks were quick they could scrape it off. . . . [I]f the gooks jumped underwater it stopped burning, so they started adding Willie Peter [WP—white phosphorous] so's to make it burn better. It'll even burn under water now. And just one drop is enough, it'll keep on burning right down to the bone so they die anyway from phosphorus poisoning.

Writing for the *Ladies Home Journal* in 1967, Martha Gellhorn reminded her readers, about napalm, that "we alone possess and freely use this weapon in Vietnam."

Foot soldier Tobias Wolff was to remember the overcoming glamour of the war in the sky. *In Pharaoh's Army* (1994) records a moment when the "jets showed up." "Such American machines, so boss-looking, so technical, so loud. *Phantoms*. When they showed overhead to lock into formation the roar of their engines made speech impossible. Down here I was in a deranged and malignant land, but when I raised my eyes to those planes I could see home. They dove screaming on the town, then pulled out and banked and did it again. The bombs sent tremors pulsing through our legs."

No one did a better job of reporting on the experience of being under American power, especially its bombs, than Jonathan Schell. In late 1966, on the way home from Japan on an around-the-world ticket, the twenty-three-year-old Schell decided to stop in Saigon. "When I landed in Vietnam I was the very definition of a pest—a graduate student who had no knowledge and who vaguely thought he might like to write something." At the *Newsweek* office he met two famous French reporters, Bernard Fall and François Sully. Fall and Sully used their connections "to perform a kind of miracle. They persuaded the military to give me a press pass on the somewhat deceptive basis that I was there for the *Harvard Crimson*." A few days later, Schell found himself on a C-5 transport that flew him straight in Operation Cedar Falls, the largest military action of the war to date. Part of the operation involved a helicopter attack on Ben Suc, and when Schell heard about the plan to bomb and bulldoze the village, he decided to "follow that particular story from start to finish." Later that summer, he accompanied Task Force Oregon as it sought to find and kill National Liberation Front (NLF) fighters in Quang Nhai, a province below the Demilitarized Zone on the South China Sea. Out of this experience Schell wrote two books, *The Village of Ben Suc* (1967) and *The Military Half* (1968).

Schell positions himself with the men in the air and on the ground, and lets them speak for themselves. "I have no wish to pass judgment on the individual Americans fighting in Vietnam," he writes. "I wish merely to record what I witnessed, in the hope that it will help us all to understand better what we are doing."

Ben Suc was a village of some 3,500 people located near the Iron Triangle, a forty-square-mile stretch of jungle northwest of Saigon that had stubbornly resisted pacification. In 1964 the NLF had expelled the troops of the ARVN from Ben Suc. "We're going to clean out the place completely," an Army major tells Schell three years later. "The people are all going to be resettled in a temporary camp near Phu Cuong."

Resettlement means being moved to a vast field empty except for a row of huts in the shade of a line of palm trees. Contained by a ring of barbed wire, and sheltered by pieces of nylon cloth, thousands of villagers are served only by open-trench latrines. Those attempting to find some privacy in the trees are often caught on the barbed wire.

Schell's book ends with demolition teams arriving at Ben Suc. Bulldozers flatten the village, and then the Air Force bombs the ruins, "as though, having once decided to destroy it, we were now bent on annihilating every possible indication that the village of Ben Suc had ever existed." *Destroy*, Schell writes. The verb "to destroy" will come to dominate *The Military Half,* a book in which Schell finds himself arrested by the "fantastic fact that we are destroying, seemingly by inadvertence, the very country we are supposedly protecting."

The bombing of South Vietnam never aroused the attention and the resistance generated by the bombing of the North. Yet the destruction rained down from the air on the South—from bombs, artillery, and chemical agents—was far more thoroughgoing than the damage done by Rolling Thunder. Rolling Thunder operated under a set of prohibitions—no bombing of the Long Bien Bridge or Haiphong harbor—that made its targets, apart from inevitable pilot error, somewhat predictable. In the South, however, the enemy was everywhere and nowhere, so mingled with and difficult to distinguish from friendly populations that the attempt to eradicate it could become endless work.

Schell first becomes aware of the destruction when he spends several days in August 1967 flying over the coastal strip of Quang Ngai and Quang Tri provinces in the back seat of a single-propeller D-1 Forward Air Control plane. Villages still stand near the main north–south road, but most of the rest "had been destroyed." The phrase "had been destroyed" tolls like a bell through Schell's pages. Yet the phrase proves not original with him, since soon after first using it Schell quotes a psychological warfare pamphlet notifying the local population that "many hamlets have been destroyed because these villages harbored the Vietcong."

Schell repeatedly asks the pilots that he meets one question: How they are able to identify someone on the ground as an enemy? After guiding an air strike toward the woods into which a man has disappeared, one pilot replies, "Well, he walked real proud, with a kind of bounce in his gait, like a soldier, instead of just shuffling along, like the farmers do." Another pilot speaks with greater certainty. "Those villages are completely infested with V.C., just like rats' nests, and the only solution is to burn them out completely." Major Billings is less sure, allowing, after directing some F-4s over a patch of jungle, "I don't know what kind of people were down there, but they're not there now."

Schell learns that "a village could be bombed immediately and without the issuing of any warning to the villagers if American or other friendly troops or aircraft had received fire from within it." When villagers are warned of attack by either leaflet or loudspeaker, they are given "a good ten or fifteen minutes to get out of there before we put in a strike." What gets hit depends on what is seen, usually from the air, and what it is then called. Villagers deemed deserving of relocation suddenly become "hostile civilians," a term coined during the Ben Suc operations. Once relocated, they then revert to the status of "refugees."

The gap between information gathered from the air and knowledge of conditions on the ground led participants into a semantic war, one with mortal consequences. The question of what to call villagers "was one of many semantic problems that the Army had to solve." In a physical landscape so difficult to decipher, and in a political situation of such profound ambiguity, it became imperative that there be "no middle ground in the semantic war. You choose sides by the words you use."

Yet, in showing how quickly the name of a thing could change, Schell's careful transcriptions reveal Americans in Vietnam as caught up in a war of shifting rather than fixed usages. Instructed to bomb "one hootch," Captain Reese drops a marker on a village. "That's not it," the ground commander replies. Reese drops another rocket, no nearer the hootch. "That's the general area," the ground commander replies. "Tired of trying to pinpoint the one house," he then instructs Reese to "cover" the general area.

Schell chooses not to dismiss such incidents as due to the fog of war. He presents them instead as the result of an asymmetry in which one side has the monopoly on "death from the sky." When it came to the air, nothing done by the U.S. could be done *to* the U.S. "Everything looks so calm up where we are," a major says. Schell discovers that in South Vietnam artillery can be fired at will at almost any time, if only to "adjust the gun's aiming device." The batteries at Duc Phu fire over 64,000 shells into the region's populated flatlands in some four months. The 105-mm. shells kill anything within a radius of 35 meters, while the 8-inch shell covers a circle 150 meters in diameter. There is counting, of a sort, and Schell is careful, even respectful, of the numbers: when Operation Benton Falls comes to a close, it has dropped 292 tons of general-purpose bombs and 116 tons of napalm. Six hundred and forty of the area's seventeen thousand people have been evacuated to government camps. Bomb Damage Assessment reports filled out by pilots have carefully tracked the percentages of targets destroyed and bombs dropped on target, but "vast 'side-effects,' such as the destruction of villages in large areas, went unmentioned."

Salisbury's reporting represented a revolt of the patriarchs. And there were older figures, Americans over forty, who did real work against the war: Spock, Coffin, Dellinger, Mailer, Chomsky, Hoopes, I. F. Stone. For the most part, however, the job of imagining and writing adequately about Vietnam fell to the young, to Michael Herr, David Harris, Frances Fitzgerald, Neil Sheehan, David Halberstam, Tim O'Brien, Gloria Emerson, Robert Stone, Ward Just, Jonathan Schell. They belonged to the "generation of writers," as the poet Robert Hass writes, "who grew up in the social and economic expansion of the postwar years" and who

> watched the planning and the confidence and the technical inventive-
> ness turn, with what seemed to the young unbelievable callousness
> and efficiency, on Vietnam. That war was, perhaps, a paradigm of
> planning without people in the plan. The Vietnamese did not fit it
> and the American young who were supposed to fight it did not fit it;
> and as the administration with a plan to win the war was replaced by
> an administration with a plan to end the war, the suffering seemed
> to go on forever. And a generation of American writers has come
> to look at the central mechanisms of American life with a deep,
> stunned, curious detachment.

Planning without people in the plan: the formulation sums up the management style of Robert McNamara. In *Backfire* (1985), Loren Baritz gives an eloquent account of the bureaucratic self and the central institutions in which "leadership has been replaced by management." In the Pentagon bureaucracy, valuing quality of achievement has been superseded by concern with body counts. Loyalty has come to matter more than doing good work. "Approval from the supervisor is won by providing him with what he considers to be desirable language or numbers." And so a "psychology of pleasing" sets in. The result is not only careerism, but "a nation without citizens, and a people without politics."

In 1995, McNamara published *In Retrospect: The Tragedy and Lessons of Vietnam.* The book presents itself as a confession, admitting on its first page that "we" got "it wrong on Vietnam." The belief that Vietnam presented a serious challenge to the West's policy of containment appears "misplaced in retrospect." The metaphor of retrospection works, however, to protect its author from having to make a full confession. It allows him to take cover behind "the lack of knowledge that existed at that time," thus reducing the "error" committed to one "not of values and intentions but of judgments and capabilities."

A retrospective stance usually assumes, however, that knowledge has been gained in the interval. Such a gain would have required McNamara to have arrived at Clark Clifford's understanding that "Vietnam was not a *management problem;* it was a war, and war is about life and death, filled with intangibles that defy analysis." In the twenty-seven years between his leaving the Pentagon and the publication of his book, McNamara lost none of his faith in analysis. "We failed to analyze our assumptions critically," he maintains. His basic mode of thinking remains unchanged: "To this day, I see quantification as a language to add precision to reasoning about the world." He continues to assert that what was needed then—in the 1960s—is what is always needed, "an orderly, rational approach."

By the mid-1990s, McNamara's conclusions about the war have changed, but his style of thinking and his sense of language have not, and so he remains wrong about how we got it "wrong" on the war. As George Ball was to conclude, the "quintessential advantage of the North Vietnamese and Viet Cong could not, however, be expressed in numbers or percentages. It was the incomparable benefit of superior *élan,* of an intensity of spirit. . . . So, with the unquantifiable omitted from the McNamara equation, the answer never came out right." The problem was not a failure of reason or quantitative analysis but rather a failure to acknowledge the inability of either capacity to take in the full complexities of human life. And this blindness to the limits of his habitual modes of thinking is in turn reinforced by McNamara's facile—even contemptuous—view of the power and value of words.

Deborah Shapley's biography of McNamara repeatedly makes the point that the secretary of defense had a "penchant for tactically useful fibs." She cites numerous instances: he lied to president-elect Kennedy about being kept from a meeting by a nonexistent December snowstorm; he made it clear to reporters that there was no missile gap with the Soviet Union, and then denied having said so; he agreed with Johnson to dissemble about the costs of the Vietnam war, hiding from Congress the size of forces to be introduced; and, above all, once his doubts about the war set in, and he came to believe it "unwinnable militarily," he refused to convey his belief to the American public. To those who say he should have resigned, challenged the president's policy, and become a leading force for change, McNamara replies: "I believe that would have been a violation of my responsibility to the president and my oath to uphold the Constitution." Despite his commitment to management and transparency, McNamara, along with Lyndon Johnson, created around himself a loyalty-based culture that ran on secrets.

Shapley's indictment assumes that McNamara comprehended the gap between what was said and what was known. McMaster also adopts this view. His index entry under "McNamara, Robert," contains a line for "deceptions and lies," followed by thirty page numbers. Yet as one reads through *In Retrospect,* the rhetorical performance reveals a self in which such misrepresentations are continually justified as expedient acts of "responsibility," while McNamara's treatment of words, to use an adjective applied to him by a Washington neighbor, bespeaks a willfully "innocent" view of language and of life, one unaware that even the most self-protective style gives its user away. To care about finding the just, pleasing, not euphemistic, accurate word—as McNamara does not—is to aim, on the other hand, for what art can sometimes achieve, a new knowledge of reality.

McNamara's words engage in a flight from the concrete. He prefers abstract nouns: one paragraph in the memoir alone features the words "assumptions," "questions," "analyses," "problems," "courses," and "consequences." He opts frequently for the cliché: the war is a "jigsaw puzzle." We see him indulging in "wishful thinking," sliding down "a slippery slope," worrying over "a serious breach in the dike," sinking "into quicksand." He invokes "ambiguities" and then refuses to explore them. And he betrays a lack of skepticism about his own motives or the motives of others, thus declaring that the Joint Chiefs he had so thoroughly marginalized "were motivated by a deep and noble desire to serve their country."

In 1966, in an interview with Henry F. Graff, McNamara addressed the matter of his habitual vocabulary. He admitted to preferring a phrase like "favorable settlement" to "such words as 'victory' or 'win'—which he called 'color words.'"

McNamara is not *in* his language. He deploys it as something received and pre-thought, a balm to be applied to unacknowledged wounds. As James Reston wrote about him, in 1963, "Something is missing: some element of personal doubt, some respect for human weakness, some knowledge of history." Because he failed to recognize that words are one of the deepest expressions of the self, and that any self worth having often finds itself torn between two conflicting goods, caught up in verbal and moral ambiguities, he also failed to develop the one thing needed in the face of the experience of Vietnam, a tragic sense of life.

In *The Masters* (1951), one of C. P. Snow's characters speaks of what he wants from a leader. "I want a man who knows something about himself. And is appalled. And has to forgive himself to get along." By continually looking within, and being appalled, and then having to forgive, such a self acknowledges the abiding presence of the shadow, the part of the self that is wayward, selfish, not to be fully known.

In 1968 there was not only division in the American house, as Johnson was to admit on March 31, there was division within the American self. A model for acknowledging this had been provided by Martin Luther King Jr.

in 1957: "Each of us is something of a schizophrenic personality. We're split up and divided against ourselves. There is something of a civil war going on within all our lives." Tom Englehardt, who loved John Wayne movies as a boy, eventually joined The Resistance. "There was a real military side in me," he remembers, one thrilled by seeing West Point's Long Gray Line. "Our image today is that there were these two sides in the war—the warriors and the antiwarriors. But the most striking thing I remember is that there were at least two sides in everybody."

Since the men who led the United States into Vietnam refused to engage in a conversation with the shadow or to acknowledge self-division, they encouraged the nation to engage in a massive projection of its own, collective shadow outward, onto a Communist conspiracy bent on world supremacy. In McNamara's case, the cost of this projection resulted in a very personal tragedy.

In July 1967, Margy McNamara was treated at Johns Hopkins for bleeding ulcers. Away on a trip to Vietnam during the early part of her hospital stay, on his return McNamara made the forty-five-minute drive to Baltimore every night. Margy recovered, temporarily, and went on to direct her Reading Is Fundamental program until her early death, in 1981.

"I think she died because of" the Vietnam War, McNamara was to say, years later. In 1967, husband and wife had tried to make light of it. " 'Bob has all the problems and I have the ulcer,' she joked before one operation. 'Margy got my ulcer,' he said." In John Frankenheimer's HBO movie *Path to War* (2002), George Ball tells Clark Clifford that McNamara's wife and son each have ulcers. "Everybody's got Bob McNamara's ulcers but Bob McNamara."

In his memoir, McNamara attempts to present himself as a hero of insight. But he is more like the man who finds God in prison. There is no sense in his life or in his writing that every time we speak or write, we are engaged in an act of building-out. So his book reduces into a gesture toward regret. But the real consequence of his belief that "to undermanage reality is not to keep it free" was paid by his wife, who did for him what he would not do for himself, internalizing the pain and the guilt and the unacceptable knowledge and feeling stirred up by the war. She, too, was a person who did not fit in to the plan.

Eight men attended the February 27 Tuesday lunch: Robert McNamara, Dean Rusk, William Bundy, Walt Rostow, Clark Clifford, Harry McPherson, Joseph Califano, and Nicolas Katzenbach. Undersecretary of State Katzenbach contributed little to the discussion; Califano and McPherson, Johnson's point man on domestic policy and his speechwriter, mostly listened. The burden of the discussion was carried by the five other men, men who under the pressure of the growing dismay had each been reduced down almost to a single, Jonsonian humour.

Secretary of State Rusk was the taciturn hawk. The son of a Georgia farmer, Rusk had secured a Rhodes scholarship and then served as an intelligence analyst in World War II, where, according to Stanley Karnow, the Nazi threat had "scarred his mind," leaving him "hostile to appeasement in any form." Recessive in meetings, by 1968 he was surviving on a diet of aspirin, scotch, and cigarettes. When he did speak, it was to resist any compromise with Hanoi, but he spoke so little that he became a vacuum McNamara easily filled.

The Bundy brothers represented the cream of the Eastern establishment. As assistant secretary of state for Far Eastern affairs, William had by 1968 replaced McGeorge in the inner councils of government, but not before McGeorge had left his mark. Dean of Harvard's Faculty of Arts and Sciences at thirty-four, McGeorge had helped Dean Acheson prepare his memoirs. Known for "an abruptness and imperious demeanor," while serving as Johnson's national security adviser he had found himself in country during the February 1965 attacks on Pleiku. Westmoreland recalled him becoming intense and arrogant, regressing to "a field marshal psychosis." He urged an immediate air strike on the North, thus helping to precipitate the bombing campaign.

In later years, McGeorge Bundy would attempt an *In Retrospect* of his own. Bundy began having conversations toward such a venture with Gordon Goldstein, a specialist in international affairs, in 1995. Bundy died in 1996; in 2002, Goldstein submitted his manuscript to Yale University Press. Then Bundy's widow decided to withdraw it. Goldstein persisted, eventually publishing in 2008 a book "composed without any involvement whatsoever from the Bundy family and its advisers."

Based on his conversations with Bundy, Goldstein argues that Kennedy would not have committed ground troops to Vietnam. "The doves were right," Bundy is quoted as saying. Goldstein brought his book to market against the backdrop of another time of presidential decision, Barack Obama's eventual choice to send thirty thousand additional troops to Afghanistan. A book club grew up in Obama's White House during those days of decision, and the manuscript advisers were reading was "Gordon Goldstein's book." Read as an allegory of the present—the summer and fall of 2009—*Lessons in Disaster* ended with an implicit caution to President Obama: "Intervention is a presidential choice, not an inevitability."

William may have been the somewhat colorless older brother, but he shared with McGeorge a pugnacity bred into both by the New England prep school tradition, that never-to-be-satisfied longing for an "activity savage enough to be classified as manly" so beautifully conveyed in the novels of Louis Auchincloss. William, too, had ties to Acheson—he was his son-in-law—and had worked his way up through Harvard Law, the CIA, the Department of Defense, and, finally, in 1964, the State Department. He was later to write a book highly critical of Nixon's conduct of foreign policy, *A Tangled Web* (1998).

Walt Rostow was the cockeyed optimist. To the bitter end, he remained an advocate of escalation and a believer in final victory. Succeeding McGeorge Bundy as national security adviser in 1966, he was gifted with a capacity for "'instant rationalization' (as one colleague put it), which amounted to a compulsion for buttressing his views by a rapid culling of the evidence immediately at hand." Paul Kattenburg, a Vietnam specialist in the State Department, recalls, "Walt Rostow in particular was completely impervious to area knowledge." He was therefore capable of saying, during the Gulf of Tonkin crisis, "You know, the wonderful thing is, we don't know if this thing happened at all. Boy, it gives us the chance really to go for broke on the bombing. The evidence is unclear, but our golden opportunity is at hand." Rostow set up a Vietnam Information Group to engage in a secret campaign to shape public opinion about the war. One of the group's prime efforts was to intervene in government debates about enemy troop strength, seeking to reduce CIA estimates of NLF capacities by almost 30 percent. McPherson was to note Rostow's "panglossian determination to see every event as part of an upward trend," a habit of mind formalized by the graph in his 1971 *Diffusion of Power* showing even at that late date a rising line for U.S. war efforts and a falling line for the enemy.

Clifford entered the room as the wise counselor and as the incoming secretary of defense, a post he assumed on March 1. A Missouri lawyer, as a young man he had been recruited by the Truman administration, where his skills as an adviser quickly brought him into the president's inner circle. It was rumored during the 1950s that he had become the nation's most highly paid attorney. As president, Johnson frequently turned to Clifford for advice. The press responded to news of Clifford's appointment by referring to him as a hawk on the war. But, according to his own account, he had early on expressed his doubts about the growing American involvement in Vietnam. "The President remembered, of course, my initial opposition to the buildup in 1965. But after that decision was made, I had consistently supported his policy in Vietnam." By the time of the Tet Offensive, however, "my perceptions of the war were changing. Fundamental assumptions on which I had based my views crumbled—not with a single dramatic revelation, but slowly and unevenly." Having spent three years looking hawkish, Clifford was about to emerge as the administration's leading dove.

McNamara held on to his post for as long as he did in part to counteract the hawkishness of Rusk and Rostow. They had long been aware of his doubts about the war, feelings, however, he did not at the time fully share with the public. The last Tuesday lunch thus served McNamara one more time as a vehicle for release—and containment. Everyone in the room assumed that what was said there, stayed there.

McNamara's outburst about the bombing marked the climax of two years of growing doubt. *In Retrospect* attempts to convert its narrator into a doubter from the start. McNamara writes that in March 1964, when the idea of bombing the North is first discussed, "data and analysis showed that air attacks would not work." "I recommended against initiating air attacks." He proceeds to represent McGeorge Bundy as the prime mover behind the retaliatory air strikes in 1965, while admitting that he too "leaned toward support of such action." By January 1967, his narrative has him testifying against the efficacy of bombing before the Senate, saying things like "I don't believe that the bombing up to the present has significantly reduced . . . the actual flow of men and material to the South." By that summer, he is in open revolt against the Joint Chiefs, elaborating again before the Senate "the inherent limitations of bombing" and calling a new air campaign against the North "completely illusory." He goes so far as to point out to the senators that one bicycle moving south could carry a load of five hundred pounds, and that enemy forces in the South—not counting food—could survive on fifteen tons a day of externally supplied matériel. A study of Rolling Thunder commissioned by McNamara and completed in December 1967 concluded that "North Vietnam's war-fighting capacity had *increased* because of the bombing."

The public record does in part support McNamara's attempt to represent himself as a doubter and gives evidence of his willingness, at times, to testify to those feelings. But the story told in his memoir contains significant omissions. Most strikingly, it contains no account of the February 27 lunch. Joseph Califano, in *The Triumph and Tragedy of Lyndon Johnson* (1991), also recalls a McNamara far more energetic in his support of bombing than his memoir suggests. Califano worked as a special assistant to McNamara until July 1965, when he joined the White House staff. A few weeks later,

Johnson received a report from McNamara on his recent trip to Vietnam, one in which he "pressed to escalate the war." Califano recalls McNamara urging the declaration of a national emergency, the calling up of 235,000 reserves, an increase in the number of draftees. He also "favored stepped-up bombing of military targets and supply routes in North Vietnam." In *The Limits of Air Power* (1989), Mark Clodfelter juxtaposes this report against an even stronger set of recommendations advanced by McNamara only a month earlier. His memo of June 26 "pressed for mining North Vietnam's harbors and for attacks on rail lines to China, POL [fuel] storage areas, port facilities, power plants, airfields, and surface-to-air missile (SAM) sites." McNamara's own summary of this memo in his memoir condenses his recommendation about air power into a single innocuous phrase, "expanded military action against North Vietnam."

So, like many of the figures on the public stage in 1968, McNamara walked a line that wavered, and his memoir is honest about this. It falls short, however, in not being willing to integrate the painful experience of this inner conflict into a more expansive, flexible, and troubled model both of the self and the good public servant. Despite the noun in its subtitle—"The Tragedy and Lessons of Vietnam"—*In Retrospect* portrays the war as a failure of management rather than as a tragedy.

The proceedings of the Tuesday lunch meetings were so tightly held that Johnson usually forbade a written report of the discussion. Four pages of notes on McNamara's last lunch do however survive. They were taken by Harry McPherson and are archived in the LBJ Library in a folder labeled "Meeting Notes File." After reading the contents of the legal-size olive folder with a little adhesive tab at the top, Paul Hendrickson concluded that they are "detailed notes, but in a sense they're the wrong notes, because they contain almost none of the emotional truth." The same reticence prevails in *A Political Education* (1988), McPherson's memoir, which devotes only two brief paragraphs to the experience. McPherson would later prove, however, to be the most vivid and concrete informant about the tone and wording of what McNamara actually said.

While the meeting had been called to discuss Johnson's upcoming speech on the war, it quickly turned into an exchange about the Army's request for more troops. For Califano, it "was the first time since early in 1966 that I had heard the President's advisers in an intimate discussion of Vietnam. McNamara, Katzenbach, and Assistant Secretary of State William Bundy were beyond pessimism. They sounded a chorus of despair. Rusk appeared exhausted and worn down."

In his memoir, McNamara gives the lunch only one sentence: "In my last official act on Vietnam, on February 27, 1968, I opposed Westy's renewed appeal for 200,000 additional troops on economic, political, and moral grounds." Califano recalls what McNamara actually said: "He called the request 'madness . . . I've repeatedly honored requests from the Wheelers of the world, but we have no assurance that an additional 205,000 men will make any difference in the conduct of the war.'" Katzenbach and Bundy appeared to agree. McNamara went on to lay out the cost of a troop increase. "This is unbelievable and futile," McPherson replied. Clifford, his doubts about the war now intensified, remembers thinking of McPherson as his "silent partner" throughout the meeting.

Rusk called for increased bombing of the North. McNamara stood up, announced that he couldn't stay, and then launched into the outburst so vividly recalled by McPherson in his interview with Hendrickson: "They've dropped more bombs than in all of Europe in all of World War Two and it hasn't done a fucking thing." Jules Witcover provides a slightly different wording of McNamara's response: "The goddamned Air Force, they're dropping more on North Vietnam than we dropped in Germany in the last year of World War II, and it's not doing anything!" In his memoir, McPherson supplies a third version: "It's not just that it isn't preventing the supplies from getting down the trail. It's destroying the countryside in the South. It's making lasting enemies. And still the damned Air Force wants more."

Whatever McNamara literally said, it is clear from all the reports of the meeting that he had finally found the words, some of them obscene, and the tone, all of it despairing, accurate to his felt experience of the war.

McNamara spoke for five minutes, in "rage and grief and almost disorientation." "We were all stunned," Clifford remembers. "Rusk stared at his drink," McPherson writes; "Clifford looked searchingly at McNamara, but said nothing." Then, trained as a devil's advocate, Clifford made a counter-suggestion. "I am not pushing it," he said, before wondering aloud whether they ought to send in "500,000 to a million men." McNamara shot back—"That has the virtue of clarity." Bundy began to argue for withdrawal, invoking a "very weak" South Vietnam and a U.S. position that had become "untenable."

Califano remembers Rusk and Rostow as still "optimistic." Tet, they argued, had actually been a military setback for the North, while Clifford reminded them that it had nevertheless won for the Communists the battle of public opinion. Reversing field, he then asked: "How do we avoid creating the feeling that we are pouring troops down a rathole?" By the end of the meeting, only Rostow seemed willing to believe that the war could still be won.

For Robert McNamara, it was almost over. He had only two more days in office. In November Johnson had announced McNamara's appointment as head of the World Bank—before telling McNamara about the change of assignment. "I do not know to this day," McNamara writes, "whether I quit or was fired." The endgame was to involve two ceremonies, the presentation of the Medal of Freedom at the White House and, on the last day, February 29, a farewell at the Pentagon.

The first of the two is the more justly famous. It marked the one moment of public breakdown McNamara allowed himself.

Margy wore a red dress. Craig, McNamara's youngest child, came down from New Hampshire. The Chief Justice attended, along with Dean Acheson, Maxwell Taylor, the Kennedy brothers and their wives. Johnson began by thanking McNamara for his "loyalty to the republic, to the president." He read the citation, and then, becoming "personal," said "I am giving the world the very best we have to win the most important war of all."

The president moved aside, and McNamara stepped to the lectern. "Mr. President," he began. Then he coughed. Continuing to cough, the words struggling out a few at a time, he managed to say, "I cannot find words to express what lies in my heart today, and I think I'd better respond on another occasion." He then moved away from the lectern and began grinning and shaking hands.

It looked like a spontaneous overflow of powerful feeling. That is perhaps how the world remembers it, as a moment of raw and awkward emotional truth. The halting admission had a kind of bitter eloquence. What McNamara said, however, was not spontaneous; he was actually *quoting himself*. He reveals this by choosing to publish in his memoir a letter sent to President Johnson on February 23, five days before the medal ceremony. The letter begins:

> Dear Mr. President:
> I cannot find words to express to you the feelings that lie in my heart.

When the moment in the East Room arrived, McNamara fell back not on upwelling feeling but on the planned, the already-said. "I cannot find words," he said on February 29, just as he had written "I cannot find words" on February 23. And yet the awkward if repeated utterance may have been his truest lie. He not only reenacted his ambivalence about the value and purpose of words but reminded his audience of the profound difficulty any thoughtful person might encounter when faced with the need to say something accurate about the experience of Vietnam. McNamara's inability "to express" was by no means unique to him alone and was to prove prophetic of John Kerry's inability to find words for his conflicted experience of the war when he ran for the presidency in 2004.

The farewell at the Pentagon, which took place the next day, was all bathos. By the appointed hour it had started to rain. Overloading an elevator, McNamara and the president spent twelve minutes stuck between floors. Once outside, the men found themselves without hats or coats. Johnson gave very brief remarks, referring to the Pentagon as the "puzzle palace." And then, in an unwitting indictment, he said: "Bob McNamara may be the only man who found the solution to the puzzle and he is taking it with him." In fact, McNamara was leaving something very important behind, an abiding belief in the efficacy of a certain kind of solution. Despite the failures of this approach in Vietnam, the nation would continue to commit itself ever more fully to the *managerial* and to the killing assumption that the things that matter are those that can be measured. Yet even the quality of the final farewell belied such a belief: on top of an unmanageable elevator and the unpredictable weather, the public address system failed when Deputy Secretary of Defense Paul Nitze stood up to speak, "carrying his eloquent words," Townsend Hoopes writes, "away on the wind."

CHAPTER

4

Thirty Days in March

On March 31, 1968, I flew from Los Angeles to New York and caught a limousine to New Haven, where I was returning from spring break to finish my sophomore year at Yale. In Davenport College I shared a two-bedroom suite with a philosophy major, an urban studies major, and an engineer who was also battalion commander of Naval ROTC. My best friend at the time studied English, like myself, and also played quarterback on Davenport's intramural tackle football team. That fall he had completed a number of passes to a senior who lived across the courtyard, George W. Bush.

The limousine left Kennedy Airport around eight in the evening. I don't remember how many of us had squeezed into the long, low station wagon, but I do recall asking the driver to turn on the radio so that we could listen to the address by the president scheduled for nine o'clock.

Lyndon Johnson had been elected to his first full term in 1964 with the highest percentage of votes yet cast in a presidential election. "Momentum is *not* a mysterious mistress," he maintained, and, carefully exploiting the sentiment for change following Kennedy's assassination, he was to push through the Civil Rights Act in 1964 and the Voting Rights Act in 1965, thus securing the two most significant pieces of legislation since the passage of the Social Security Act thirty years earlier. The black activist Bayard Rustin later claimed that "Johnson was the best we ever had."

Johnson had also inherited a war. But from whom? For George Herring, in *America's Longest War,* it is Truman, then Eisenhower, who passed it along to Kennedy and under whom the number of U.S. advisers in Vietnam increased sixteen-fold. Some historians speculate that Kennedy, by the time of his death, was ready to begin a draw-down in Southeast Asia. "We don't have a prayer of staying in Vietnam," he said to a friend in 1963. Earlier, he told Arthur Schlesinger Jr. that sending men into war was like "taking a drink. The effect wears off, and you have to take another." But Dean Rusk, Kennedy's secretary of state, also maintained that in hundreds of talks with the president "not once did he ever suggest or even hint at withdrawal." Three weeks before Kennedy was assassinated, a U.S.-sanctioned coup was carried out against Ngo Dien Diem, the South Vietnamese president. Diem's bullet-riddled body was later found in an armored personnel carrier.

These were not events about which, as a sophomore in high school, I could read in the *San Bernardino Sun,* my local paper. I knew nothing about them five years later, even though I had by then taken Bradford Westerfield's course on modern American international relations. For the unit on Vietnam, Westerfield assigned a textbook called *Viet Cong* (1966), by Douglas Pike, a former USIA officer, which argued that the conflict in the south was the result of a Communist invasion from the north.

I had entered college with a high-school-textbook sense of American history, a belief in the righteousness of the country's foreign wars and in the nation's essential purity of intent. I recently had been shaken out of such convictions after attending a teach-in at the Yale Law School, where many of my professors, one after the other, stood up and denounced the conduct of the war. Always the good student, I took their lessons to heart. I also ran across a copy of a book called *Air War—Vietnam* (1967), and was stunned by the ability of our air power to inflict such harm from so great a distance. Once having changed my mind about the war, I looked around for an object for my aroused emotions. Knowing little about Kennedy's involvement in the war, and dazzled by the hagiography being pumped out by Kennedy loyalists—he was a man of "brilliantly controlled . . . toughness and restraint . . . nerve and wisdom"—it was easy to look on Vietnam as Johnson's war, and to hate him for it.

By late March, I was firmly committed to the candidacy of Eugene McCarthy. While I hadn't made the trek north to New Hampshire, I had been thrilled by McCarthy's "victory" there, despite the fact that Johnson actually won the primary by a spread of seven points. Few who shared these emotions were then likely to have been aware of the irony, uncovered in later polling, that the majority of votes for McCarthy had come from hawks angry with Johnson for not fighting harder in Vietnam. There is a happy memory of attending a McCarthy rally at the New Haven Armory, where the crowd threw so much money at the candidate that it filled a trash can eventually dumped onto the stage.

All this lay behind or ahead as the limousine sped toward New Haven. Finally we heard the words "Good evening, my fellow Americans." Johnson began by laying out his latest thinking about the conduct of the war. This part of the speech reflected his delayed response to the January Tet Offensive. Johnson went on to assert that Tet had "failed to achieve its principal objectives." He nevertheless gave reluctant consent to two tactical compromises: he would call a partial bombing halt above the 20th parallel, and he was ready to engage in peace talks with the North Vietnamese. Here Johnson fell back on the words of another president, the man he had succeeded: "I believe that now, no less than when the decade began, this generation of Americans is willing to 'pay any price, bear any burden, meet any hardship, support any friend, oppose any foe to assure the survival and the success of liberty.'" In quoting Kennedy's 1961 inaugural address, Johnson attempted to reach back, in the words of James T. Patterson, to a time of "grand expectations." And in quoting a past strong speech, he also signaled his awareness that effective presidential rhetoric often builds on ancestral voices. But Johnson's chosen repetition sounded with a dying fall; in the seven years that had elapsed between the one speech and the other, Kennedy's words had been proven, in part because of his own ambivalent efforts in Vietnam, simply untrue.

The mind might have faded in and out while Johnson discussed the international monetary system and development of the Mekong Valley, but as he approached the end of the speech, the refrain "I believe" began to sound a more personal note. Then Johnson made a striking admission: "There is division in the American house now." He was going to conclude by invoking one of the most powerful metaphors ever deployed in a speech by an American president: "A house divided against itself cannot stand," Lincoln had argued in his speech before the Illinois Republican State Convention in 1858. And this repetition, unlike the quoting of Kennedy, would do real and serious work.

Lincoln's speech laid out the comparison of a country to a house in striking detail. Citing the use of timbers, tenons, and mortises, he carefully worked out the logic of the metaphor. The detail alone had been impressive, all of it meant to serve Lincoln's case about a "string of historical facts," facts perhaps by 1968 lost to everyday American memory, like the Kansas-Nebraska Act or the Dred Scott case. The facts cited by Lincoln pointed to slavery as the provoking issue in the thirty years of Supreme Court cases and legislative compromises and backroom dealings that were leading the nation inexorably toward civil war. Just as impressive as Lincoln's carefully assembled historical analysis was the force and aptness of the metaphor itself. To imagine the United States as a house was to argue that its citizens live under the same roof, that the country is a family, and that however divided that family, the fortunes of its members cannot be separated.

So Johnson arrived at something beautiful, and true. The American nation-as-house *was* divided in 1968; a kind of civil war had come again. To invoke Lincoln was then also to assure the country that it had a leader who did know how to listen to the voices of the past and who had an understanding, perhaps, of how once again to bind up the nation's wounds.

As the voice on the radio began to wind down, it gave no hint of the further surprise to come. Johnson's timbre remained soft, and grave. That morning he had been up early to meet his daughter Lynda, just back from sending her husband, Marine officer Charles Robb, to Vietnam. The daughter had questioned the father about the necessity of the war. Lady Bird Johnson was later to write of seeing "such pain in his eyes as I had not seen since his mother died."

The key word in Johnson's speech, a word also derived from Lincoln, was the word "united." Through the bitterly "educating" experience, as Frederick Douglass was to call it, of the Civil War, *union* became for Lincoln that for which it truly was worth paying any price. A country becomes united, Lincoln had learned, and Johnson now remembered, through the experience of suffering and loss. When Johnson went on to speak of "what we won when all of our people united," he meant to invoke the coming together of the country in the terrible fall of 1963, a solidarity won through grief. "Believing" that this sense of unity "must not now be lost in suspicion" and distrust, Johnson had concluded that he "should not permit the Presidency to become involved in the partisan divisions that are developing in this political year." A sense of anticipation began to build as we took these words in. Then Johnson came to his turn, to the word "Accordingly."

I cannot remember whether with the sounding of this word my heart leapt up. After the fact, and to this day, the word in just that place in its sentence remains for me one of the most moving pivots in the American language. *Consequently,* it could be taken to mean. As in: I make this announcement as a consequence of the careful consideration of the unassailable logic of a string of historical facts, now fully understood. But "consequently" is too coldly rational; "accordingly," with the word "accord" in it, connotes an instinctive response, and harks back to the speech's earlier word, "united." And there was something inevitable, and modest, in the tone of Johnson's conclusion: "Accordingly, I shall not seek, and I will not accept, the nomination of my party for another term as your President."

As he finished uttering that sentence, the limousine exploded. All of us strangers, we were suddenly united in deafening cheers—for the classmates who had braved New Hampshire snow, for our university chaplain, soon to be convicted in a Boston court of conspiracy to aid draft dodgers, for those who had marched on the Pentagon and gathered on the Mall to listen to a speech about having a dream, for the Union Dead and the Vietnamese Dead. It seemed, for a moment, as if the peace movement had won. On that cold March night, as we barreled through the Connecticut dark, it was impossible to believe that there would be seven more years of war.

"You just cannot resign from the office," Hubert Humphrey had told the president, when shown the ending to the speech earlier that day. Yet what Johnson had done bore no resemblance to a resignation. Instead his decision not to continue resembled George Washington's after the end of the Revolutionary War. "I take my leave of all the employments of public life." In speaking these words to the Continental Congress, Washington ensured that power in America would not be transferred through a succession of military strongmen. Johnson's act was also a voluntary giving up of power, although the act of letting go also required a persistence in the task of governance for nine more long and public months. An act arising out of the pressure of incalculable forces, Johnson's decision not to run was nevertheless also an act of considerable moral and political imagination. There is no way to parse it without conceding its origin in something selfless, a transcendence of the vaunted Johnsonian ego. Looking back, it is difficult to locate a commensurate act of statesmanship in the subsequent forty years of American political life. Six years later, a real "resignation" by a sitting president would take place, but by then it was nothing like a surprise.

March 1968 presents, in the words of Townsend Hoopes, a "remarkably taut time span of thirty days." On the first day of the month, Clark Clifford was sworn in as secretary of defense; on the last day, Lyndon Johnson announced that he would not seek or accept his party's nomination for president. These are the bounding events for this chapter, a story centered in the White House. Yet March contains many other stories: McCarthy's "win" in New Hampshire on the 12th; Robert Kennedy's "I will run" announcement four days later; Nelson Rockefeller's decision not to run on the 21st, followed by Spiro Agnew's first meeting with Richard Nixon on the 29th; the student boycott at Bowie State, in Maryland, beginning on March 27th; and, behind it all and unreported for some twenty months, and occurring on the same day as Kennedy's announcement, the story of an Army company moving into a village in the coastal province of Quang Ngai named My Lai.

Lyndon Johnson entered March knowing he had to make a decision, and, in *The Vantage Point*, he places considerable emphasis on the very word. He titles the chapter leading up to his speech "The Making of a Decision" and begins it by asserting that "a President reaches a major decision through a complicated process." Throughout his memoir, Johnson attempts to represent himself as a careful decider. "After long discussion," he will write, "I authorized the strikes."

While *The Vantage Point* means to depict its author as cautious, measured, and decisive, its rhetoric and its deep narrative argue something far different, revealing a man who, in Doris Kearns Goodwin's words, seeks "insulation from choice." And the confusions in Johnson's behavior—his entirely human capacity for self-mystification—have everything to do with his ambivalence over the responsibilities that come with the using and choosing of words.

When did Johnson decide not to run? The answer is inseparable from another question: How did Johnson make decisions about the war in Vietnam? In his March 31 speech, the two matters are conjoined. What began as a war speech turned into a "peace speech" and then into a surprise announcement. The strength it took to embrace these decisions was to prove inseparable, for Johnson, from the weakness displayed in making them, while the sheer scale of the self-division at play reveals him as one of the era's most complex and looming figures.

Gifted at the art of private persuasion, Johnson had little interest in formalized public knowledge. He had never been a reader; Robert Caro cites Johnson's "lifelong reluctance" about picking up a book. After his first heart attack in 1955, Lady Bird did read to her husband aloud, in "the very small doses" he would tolerate. Recovering back at the ranch, he maintained that "he'd always been too busy to read books before" and admitted to having read no more than six since leaving college.

A determined self-narrower, Johnson succeeded in reducing his interests to one thing: political ambition. In 1951, an article in the *Saturday Evening Post* depicted him as "entirely preoccupied with the science of politics" and as a man who "refuses to be trapped into thinking about or discussing sports, literature, the stage, movies, or anything else in the world of recreation." With no other realm to which his imagination could appeal, Johnson became a wholly political creature, and his politics, unmoored to any other set of concerns or experiences, were to reduce, inevitably, to an exercise of manipulation and power. As a consequence, Kearns Goodwin writes, Johnson came to "view words as sticks for action, as tools for persuasion. The words themselves mean nothing divorced from the object of persuasion." In conceiving of language as mere rhetoric, Johnson came to treat words as instrumental, functions in a power play rather than as expressions of perceived realities or a revealable self.

So, when it came to writing *The Vantage Point*, "the man who talked for the memoirs was the man Lyndon Johnson thought he should be." The awkward deadness of the performance—its revelation of a terrifying inner emptiness—reminds us that a working self depends for its construction and maintenance on a care for words. Yet Johnson proceeded "as if the spoken word were vapor." Unable to bring himself to write them down, he insisted on dictating his sentences to Kearns Goodwin. "I was listening to a man," she concluded, "who had always had a peculiar relationship with words."

Which came first: Johnson's fugitive center or his disdain for words? It is impossible to know. But it is also difficult to separate the two, or not to conclude that Johnson's refusal to be in his language led to a "lack . . . of any moral foundation whatsoever," as Robert Caro puts it, or, in the words of Townsend Hoopes, to a record which shows "no solid core of philosophical principle."

And yet Johnson did great things. He proposed and helped to enact the most important social legislation since the New Deal. He was to give three of the era's greatest speeches. But he was betrayed, finally, by his commitment to results rather than ideals and processes, as Kearns Goodwin argues, by his seeing "preoccupation with principle and procedure as a sign of impotence." The speechwriter Harry McPherson, who joined the Johnson team in 1965, would here add a qualification. He too came to see Johnson as invested more in ends than in means. "Quite obviously he believed that some ends—particularly the enactment of progressive legislation—required generosity in judging the means that produced them, but he gave no sign that he rejected the legitimacy of judgment. . . . Ingenious and practical as he was, he was also ethically sentient; he wished to be thought a good man as well as a clever one." McPherson's memoir, *A Political Education*, displays throughout this generous and affectionate view.

How much better it would have been for Lyndon Johnson, in looking back on his presidency, to have come to rest "in the ambiguity." It is there, in the ambiguity, McPherson believes, that "the best political men" do, eventually, locate themselves. The truth is that Johnson was a terrible decider, and that this very personal characteristic played a crucial role in the failure of U.S. policy and practice in Vietnam. Seeing this, and owning up to it, was of course beyond him. It remained for Robert Dallek, H. R. McMaster, Herbert Shandler, and Townsend Hoopes, along with insiders Kearns Goodwin and McPherson, and perhaps above all his wife, to reveal the true nature and effects of Johnson's way of "deciding."

In a word, the problem was "consensus." As a senator, Johnson had been effective because he knew how to broker deals, to reconcile the pull of conflicting interests. Success in the Senate depended on the finding of a middle ground, but disaster resulted when Johnson applied these methods to his role as an executive. His habit of attempting "to compromise conflict instead of choosing sides" led him to build into his presidency a system of "anticipatory feedback." The process worked to discourage the expression of dissenting views. And the fiction of consensus persisted to inform Johnson's behavior and thinking even once he was out of office. As Herbert Schandler argues, in *The Unmaking of a President* (1977), Johnson constructs in *The Vantage Point* a narrative showing "everyone agreeing with each other and agreeing with him." Thus he was able to say, about his Tuesday Lunch advisers: "That group never leaked a single note. Those men were loyal to me. I could control them." One reason Kearns Goodwin may have felt compelled to write *Team of Rivals* (2006) some thirty years later, a book about Lincoln's adept handling of the competitors he brought into his cabinet, was to create a counter-allegory of the conflict-denying administration in which she had worked as a young woman.

Johnson's recollections about the Gulf of Tonkin incident make no reference, for instance, to the controversy about whether the attacks on U.S. naval vessels really did occur. Within a month of the incident he was saying to McNamara, "You just came in a few weeks ago and said they're launching an attack on us—they're firing at us, and we got through with the firing and concluded maybe they hadn't fired at all." Such doubts are not allowed to enter Johnson's memoir. Instead, he writes that "Admiral Sharp . . . had no doubt whatsoever that an attack had taken place." As we have seen, Sharp had at the time of the alleged attacks expressed to McNamara a strong sense of uncertainty, one only conveyed to Johnson after the fact. The ensuing debate over possible misreadings or misrepresentations of enemy maneuvers

and intentions is part of the story, part of the "perspectives," to borrow a
word from Johnson's subtitle, afforded by elapsed time. Instead of perspective, however, Johnson offers up his presidency as a decision-laden process
apparently immune to afterthought.

Suppression of conflict led to a splitting-of-the-difference on big decisions regarding the war, which in turn produced a strategy of "graduated
response." McMaster is the most eloquent student of this failed approach,
and his *Dereliction of Duty* carefully traces the baby steps by way of which
Johnson allowed himself to be drawn into a war he never fully decided
to fight. "Graduated Pressure," his chapter on Johnson's early approach
to Vietnam, shows how a strategy growing out of the Cuban missile crisis
found itself applied by Kennedy holdovers, and therefore by Johnson as
well, to Southeast Asia. According to Robert Dallek, "Johnson wanted the
freedom to push ahead and pull back in Vietnam as he believed necessary."
Such an approach allowed him to avoid "a difficult choice between war
and withdrawal from South Vietnam." But this tentative military strategy
was the result of a personal style, not a calibrated response to facts on the
ground. It overlooked the most important fact about the enemy—that it
had no interest in compromise.

Near the beginning of "The Making of a Decision," Johnson offers up
an unambiguous sentence: "The decision to finish my term and go back to
my ranch in January 1969 was as firmly fixed in my mind as any decision
could be." In the chapter following, "A Beginning and an End," he indicates
that the decision not to run had been made months and perhaps even years
before the spring of 1968. The decision thus emerges as uninfluenced either
by the Tet Offensive or by the McCarthy campaign. But the phrase "as any
decision could be" proves the fatal qualification, since Johnson's narrative
finally reveals that for him no decision is ever "firmly fixed." He will in fact
argue that "no President, at least not this President, makes a decision until
he publicly announces that decision and acts upon it." Any of the decisions
announced in the March 31 speech "I could have unmade . . . right down
to the time I sat behind my desk and began to speak on television."

Johnson here advances a decision as a thing largely external to the person
making it. It remains unfixed up to the moment of public utterance—as
if only saying it can make it true. By claiming to have made a firmly fixed
decision before the cascading troubles of 1968, Johnson attempts to present himself as above the pressure of events. Yet by mystifying the issue of
when a thing is decided, he instead creates a character wholly vulnerable to
what he calls "a dramatic change in circumstances." As he writes, in the last

paragraph of "The Making of a Decision," "any one of dozens of things *could* have happened, and in each case I would have reconsidered my decisions and changed my course if necessary." Abigail McCarthy saw it quite differently, writing in her memoir that while in *The Vantage Point* Johnson's decision to withdraw from the presidential race "was all supposedly explained," his primary concern was to withhold it from the public until the last minute "for the sake of an effect."

Johnson might have done better simply to have quoted Theodore Sorensen: "The essence of ultimate decision remains impenetrable to the observer—often, indeed, to the decider himself." Still, few presidential decisions appear as overdetermined as the two linked announcements Johnson made on March 31. What remains remarkable about the story is Johnson's ability to remain so *undecided* in the face of such a torrent of advice and events.

Lady Bird Johnson's *A White House Diary* (1970) provides a detailed account of her husband's wavering approach to the "big decision." Lady Bird began talking her diary into a tape recorder a few days after November 22, 1963. "I *like* writing," she says, in her preface; "I like words." Out of the 1,750,000 words she eventually generated, Lady Bird produced a 783-page "sampler," "using about one seventh of the material."

Published a year before *The Vantage Point,* the wife's diary is careful not to usurp the husband's narrative of events. "As far back as the summer of 1965," he can write, "I told a number of people of my intention not to run again." Despite having shared such thoughts over the years "with others," Johnson admits, "I doubt that any of them would have bet his life on the outcome."

Lady Bird first makes mention of "coming down off the mountain" in an entry on May 13, 1967. Likening another campaign to an open-ended stay in a concentration camp, she writes, "I have thought that Lyndon was of the same mind—that he would at some proper time announce that he would not be a candidate for reelection—but I do not know." She talks with trusted counselor Abe Fortas, who insists that "Lyndon must not make a decision, and certainly not an announcement, before next March." Anything done earlier would hamstring the war effort and the president's domestic program.

By July, a corner appears to have been turned: "Our decision, our hope, our determination, is to leave when this term ends." And she now concurs with Fortas, thinking the announcement should wait until the following March. By saying so, of course, Lady Bird brings her wishes for the future into conformity with what actually did happen.

By September she can write "about Lyndon's big decision—when and how to announce that he is not going to run again for the Presidency." Despite his "roaring energy," she fears for her husband's health. In a meeting at the ranch, she talks about her "feelings" about not wanting to face another campaign. She orders dinner on trays, and "there I sat in my sausage curlers, eating and trying to help my husband and two good friends decide his future. I think we all knew that we would only really know what was going to happen when we heard it happen."

Four months later, and again at the ranch, the Johnsons and the Connallys talk without interruption for almost three hours. "John said, 'You ought to run only if you look forward to being President again—only if you *want* to do it.'" Johnson worries about what history, and the soldiers in Vietnam, will say about him. "And so we went round and round on the same hot griddle, finding no cool oasis, no definite time for an acceptable exit."

"What shall I do?" her husband asks Lady Bird, on the evening of January 17, 1968. He is to deliver the State of the Union address in fewer than three hours. She answers that she cannot tell him what to do, although both she and Johnson's press secretary at the time, George Christian, have written statements about not running again. Christian gives her his draft, which she prefers to her "feeble" one. All day she has Christian's statement "in my keeping and I held it like a coal of fire. . . . I wanted to get it back into Lyndon's pocket."

Lady Bird never makes it clear whether or not she accomplishes her goal. There is a hurried exchange with her husband outside the Fish Room. That night, "as he approached the end" of his speech, "I tightened up in my seat. Would he end with his statement? Did I want him to?" She does not answer these questions. "He ended on a strong high note," she writes, "and there was a great roar of applause." The entry for January 17 makes no more mention of the fate of the statement, or of the "big decision." Lady Bird will not recur to the subject in her diary until the entry for March 31, when her husband reads to her and two friends "a very beautifully written statement" which begins with the word "Accordingly." Despite having "talked about this over and over . . . somehow we all acted and felt stunned."

Tet intervened soon after the State of the Union address, calling upon all of Johnson's capacities for self-persuasion. Knowing that the war had damaged his popularity and perhaps even his capacity to govern, he once again believed success into being. It was an old pattern, according to Robert Dallek: "Because so much of what he hoped for in the war was at variance with the realities of the conflict, his expressions of faith, which rested on sincere convictions about what the U.S. military could achieve in Vietnam, made him seem devious."

Having become a prisoner of a rhetoric of "unrealistic optimism," Johnson thus chose to respond to the disaster of Tet by casting it as a victory. Meanwhile, in early February, the strains of Tet found him crying uncontrollably during a visit from his old Senate friend Richard Russell.

In describing Tet as a defeat for the enemy, Johnson was simply echoing General Westmoreland, who accompanied his claim with a request for an additional 206,000 troops. It was this request, forwarded through General Wheeler to Washington in late February, that set off the intense reevaluation of Vietnam strategy culminating in Johnson's March 31 speech.

On the day he was sworn in as secretary of defense, Clark Clifford commissioned a task force to review Wheeler's request. The resulting report was presented to Johnson on March 7. Townsend Hoopes characterizes the report as "entirely silent on the matter of the relevance and adequacy of U.S. political objectives in Vietnam." The report supported the troop request, one bound to involve the mobilization of reserves as well as increased draft calls. It also advocated intensified bombing in the North and the mining of Haiphong harbor. While the report may have seemed to ratify much of the existing approach in Vietnam, in the process of assembling it, as Herbert Schandler has shown, a change was worked in Clifford's mind. When the new secretary of defense met with Johnson on March 8 to address the troop request, he expressed doubts about the ongoing strategy. On the same day, Johnson told his political aides to begin organizing for the primaries and the summer convention.

Two days later, on a Sunday, the *New York Times* broke the story about the new troop request. "206,000 More Men," the headline read. "The request has touched off a divisive internal debate within high levels of the Johnson Administration," the *Times* reported. The next day, March 11, Ted Sorensen, one of Robert Kennedy's closest advisers, met with Johnson at the White House. When he indicated the likelihood of a Kennedy candidacy, Johnson asked whether Sorensen "had any suggestions—presumably to avert that occurrence." Sorensen proposed appointing a blue-ribbon commission to review the entire Vietnam policy. Still undecided about whether to run, Kennedy had delivered a Senate speech in the week previous questioning whether "we can decide in Washington, D.C., what cities, what towns, what hamlets in Vietnam are going to be destroyed." On Tuesday, March 12, McCarthy "won" in New Hampshire by losing to Johnson by almost seven percentage points.

In *Up 'Til Now* (1987), McCarthy was to write, about Johnson's March 31 announcement, "I do not know what the immediate motivation for the

Johnson withdrawal was." The following sentence reads: "The polls indicated that I would get 60 percent of the vote in the Wisconsin primary." The implied conclusion is clear: I drove Johnson out of the race. Johnson makes no mention of McCarthy or of New Hampshire in his chapters about the making of a decision. Near the end of his memoir, in "The Last Year," he finally brings up the subject, asserting that he "would have preferred to announce my intentions not to run before that primary." He had been prevented from doing so, he implies, by larger considerations, the Tet Offensive, discussions of a bombing halt, his legislative program. "The fact that I received more votes, as a write-in candidate, than Senator McCarthy," he adds, "seems to have been overlooked or forgotten."

An economic crisis that had been gathering for months, if not years, came to a head in mid-March. The country had been running trade deficits in seventeen of the previous eighteen months, and, as the costs of the war continued to lead to a fall in the dollar on world markets, a run on gold began. On March 14, the Treasury closed the gold markets. Johnson had been pressing since September for a 6 percent tax surcharge to cover the gap between spending on guns and his continuing commitment to more and more butter. Now, the crisis in the markets made it clear that the country simply could not afford anything close to Westmoreland's requested troop increase.

Dean Acheson lunched with Johnson on Friday, March 15. The old Cold Warrior had long since concluded that "the Joint Chiefs of Staff don't know what they're talking about." He presented Johnson with the findings of a group of experts he had privately convened. According to Hoopes, "he told the President that his recent speeches were quite unrealistic and believed by no one, either at home or abroad. He added the judgment that the country was no longer supporting the war."

Robert Kennedy entered the race for the presidency on the following day. Johnson had long been haunted by Kennedy and his belief that Bobby saw himself, in Johnson's words, as the "rightful heir to the throne." James Rowe, one of Johnson's oldest friends, was now convinced that Johnson had to run. "He is not about to turn the country over to Bobby." Johnson flew back to his Texas ranch on Sunday, and then traveled to Minneapolis, where he gave a "we are going to win" speech before the National Farmer's Union. Dallek interprets the speech as meant to intimidate Hanoi and therefore to convince it that the "only hope for a settlement was through negotiations." Despite the martial rhetoric, Dallek argues, "Johnson was desperately eager for an honorable way out of the war."

But politics continued. On Tuesday, March 19, the leaders of Johnson's campaign met and discovered that only 32 percent of the nation approved of Johnson's handling of the war. That Friday, Johnson announced his promotion of Westmoreland to Army chief of staff. In a letter appearing that morning in the *Times*, Arthur Schlesinger Jr. pointed out that Lincoln, unlike Johnson, knew how to fire generals who could not win. Johnson also met on the 22nd with his inner circle to discuss the speech that McPherson had been asked to prepare, almost a month earlier, as a response to the Tet Offensive.

Clifford was dismayed by what McPherson later called his "We Shall Overcome draft." He now argued for a partial bombing halt. The group seemed paralyzed between "the broad desire to make a gesture toward peace and the fear of its rejection by Hanoi." At home, that night, McPherson hit upon the notion of an unconditional bombing halt north of the 20th parallel, an idea Johnson was quick to endorse.

The "Wise Men" assembled at the White House on March 25 and 26. McGeorge Bundy led off by summarizing "the general view," which held that the present war policy no longer engaged the support of the American people and "therefore required significant change." When, on the second day of the meetings, General Wheeler asserted that the United States was "not seeking a military victory, only helping the Vietnamese avoid a communist victory," Acheson exploded. "Then what in the name of God are five hundred thousand men out there doing—chasing girls? This is not a semantic game, General; if the deployment of all those men is not an effort to gain a military solution, then words have lost all meaning."

But of course, as Henry James had said some fifty years earlier, war always leads to "a depreciation of all our terms." In an environment so corrupted by euphemism and acronym, Michael Herr was to despair of the power of conventional journalism to reveal anything true about the war. Perhaps all a writer could hope to provide was a single, piercing metaphor, like the one first imagined by Hemingway and then remembered by Herr on the last page of *Dispatches*, "the glimpse he'd had of his soul after being wounded, it looked like a fine white handkerchief drawing out of his body, floating away and then returning." Why this metaphor, for that war? Why an image of suffering indistinguishable from the white flag of surrender? Because Hemingway saw how necessary it had become, in a war of such appalling and ineffectual attrition, to declare a truce. In *A Farewell to Arms* (1929) Frederic Henry will call this "a separate peace" and will choose the antiheroism of desertion over the heroism of combat. As he retreats from the front, he also seconds James's insight into the depreciating effect of war on words:

> I was always embarrassed by the words sacred, glorious, and sacrifice
> and the expression in vain. . . . There were many words that you
> could not stand to hear and finally only the names of places had
> dignity. Certain numbers were the same way and certain dates and
> these with the names of the places were all you could say and have
> them mean anything. Abstract words such as glory, honor, courage,
> or hallow were obscene beside the concrete names of villages, the
> numbers of roads, the names of rivers, the numbers of regiments
> and the dates.

"No words are strong enough," Johnson had said in the first major speech
of his presidency, on November 27, 1963. No words are strong enough,
he meant, to express the nation's grief over John Kennedy's death or its
determination to go forward. Having renounced, at the very beginning
of his presidency, the power of words, and having always had a "peculiar
relationship" with them, Johnson found himself, at the end of March 1968,
caught up in a search for just the right ones. It was not, as Acheson said,
a semantic game. By the evening of March 26, Johnson saw that the Wise
Men had deserted him. In *The Vantage Point,* he tries to rationalize their
gloominess by blaming briefers who had used, he concluded, "outdated
information." Still, these were "intelligent, experienced men. . . . If they had
been so deeply influenced by the reports of the Tet Offensive, what must
the average citizen in the country be thinking?" The big thing left to do was
to write and to deliver a dignified speech.

Johnson gave three great speeches during his presidency, the last on March
31, 1968. The tragedy of that final occasion can best be understood after
looking back at the two speeches in which Johnson laid claim to a legacy
that had nothing to do with the war. Both earlier speeches had been written
by Richard Goodwin.

Goodwin liked to live on the cutting edge of hope, and he chose to do
so by writing speeches. Joining the Kennedy administration in 1961, at the
age of thirty, he felt "poised for a journey of limitless possibility." Under
JFK he helped conceive the Alliance for Progress and met secretly with Ché
Guevera. After the assassination he stayed on in the White House, coined
the phrase "The Great Society," and wrote the great civil rights speech of
March 1965. Leaving government later that year, he joined the McCarthy
campaign in February 1968. In the same month he also published a piece
on the domino theory in the *New Yorker's* "Talk of the Town," declaring it
"not a theory at all but rather a selective metaphor with almost no support

in contemporary history." Abandoning McCarthy for Robert Kennedy a month later, Goodwin stayed with the campaign until the assassination in June, after which he withdrew from public life.

Goodwin's *Remembering America* (1988) offers itself as an "exhortation to remembrance, written in hope that by recollecting what we were, we may remember what we can be." He looks back on the 1960s as "a decisive turning point in the American story," a history in which he played a crucial part. Goodwin "saw his role as far more than that of a creative amanuensis," Harry McPherson writes. "He meant to influence the direction of government." But Goodwin could only remain loyal to this ambition by turning to fresh tasks, and so became the decade's most adept side-changer. At least one of the politicians he wrote for carried no grudge. "Goodwin is like a professional ball player," Eugene McCarthy said. "You could trade him . . . and he wouldn't give away your signals to the other team."

"A speech," Goodwin argues, "is not a literary composition. It is an event, designed not to please the exegetes of language, but to move men to action or alliance." As the decades pass, however, and the memory of actions and alliances fade, presidential speeches, especially the strong ones, take on a persisting power, the recorded words as durable as any other form of survival.

In April 1964, Johnson invited Goodwin for a naked swim in the White House pool. There the president instructed a speechwriter inherited from the Kennedy administration to "put together a Johnson program." As they left the pool, Johnson looked back and said, "They're trying to get me in a war over there: It will destroy me. I turned them down three times last week."

Goodwin approached his task by recurring to a phrase he had earlier slipped into a minor speech: "the Great Society." After first hearing it, Jack Valenti and Johnson realized they "could fit a lot of what we were trying to do within the curve of this phrase." Goodwin, encouraged, made it the centerpiece of an upcoming commencement address to be delivered at the University of Michigan on May 22.

All writers quote, but the strongest do so in such a way as to seem to anticipate what has been received. As Borges says, "every writer *creates* his own precursors." In reconstructing the influences behind the Ann Arbor speech, Goodwin cites Albert Camus, Betty Friedan, and Ralph Nader. But he gives most credit to the Port Huron Statement of 1962. The SDS manifesto had been written, after all, on Michigan ground. "I had no intention of calling for a spiritual rebirth," Goodwin admits, but that is exactly what he did, taking off from Port Huron's claim that "the life of the nation is spiritually empty." While the speech focused on the enhancement of urban life, the restoration of natural beauty, and the improvement of education, it finally looked beyond changes in the material world toward issues of "spirit and soul." The Great Society, as Goodwin envisioned it, was a place "where men are more concerned with the quality of their goals than the quantity of their goods." In the best Emersonian tradition, to which the Port Huron Statement also had recurred, the speech appealed less to the wants of the body than to the "needs of the spirit." It was time to stop confusing "the good life" with a "soulless wealth." Out of these ambitiously spiritual promptings would come the very concrete interventions of Medicare and Medicaid, Head Start, Upward Bound, the Legal Services program, the College Work-Study program, the Water Quality and Clean Air acts, the NEA and the NEH, the food stamp program, and the Highway Beautification Act.

"I wanted power to give things to people," Johnson was to tell Kearns Goodwin. Much of what Johnson gave the nation remains of lasting value and has become a permanent part of American life. But in the generosity of the Great Society lay, as well, its fatal flaw. Within Johnson's giving—perhaps in any giving—there lay a will to control. Johnson was "a generous and demanding giver," Kearns Goodwin writes; over time he was to burden her with twelve electric toothbrushes. "The giver decided what he wanted to give, not what the recipient wanted to receive." The cost of the gift was that it be "appreciated." What Johnson failed to imagine was a "resentment based, not on objections to his social goals or to the practicality of specific measures, but on hostility to the implicit assertion of increased central authority to define the general welfare and confer benevolences which, however desirable in themselves, should not be imposed by presidential will." Kearns Goodwin here articulates the attitude toward federal "giving" that would become the core of the Reaction. And whether or not one remained a Democrat or a Republican in the ensuing decades, the growing resistance to Johnson's gifts invoked one of Emerson's hardest sayings: "We do not quite forgive a giver."

In *Power and Protest* (2003), Jeremi Suri reads Johnson's involvement with Vietnam as a romance of generosity. "Johnson believed that the United States had to sponsor an international New Deal," and Vietnam was the place where it seemed most obviously on demand. "Development" consequently became a keyword in Johnson's statements about Southeast Asia. If the Vietnamese resisted our gifts, they would need to be coupled with a "limited war" that would allow American largesse to operate. But, since "no one could make over South Vietnam in the image of Texas," graduated response followed upon graduated response. "Washington's efforts produced devastation instead of development." The attempt by the United States to punish Vietnam into accepting its help led, in Suri's words, to "the illiberal consequences of liberal empire."

Johnson's next strong speech worked even better than the one on the Great Society because it gave nothing that had not already been taken. By the time he stood up before a joint session of Congress to deliver an outline of the Voting Rights bill, African Americans had themselves put their bodies on the line in order to claim the franchise so long denied them. Johnson's speech, also written by Goodwin, merely recognized a social change already accomplished that now deserved to be formalized into law.

Martin Luther King Jr. first heard the song "We Shall Overcome" on Labor Day weekend in 1957, when Pete Seeger sang it at the Highlander Folk School in Tennessee. By 1965 the old Negro spiritual had become the anthem of the civil rights movement. King repeatedly borrowed the phrase from the song, and Johnson, through Goodwin, borrowed the phrase from King. Even more than the repeating of the "house divided" metaphor on March 31, a figure Lincoln had of course borrowed from the Gospel of Mark, Johnson's assumption of the phrase "We shall overcome" once again revealed the nation as bound together by the echoing power of ancestral voices.

Goodwin had less than a day in which to write the voting rights speech. Johnson was scheduled to address Congress at 9 p.m. on Monday, March 15. At 9:30 that morning Valenti called Goodwin, who knew a speech was being contemplated, and said to him, "He needs a speech from you . . . right away." Under "the constraint of time," Goodwin quickly realized that in this matter "there was no other side." It was not an occasion calling for balance. The speech he went on to write, while in his words, "was pure Johnson." And it would turn on an unassailable fact: "that in many places in this country men and women are kept from voting simply because they are Negroes."

A unique moment of crisis, Goodwin saw, is also always an experience of repetition. He therefore began by reminding his audience that the decade through which it was living marked the third of the nation's civil wars. It was a new moment of founding, one also requiring a recommitment to the "work we are in," to use Lincoln's moving and yet modest phrase for the collective and always unfinished activity of building a more perfect union. "At times history and fate meet at a single time in a single place to shape a turning point in man's unending search for freedom. So it was at Lexington and Concord. So it was at Appomattox. So it was last week in Selma, Alabama." This was a crisis, like the Revolution and the Civil War, that "lay bare the secret heart of America itself." In a country founded on a claim of all men being equal, the lack of equal rights for African Americans had always been, and still continued to be, the contradictory heart of the matter. It was a question of integrity, of a failure to be one with the founding ideals. The country was experiencing a failed spiritual integration for all, not only a failed legal integration for some. Then Goodwin fell back on the eloquence of the Bible: "For with a country as with a person 'what shall it profit a man, if he shall gain the whole world, and lose his own soul'?" All politics may be local, the coming wisdom would go on to claim, but by way of Johnson's voice, and through Goodwin's claim, all politics are revealed as also spiritual.

A central refrain in Martin Luther King Jr.'s recent speeches had been an end to waiting. "How long?" he had asked; "Not long," he had answered. Now Johnson picked up the theme, and made it an issue for every American rather than for black Americans alone. The nation had reached a moment of timely untimeliness. "The last time a president sent a civil rights bill to Congress . . . the heart of the voting provision had been eliminated." He was referring to the Civil Rights Act of 1957, the one he had been so instrumental in limiting and then in getting passed. He would not make the same mistake again. "This time, on this issue, there must be no delay, no hesitation, and no compromise. . . . We cannot . . . refuse to protect the right of every American to vote . . . must not wait another eight months. We have already waited a hundred years and more, and the time for waiting is gone."

The key shift in the speech is the move from "they" to "We." In the phrase "We have already," Johnson suddenly and swiftly includes all Americans into the felt and painful experience of waiting. This shift will in turn set up the biggest surprise of the speech, one involving the quoting of another famous "we" construction. The present struggle is about "all of us," Johnson goes on to say; we must all "overcome the crippling legacy of bigotry and injustice." There, in one word—"overcome"—the upcoming claim had been quietly sounded. So Johnson paused, and then said, carefully spacing out the words: "And we . . . shall . . . overcome."

"There was an instant of silence," Goodwin writes. Then seventy-year-old congressman Emmanuel Cellar leaped to his feet. Soon the entire chamber was standing. Senator Mike Mansfield was weeping; in Alabama, Martin Luther King Jr. also wept. Jack Valenti was later to total up fifty-six interruptions for applause during the speech. But this interruption went on and on. Senator Richard Russell of Georgia, an implacable foe of civil rights legislation, would call Johnson and say that while he could not be with him on the bill, it was the best speech he had heard any president ever give.

Undersecretary of the Air Force Townsend Hoopes was so dismayed by the "galloping distortions" dominating Johnson's approach to Vietnam that, but for the appointment of Clark Clifford as secretary of defense in February 1968, he would have resigned from his position. Instead, he stayed on in the administration and was therefore able to leave us *The Limits of Intervention: An Inside Account of How the Johnson Policy of Escalation in Vietnam Was Reversed* (1969). Hoopes had been right to hope; by the time the Wise Men delivered their gloomy findings to Johnson on March 26, Clifford had taken firm control of the discourse on the war.

Clifford's change of heart after assuming his new post came as a surprise to those who assumed him to be a hawk on the war. As Herbert Schandler writes, "the McNamara men in the Pentagon did not want a political dilettante, a Mr. Smooth, a man reportedly interested mostly in money and creature comforts." But Clifford turned out to be other than what he appeared to be. Early on he had expressed doubts about escalation in Vietnam. But in his role as an unofficial counselor, not a paid adviser, Clifford believed it appropriate to support the president once directions had been set. He thus entered government with a usefully divided mind, one long privately skeptical if publicly supportive of Johnson's policy on the war. As a result, he was perhaps not entirely surprised to find himself soon entertaining positions that "seemed internally contradictory."

Clifford also possessed an intense form of piety. He opens *Counsel to the President* by claiming to hold the "office of President . . . in special reverence." *Office,* he writes, not *man.* While Johnson called Clifford "old friend" and had begun cultivating him as early as 1946, it was, according to Clifford, "a slowly developing relationship." For Johnson, Clifford was to prove above all a fixer, someone brought in to develop talking points for an awkward meeting with Robert Kennedy or to devise an advertising strategy against Barry Goldwater. Johnson began turning to him for advice on Vietnam in 1964, often inviting him to working meetings at Camp David. Friendship may have played its part, but the man who eventually took over at the Pentagon continued to define himself as the disinterested counselor not to the man but to the position.

"Give me the lesser of evils," Johnson said to Clifford, when asking him to set up a task force on Vietnam in late February. "I was thrust into a ruthlessly frank assessment of the situation by the men who knew the most about it," Clifford was to write, in a 1969 article in *Foreign Affairs.* "Try though we would to stay with the assignment of devising means to meet the military's requests, fundamental questions began to recur over and over." Schandler again: "Clifford's reaction was one of shock."

Hoopes remains impatient with the limitations of the task force report, but Schandler depicts the deliberations surrounding it, and the various drafts leading up to it, as comprising the important first stage in Clifford's reeducation. Most of the work of the task force was performed by young men in the Pentagon, men who had finally decided "to write what we thought even if that meant we all got fired." The result was the "first memo . . . which really attacked the fundamental motives in the Vietnam war—and the military had no answer to it."

While the report itself was to make only "modest recommendations" for change, the heated debates involved in constructing it, especially the doubts expressed by the Defense Department civilians, became known to the press. On the evening of Saturday, March 9, 1968, much of the Washington press corps had gathered at the Gridiron Club dinner. Just before 10 p.m., the early editions of the *New York Times* hit the room. The newspaper carried a story by Neil Sheehan and Hedrick Smith summarizing the Task Force report. "The scope and depth of the internal debate within the Government reflect the wrenching uncertainty and doubt in this capital about every facet of the war." As Smith recalls, "It moved like wind through a field of wheat." George Christian soon found himself surrounded by reporters. Walt Rostow later admitted that the story "churned up the whole eastern establishment."

Clifford had begun talking to Senator Richard Russell, who had come to believe that "we shouldn't have gone in in the first place." Asked to testify before the Fulbright Committee, Clifford begged off, in part because of his growing doubts about administration policy. Schandler argues that as Clifford confronted the possibility of public testimony, his "thoughts coalesced." He came to see the course being pursued in Vietnam as "not only endless, but hopeless." In a private meeting with Fulbright, it was agreed that Clifford would not have to testify.

Johnson soon became dismissive of what he called the "Clifford approach." In McPherson's view, Johnson felt that he had invited in "an extremely able, loyal, and effective advisor" only to discover him showing "signs of not having his head on straight on this issue." As Clifford recalled in a later interview, "The president made a great deal out of our differences. He was upset with me. The bloom was off our relationship."

By mid-March, McPherson had been at work on Johnson's Vietnam speech for almost six weeks. After circulating a fourth draft, he received a phone call from Clifford. He was calling "to ask what I really thought about the war." McPherson shared his views, and Clifford then said, "we must be watchful for any sign that the war is to be wound up again, and not down.

That would be tragic—for the country, and for the man himself." Clifford's next major move was to convene the Wise Men, a meeting that "served the purpose that I hoped it would. It really shook the president." Clifford now had to make sure that the country got the speech he believed it needed.

By this point in the Johnson presidency, preparing a presidential address had "become a vast collective enterprise." Horace Busby had worked for Johnson as a speechwriter and political analyst since 1948 and would weigh in on the final product, especially on its ending. George Christian had the right of review, and most of Johnson's major advisers had been tinkering with the speech since February 27. Even Lady Bird would contribute some essential wording. Despite all this, McPherson claims that "when the President was preparing a major address—the final product usually belonged more to him than to his writers."

On the evening of Wednesday, March 27, the day after the Wise Men delivered their views, Johnson met with Senate majority leader Mike Mansfield at the White House. "Madness," Mansfield said, about the requested 206,000 troop increase. Johnson claims to have told Mansfield that he intended to halt all bombing north of Vietnam's 20th parallel, an idea originating with McPherson and one that would eventually make it into the final version of the speech. In later correspondence, Mansfield wrote that Johnson only mentioned the "possibility" of a bombing halt.

On the next day, March 28, the speech finally coalesced. In a meeting with Rusk, Clifford, Rostow, and Bill Bundy, McPherson presented his eighth draft, "still essentially a defiant, bellicose speech written to be delivered between clenched teeth." Clifford exploded. "The President cannot give that speech! It would be a disaster! . . . What the President needs is not a war speech, but a peace speech." What Clifford said in that fateful meeting will never be known entirely, but how he said it has been nicely captured by Townsend Hoopes: "The Clifford manner is deliberate, sonorous, eloquent, and quite uninterruptible. It gathers momentum as it proceeds, and soon achieves a certain mesmerizing effect; the perfection of the grammar is uncanny." Clifford spoke slowly, for over two hours. He described Vietnam as "a hopeless bog." McPherson was to describe it as a "brilliant and utterly courageous performance." Afterward, not even Rusk and Rostow spoke against "winding it down."

"It was decided," McPherson recalls, "that I should write a different speech." Clifford suggested that Johnson be given a choice between the "current draft" and the "different speech." McPherson, now an ally of Clifford's, "left the State Department wanting to holler."

That afternoon, Johnson met with Joseph Califano to discuss the issue of the tax surcharge, itself a major feature of the upcoming speech. "What do you think about my not running for reelection?" Johnson asked. Califano said he thought the president had to run, that only he could push through the necessary legislation. "Others can get things done," Johnson answered. "The Congress and I are like an old married couple. We've lived together so long and we've been rubbing against each other night after night so often and we've asked so much of each other over the years we're tired of each other. They'd have a honeymoon. Any one of them. I wouldn't have one."

At six thirty that evening, Johnson went over the two versions of the speech with the working group. The first began, "I speak to you tonight in a time of grave challenge to our country." The second opened with the words, "Tonight I want to speak to you of the prospects for peace in Vietnam and Southeast Asia." Johnson saw that the newer version also contained what he called a "peace offer"—the confining of air and naval attacks to military targets south of the 20th parallel. "It was what I had decided needed to be done," he claims in *The Vantage Point,* although he admits to not then saying so "flatly for fear of another damaging press leak."

March 29 proved quiet except for a phone call from Johnson to McPherson in which he queried one passage. In looking at the two versions of the speech, McPherson was jubilant to discover that Johnson was now working with the alternative draft.

The president and his advisers spent all of Saturday "painstakingly" going over the speech's every word; it was this kind of obsessive combing through of McPherson's constructions that made the final product belong as much to Johnson as to his writers. McPherson remembers that at around nine, "the President asked, 'Where's the peroration?'" McPherson said he had not liked it, and so had removed it. "That's O.K.," Johnson replied. "Make it as long as you want. I may even add one of my own." McPherson took Johnson's question as a request for a summary on a peaceful Southeast Asia, which is what he then promptly wrote. It was not quite what Johnson had in mind.

On a trip to Australia in December 1967, Johnson had told Horace Busby "what I planned to do and what I wanted to say. I asked him to try his hand at a statement." Two days before the State of the Union speech in January, Busby handed him a draft:

> I shall not seek—I have no desire to accept—the nomination of my party for another term in this great office of all the people.

Johnson then showed the statement to his wife. After reading Busby's sentence, Lady Bird penciled in "will not accept" over the phrase "have no desire to accept." This language, which would finally stand, was then merged into a withdrawal statement being written by George Christian, the one Lady Bird remembers carrying around on January 17 like a coal in her pocket. When he had arrived at the Capitol to give the State of the Union speech, Johnson writes in *The Vantage Point,* "I thought I had the statement with me but I discovered that I had failed to bring it. Frankly, I cannot say what I would have done that night if the paper had been in my pocket." So in whose pocket did the statement end up? Robert Dallek provides one answer: "At the last minute Johnson decided against using the statement. He handed the text to Mrs. Johnson before leaving for the Capitol and did not have it with him during his speech." Neither the husband's nor the wife's memoir contains any record of this exchange.

"I was never more certain of the rightness of my decision." This sentence from *The Vantage Point* refers to sharing the withdrawal statement with his daughter and her husband on the way back from mass on the morning of Sunday, March 31. Johnson then describes driving to Hubert Humphrey's apartment and telling him of his plans.

Johnson took Humphrey into a room and read him the speech he had in mind. In *The Vantage Point,* he omits what then followed. As Humphrey recalled in 1971, Johnson then said, "'I've got two endings for this speech, and I want you to listen to them.' He read both of them to me. I said, 'Mr. President, you can't take that second ending. You just can't do that. You just cannot resign from the office. Because that's what you would be doing.' He said, 'Hubert, I've got to tell you something. Nobody will believe that I'm trying to end this war unless I do that.'" Had the decider finally decided? In a posthumously published memoir, *The Thirty-First of March* (2005), Horace Busby provides an intimate sense of the crosswinds still blowing through the White House on the last day of March.

On Saturday morning Johnson had called Busby and asked him to "sit down and write out for me what you and I were talking about in January." Not running again was what they had talked about then, and earlier in December, and Busby had sent Johnson a draft of a withdrawal statement. Now he wrote another draft and had it delivered to the White House. A little after midnight, Johnson called Busby and asked him to come in by nine that morning.

"I want out of this cage," Johnson said to Busby when they met on Sunday. He also claimed to prefer Busby's January statement to "what you wrote yesterday," and informed Busby that George Christian still had the first statement, saved from the day of the State of the Union address. Johnson added that the odds of his using either statement were "Eighty–twenty, against it."

Still, the president and his longtime aide continued to labor over wording, with Johnson, over Busby's objection, changing "will not" to "would not accept." Debate surged around the lunch table, with family and friends nearly all opposing withdrawal. Around three, Busby found himself rewriting the statement. "This is me," Johnson said, when he read it.

Still conflicted, Johnson wondered during his afternoon lie-down whether he ought to postpone the announcement until a Thursday fundraising dinner. Busby argued against the idea. Just before six, Johnson finally read the statement aloud to those who had gathered to support him, with Busby's last service being to convince the president to change the "would" back to a "will," thus restoring the revision of Busby's draft originally proposed by Lady Bird back in January.

Out of consideration for the principal author of the speech, Johnson phoned Harry McPherson around five "and asked if I thought the speech was any good." McPherson replied that he thought it was. Then Johnson informed McPherson that he had supplied an ending of his own. "Did I know what he was going to say? I thought so. What did I think about that? 'I'm very sorry, Mr. President.'

'Well, I think it's best. So long, podner.'"

A few minutes before nine, Rostow and Clifford arrived at the White House. "I showed them the statement for the first time," Johnson writes. "After what you've been through," Clifford said, "you are entitled to make this decision." In his own memory of the occasion, Clifford is not so composed. "You could have knocked my eyes off with a stick," he was later to say. When Clifford passed the news to his wife and to Mrs. Rostow, "they were absolutely and completely destroyed."

So Johnson sat before the cameras and delivered his speech. What he said matters, but no more, perhaps, than how he came to say it. The process as well as the product is part of the final meaning of the speech.

Johnson may have been trying to end the war, but the war would continue. The number of troops in Vietnam rose by April of the following year to a ceiling of 543,000, a stunning figure but one that fell far short of what it might have been if Johnson had not chosen to whittle down Westmoreland's request. In the end, he sent only 23,000 additional troops to Vietnam. From mid-1969 on, troop levels in Vietnam began to decline. But the machine ground on: in the ten months after McNamara's retirement, Clifford was to authorize the dropping of more bombs on Indochina than had been dropped in the three previous years. April 1968 saw the largest offensive operation of the war. The over 14,500 Americans killed in Vietnam during 1968 would make it, for the United States, the war's bloodiest year.

Still, after Johnson's March, Nixon was never able to reescalate the war. While he did expand the conflict into Laos and Cambodia, and with disastrous results, he was still fighting, as Thomas Powers maintains, and despite any other words that might be used to describe the case, "what amounted to a retreat." The "decisions made in March of 1968," despite the ongoing indecision of the Decider himself, "set the stage for the withdrawal of American troops from Vietnam." In accepting his own defeat, and in finally deciding to acknowledge it in publicly spoken words, Lyndon Johnson helped prepare the nation for the need to face its own.

5

Fourteenth Street

A week after Barack Obama's 2009 inauguration, on a cold January morning, I drove up Fourteenth Street, which runs due north through Washington, D.C., passing a few blocks to the east of the White House and bisecting the Mall, at its southern end, alongside the Washington Monument. It was not a street I knew well, despite having spent the middle of my work week for almost twenty years in an apartment in Adams Morgan, a neighborhood not far to the west. For me, Fourteenth Street was where my son Luke had worked at Sparky's Espresso after moving to the District in 2001, and where he later played gigs with his girlfriend in their duo, Big Gold Belt, at a venue called the Black Cat.

I did know that Fourteenth Street had been the heart of black Washington and that after the riots of April 1968 it had taken the neighborhood over three decades to begin to recover. Now, the signs of urban uplift were everywhere. At P Street, I came to the Studio Theatre, founded in 1978 by Joy Zinoman, where I had seen Ricky Jay impale a watermelon with playing cards thrown from a distance of twenty feet. A little way down P there was a Whole Foods supermarket. A block further north, the Central Street Mission still offered its services to the poor. Across Fourteenth, Cork, a wine bar, had replaced

Sparky's Espresso. I drove by the Black Cat, and then saw that Source, the recently relocated performing arts center, was doing *The Marriage of Figaro.*

At Fourteenth and U Streets I parked my car and explored the sidewalk around the ten-story Frank D. Reeves Center of Municipal Affairs, which had gone up in 1986 as the first token of the will to renew. A historical marker out front carried the title "Riots to Renaissance." The renaissance included, to the south, a McDonalds, a Taco Bell, a KFC, and a Foot Locker. Across the street, a dry-cleaning shop had replaced the People's Drug Store, which had been badly damaged in 1968.

The riot had in fact begun at this very spot. In 1968, the twenty blocks on Fourteenth above U were home to some three hundred businesses, many of them black-owned. Both the Southern Christian Leadership Conference (SCLC) and the Student Nonviolent Coordinating Committee (SNCC) had their offices within steps of Fourteenth and U. The third-busiest drug store in the area stood on the northwest corner of the intersection, catty-corner from National Liquors. The London Custom Shop occupied another corner, up the street from a Safeway, Rhodes Five and Ten, and Sam's Pawnbroker. The Zanzibar Restaurant and the Jumbo Nut Shop were nearby. According to Ben Gilbert, in his *Ten Blocks from the White House* (1968), "police considered this intersection the most volatile in the city's crowded Negro sections."

April 4 was a Thursday, a work night. At 7:16 p.m., transistor radios picked up the news that Martin Luther King Jr. had been shot in Memphis. By this time in the evening, black Washingtonians on their way home were changing buses at Fourteenth and U, stopping to buy liquor or supplies at the drug store, or simply enjoying a warm spring night. At 8:19, the radios reported that King had died of his wounds. At 9:25, the first windows were broken, in the People's Drug Store.

Meanwhile, former SNCC chairman Stokely Carmichael had hit the pavement, telling the crowd to "go home" and asking businesses to close their doors. He moved up and down Fourteenth, shouting "Get off the streets. This is not the time, brothers." Five blocks north of U Street, he watched a woman lean against the window of Belmont TV and Appliance and begin "bumping it with her broad backside." When the window broke, Carmichael grabbed a teenage looter, brandished a revolver, and told him, "You're not ready for the 'thing.' Go home. Go home."

A few minutes later, looters began pouring out of Sam's Pawnbroker and Rhodes Five and Ten, carrying jewelry, radios, watches, TVs. By midnight, Fourteenth and U had been sealed off by the police. Fires were started further north in two food markets, and police began wielding nightsticks and deploying tear gas. The last major confrontation occurred at 3 a.m.; by sunrise, Fourteenth Street was quiet. But the anger surged again the following day, spreading across the city. Many of the blocks along Fourteenth looted the night before were now destroyed by fire. "White merchants scurried around for pictures of Dr. King to place in their windows," Gilbert reports. A "vengeful selectivity" may have been exercised early on, but as the violence spread across the city it evidenced "little concern about ownership of property."

On Friday, April 5, Horace Busby and other members of the president's staff gathered around Lyndon Johnson to wait out the day. The disturbances of the night before in Washington appeared to have subsided, and the hope was that the trouble had passed. As the group sat down to lunch, messages coming into the White House indicated that major cities were calm. Then secretaries returning from noontime shopping reported downtown department stores being quickly cleared. Someone called in to say that whites in the business district were surrendering the sidewalk. The uprising that had begun the night before now flared again and spread across the city, to 7th Street, H Street, and Anacostia.

Busby moved to the window:

> The eastbound lanes of Pennsylvania Avenue, carrying traffic toward the shopping district, stood starkly empty, but the westbound lanes were a river of fright, bumper to bumper, curb to center stripe, with Washingtonians surging out toward the sanctuary of their suburban homes.
>
> No one spoke. The sight below told a story the yellow message sheets could not tell. We could only stand mute and motionless, watching a nation divide.

An assistant leaned forward, to look toward the east. The rest followed, "smoke leaped into the sky, and we could see the first flames."

In Washington to meet with Averell Harriman, envoy to the upcoming Paris peace talks, the activist Tom Hayden, who had contacts with the North Vietnamese, "briefed him as clearly as I could with the drama of urban rage flaring behind his silver hair." William Westmoreland was also in town. He helicoptered with Johnson over Washington while the fires were still burning. "It looked considerably more distressing," he offered, "than Saigon during the Tet Offensive."

The fires seen by Busby were the second wave, one that crested during the next twenty-four hours and subsided only on Palm Sunday. That April weekend was to see riots in 110 American cities. According to Stephen Oates, "the hardest hit was Washington, D.C., where 711 fires blazed against the sky." By the time the riots in Washington had ended, 760 people were arrested, more than in Watts in 1965 or Detroit in 1967. Twelve people lost their lives. And the neighborhoods that did recover came back as something quite other than they had been before the fire.

Riding a bus north up Fourteenth Street soon after the riot started, twenty-one-year-old Bob King saw a crowd tearing down the iron gates in front of a liquor store, looters carrying caskets out of Himes Funeral Home, and families careening out of Safeway, carts filled with steak and chicken. "I felt so sad that my community was being destroyed," he said. A few months later, King converted a destroyed pawnshop into a community center. He spent years attending meetings about reconstruction of the Fourteenth Street corridor. Interviewed in 2008 by the *Washington Post,* King recalled that residents "always had the same question." "How long? How long will we have to wait? And I always gave them the same answer: 'Not long.'"

In saying "Not long," Bob King was quoting Martin Luther King Jr. In what many see as his greatest speech, one given on the steps of the Alabama state capitol building in 1965 after the triumphant march from Selma to Montgomery, King had addressed the crucial issue of waiting. His 1963 "Letter from Birmingham Jail" had also dealt with "why we find it difficult to wait." In Montgomery, King both asked and answered this abiding question.

It had taken three tries for the marchers to get to Montgomery. The aim was to dramatize the lack of progress on voting rights in the South, and Selma had been chosen as a departure point since, in a city more than half black, 99 percent of its voters were white. In a February 1965 meeting with King, Lyndon Johnson had promised him a voting rights bill and had asked him to wait. But King had also come to believe that legislation would only result from "dramatic confrontations" with white supremacy, and, when the Dallas County Voters League approached him with the idea of a march from Selma to Montgomery, he quickly agreed to an action calculated to provoke violent retaliation from local sheriff Jim Clark.

When marchers set out on Sunday, March 7, 1965, on the first attempt to cross the Edmund Pettus Bridge, on the outskirts of Selma, King was in Atlanta. The SCLC leadership had judged that his presence in Selma would be too provocative. As John Lewis and Hosea Williams led some five hundred people across the crest of the bridge, they were met by Alabama state troopers and members of Clark's posse. Lewis and Williams were knocked to the pavement and suffered severe head injuries; the column was attacked with tear gas and bull whips. King returned to Selma to comfort the injured and reiterated his call for a second march on Tuesday.

Meanwhile, after Judge Frank Johnson issued a restraining order against further marches, King found himself torn between compliance and defiance. One adviser urged him to violate the injunction; another counseled him to submit. In a compromise solution, King decided on a "symbolic march" in which he would lead his followers only to the far side of the bridge. He even accepted a map drawn up by local authorities showing him where he should stop. "I'll try my best to turn them back," King said, as he set out on Tuesday afternoon from Selma's Brown Chapel. Informing only SCLC leaders about his plan, King, after carrying it out, was accused by an angry ally of indulging in a "Tuesday turnaround."

The third attempt finally made it to Montgomery. After Judge Johnson lifted his order, King, on March 21, led a column of three thousand safely across the Alabama River. Covering fifty-four miles, the march reached Montgomery on March 24, and the next day King gave his "How long? Not long" speech.

King's speech in Montgomery celebrated the completed march and owned up to his recent display of wavering. "We will go back to the church now!" he had commanded, on that fateful Tuesday afternoon, executing a U-turn that lost him many hearts. The choice was real: King was caught between the need to placate federal authorities to whom he looked for redress on voting rights and the passion of his followers, many of whom had been injured during the first attempt to cross the bridge two days earlier, on Bloody Sunday.

Among the public figures of the 1960s, King was one of the most willing to acknowledge his self-divisions. "Each of us is something of a schizophrenic personality," he had argued, as early as 1957. "We're split up and divided against ourselves. There is something of a civil war going on within all our lives." As the completing act of the Civil War, the civil rights movement had found a leader, like Lincoln, willing to body forth, in his hesitations and sadnesses and capacity for self-rebuke, the larger national divisions he sought to reconcile. Lincoln had argued in the Second Inaugural that the war had been *given* "to both North and South." Each party to the conflict was implicated in the "fundamental and astounding result." The effective leader did not simply pursue the interest of one side against the other, but entered actively into "the enemy's point of view," in King's words, and even struggled to love him.

King began his speech in Montgomery by imaging the struggle for civil rights as "a mighty walk," just as he ended it by claiming that the cause was "marching on." The words of "The Battle Hymn of the Republic" invoked mythic time, the end of days in which all divisions would be healed. King would turn again to the words of the song in the last sentences of his last speech, in Memphis in 1968, where his eyes looked toward a promised land into which he would never walk. But in the case of the march from Selma to Montgomery, the word "walk" also denoted an actual fact. Thousands of people had walked all that way, and now, although their feet were tired, their souls were rested.

King's major form of civil disobedience was the public march. Harris Wofford was to describe King as a genius at "the politics of walking." But what to say when by one's own actions that very politics looked to have been publicly repudiated? King faced the question head-on: We are now here, he says, "standing before the forces of power." And "we ain't goin' let nobody turn us around."

Turn us around. In saying this, King acknowledged the fact that he had initially turned around. The eventual completion of the march had afforded him a second chance to overcome his original diffidence. "Put it in the center of your mind and dare—stare daringly at it," King preached later that spring, about shame and failure. The combined experience of a turning around and of an eventual marching on is a pattern often lived out by the true wayfaring Christian, a figure who continually reenacts a kind of fortunate fall in which limits are discovered and who then summons the courage to face the mistake and to persist in what King goes on to call the "long way."

King does not flinch from reminding his listeners of his conflicted behavior. He repeats himself: "We are not about to turn around." He even goes so far as to admit having led his people into "a trail wound in a circle." By so openly acknowledging the civil war in his own life, King purchases the authority to embrace the full potential of the simple words *here* and *now*. "We are here," he says. "We are on the move now." As the speech unfolds, King's emphasis shifts from the first word to the second. The physical fact of overcoming space, by marching and arriving, gives way in King's argument to the even more pressing matter of fulfilling a nation's promises within historical time.

As King spoke on March 25, 1965, he made reference to a speech given ten days earlier, Johnson's "We Shall Overcome" address to Congress about the Voting Rights Act. He judges it "an address that will live in history." But Johnson's address would never have entered history had it not been for the Bloody Sunday on the bridge, where "the tiny community of Selma generated

the massive power to turn the whole nation to a new course." It was the pho-
tographed and televised violence, from which King had absented himself, that
had aroused the nation and afforded Johnson the political capital he needed in
order to make the speech. By *not* turning back, the marchers assaulted on the
bridge had already effected, as King calls it, the most important "turn" of all.

All this prepares him for his peroration: "How long will it take?" The
question could be heard as addressing both the realization of the good
society King and his followers were trying to create and a hoped-for future
in which the divided self might merge with its ego-ideal. "It will not be
long," King answers.

But he was not yet done. Immediately, as if the very word "long" had
begun to sound an echoing bell, he continues:

> How long? Not long. Because no lie can live forever.
>> How long? Not long. Because you shall reap what you sow.
>> How long? Not long. Because the arc of the moral universe is
> long, but it bends toward justice.
>> How long? Not long. Because mine eyes have seen the glory of
> the coming of the Lord. He is trampling out the vintage where the
> grapes of wrath are stored. He has loosed the fateful lightning of his
> terrible swift sword. His truth is marching on.

At the end of perhaps his most timely speech, the one in which an achieved
historical destiny can be felt to coincide with a Biblical moment of revelation, King fell back on the eloquence of refrain. Refrain is so often what we
listen for, in poetry and in song. As time moves inexorably forward, in any
verbal or musical medium—in any life—refrain reaches back, returns to the
something already heard, and thereby consoles the listener with the sense
that there remain still and recoverable points in experience, that time is not
simply the sum of everything that runs away. The sublime irony carried by
King's refrain is that the content of the repeated words directly addresses
our longing and need for refrain itself, our helplessness before the march of
time, our need to conserve and to remember, and our abiding impatience
at having, as humans, to wait. For all that had been achieved by March 25,
1965—and much indeed had been—there awaited an uncertain future, as
King knew, and in such a moment sometimes the most that can be asked
for is the reconciling power of the wished-for words.

King's speech in Montgomery marked the high point of his public career and
the beginning of a difficult three-year period culminating in his assassination

in Memphis in April 1968. These were the years in which the movement's efforts "nationalized race" as it shifted attention from the South to the North and began to reveal racism as a national rather than solely a regional problem. But they were also the years of destructive urban riots, the rise of black power, squabbling within the SCLC, an ambitious but largely unsuccessful campaign against poverty in Chicago, and King's outspoken and unpopular opposition to the war in Vietnam.

The theme of the three years was backlash and resistance to change. While the 1964 Civil Rights Act and the 1965 Voting Rights Acts dismantled legal segregation, they could do little to promote social or economic integration or to soften human attitudes. Lyndon Johnson grasped the difficulty of a nation being called on to embrace equality not only "as a right and a theory, but equality as a fact and as a result." Yet "massive resistance" to school integration did not end in states like Virginia until 1968, after which the ensuing white flight from the inner cities eventually resegregated many urban public schools. In June 1966, while walking through DeSoto County, James Meredith was shot with a 16-gauge automatic shotgun wielded by a forty-year-old hardware contractor. A month earlier, Private First Class Jimmy Williams, who had been killed in Vietnam, was refused burial in his hometown cemetery of Wetumka, Alabama. As a result of the Civil Rights Act, Whalest Jackson was hired by the Natchez Armstrong Tire and Rubber Company. His job was to mix cement. On February 27, 1967, a car bomb exploded under his pick-up. His murder was never solved. What had seemed, in 1965, like an end to waiting, began to look, as the decade wore on, like a dream deferred.

The biggest shock to the movement came five days after the signing of the Voting Rights Act, when Watts went up in flames. The rioting that began in Los Angeles on August 11, 1965, was the first large-scale urban uprising of the 1960s, and its following so close on the culminating piece of civil rights legislation can invite a retreat into baffled irony. How is it that as things were getting truly better, they also became so dramatically worse?

In Chicago, in March 1967, King was to maintain that "a riot is the language of the unheard." While riots release, incite, and destroy, they also *express*. King went to Watts in the days after the rioting and walked and talked with the people there. He noted that Watts was "closer to" and also "further from" a major city and its "luxurious living" than "any other Negro community in the country." He found himself again drawn to an insight imparted two years earlier during a television interview on the day of his "I Have a Dream" speech, where he invoked the key problem: "a revolution of rising expectations."

Those who persisted in a "search for causes," as did the report on the riots commissioned by Governor Pat Brown, had not far to seek. In 1963 California had passed a fair housing act. In 1964 the law was revoked by a public referendum. In 1965 almost one in three men living in Watts was unemployed. Watts had the highest population density of any city in Los Angeles County. Dorsey High School, once one of the best schools in the region, "sleighrode from 35 per cent Negro in 1961 to 85 per cent in 1965." Alameda Street, which ran along the western edge of Watts, marked the line beyond which blacks were discouraged from migrating. Residents called it "the Berlin Wall."

Authored by Nathan Cohen, the most compelling study to come out of the Watts uprising directed attention beyond material conditions toward what it called "the structure of discontent." "Why Los Angeles?" the government-commissioned McCone Report had plaintively asked, and, as if to dismiss an attempt at a serious answer, it fell back on the "riffraff theory," the belief that only 2 percent of the county's 650,000 African Americans had directly involved themselves in the riot. Cohen's *The Los Angeles Riots: A Socio-Psychological Study* (1970) found instead that within the curfew zone up to 15 percent of the adult Negro population admitted to being active at some point in the rioting. Cohen agreed with the McCone Report on one point, however: in Watts, appearance might seem to belie reality. "A drive through the main streets" of Watts "may give the impression of a fairly comfortable lower-middle class community, for the main streets are wide and paved, the parks appear attractive and well-cared for, and many of the houses are neat and well-groomed, with lawns, trees, and flowers." But Cohen also knew, with William Blake, that we must look not with but *through* the eye.

There was no denying that by 1965 for many blacks in America conditions were beginning to improve. Between 1960 and 1970 the proportion of blacks in the middle class rose from 13 to 25 percent. Yet economic gains alone did not appear to lessen discontent. As James T. Patterson concluded, during the 1960s "there was no clear correlation between the incidence or depth of poverty and disorder." Just as likely to fire black anger, he argued, was "a sense of relative deprivation," a conclusion in which Cohen precedes him. Why the "high level of discontent" pervading the curfew community? Cohen delivered an unsettling answer: "Discontent increases as social contact increases." Blacks in Los Angeles, as in so much of the country, were beginning to better themselves, and this became the heart of the problem: as conditions improved and awareness of options grew, more was expected, and as these expectations were not met, anger was the result. As early as the

1963 march on Washington, King noticed that he was "running into more and more bitterness because things haven't moved fast enough." In time, King himself became the object of such feelings. "Bitter hatred develops toward the very people," he came to believe, "who build up the hope."

Cohen's work pointed to the anguishing paradox that things had gotten worse *because* things had gotten better. In his memoir, Harry McPherson quotes a "scholarly friend" who maintained that the Johnson administration, in its will toward change, "unwittingly teased and taunted Negro aspirations." One of Joseph Califano's assistants asked: "Why have law and order broken down now, when we've begun to move? McPherson answered: "Because we've begun to move."

Solemn reports like that of the Kerner Commission, released in February 1968, would not stint from laying blame. White racism lay at the bottom of urban disorder, it argued, and "white society is deeply implicated in the ghetto." Richard Nixon responded by saying that the report "blames everybody for the riots except the perpetrators of the riots," and this became the rallying cry of the Reaction, one founded on notions of personal responsibility and self-bootstrap-pulling-up that had been authoritatively demolished by Lyndon Johnson in a 1965 speech at Howard University. "You do not take a person who, for years, has been hobbled by chains, and liberate him, bring him up to the starting line of a race, and then say, 'you are free to compete with all the others,' and still justly believe that you have been completely fair." The very process of liberating or "giving" in which the federal government had so recently been compelled to engage also served to draw attention to the century of waiting that had preceded it. Cohen's assessments invoked this dynamic, one perhaps built into any culture's attempt at massive social uplift. His findings led to the hard conclusion that ameliorative legislation, for all the good it does, also serves to elevate more people into the realm of discontent. It was within this period of "creative tension" that Martin Luther King was to live out his last three and difficult years.

What King had seen as a crisis of proximity in Los Angeles—the living "closer to" and yet "further from" syndrome—was certainly in evidence as I continued my drive up Fourteenth Street. Statistics did show a steady black flight from this section of the inner city, and a countervailing influx of white and Hispanic residents. But the neighborhood was still about 50 percent black. And as their numbers had diminished, their buying power had not increased. The *Post* was reporting that between 1960 and 2006, the percentage of black-owned homes in the District had actually gone *down*.

Logan Circle might have its Whole Foods and its urban professionals, but the biggest change had come further north on Fourteenth Street, in Columbia Heights. When I had first purchased my Adams Morgan apartment, in 1987, one did not walk to the east at night: Sixteenth Street was our "Berlin Wall." Yet here I was, two blocks beyond that once tacit barrier, passing an odd combination of boarded-up storefronts and stylish new condominiums.

Washington Metro, the city's subway system, had opened a station on the Green Line in Columbia Heights in the late 1990s, and over the next decade the area had been transformed. Between 2000 and 2005, the median income of home-buyers in the area had risen from $76,000 to $103,000. Units in Kenyon Square, finished in 2008, had recently been priced, before the economic downturn, as high as $700,000. Across from them, a huge cube of a building hosted a Target, a Marshalls, the Washington Sports Club, and a Best Buy. While the problem of urban decay had been "solved," it appeared to have been accomplished through bypassing rather than empowering many of the area's black citizens. What good was all this, I wondered, when so many of the people lingering on the sidewalks still clearly lacked the money to buy things?

"The money to buy things" is King's phrase. This had become the pressing need, he began to argue in 1965, the business left unfinished by the passage of the great civil rights legislation. After the triumph in Montgomery and the trauma of Watts, King turned his attention away from statutory discrimination and toward jobs, homes, and schools. The problems faced by African Americans were, in a word carefully chosen by King, "structural." Seeing Mayor Richard Daley as a version of Lyndon Johnson, a liberal with the power to compel change, King and the SCLC decided to bring a campaign for fair housing to the heavily segregated city of Chicago.

King moved his family into a derelict apartment in the neighborhood of North Lawndale in January 1966. The plan was to mobilize one million black Chicagoans against discriminatory landlords, realtors, and employees. The tactic was to gain attention through a series of open housing marches.

The marches King led into the white neighborhoods of Gage and Marquette Park sparked a violent white counterreaction. Columns of protestors were assaulted by bottles, cherry bombs, and hate songs. In July, "insensitive policing provoked widespread violence in the West Side ghetto," and King made ineffectual calls for calm. During an August march, King was brought to his knees by a rock that struck him in the right temple. "I have to do this," he said, "to expose myself—to bring this hate into the open."

By mid-September the movement began negotiating with authorities toward the goal of a well-enforced open housing initiative. Daley outmaneuvered King by having negotiators promise to build "non-ghetto low rise," while the Mortgage Bankers Association agreed to grant mortgages to applicants regardless of race. The problem then came down to the behavior of realtors.

As negotiations continued, Daley secured an injunction against further marches. Meanwhile, Congress passed a watered-down fair housing bill, one exempting nearly 60 percent of privately owned homes from its scope. The agreement finally reached with the Chicago Real Estate Board paid lip service to "the best housing" for welfare recipients, nondiscriminatory loan policies, and more scattered low-density housing. But the board had little enforcement authority, and after the white backlash of that summer, it could seem a pyrrhic victory for blacks to now be free to move into neighborhoods where they were hated and into houses they still could not afford. In April 1967 Mayor Daley was reelected to a fourth term, receiving a substantial black vote.

In Chicago in 1966, as in Memphis in 1968, King mobilized energies he could not control. Moreover, Chicago was the place where the Reaction, beyond the South, first fully surfaced. As Peter Ling was to write, "the Civil Rights Movement in the North sparked a counter-movement, which ultimately swelled into a powerful neo-conservatism that questioned state interference into what it considered the private sphere of home and family."

The Watts riot challenged the ethic of self-help at the heart of the civil rights movement. King and his fellow marchers had taken it upon themselves, especially through a willing exposure of their bodies to physical harm, to help themselves. The federal government was imagined by them as the necessary, reactive partner, one with the power to codify into new law the empathy generated by black initiative and suffering. But the real work was done, and the mortal risks were taken, by the marchers themselves.

In the years between 1955 and 1965, white Americans were invited to school themselves in the expressive capacities of nonviolence. Then, beginning in August 1965, rioting began to rival marching as the "language" of the unheard. As John Lewis was to write about the movement after Selma: "The road of nonviolence had essentially run out." The primary casualties of the violence were black neighborhoods and black lives; a decade of self-help gave way to an interval of self-hurt. One of the most destructive of these riots took place in the summer of 1967, in Detroit.

As in Watts, the Detroit riot was sparked by a police action, an attempt to arrest some eighty people celebrating the return of black servicemen from Vietnam. In the six days that followed, much of downtown Detroit was burned to the ground. Michigan governor George Romney, unwilling to admit a situation beyond state control, hesitated to call for federal troops. Two thousand Army paratroopers eventually helped to calm the city, by which time forty-three people had been killed, twenty more than had lost their lives in the riots in Newark, which had occurred two weeks earlier. "There were dark days before," King told his people on the night after the Detroit riot began, "but this is the darkest."

In August 1967 John Hersey "went to Detroit, with a general intention of writing overall about the devastating uprising there." Hersey went to Detroit in the spirit of King's visit to Watts, in order to open himself to the "language" of a riot and in search of a new way of covering one. "Uprising" is Hersey's chosen term for what happened in Detroit, and his insistence on the descriptor indicates the scope of his project—to defamiliarize a reader's sense of what a riot is. Out of his experience he wrote *The Algiers Motel Incident* (1968).

The Algiers Motel was a transients' hostelry on Woodward Avenue, the street that divides eastern from western Detroit. The motel was located a few blocks from where the black uprising had started. On the third morning of the rioting, police officers from the Thirteenth Precinct learned that patrolman Jerome Olshove had been shot and killed near the Algiers Motel. Tanks were by now cruising the city's streets. That evening, Theodore Thomas, a warrant officer in the Michigan National Guard, found himself assigned to protect the Great Lakes Mutual Life Insurance Building, at the corner of Euclid and Woodward. Hearing what he thought was gunfire coming from the vicinity of the nearby Algiers Motel at about midnight, Thomas called his commander to report that he and his men "were being fired upon." A dispatcher forwarded the message to police as "Army under heavy fire." City and state police then entered the motel. By the time they left, three young black men had been killed, while ten black men and two white women had been lined up against the motel wall and beaten with rifle butts and black jacks. The girls were also stripped of most of their clothing.

Nowhere does Hersey provide such a brutal summary. Instead he begins *in medias res,* with the surviving members of "the line" told to go home and not look back. He then deals with the dispersal of the news into the black community, the reporting of the three dead bodies, the arrival of investigating police, the media response to the incident, and the grief of the bereaved families.

Hersey works through juxtaposition, intermixing the voices of black relatives and friends with police and news reports. The raw honesty of the one kind of language highlights the hype and hysteria of the "news," where the local paper compares "Negro snipers" to infiltrating "Viet Cong." Hersey describes the motel as a place "where most of the action of this narrative hid itself." His patient and empathetic reporting *unhides* the narrative by asking the reader to collaborate with the author in piecing together an adequate account.

Chapter 2 begins with the following sentence: "At this point in the narrative, enter myself. Reluctantly. I have always, before this, stayed out of my journalism. . . . I cannot afford, this time, the luxury of invisibility." As Mailer and Didion also did in 1968, Hersey here decides to come out into his narrative. Conventional journalism can no more cover John Hersey's Detroit than it can Michael Herr's Vietnam. In the face of what he experiences there, Hersey feels compelled to argue that conventional journalism has never really existed: "There is no such thing as objective reportage. Human life is far too trembling-swift to be reported in whole; the moment the recorder chooses nine facts out of ten he colors the information with his views."

Hersey presents himself not as an objective knower but as a subjective learner. "At the outset I learned how little I knew. . . . Now I learned all sorts of new things . . . and I learned how much more I have to learn about issues of race in my country." He is aided in this work by reading *The Autobiography of Malcolm X,* but above all by consenting to listen to the city's voices. As with Anna Deavere Smith's *Twilight* (1994), itself the response to another urban uprising, Hersey's book becomes a record of what a writer "*heard*" in Detroit.

Hersey's willingness to remain in uncertainties, to embrace a certain negative capability with respect to the facts of the incident, confers on his project an answerable if self-interrogating form. "My reliance in this narrative on the statements of witnesses tends to fragment the story; it is not so much written as listened to, in bits and pieces." The story resided "as much as possible in the words of the participants," and since, as Hersey admits, "I was all too aware that the truth had not always been told me," the reader is left to arbitrate between the conflicting testimonies. It is a history with holes left in it, to indicate what it does not know. "There could be no 'creative reconstruction.' Doubts about chronology could only be revealed, not resolved."

Hersey's uncertainty about what happened at the Algiers Motel liberates him and his reader into a speculative space where the pieces of evidence that can be adduced lead to strong conclusions about motive and feeling. As we are absorbed into his open form, we are invited to enter into each human, baffled subject position. But this very motion toward the participants in the story provokes a critical pulling back, as we become burdened with unavoidable awareness. Empathy, for Hersey, as for any committed practitioner of new journalism, is the precondition not for neutrality, but judgment.

Hersey concludes that the violence dealt out at the Algiers Motel had much to do with the fact of black men partying with white women. Members of the police and the Army Airborne ripped at the girls' dresses as they stood in the line, reducing them to their underwear. Roderick Davis reported a policeman saying to the girls, "Why you got to fuck them? What's wrong with us, you nigger lovers?" Once the girls had been stripped, two of the black men in the line were told by police to look at the girls, and were then asked, "Ain't you shamed?"

A report of sniping in the vicinity brought police to the Algiers in the first place. Hersey discovers that one of the three boys killed at the motel had been playing with a starter pistol at the time Warrant Officer Thomas reported himself under fire. So were the boys killed because they had been sniping with a gun from which it "was not even possible to shoot bullets?" Hersey asks. "Except, of course, that as it turned out the boys were not executed as snipers at all. They were executed for being thought to be pimps, for being considered punks, for making out with white girls, for being in some vague way killers of a white cop named Jerry Olshove, for running riot—for being, after all and all, black young men and part of the black rage of the time." To locate "sexual jealousy," as Hersey does, along a continuum including "racist abuse," was to risk a rejection of his project as unduly speculative. Yet the black male in America had been, from the start, repeatedly consigned to a "scene of violence," as Houston Baker calls it, a scene in which sexuality played an essential part.

Faulkner's "Dry September" (1931) tells the story of a black man accused of molesting a white woman. Informed that the rape may not have happened, the leader of the lynch mob answers: "Happen? What the hell difference does it make? Are we going to let the black sons get away with it until one really does it?" Faulkner's story reveals the act of physical intimidation designed to keep the black man in his place as reliant on the projection of a sexual interest in white women that may not, in fact, have existed, and which in any case was unlikely to have been acted on. The treatment of the bodies of the white women by the police and Army officers in Detroit, and their staging of a scene of humiliation in which black and white bodies on the scene were drawn into a sexual relation, reenacted this abiding American tradition. Only a writer unbound by literary and journalistic convention, like John Hersey, was likely to notice this.

The triangle of black man–white woman–white man, a dynamic from which the black woman has been routinely excluded, is the focus of another brilliant and obsessive book published in 1968, Eldridge Cleaver's *Soul on Ice*.

Cleaver's story is of a man who sets out to literalize the lynching plot. What would it mean to surrender to this cultural narrative, to agree that my imagination is dominated by "the Ogre," the body of the white woman, and then to actually do what black men have too often been falsely accused of doing? "I became a rapist," Cleaver writes, in a sentence as frightening as it is honest. He becomes so less out of desire than out of anger, in rage at an imagination that has been colonized by an image. "A black man growing up in America," he maintains, "is indoctrinated in the white race's standard of beauty." Having acted out the projected fantasy, and been caught and imprisoned for doing so, Cleaver decides to write his way free. The ready way to decolonize his mind is to think—not to act out—to read and to study and to recover "the history that has placed those tensions of lust and desire in my chest."

Cleaver thereby becomes a hero of analysis. He comes to understand his behavior as his own responsibility, surely, but as also having its origin, to use King's word, in the "structural." One must analyze the nation's social and political structures, but one must also work to change them. In 1968, Cleaver not only published a book but declared himself a candidate for the presidency. In the same year, the authors of *An American Melodrama* concluded that *Soul on Ice* "displayed a better appreciation of America's structural problems than anything said by any of the other candidates."

As if to make Cleaver's case, the FBI, by 1968, had sexualized its campaign against Martin Luther King. In 1962, the bureau assigned King "full enemy status." As Taylor Branch reports, "Thereafter, upon receiving intelligence that someone was trying to kill him, the Bureau would refuse to warn King as it routinely warned other potential targets." Growing out of a belief that a massive social revolution was somehow the result of a conspiracy with Communist roots, the FBI's daily surveillance of King began in 1961. According to Gerald McKnight, even Lyndon Johnson eventually convinced himself that "the ghetto rebellions of the 1960s were the work of a small cadre of black conspirators." Under intense pressure from J. Edgar Hoover, attorney general Robert Kennedy authorized wiretaps of Stanley Levison, a New York lawyer and close adviser to King, in February 1961. A year later, he allowed Hoover to begin wiretapping King directly. On his own authority, Hoover also began bugging Levison, and, eventually, King. The FBI file amassed on King ran close to a million pages, a record of his movements so complete that Taylor Branch builds much of his three-volume narrative out of the Bureau's minute-by-minute accounts.

Hoover became convinced that King was a "tom cat" driven by "obsessive degenerate sexual urges." King did maintain a number of mistresses and occasionally disappeared with one for a night or two, just as he routinely berated himself before his aides for his sexual "sins." On the night of his "I Have a Dream" speech, a microphone planted in King's room at the Willard Hotel yielded evidence of "sexual activity" with a white woman. In 1964, the FBI manufactured a tape, complete with "sex groans and party jokes," purporting to record King's activities in the Willard. Assistant director William Sullivan actually prepared the tape out of "highlights" from recordings the FBI had gathered over a period of ten months. The tape was delivered to the SCLC offices in Atlanta, where Coretta King was the first to open the thin box. What came to be known as the "suicide package" also contained an anonymous letter warning her husband, "Your end is approaching . . . You are done. There is but one way out for you. You better take it before your filthy, abnormal fraudulent self is bared to the nation."

In brooding over the intensity of the FBI harassment, Andrew Young, the Congregationalist minister who became one of King's closest advisers, arrived at the conclusion that "the campaign against Martin and the movement was less about sex than about fear of sexuality," one coupled with a "deeply buried but intense sexual fear of black males. . . . The theme was ever-present at lynchings of black men for allegations of rape or for flirtation with white women, and is always evident somewhere in the heavy punishment awaiting black men who assert or advocate the interests of their people." Lyndon Johnson, so often in touch with his own dark patches, complained after one of his last conversations with King "that he was so hurt by Martin's criticisms that he felt as if he had discovered that Martin raped his daughter."

By late 1965, Johnson and King had stopped speaking. Their estrangement had largely to do with King's outspoken criticism of the war in Vietnam. In 1967, at the Riverside Church in New York, King made his most thoroughgoing case against the war, calling the United States "the greatest purveyor of violence in the world today." The claim is less interesting for its truth than for its force. It was remarkable that such a thing could be said by a man of such hard-earned moral authority. John Lewis admired any utterance with "*sting*" in it, and later judged King's performance at Riverside "the best speech of his life in terms of sheer tone and substance."

King voiced his first public comment about Vietnam a few days after the air strikes on the North were announced, at a speech at Howard University. "The war in Vietnam is accomplishing nothing," he said. The blanket condemnation would evolve into a deeply informed knowledge of the history of Vietnam, one accompanied by specific policy proposals for ending the conflict. It was important to feel with the enemy, "to know them and hear their broken cries." But while he was appalled by the June 1967 photographs in *Ramparts* magazine of Vietnamese bombing victims, as he was by all of the suffering of "helpless and outcast children," King's galvanizing concern was that the war had "broken and eviscerated" the civil rights movement.

King knew that the country could not conduct a war on poverty at home while fighting a shooting war abroad. By the end of 1966, Congress had in fact reduced funds for the War on Poverty by half a billion dollars. It failed to pass a strong fair housing bill; it even refused to appropriate money for rat extermination. Irony was being added to insult: while "devastating the hopes of the poor at home," the war "was sending their sons and their brothers and their husbands to fight and to die in extraordinarily high proportions relative to the rest of the population." "The whole structure of American life must be changed," King argued. "We must see now that the evils of racism, economic exploitation, and militarism are all tied together."

In "A Time to Break Silence," the name given to his address at the Riverside Church, King calls for a national moment of turning. "We must be ready to turn sharply from our present ways." To admit "that we have been wrong" will demand of Americans "a maturity," however, "that we may not be able to achieve." In the sequence of the speech, King invokes this new turning only after having confessed to his own "sins and errors." Earlier that year, in a retreat with his advisers, King had admitted to his "vacillations" over speaking up about the war. Now, in New York, he admits being moved to preach in part "to break the betrayal of my own silences." "The ambiguity of the total situation" may have inhibited him, but the time has come. "There is such a thing as being too late." As in Montgomery, and as he was again to do in Memphis, King invites his listeners to step into "the fierce urgency of now."

King's response to the war in Vietnam enacted his belief in criticism as love. He offered up his analysis of the war as a "plea to my beloved nation." It was also a plea against segregation of thought. The world was a web; there could be no compartmentalizing of concern. The war and civil rights were tied together, if only because the cost of the one made it difficult to finance the reforms won by the other. Attacked by the *New York Times* for trying to fuse two "distinct and separate" problems, King shot back: "I've fought too long and too hard now against segregated accommodations to end up segregating my moral concerns."

As King's thinking became more attentive to the world as a "network of mutuality," he began to see the problem of race as entangled with the problem of class. American poverty, while oppressive to blacks, cut across racial lines. His final project, one proposed by Marion Wright in the fall of 1967, was to be a second march on Washington to take place in the spring of 1968, a Poor "People's"—not solely a Negro—Campaign. In response to the announcement of the campaign, a St. Louis motel operator offered $20,000 to anyone who would kill "the big nigger," while a patent attorney in the same city put up his own bounty of $50,000. Active in the St. Louis wing of George Wallace's American Independent Party was an escapee from the Missouri state penitentiary named James Earl Ray.

By the winter of 1968, King was "spiritually exhausted." He was gaining weight and he often could not sleep. Friends detected in him a "profound sadness." King's conversation had often displayed "a conspicuous thread of thanatopsis," and thoughts of dying seemed more frequently to assail him. After John Kennedy had been shot, King had said, "This is what is going to happen to me." "Somehow he always felt that he would die early," Coretta was to recall. King's "Mountaintop" speech, delivered on the night before he was killed, was the last in a series of self-elegies in which he anticipated and forgave the prospect of his own death.

King went to Memphis in the spring of 1968 at the request of a Methodist pastor and activist, James Lawson, who called King about a garbage worker's strike. AFSCME local 1733 had walked off the job after twenty-two black sanitation workers had been sent home in a rainstorm while white workers had been kept on the job.

The climactic moment came on March 28, when King arrived late for a planned protest march. He placed himself at the head of nearly a thousand union members carrying signs that read, "I AM A MAN." Then, somewhere near the rear of the column, storefront windows began to be broken. Sticks were stripped from their placards and used to attack police. Echoing King's words on the Pettus Bridge, Lawson called for "everybody . . . to turn around and go back to the church." King was torn. The march tried to reverse itself, and the pile-up further inflamed the crowd. King's aides finally dragged him into a Pontiac and delivered him to a nearby Holiday Inn. A local youth gang called the Invaders bore the initial blame for the violence, but both Lawson and the FBI later concluded that the trouble had been started by "the petty criminal class" that hung out on Beale Street. Nevertheless, King and his people had failed to take control of a march they had agreed to head. "What was supposed to have been a brief detour in support of comrades-in-arms," Andrew Young wrote, "had turned into an absolute disaster."

In his hotel room, King drew the bed covers over his head. "Maybe we just have to admit that the day of violence is here," he said. After meeting with the Invaders, he flew out of Memphis, returning on Wednesday, April 3, in a flight delayed by a bomb threat. His intention was to participate in a second march scheduled for April 5. That night he gave his last speech, at the Mason Temple, and then returned to his rooms at the Lorraine Motel.

Four friends kept company with King on his last night and day. Elected to the SCLC staff in 1962, Hosea Williams had led the first march across the Pettus Bridge, emerging with a fractured skull and a severe concussion. In 1972, he was to stage an unsuccessful run for a Georgia U.S. Senate seat. In the late 1980s, Williams helped integrate all-white Forsythe County, outside Atlanta, by leading two marches there. Shortly before he died, in 2000, Boulevard Drive in southeastern Atlanta was renamed for him.

Bernard Lee first met Martin Luther King in 1960, while leading a student sit-in at Alabama State. Friends called him "Jelly" because of his love of food. He became King's valet and shadow, the ever-present sideman. Lee was arrested and jailed during both the Freedom Rides and the Albany Movement demonstrations. In later life he received a Master of Divinity degree from Howard University, worked as an assistant of religious affairs for D.C. mayor Marion Barry, and served as chaplain at the Lorton Correctional Facility in Virginia. He died of heart failure in 1991, at the age of fifty-six.

Fellow Baptist minister Ralph Abernathy was King's boon companion, the man King could joke and relax with, the keeper—and revealer—of King's secrets. At the opening of his last speech, in Memphis, King told the crowd that Ralph was the best friend he had in all the world. Abernathy continued the work, leading the Poor People's Campaign into the capital in the summer of 1968 and earning a three-week jail term for refusing to disband the protest. In 1980, he endorsed Ronald Reagan for president. In 1987, thirty years after cofounding the SCLC with King, Abernathy helped organize the American Freedom Coalition, an organization dedicated to "traditional values" and funded by Sun Myung Moon's Unification Church.

Andrew Young came to the movement through his work with Septima Clark's Leadership Schools. Becoming a trusted aide during the Albany Movement, Young quickly adopted the role of resident intellectual, the man who dealt with politicians and judges. He was a principal architect of the Birmingham campaign. In 1977, Jimmy Carter appointed Young ambassador to the United Nations, a post he was forced to resign after holding a secret meeting with the Palestine Liberation Organization. Young went on to serve two terms as the mayor of Atlanta. On September 13, 2001, asked by NBC's Tom Brokow about the message in the terrorist attacks, Young responded: "The message is that we shall overcome. We have things well integrated here, and some people resent that." When Brokow mused about now being considered a sort of wise elder, Young replied, "That makes two of us. Whatever happened to Huntley and Brinkley? The giants that we looked to are gone, and, well, we've got to perform."

On the morning of April fourth King slept in, lunched with Abernathy, and then joined his brother, A.D., in a long phone conversation with their mother. He kidded local pastor Billy Kyles about the dinner his wife had promised them, insisting that it be soul food. Around five in the afternoon, King playfully wrestled with Andrew Young, and a pillow fight then broke out between Abernathy, Williams, Lee, and A.D. While King went upstairs to dress for the evening, Young went down to wait for Kyles's car in the motel parking lot. Kyles arrived and went up to fetch King, who soon appeared on the second-floor balcony. "I want you to come to dinner with me," he yelled down to Jesse Jackson. "Suddenly," Young remembers, "we heard what sounded like a car backfiring, or a firecracker. I looked across from the motel to see what might have caused the noise, then I glanced quickly up to the balcony where Martin had been standing at the railing. He was no longer standing."

King organized his great speeches around the tropes of waiting, turning, and standing. On the night of April 3, he spoke of the Memphis sanitation workers "standing up for the best in the American dream," just as he had called his listeners to "stand up for freedom together" in his speech before the Lincoln Memorial. The image went all the way back to King's crucial epiphany of 1956, the long night spent in his Montgomery kitchen alone, when God visited him and said: "Martin Luther, stand up for righteousness. Stand up for justice. Stand up for truth." The night on which the career had been initiated prefigured its ending as well as the prophecy King had made in Birmingham, in 1963: "I will die standing up for the freedom of my people."

In *A Testament of Hope,* King's last speech is titled "I See the Promised Land." Whatever he might have chosen to call it, King would not have resisted a title placing the speech in a chain of utterance. He had in fact built much of his oratory out of refiguring his own voice and the voices of others. In *Voices of Deliverance* (1992), Keith Miller reveals King as speaking within a profoundly typological tradition, one in which originality matters less than the ability to repeat and refigure the burdens of African American history and rhetoric. It was a tradition organized around the theme of deliverance. And, as in the great Negro spirituals, Moses was its central figure, and Exodus its guiding story.

In his 1967 book, *Where Do We Go from Here?,* King had invoked Exodus as a "continuing story" and invited his readers to view "the present struggle in the United States" as "a later chapter in the same story." By the time he returned to Memphis, King had led his people to Canaan's Edge, as Taylor Branch has called it, and while it was a moment filled with hope, it was also an evening for self-refrain. The moment was not so much new, as *now,* an interval of possibility always available to the willing heart. King therefore built the central claim of his speech out of a repetition. "I've been to the mountaintop," he said. But he had already said this, three years earlier, on a Sunday in Atlanta. The words of King's closing paragraph in 1968 were first tried out in 1965: "I've been to the mountaintop now. God allowed me to live these years. It doesn't matter now. Whatever happens now doesn't matter, because I've seen the promised land."

King's lifelong identification with Moses contained an implied recognition—that he, too, would not get to the promised land. In the Biblical story, Moses climbs Mount Pisgah and looks over into the place God has set aside for his people. He goes to the mountaintop. But he is not allowed to cross over. He, like King, has sinned, and part of the punishment is not being allowed the experience of literal return: as the King James Version puts it, "Thou shalt not go over this Jordan." The sense of self-elegy in each career arises from the foreknowledge that being privileged to lead a people on a mighty walk will not translate into being present at the moment of arrival.

As King's last speech, "I See the Promised Land" was bound to acquire the status of a valediction. As if in anticipation of this, the speech begins and proceeds out of an uncanny sense of an ending. Ever since his "Letter from Birmingham Jail," King had directed attention toward a prevailing American "myth of time." The myth held that, in time, problems would take care of themselves. It counseled a wise patience. It asked black Americans to *wait.*

Now, on the night of April 3, 1968, as rain beat on the roof of Memphis's Mason Temple, King spoke as if he stood at the end of *his* time. It is not a moment of sad farewell but rather of an active re-choosing. "If I were standing at the beginning of time," he asks himself, in which historical interval might I choose to live? Now, he answers: I choose now. "If you allow me to live just a few years in the second half of the twentieth century, I will be happy."

Happy? King admits this to be a strange statement to make. The nation is sick. Trouble is in the land. And yet something is happening, a massive act of "rising up." And so he is happy to live in this period of time, "to see what is unfolding." He is happy simply to have "been around."

Because he almost hadn't been around. As he nears the end of his speech,

King recalls being stabbed in New York by a "demented woman." The tip of the blade ended up resting "on the edge of my aorta." "If I had sneezed, I would have died." He goes on to remember the letter from a ninth-grade girl who wrote to say, "I'm so happy that you didn't sneeze."

The stabbing was one in a series of wounds. In 1958, a Montgomery police officer hustling King away from a courtroom almost broke his arm. In 1960, in Atlanta, a cross was burned on his front lawn. In Birmingham, in 1962, he was punched in the face by a member of the Nazi party. In 1963, a bomb exploded under King's recently vacated motel room. Later that year he was assaulted on a plane. Attempting to register as a guest at Selma's Albert Hotel in January 1965, King was hit twice in the temple by another young Nazi. He was struck again, in the temple, by a stone thrown in Chicago.

But all of this is behind him now. "It doesn't matter now," King says. "It really doesn't matter what happens now." As he approaches his close, King arrives at the radical position that a certain amount of experience might be enough. He has, he is saying, completed his part of the work we are in.

King's embrace of the American present allows him to move through the general word "now" to the more specific word "tonight." He is here, in this time, and in this place, with his chosen "we." He is improvising by now, remembering and inventing all at once. It is the word "we" that he adds to the sentences being refigured from 1965, as if to hand over his long walk to the next, the Joshua generation:

> Well, I don't know what will happen now. We've got some difficult days ahead. But it doesn't matter with me now. Because I've been to the mountaintop. And I don't mind. Like anybody, I would like to live a long life. Longevity has its place. But I'm not concerned about that now. I just want to do God's will. And He's allowed me to go up to the mountaintop. And I've looked over. And I've seen the promised land. I may not get there with you. But I want you to know tonight, that we, as a people will get to the promised land. And I'm happy, tonight. I'm not worried about anything. I'm not fearing any man. Mine eyes have seen the coming of the glory of the Lord.

On the evening after my drive up Fourteenth Street, Luke walked over from his apartment on Sixteenth and we had dinner at one of the restaurants in Target's shadow. The theme was English pub; we shared a flight of four Scotches for fifteen dollars. Luke said he enjoyed shopping at the recently opened Giant and that most of the new restaurants were not bad. "But the neighborhood skipped a step," he added. "A huge, middle-class mall has just been dropped into it; very little of what you see is indigenous business development."

I thought about destroying a city in order to save it, about the Jumbo Nut Shop and the Zanzibar Restaurant, about all the still boarded-up and fenced-off buildings I had driven by on my ride uptown. And I remembered something from Abigail McCarthy's memoir, something said to her in the days after the 1968 riots by her black maid, Kathryn Dodson. "Fourteenth Street was our town, Mrs. McCarthy. You don't know how it feels to have it gone."

CHAPTER

6

RFK

In the summer of 1968, the last one spent living in my parent's house, I walked the hot streets of San Bernardino campaigning for Eugene McCarthy. My canvassing took place on the eastern outskirts of the city where the houses gave way to vacant lots and tumbleweeds. Air conditioning had not yet colonized the Inland Empire, so most homes were equipped with swamp coolers and their big rotary fans. When people opened the doors of their darkened houses, I was often hit with a blast of humid wind.

My father was a supporter of Robert Kennedy. He had taken my sister to see Kennedy on a campaign swing through our downtown and had come home saying, "He's the most beautiful man I've ever seen." At the dinner table we abided our differences. On the evening of June 5, after my parents had gone to bed, I stayed up late to watch the primary election returns. To this day I cannot recall the emotions I felt as it became clear that Kennedy had won California. All the tensions ghosting our household were swept away a few minutes after midnight by a revolver fired in the kitchen of the Ambassador Hotel. I remember knocking on my parent's bedroom door and sitting with them in silence before the glowing screen. What I could not know was that Sirhan Sirhan's bullet had also blown away McCarthy's chances and was to leave the field open to two candidates who had no capacity for imagining how or why we needed to end the war.

By the fall of 1963, Robert Kennedy had become the man who knew too much. On the day his brother was killed he remained, however, not at all certain of what he suspected. According to Daniel Talbot, author of *Brothers* (2007), RFK placed three investigative phone calls on November 22. Reaching a "ranking official" at the CIA, he asked, "Did your outfit have anything to do with this horror?" That evening, he called Julius Drazin, an expert on union corruption, to inquire whether the Mafia had been behind the assassination. He also spoke to Enrique Ruiz-Williams, a veteran of the Bay of Pigs invasion of 1961, "telling him point blank, 'One of your guys did it.'"

In *Of Kennedys and Kings* (1980), Harris Wofford invokes the "burden of knowledge—even of guilt that Robert Kennedy was carrying in the last years of his life." Only after the 1975 findings of the Senate Select Committee on the CIA did these feelings begin to make sense. The committee revealed secrets the younger brother had worked hard to keep, secrets providing "motives for Castro, or the Mafia, or the CIA's Cuban brigade, or some people in the CIA itself to have conspired to kill the President." Once his brother had been shot, Robert Kennedy realized that "there was no way of getting to the bottom of the assassination without uncovering the very stories he hoped would be hidden forever."

The secrets went a long way back. Because of John Kennedy's habitual sexual buccaneering, an activity faithfully monitored by the FBI, the Kennedys faced a continual threat of blackmail from J. Edgar Hoover. As a consequence, attorney general Robert Kennedy was unable to resist the pressure Hoover exerted on him, in the early 1960s, to authorize wiretaps of Martin Luther King Jr. And because the Kennedy administration chose to enlist both the CIA and the Mafia in assassination attempts against Fidel Castro, and because of his fears that these activities might become public, Robert Kennedy chose to defer to the Warren Commission's lone gunman theory rather than to pursue a vigorous investigation of the story behind the assassination in Dallas. These interconnected networks of secrets provided much of the "pain" Robert Kennedy spoke of in Indianapolis in 1968, the pain which, in the days and years following November 22, 1963, seemed to fall "drop by drop" upon the younger brother's heart. Behind it all was the more primal guilt to which he also began to give expression, as when he read Henry the Fourth's death speech to the poet Robert Lowell. "Henry the Fourth, that's my father," he said. The remarkable rise of John, Robert, and soon, enough, Edward was, like the rise of Henry V, in some part due to and funded by a father's "canker'd heaps of strange-achieved gold."

If, as Henry James maintains, "relations stop nowhere," when it comes to the Kennedy years, "the whole thing goes back to Cuba." Cuba became for both brothers "the moonlit fixation in the emerald sea." It was the embarrassment over a communist revolution ninety miles offshore that drew the Kennedy administration into the failure at the Bay of Pigs and the failure of Operation Mongoose, the official but clandestine attempt to kill Castro. The botched invasion, for which President Kennedy refused to approve last-minute air support, left both the CIA and the Cuban exiles in a rage. Operation Mongoose enlisted the Mafia at the same time that the president was "fucking the girlfriend of Momo Giancana." These two failures inspired the brinkmanship of the Cuban missile crisis in 1962, a facing-down of the Russians which many historians judge as a "ripening" of American leadership in which the president showed "toughness and restraint." This reading overlooks the fact that Nikita Khrushchev was the leader who showed considerable restraint, permitting himself to be humiliated in agreeing to back down. Rather than learning "pacific ways in this 'restrained' success," Garry Wills argues, John Kennedy "must have learned that his own and his party's popularity soars when he can make an opponent visibly 'eat crow,' even if the only way to serve up that menu is to risk the national safety." The lesson thereby learned was one then applied "year after year in Vietnam: 'We must never negotiate from weakness'"; we must in fact only agree to negotiate the other side's surrender or defeat.

"When Jack sent out word to get Castro, he put himself in a world of blood and pain. Nobody told him he had to live there. He made the choice with his brother Bobby." These sentences can be found in Don DeLillo's *Libra* (1988), a book of generous speculation on the complex of forces out of which the assassination sprung. The quoted sentences are spoken by an anti-Castro conspirator, a man who really wants John Kennedy dead, while the original plot in the novel, set in motion by a semiretired and disaffected CIA agent named Win Everett, is intended merely to "lay down fire in the street." The various plots spin out of control and Lee Harvey Oswald materializes as if in response to them and then goes off mission, failing to grasp that what was wanted, by Everett at least, is only a "spectacular miss."

DeLillo's self-character in *Libra* is a man named Nicolas Branch, a retired senior analyst hired by the agency "to write the secret history of the assassination of President Kennedy." Branch stands in for the speculating reader as well, the figure who comes after and who struggles to make sense of the historical debris. Branch eventually breaks off from a strong reading, concluding that "the conspiracy against the President was a rambling affair that succeeded in the short term due mainly to chance." What then to make of DeLillo's hard work, his carefully researched attempt to reimagine and weave together so many of the assassination "plots"?

One response is to keep speculating. The word "speculation" comes from *speculum,* mirror. To be a speculative reader is to acknowledge that any text reflects—that it mirrors a reader's capacity and will to keep speculating, even in the face of the ambiguous and the partial. There are limits to speculation, surely, limits that involve both courage and tact, and they are limits that can be learned and applied by setting the self before the most challenging and difficult fictions. *Libra's* speculations comprise a *"might-have-been which is more true than truth,"* in Faulkner's phrase, an offered fiction capable of piercing to the dark heart of America in the way no straight history can. Fiction committed to the interplay of fact and surmise comprises an invaluable "secret history," a phrase DeLillo shares with Michael Herr. The speculating reader becomes an essential party to the creation of this secret history when he or she accepts the invitation to enter in, to play along, and to feel with. And in so doing we find ourselves revealed in our speculations, in what we can believe is true.

"Some things are true," a voice in the novel opines. "Some are truer than true." The truth of Imagination looks beyond the probities, the received notions of "balance" and "objectivity" and toward an unassailable claim about American history here made by DeLillo's fiction, a claim especially true of the history of the Cold War: "plots were devised." The achieving of this recognition is the actual object of Everett's plan, not to kill the president, or even to miss him, but to perform an act of *uncovering:* "This was the little surprise he was keeping for the end. It was his personal contribution to an informed public. Let them see what goes on in the committee rooms and corner offices. The pocket litter, the gunman's effects, the sidetrackings and back alleys must allow investigators to learn that Kennedy wanted Castro dead, that plots were devised, approved at high levels, put into motion, and that Fidel or his senior aides decided to retaliate. This was the major subtext and moral lesson of Win Everett's plan."

Norman Mailer, hard at work in 1988 on his own novel about the CIA, was so moved by DeLillo's accomplishment of *his* plan that he sent him a letter of praise. "I think you're fulfilling the task we've just about all forgotten, which is that we're here to change the American obsessions—those black holes in space—into mantras that we can live with. . . . Whether history will find you more wrong than right is hardly to the point: what counts is that you brought back to life a place in our imagination that has been surviving all these years like scorched earth."

Libra may well turn out to be one of the strongest novels written about the Cold War because it exposes the passions and loyalties and sheer romantic dreaming that propelled the United States to erect a Secret World with which to fight a largely nonexistent or, at best, overestimated enemy. And the time called up by the novel is crucial to an understanding of Robert Kennedy's last five years of life, since this is the period in which he put off his Cold War "illusions," to use a word he repeated twice in his March 1968 speech at Kansas State University, and came to embrace fully the cause of the dispossessed.

It was the accumulating sense of his own complicity in "the darker impulses" of the American spirit," impulses of which he spoke at the Greek Theater six days after Kansas State, that funded Robert Kennedy's access of empathy in the years following his brother's death, an empathy which in turn opened the way for dramatic personal growth. The inner shadow became the theme. "It is not upon you alone the dark patches fall," Whitman had written in "Crossing Brooklyn Ferry," and the recognition, with its accompanying "me also," led RFK into an ever-increasing sense of solidarity with the fellow fallen.

RFK began his public career as a man committed to certainties. His zealous pursuit of labor racketeers for the Senate Permanent Subcommittee on Investigations led law professor Alexander Bickel to remark that "Mr. Kennedy knows, and when he knows he is very sure that he knows." His harrying of witnesses before the committee led to the charge of "ruthlessness," while his willingness to play fast and loose with the Fifth Amendment recalled the antics of Joe McCarthy, the man he had served as minority counsel and for whom he retained a lifelong affection. Kennedy even made a point of flying to McCarthy's interment. Eight years after leaving the Senate committee, the same man found himself in a "charismatic protest against the legal system." As Garry Wills observes, "There is nothing stranger in our recent history than the way this puritanical Catholic became, in his final months, a hero to people whose earlier heroes were Ho, Mao, Fidel, and Ché."

Kennedy learned to connect to people by crediting them with the power his own losses had brought to him, the capacity to feel and register pain. The hard-hitting questioner could attend a Lithuanian mass in Sheboygan and then write, in *The Enemy Within* (1960), about "the strong, stern faces of people who have worked hard and who have suffered." Despite Kennedy's skepticism about labor unions, especially the Teamsters run by Jimmy Hoffa, United Auto Workers president Walter Reuther saw in him a shared sense of "human compassion." The experience of working for the Rackets Committee "helped strengthen the instinct of sympathy within him—that instinct more or less repressed since childhood—and gave it for the first time," as Arthur Schlesinger writes, "social direction." "You know you fellows are educating Bobby," Jack said to Reuther.

The educating of RFK was accomplished largely through his experience of race. As his brother's attorney general, he began with a go-slow approach on civil rights. During the first Freedom Ride, in May 1961, he urged "a cooling off period." Yet his inner caution remained vulnerable to the spontaneous overflow of powerful feeling, as when he placed a phone call to a Georgia judge during the 1960 campaign. The call was made a few hours *after* he had objected to an earlier call made by his brother to Coretta King, a call meant to comfort her over her husband's recent jailing. "Do you know that this election may be razor close," Robert raged at the instigators of the call, "and you have probably lost it for us?" Worried one minute that the candidate might be associated with a national symbol of black activism, RFK then found himself interceding as well. He phoned Judge Mitchell and informed him that, as a lawyer, he believed that the defendants—King had been denied bail and was serving a four-month sentence for violating the terms of an earlier probation imposed by Mitchell—had a right to release on bond while appealing conviction. The two phone calls were later credited with swinging the black vote in Chicago that put the older brother in the White House.

One of John Kennedy's ambassadors later called RFK "the most attentive listener in town." Meeting with the attorney general in the summer of 1963, John Lewis found him "willing to listen." This emerging capacity had been put to the test a few months earlier, in a May meeting with prominent black Americans at the Kennedy family apartment in New York.

Held a few days after the Birmingham settlement, the meeting grew out of ongoing conversations between RFK and James Baldwin. Feeling that their talks at Hickory Hill had been cut short, Kennedy asked Baldwin to convene a discussion about conditions in the cities of the North.

Kennedy was interested in policy, in statistics and legislation. While the group Baldwin pulled together did include the sociologist Kenneth Clark, Edwin Berry of the Urban League, and Clarence Jones, King's personal attorney, it was dominated by three artists—Lorraine Hansberry, Lena Horne, and Harry Belafonte—and above all by a young CORE field worker named Jerome Smith.

At the age of ten, in 1950, Smith had experienced his own Rosa Parks moment when he removed a barrier separating blacks from whites on a New Orleans streetcar. Later he was badly beaten during voter registration drives in McComb, Mississippi. In Baldwin's memory of the day in New York, "Smith set the tone." Being in the same room with Kennedy, Smith said, made him feel like throwing up. He spoke of coming to the end of nonviolence. "When I pull the trigger, kiss it good-bye." He shocked Kennedy by saying he would never fight for his country. When Kennedy protested, "that made everybody move in to protect Jerome and to confirm his feelings," Clark recalled. "And it really became an attack!"

Lena Horne felt as if Smith's remarks had awakened "primeval memory," the awareness of "the common dirt of our existence." Hansberry then said to Kennedy, "Look, if *you* can't understand what this young man is saying, then we are without any hope." Kennedy fought back by invoking the humiliations in the Irish immigrant experience, and argued that a Negro would be president within four decades. "Your family has been here for three generations," Baldwin replied. "My family has been here far longer than that. Why is your brother at the top while we are still so far away?"

In looking back on the gathering, Kennedy said, "They seemed possessed. They reacted as a unit. It was impossible to make contact with any of them." But they had made contact with him; the standoff gave example once again of Kennedy's willingness to open himself to experience. The emotions displayed started to sink in. "He began," Schlesinger writes, "to grasp as from the inside the nature of black anguish." If the Civil War had had for Lincoln an "educating" force, the civil rights movement would educate Robert Kennedy. When he met John Lewis later that year at the White House, he admitted as much: "The people, the young people of SNCC, have educated me."

He stopped fending things off and began taking them in. He refused to focus on the violence of black rioting as mere violence; with King, he took it to be the language of the unheard. "The violent youth of the ghetto is not simply protesting his condition, but making a destructive and self-defeating attempt to assert his worth and dignity as a human being—to tell us that though we may scorn his contribution, we must still respect his power. In some ways it is a cry for love." After the Detroit riots, Kennedy proposed that the networks produce documentaries. "Let them show the sound, the feel, the hopelessness."

"I want to see it," Kennedy said about poverty in Mississippi, after hearing Marian Wright testify before a Senate committee in 1967. In a windowless shack in the Delta, he saw a small child playing with rice grains on the floor. Its stomach was distended from hunger. He picked up the child, and began rubbing its stomach. "My God," he said, "I didn't know this kind of thing existed." Charles Evers saw tears on his cheeks. "I had the feeling that he was serious in trying to say how he would feel as a black person," the black historian Vincent Harding observed, "even though I thought that at certain levels it was really impossible for him to do more than *want* to feel that."

In September of that year, having lost all "influence" with President Johnson, Kennedy said: "Now I know how Negroes who riot feel." The wanting to *feel with* counted for more, perhaps, than the inexactness of the comparison. In April 1968 he flew to Washington to walk its riot-torn streets. "Troops saw us coming at a distance," Walter Fauntroy recalls, "and they put on gas masks and got the guns at ready, waiting for this horde of blacks coming up the street. When they saw it was Bobby Kennedy, they took off their masks and let us through. They looked awfully relieved."

Teddy Kennedy later came to see his brother Robert as a hero of feeling. "People who have to live so much by emotions, who depend on their feelings, can see sincerity in others. He felt deeply about the things he talked about, and he showed it." He had decided to run for the presidency, he said on March 16, 1968, "because I have such strong feelings about what must be done." In the eighty-five days left to him, the experience and language of feeling became the core of the campaign. Something said by Martin Luther King Jr. about John Kennedy proved even more true about his brother Robert: he had "the ability to respond to creative pressure." Running for the presidency became a discovery procedure, one in which "he defined and created himself in action." But the action was always in the service of a wider access to feeling, especially the experience of suffering. With Wordsworth, Robert Kennedy came to see that action is transitory, a step, a blow, the motion of a muscle this way or that, but suffering is permanent, obscure and dark, and shares the nature of infinity.

Kennedy entered the race for president because of Vietnam. His reasons for running changed as he ran, especially after Johnson withdrew. With the target of anger suddenly removed, and the war issue no longer as squarely on the table, Kennedy quickly expanded his circle of concern, homing in on various forms of American lack. But Vietnam was the trigger, and, as with issues of race and class in America, his sense of the problem evolved.

He asked his listeners to empathize with the enemy, with our "small and difficult adversary." In bombing "cities and villages" Americans had taken on "the awful majesty of God." We had "to visualize 'the horror,'" the "moment of amazed fear as a mother and child watch death by fire fall from an improbable machine sent by a country they barely comprehend." He appeared to recoil from the sheer aggressiveness of American power, its indiscriminate strength. If Lyndon Johnson saw the war as an occasion for proving his manliness, it allowed for Robert Kennedy, as Harris Wofford writes, the finding of "a new kind of courage—the courage to appear soft."

RFK was not an innocent bystander of the war he came to oppose. His dismay at his brother's embarrassment over the Bay of Pigs had only made him a greater fan of counterinsurgency. On weekends he imported Green Berets into Hyannisport, where they entertained the children by swinging from trees. As part of Operation Mongoose, the get-Castro project, Kennedy recruited Edward Lansdale, the former CIA operative who, during the early 1950s, had set in motion the American secret war in Vietnam. Lansdale sought guidance from CIA higher-ups on "liquidation of leaders," a go-ahead that blew back on the Kennedy administration in November 1963, when South Vietnamese premier Ngo Dien Diem was assassinated by a CIA-supported coup.

In mid-1964 Kennedy expressed to President Johnson his willingness "to go to Viet Nam in any capacity." A year later, he told an audience at Queens College that "it is not helpful, it is not honest, to protest the war in Vietnam as if it were a simple and easy question." Yet, the previous month, in brief remarks in the Senate, he spoke of the United States as having "erred" in regarding Vietnam as "purely a military problem." In July 1965, Adam Walinsky wrote a speech for Kennedy about guerilla warfare. It included a protest against "air attacks by a government of its own villages." The words were cut from the speech Kennedy eventually delivered, but the unrevised advance copies encouraged the wire services to invoke Kennedy's "break" with the Johnson administration.

Kennedy's "watershed decision" on Vietnam came in February 1966, in a press conference where he called for the National Liberation Front to have "a share of power and responsibility" in any emerging government. The resulting counterattack by the press and the White House quieted Kennedy for the remainder of the year, although he did call for an end to the bombing of the North in some remarks made that fall. Meanwhile, he intensified his reading about the war, digesting Douglas Pike's *Viet Cong* and Kahin and Lewis's *The United States in Vietnam* (1967). He met with Tom Hayden and Staughton Lynd, coauthors of a book about their illegal trip to Hanoi in 1965.

The big break with Lyndon Johnson came in a speech delivered in March 1967. Kennedy began by taking a "me also" position. As one who had been involved in decisions on Vietnam, "I can testify," he said, "that if fault is to be found or responsibility assessed, there is enough to go round for all—including myself." So the buck stopped with everyone: "We are all participants," he argued; the war was "not just a nation's responsibility, but yours and mine." He went on to call for a bombing halt and a settlement including all major political elements.

Having taken a stand, Kennedy then chose to delay. For an entire year he wavered between running and not running, anguishing over the war and yet fearful of being seen as ruthless and opportunistic in taking on a sitting Democratic president. The delay speaks to some excess in Kennedy—of scruple, or caution, or sheer political cunning—as well as to an abiding conflict between a belief that action is existential and a wish that outcomes might be controlled. Whatever the sources of the hesitation, "it's hard," as Robert Lowell was to say during the Oregon primary, "to forgive Kennedy his shy, calculating delay."

When McCarthy announced his decision to run as an antiwar candidate on November 30, 1967, RFK was taken aback. "I think he thought," George McGovern said, "'My God, I should have done this.'" The first approach from the peace movement had come in late 1965, from Benjamin Spock. Al Lowenstein, head of the Dump Johnson movement, only went with McCarthy after Kennedy turned him down. To his journal Arthur Schlesinger Jr. confided his fear that "Gene will make himself the hero and leader of the anti-war movement and cast RFK as Johnny-come-lately."

It is impossible to date the day on which Kennedy decided to run, although the various surmises pivot around March 12, the date of the New Hampshire primary. The journalist Jack Newfield located the moment a week earlier; "Kennedy decided, in his own mind, to enter the race on Tuesday, March 5." He did so, Newfield argues, after the "first hard talk about how to run" with his brother and his closest advisers. Schlesinger goes with March 10, the day Kennedy took communion with César Chávez in Delano, California. He listened to the words of Chávez's speech: "So it is how we use our lives that determines what kind of men we are. It is my deepest belief that only by giving our lives do we find life." On the plane back, he told his legislative aide Peter Edelman, "Yes. I'm going to do it." In *85 Days* (1968), Jules Witcover has RFK announcing his run on the day after the McCarthy "win" when, in some informal remarks to reporters, he admitted he was "reassessing the possibility of whether I will run against President Johnson." Kennedy himself chose March 14, the day on which Johnson rejected his idea of a Vietnam commission, as the clutch date. "That night I decided to run for President."

And yet there still remained one last act of indecision, the meeting with Eugene McCarthy in Green Bay.

Teddy Kennedy had long resisted his brother's impulse to run. In a December 1967 "council of war," Teddy had expressed the view that Johnson was unbeatable and that to run in 1968 would be to jeopardize "Bobby's future." Before the hard talk with his brother on March 5, he had remarked, with resignation, "Bob's just about made up his mind to run. The thing now is to make sense of it." Five days later, Robert could still say, "All of my sisters are for it, Teddy is against it." So it was Teddy, the most ambivalent of his brother's supporters, who was tasked with the assignment of informing McCarthy of his brother's decision. The plan was to work out a deal in which the two men would divide up the remaining primaries, damage Johnson, and then go up against each other in the last big primary, in California.

Teddy was dispatched to Green Bay on Friday, March 15. He was accompanied by Richard Goodwin, who had joined the McCarthy campaign in late February, as well as by two of McCarthy's campaign managers, Curt Gans and Blair Clark. Each man had agreed to act as a broker between Kennedy and McCarthy. By the time the flight took off at 7 p.m., the *CBS Evening News* had carried the story that Kennedy planned to announce his candidacy on the following day. Abigail McCarthy learned of the loyalists now traveling with Kennedy: " 'But why, why are they with Teddy?' I asked blankly. 'Could they have all gone over to Bobby so soon?' "

They whirl asunder and dismember me. John Kennedy carried in his pocket this line from Shakespeare's *King John.* The year 1968 was one in which good men found themselves torn asunder, and of no one is this more true than Richard Goodwin. Goodwin entered the year as a Kennedy loyalist. He had begun trying to convince RFK to run in mid-1967. In early January, with a decision still unmade, Goodwin met with Bobby, Teddy, and some Kennedy advisers at Hickory Hill. "In the mild chill of a Virginia winter, a small group retreated to the most unlikely of council chambers—the wood-framed bathhouse that adjoined the swimming pool." Bobby concluded that "the support just isn't there," and that afternoon Goodwin told him he was going to New Hampshire to help McCarthy.

A jubilant Goodwin called RFK on the night of the New Hampshire primary. Kennedy said, "Well, what do I do now?" "I don't know what you should do," Goodwin replied. "But there's one sure thing, Bobby. You can't keep saying that you're neutral. . . . Either you run or you support McCarthy." In *Remembering America,* Goodwin omits any mention of the meeting in Green Bay. He does report a phone call received on the morning of March 16, in which RFK said to him, "I'd like you to be with me." Goodwin resisted, deciding to stay with McCarthy through Wisconsin. On April 5, the day after Martin Luther

King had been shot, Goodwin found himself on the debris-strewn streets of Washington, D.C. He got in his car and set out for Hickory Hill, stopping on the way at McCarthy's home. "I'm sorry, Senator," he said. "But I just can't be part of a campaign whose purpose is to end the political career of one of my best friends." McCarthy gracefully released him—"Maybe we'll meet again"— and Goodwin drove on into Virginia. He wrote for the Kennedy campaign until the assassination, and then rejoined McCarthy.

Teddy's flight to Wisconsin landed in the early hours of March 16. McCarthy had gone to bed, leaving word he did not want to be awakened. During the "bitter interlude when Blair and Dick Goodwin arrived," Abigail was to write, McCarthy's daughter Mary was convinced to wake up her father. Teddy, waiting in a nearby hotel, then slipped into McCarthy's room by way of a freight elevator.

The men met at two in the morning. Teddy offered to "help" in Wisconsin, while McCarthy proposed to have RFK enter some primaries "which have not been entered." McCarthy summed up the experience: "Like the walrus and the carpenter, Senator Kennedy and I talked of many things." Curt Gans was more cutting: "When they talked there wasn't anything to talk about." McCarthy noticed his fellow senator's black briefcase, and told him to fasten the clasp. Teddy laughed, and did so. The McCarthy people concluded that the briefcase contained a tape recorder. No agreement to cooperate was reached, and, once the Kennedy people had left, McCarthy said, "They never offer anything real." When Teddy arrived back at Hickory Hill, around dawn, a friend asked, "How did it go?" Teddy replied, "Abigail said no."

The Green Bay meeting has it all: A sense of entitlement so extreme as to imagine a man might make a "deal" three days after a historic victory; the backroom politics, with last-minute plane flights, family intermediaries, and freight elevators; the ability to inspire a loyalty so deep as to commandeer another candidate's very best men; and the price to be paid, in loss of dignity and loss of face, for a prolonged season of wavering and delay. Kennedy reached out one last time to the man who had made the courageous first move, as if to acknowledge him, to coopt him, perhaps even to find one last reason for not running. It looked like more delay, and it was, but it also signaled an ongoing process of relinquishing certainty. "Depth had come to him," Garry Wills writes, "and with it indecision."

Robert Kennedy had never been known as a strong speaker; he had a high-pitched voice and a tendency to mumble. Lem Billings had said in 1955 that "Bobby was the worst speaker that I *ever* . . . it was just horrifying to hear him." After speaking at the 1964 Democratic convention, Kennedy sat on a fire escape and wept. He learned to offset his awkwardnesses by making fun of them, as when he joked with a crowd about his Massachusetts way of saying "Indian-er" and then dramatically corrected it with an "Indian-uh!" By 1968, a Republican operative was hearing in his sentences "the sound of steel." While to Joseph Alsop Kennedy's delivery might still sound "staccato," he also allowed that the candidate had mastered a way of speaking in which "what comes through most strongly is a sense of deep and true concern." His gift was for connecting with people on the stump in an almost visceral way, and the best speech of his 1968 campaign was to be an extemporaneous one.

For a man not much given to rhetoric, RFK called up an eloquence in others. Richard Goodwin saw his "imagining heart" as "always in the hills, leading some guerilla army." Murray Kempton wrote of a man taught to hate by his father and his brother, but "unskilled at hating on his own." Norman Mailer discerned in Kennedy a "subtle sadness." For Shirley MacLaine, RFK was possessed of a "psychic violence" which Arthur Schlesinger Jr. attributed to "an almost insolent fatalism about life." "Unless you include the fact that he could put people off horribly," William Styron maintained, "you're not going to get an honest picture."

In 1968 Robert Kennedy finally did find the wished-for words. His public utterances during that year center around three of them: "feel," "responsibility," and "illusions." Put together, the three words might have produced the following sentence: *It is our responsibility to feel our way out of our illusions.* Illusion was the problem, feeling the solution, and responsibility the goal.

Throughout his run for the presidency, RFK would "measure" himself "against ancient tests"—and texts. He promised to do so in the first big speech in the campaign, at Kansas State University, where he talked about his reading and quoted Tacitus. After November 1963, Jackie Kennedy had given her brother-in-law a copy of Edith's Hamilton's *The Greek Way* (1930), which he read with great attention. He also acquired an edition of Hamilton's *Three Greek Plays* (1937). "He knew the Greeks cold," one staffer said. Kennedy became especially fond of six lines from Hamilton's translation of *Agamemnon:*

> Drop, drop—in our sleep, upon the heart
> sorrow falls, memory's pain
> and to us, through our very will,
> even in our own despite,
> comes wisdom,
> by the awful grace of God.

To believe that wisdom comes through suffering was to enter into a tragic sense of life. And the tragic hero appealed to Kennedy because, in a moment of deep feeling, such a hero casts off his illusions and takes responsibility for his fate.

At Kansas State, on March 16, Kennedy began and ended with illusions. His opening supposition—"If in this year of choice we fashion new politics out of old illusions"—was balanced by his closing appeal, "to learn the harsh facts that lurk behind the mask of official illusion." The illusion being addressed was the self-consuming illusion of power, the terrible fact that for all "we have done . . . our problems seem to grow not less, but greater." Kennedy went on to admit to his "responsibility" for past Vietnam policy, and called it *error*. "But past error is no excuse for its own perpetuation." Error persisted in will lead not only to the destruction of South Vietnam but of America's "soul." And the error has long since ceased to belong to any one administration. "I'm responsible and you're responsible because this action is taken in our name." The way out is a matter of feeling, of asking ourselves how much "we care." "And if we care so little about South Vietnam" that we are content to destroy it in order to save it, "then why are we there in the first place?"

Responsibility was especially on Kennedy's mind when speaking to the comfortable. He was troubled by the inequities of the draft, the ability of the privileged to avoid it and the liability of the poor, and the black and the brown, to be required to serve. At Creighton University, in Omaha, a student suggested that the draft might help to lift people out of the ghettos. "How can you say that we can deal with the problems of the poor by sending them to Vietnam," he answered. "Look around you. How many black faces do you see here, how many American Indians, how many Mexican-Americans? . . . How can you accept this? . . . You're the most exclusive minority in the world. Are you just going to sit on your duffs and do nothing?"

In talking to a group of medical students at Indiana University, some days earlier, Kennedy's responses had been even more pointed. A black maintenance man shouted out "We want Kennedy," while a number of students shouted back, "No we don't." Kennedy joked about trying to form a Doctors for Kennedy Committee in Indiana. Then a student asked him where he would find the money to fund his health program. "From you," he shot back. "Angry at the smugness," as David Halberstam writes, Kennedy went on: "The fact is there are people who suffer in this country and some of the rest of us have a responsibility. I look around me here and I don't see many black faces. Frankly, the poor have difficulty entering your profession. You can say that the federal government does this or fails here or doesn't do that, but it is really our society that is responsible. . . . [T]he poor are the ones who are doing most of the fighting in Vietnam, while white students sit here in medical school."

Even though Kennedy worried that the "A" students had already committed themselves to McCarthy, he proved adept at connecting with them when given a chance. Sometime after midnight on the day of the Indiana primary he ran across two student volunteers from the McCarthy campaign in the Indianapolis airport. He tapped a dozing Taylor Branch on the shoulder. "I see you're for McCarthy," he said, inviting Branch and his friend, Pat Sylvester, to talk. Convincing the coffee shop to reopen, Kennedy spoke with the two volunteers into the wee hours. Branch told Kennedy that his draft physical was coming up and that if he passed it he would apply for C.O. status or flee to Canada. Kennedy argued that he should serve but added, "I'm against the war just as much as you are." They talked about civil rights, about why McCarthy had a hard time going into a ghetto. "We were bowled over by him," Branch later said, "but at the same time proud of ourselves that we held to our position." Fred Dutton was to recall that Kennedy "had won in Indiana, but he couldn't win over those kids, and they really got to him."

Kennedy's response to the privileged students at Creighton and Indiana University raises a question in the mind of any reader who, similarly positioned in 1968, managed to avoid the draft. No one better captured the immediate relief and the complicated after-feelings of such avoidance than did James Fallows in his 1975 essay "What Did You Do in the Class War, Daddy?"

In the fall of 1969, Fallows tells us, he was a senior at Harvard. In the newly instituted draft lottery, he draws the low and therefore vulnerable number of forty-five. Reinforced by a widespread consensus that the war is wrong, and to be avoided, Fallows decides to gain a physical deferment by starving his 6'1" frame down to a weight of 120 pounds. On the day of his physical, Fallows is bused from Cambridge to the Boston Naval Yard along with other students from Harvard and MIT. There he witnesses potential draftees throwing urine samples at orderlies. A doctor who appears to have "understood exactly what I was doing" asks him if he has ever contemplated suicide. "'Oh suicide—yes, I've been feeling very unstable and unreliable recently.' He looked at me, staring until I returned my eyes to the ground. He wrote 'unqualified' on my folder, turned on his heel, and left. I was overcome by a wave of relief, which for the first time revealed to me how great my terror had been, and by the beginning of the sense of shame which remains with me to this day."

The brilliance of Fallows's account inheres in a narrative turn occurring at just this point, one in which he confronts two very different kinds of shame. Fallows proceeds to tell us that the shame he feels is in "having gotten away with my deception." But something then happens to Fallows that deepens and complicates his shame, bringing it "into sharper focus." As the last of the Cambridge contingent continues its various forms of resistance as acting out, "buses from the next board began to arrive. These bore the boys from Chelsea, thick, dark-haired young men, the white proles of Boston. Most of them were younger than us, since they had just left high school, and it had clearly never occurred to them that there might be a way around the draft." "We returned to Cambridge that afternoon," Fallows continues, high-spirited but also haunted by "something close to the surface that none of us wanted to mention. We knew now who would be killed."

In the aftermath of the experience at the Navy Yard, Fallows falls into an acute case of class-consciousness. "Class" is not a word often used in America, he implies, but it comes to apply. He sees himself as part of a "we," part of "the mainly-white, mainly-well-educated children of mainly-comfortable parents." "What makes them a class is that they all avoided the draft by taking one of the thinking-man's routes of escape." He is not talking, he admits, about those who, like David Harris, chose to resist the draft and to pay the price; he is talking about those who chose to avoid it.

And this class division, within his generation, will persist, Fallows argues, and can be located in the "very different fates of the different sorts of people I had known in high school and college." It was to persist in the starkly different numbers of deaths suffered among these different sorts of people, in how one felt, in after years, when visiting the Vietnam Veterans Memorial, and perhaps most of all in the backlash I have called the Reaction, the *turning against* the Turning. The proles of Boston, as Fallows calls them, were the very "white ethnics" that only Bobby Kennedy, among the Democratic candidates for president in 1968, could reach out to, as he did so powerfully in the motorcade in Gary, Indiana, riding in the back seat of a car with former boxing champion Tony Zale. "We have to convince Negroes and blue-collar whites that they have common interests," Kennedy told Jack Newfield during the campaign, a coalition the hope for which was blown away in Los Angeles, on June 6, 1968, and again, according to James Fallows, on a spring day in 1970 at the South Boston Naval Yard.

John Lewis first met Martin Luther King Jr. in 1957 at the age of seventeen, after he and some friends began planning to desegregate Troy State University in Alabama. He went on to become a founding member of the Student Nonviolent Coordinating Committee (SNCC) and its chairman in 1963. Lewis was badly beaten on a Freedom Ride in the spring of 1961; four years later he was clubbed unconscious while walking shoulder to shoulder with Hosea Williams across the Edmund Pettus Bridge. Lewis believed in striving through nonviolence for what he called the Beloved Community. Never a man to be "patient," however, he also wrote and was prevented from delivering a speech with "some *sting*" in it for the "I Have a Dream" rally. In the service of his cause, Lewis was arrested forty times.

For thirteen years, Lewis's life had been "entirely about the work," but, by 1968, he had been drummed out of SNCC and alienated by the growing rejection of nonviolence. Once RFK declared his candidacy, Lewis immediately sent him a telegram of support. While many friends still harbored resentment over the "inactions" of the Kennedy Justice Department, Lewis had come to believe that Kennedy "had dramatically changed, that he had grown." Lewis would be the "only major figure from what was left of the movement to come out for Kennedy."

On the evening of April 4, 1968, Lewis found himself outside the Broadway Christian Center in the heart of the Indianapolis ghetto. He had been sent to Indiana by the Kennedy campaign to get out the black vote. "Near sunset," he writes in *Walking with the Wind* (1998), "we were gathered at the rally site, a large open lot in the shadows of several tall, run-down brick buildings." One of Kennedy's advance men rushed up and told Lewis that King had been shot. "I just stood there, not moving, not thinking, as the cold Indiana wind stirred the dirt around my feet."

Meanwhile, Robert Kennedy was making his way to the rally site. He had been told about the shooting just before taking off from the Delaware County Airport. When the plane landed in Indianapolis, he was told that King had died. "I'm sorry, John," he said to Lewis, over a two-way radio. "You've lost a leader." Then he corrected himself. "*We've* lost a leader."

On the drive to the rally, Kennedy stared out the car window. "What should I say," he asked Fred Dutton. Lewis had an answer—and it was not "nothing," despite the arguments made by a number of staffers that any remarks made might incite the crowd. "Somebody has to speak to these people," Lewis said. "You can't have a crowd like this come, and something like this happen, and send them home without anything at all. Kennedy has to speak, for his own sake and for the sake of these people." So Kennedy gave his speech. Lewis listened, and then returned with him to the hotel, where "Kennedy broke down on a bed, lay there on his stomach and cried."

"I'm only going to talk to you just for a minute or so this evening," Kennedy began. He spoke without notes; those handed to him by Adam Walinsky he had shoved into his pocket. The speech he was about to give lasted a little less than five minutes. "He spoke simply and extemporaneously," Lewis recalled, "straight from his heart." He certainly spoke about the heart, especially in the lines he quoted from Aeschylus, lines Lewis elides from his quoted version of the speech, and that Kennedy remembered not perfectly, but accurately enough. The "pain" that had been building in him finally found its complete expression: never before had Robert Kennedy spoken publicly of his brother's murder. He had already done so even more directly earlier in the speech, when comparing his pain to the pain of black people on this night. "I had a member of my family killed." So he spoke to both the simple loss and to the complex guilt, the sheer missing of someone he had loved as well as the slow dripping on the heart, over the four and one half years since November 1963, as he came to acknowledge and accept his part in setting loose the forces behind that loss and in helping to cover it all up.

But the speech was not primarily an act of identification, as in "I am like you." It reached instead toward a strenuous kind of empathy, as in "I am not like you, but I can try to imagine how you feel." This is why Kennedy makes such a clear distinction throughout the speech between being "black" and being "white" in America, and why he repeats the one word five times and the other word six. The black and white responses to the death of Martin Luther King Jr. will be necessarily different. But they can be linked by the sheer intensity of the feelings thereby called up, an insight which allows Kennedy to say, in response to his imagining a black heart "filled with hate," what he did go on to say: "I would only say that I can also feel in my own heart the same kind of feeling."

The word "hatred" vies with the word "love" throughout Kennedy's speech. "You can be filled with bitterness, with hatred," he tells his audience. The "you" here addressed are black people; in saying this, Kennedy almost gives a sort of permission to react and to feel in this way. He poses before his audience a choice, one inflected but not determined by race. So, at the end, the word "we" replaces the word "you," as Kennedy moves toward his closing words, to the phrase "our people."

The people standing in front of the flatbed truck from which Kennedy spoke had come with expectations, and then life intervened. As one watches the faces in the crowd, faces captured in the film surviving from that night, it is as if they sense something has been unleashed that is not going to stop for a long time:

> I'm only going to talk to you just for a minute or so this evening, because I have some—some very sad news for all of you—Could

you lower those signs, please?—I have some very sad news for all of you, and, I think, sad news for all of our fellow citizens, and people who love peace all over the world; and that is that Martin Luther King was shot and was killed tonight in Memphis, Tennessee.

Martin Luther King dedicated his life to love and to justice between fellow human beings. He died in the cause of that effort. In this difficult day, in this difficult time for the United States, it's perhaps well to ask what kind of a nation we are and what direction we want to move in. For those of you who are black—considering the evidence evidently is that there were white people who were responsible—you can be filled with bitterness, and with hatred, and a desire for revenge.

We can move in that direction as a country, in greater polarization—black people amongst blacks, and white amongst whites, filled with hatred toward one another. Or we can make an effort, as Martin Luther King did, to understand, and to comprehend, and replace that violence, that stain of bloodshed that has spread across our land, with an effort to understand, compassion, and love.

For those of you who are black and are tempted to fill with—to be filled with hatred and mistrust of the injustice of such an act, against all white people, I would only say that I can also feel in my own heart the same kind of feeling. I had a member of my family killed, but he was killed by a white man.

But we have to make an effort in the United States. We have to make an effort to understand, to get beyond, or go beyond these rather difficult times.

My favorite poem, my—my favorite poet was Aeschylus. And he once wrote:

>Even in our sleep, pain which cannot forget
>falls drop by drop upon the heart,
>until in our own despair,
>against our will
>comes wisdom
>through the awful grace of God.

What we need in the United States is not division; what we need in the United States is not hatred; what we need in the United States is not violence and lawlessness, but is love, and wisdom, and compassion toward one another, and a feeling of justice toward those who still suffer within our country, whether they be white or whether they be black.

So I ask you tonight to return home, to say a prayer for the family of Martin Luther King—yeah, it's true—but more importantly to say a prayer for our own country, which all of us love—a prayer for understanding and that compassion of which I spoke.

We can do well in this country. We will have difficult times. We've had difficult times in the past, but we—and we will have difficult times in the future. It is not the end of violence; it is not the end of lawlessness; and it's not the end of disorder.

But the vast majority of white people and the vast majority of black people in this country want to live together, want to improve the quality of our life, and want justice for all human beings that abide in our land.

And let's dedicate ourselves to what the Greeks wrote so many years ago: to tame the savageness of man and make gentle the life of this world. Let us dedicate ourselves to that, and say a prayer for our country and for our people.

Thank you very much.

The Indiana campaign was the high-water mark of the Kennedy candidacy. He won, too, in California, a victory that might well have delivered him the nomination. But Indiana was where he found his voice and his ability to inspire an audience. He visited every town in the state with a population of over five thousand. As McCarthy became "curiously withdrawn from the race," Kennedy caught fire. What he had confirmed in himself on that fatal night in Indianapolis was simple: "I want to work for all the under-repre-sented people." His run in Indiana ended on a sunny day with a nine-hour motorcade through the northern part of the state. "Kids ran alongside the car or rode their bikes for blocks at breakneck speed with seemingly end-less endurance," Jules Witcover remembers. Two girls tailing the motorcade appeared at thirteen different spots along the route. Crowds were so thick that Kennedy simply held out his arm, "letting it run along through the out-stretched hands." His security guard, Bill Barry, lost all feeling in his knees from a day spent kneeling behind Kennedy and holding his arms around him to prevent his being pulled out of the car. "Well," Kennedy said that night, "I've done all I could do."

"To *love* the man who stands before us," John Lewis was to write, "—a King or a Kennedy—I don't think has ever been regained." The very shape of Lewis's narrative reminds us of how closely the loss of the one loved man followed upon the loss of the other. "O my God," Lewis writes, on page 386 of *Walking with the Wind*, after hearing that Dr. King had been shot. "I can say those words today," he continues. "They are what I feel when I think of it now, thirty years later. But at that moment I had no feeling." Fewer than ten pages later, as his narrative advances into June, he hears a woman cry, "Oh my God!" It is the voice he overhears in a fifth-floor suite at the Ambassador Hotel, close to midnight.

Lewis had spent two weeks in California, going deep into the poorest neighborhoods in Los Angeles, working the vote for Kennedy. On election night, as he headed downstairs to declare victory, Kennedy ducked in to the room where Lewis was watching the returns:

> "John," he said as he shook my hand, "you let me down today. More Mexican-Americans voted for me than Negroes."
>
> We all laughed, including Bobby. Then he turned to the room and said, "Wait for me. I'll be back in fifteen or twenty minutes."

Lewis listened to the victory speech, turned away from the TV, and then heard the "Oh my God!" Looking back at the screen, he saw Kennedy falling to the floor. "I dropped to my knees, to the carpet, I was crying, sobbing, heaving as if something had been busted open inside."

Lewis wandered back to his hotel room. "I felt dead," he writes. "When I awoke in the morning Kennedy was still alive. But there was no hope."

Lewis caught a plane home that afternoon. "That was the loneliest, longest flight of my life. Coming over the Rockies, I looked down and could see snow. Snow in June. I cried some more."

The family telegrammed, asking Lewis to come to New York to be an honor guard at the funeral. After the mass at St. Patrick's, where Tom Hayden saw William Sloane Coffin at the altar rail and "started to cry hard," Lewis took his place on the funeral train and "rode south," as Arthur Schlesinger remembered it, "under the savage sun." All along the way were crowds holding up signs that read "We Love You, Bobby," "Goodbye Bobby." Lewis felt "as if it was a dream, as if I was floating. I didn't want that train to stop in Washington. I wanted it to just keep going, keep going forever."

7

The Ditch

Scattered throughout Tim O'Brien's *In the Lake of the Woods* (1994) are seven chapters called "Evidence." The evidence given in the fourth of these chapters is about the My Lai massacre. O'Brien's reader has known for some time that such evidence is looming and has begun to suspect, perhaps as early as page 10 of the novel and if he knows anything about the case, that John Wade's having served in Company C in Task Force Barker is likely to have involved him in the events that took place on March 16, 1968, in Quang Ngai province in South Vietnam. There has been mention of John's going to war, and of finding himself, in a phrase O'Brien will repeat at three different points in the novel, "at the bottom of an irrigation ditch." By the time the evidence in chapter 16 is produced, we know that Wade has lost at the age of forty a race for a Senate seat in Minnesota and that his wife, Kathy, has gone missing in the great north woods, a wilderness into which John, too, will eventually disappear.

We have also learned that the lists of facts and quotations making up the "Evidence" chapters fall short of achieving an adequate representation of the feelings and historical events summoned in the novel proper, and that such evidence is often conflicting, fragmentary, and ambiguous. John Wade's story remains a "mystery" about which O'Brien seems to invite us, in Keats's phrase, to remain "capable of being in uncertainties." O'Brien even comes out into his narrative, in a footnote on page 30, where he admits that "fact in this narrative . . . must ultimately be viewed as a diligent but still imaginative reconstruction of events." So we perhaps hold off from judging John, refrain from convicting him of the murder of his wife a number of informants believe him to have committed, and therefore consent to entertain the thought that with material so hot to handle a novel may be a more adequate vehicle for getting at the past than is a trial.

By placing My Lai at the center of his novel, O'Brien would seem to invite us to remain in uncertainties about the massacre as well. His public comments on the subject support this hypothesis. At a conference held in 1994 at Tulane University, O'Brien insisted on the one hand that "there were no mitigating circumstances" for the massacre, while also going on to conclude that "it's a mystery." "There are seeds of evil" in all of us, he maintained. Clearly conflicted about how to think and feel about the massacre, O'Brien contented himself with saying, "Evil is a mysterious thing."

O'Brien's novel moves toward a more refined sense of complicity, however, than these comments would suggest. It does so by asking its reader to remain in a hypothetical relationship to the narrative. If "Evidence" is the title of seven chapters, eight others receive the title "Hypothesis." Faced with the "implacable otherness of others," even an other like John Wade, a character he himself has invented, O'Brien admits in one of his footnotes that "we wish to penetrate by hypothesis." There is an authorial desire to perform "miracles of knowing." But the word "hypothesis" has already ceded away any such achievement, embracing instead the contingent and constructed nature of any take on anything.

So O'Brien ends the second "Hypothesis" chapter with a *maybe:* "Maybe she's still out there." The question of Kathy's disappearance and possible survival merges, in O'Brien's novel, with the question of what happened, in Vietnam, at the ditch. John Wade has been present at each occasion. He has also engaged in a cover-up of his involvement in each event, to the extent that he hides from the authorities the trouble in his marriage, just as he had failed to mention his presence at My Lai to his campaign manager, Tony Carbo. "All you had to do was *say* something," Carbo later tells him, after the secret has come out and Wade has been forced to give his brisk concession speech.

Despite his character's insistence on the manifold "uncertainties" surrounding Kathy's disappearance, O'Brien as interrogating commentator remains uneasy with John Wade's negative capability. Such a capability is possessed, John Keats argues, "when a man is capable of being in uncertainties, mysteries, doubts, without any irritable reaching after fact and reason."

O'Brien chooses instead to reach after facts and reasons. In the big foot-note on page 203, he tells us that he arrived in-country—and O'Brien did in fact see combat in Vietnam—a year after John Wade and walked the terrain around Pinkville, as the GIs called the My Lai area. "I know what happened that day," he writes. "I know how it happened. I know why." Having achieved this moment of "perfect knowledge," the fantasy, again expressed by way of Kathy, that "the burden of secrecy would be lifted," O'Brien proceeds to blow his climax. "It was the sunlight," he explains. "The wickedness." The "frustration." The "rage." These are reasons for what happened that fail, ostentatiously, to explain.

But O'Brien does not stop there. He proceeds to fall back on his will to invoke "something more," on the "mysterious." And it is this word that almost makes a wreck of an otherwise brilliant book. It is a word with which we have already seen O'Brien willing to be publicly identified. But does falling back on "the mystery of evil" in any way assist us in apprehending anything useful about either the marriage or the massacre?

It is one thing to embrace negative capability and to acknowledge the "inconclusiveness" of the facts. It is quite another to say, in the very next sentence, "Mystery finally claims us." The word *mystery* does provide an explanation, even if it is a mystifying one. And to deploy the word might seem an honest admission of the limits of knowing. But in fact it is really an act of ambitious positing, one expressly dedicated to fudging the question of corporate and personal responsibility. Given O'Brien's will to mystify the case, we can put down his novel with great admiration while also concluding that in the case of My Lai—if not John's marriage—perhaps what is needed is a trial after all.

Part of what gave My Lai its terrible force was its being kept a secret. Deciding on his honeymoon that "his secrets would remain secret," John Wade keeps his part in the massacre from his wife as well. When Kathy leaves, she may do so for a very simple reason: her "frustration" and her "rage" over her husband's cover-up of his past. While a comparison may appear to be building, it is on the issue of secret-keeping, however, that any parallel between the fate of the Wades' marriage and the American experience of My Lai breaks down. Keeping such a secret from a spouse may be—for the spouse—"worse than the terrible thing itself." But this can hardly have been the case for those to whom the terrible thing was done. To in any way suggest that the cover-up was worse than the My Lai massacre itself is to engage, once again, in the ongoing failure of imagination to which this chapter will address itself: it is to fail to acknowledge the suffering of the Vietnamese.

As O'Brien puts it, the fact of "what happened that day" has too often been obscured by the attempt to "know why." The endless plumbing of motive conveniently distracts attention away from the simple acknowledgment of the thing done. Yet what happened at My Lai can be pretty well ascertained, and O'Brien acknowledges this by restaging the massacre at three different points in his book. Each staging is filtered through John Wade's memory, and the memories inevitably differ. Each shares however a high degree of specificity, including names of the actual participants in the massacre, names like Meadlo, Conti, and Calley. This is valuable, and worth doing: to say *We did this*. The Peers Commission, the official Army panel set up to investigate what was done, is unambiguous on the fact of a massacre:

> During the period 16–19 March 1968, US Army troops of TF Barker, 11th Brigade, Americal Division, massacred a large number of non-combatants in two hamlets of Son My Village, Quang Ngai Province, Republic of Vietnam. The precise number of Vietnamese killed cannot be determined but was at least 175 and may exceed 400.

It is equally clear about the cover-up:

> At every command level within the Americal Division, actions were taken, both wittingly and unwittingly, which effectively suppressed information concerning the war crimes at Son My Village.

There is something comforting in such direct, responsibility-taking language, a degree of official eloquence reminiscent of the brief statement issued on the eve of the invasion of Normandy by Dwight D. Eisenhower and one singled out by Paul Fussell in *Wartime* (1989) as a "noble acceptance of total personal responsibility":

> If any blame or fault attaches to the attempt, it is mine alone.

My Lai proved difficult to represent less because of some intrinsic ambiguity in the event than because of official attempts to obscure and suppress a knowledge of it. The three historical accounts I have found most useful in uncovering its secrets are Seymour Hersh's *My Lai 4* (1970) and *Cover-Up* (1972), and Michal Belknap's *The Vietnam War on Trial* (2002). These are works of courageous journalism and eloquent scholarship. In the very specificity of these accounts, however, another kind of obscuring can take place. Response may become blurred in the sheer flurry of proper names. Why not recall it all as generic; why not treat everyone involved, on the American side, in the way in which our side treated the Vietnamese? This would be to honor the fact that at the court-martial, the prosecutor, in his opening statement, was unable to supply names for any of the "Vietnamese human beings Calley was alleged to have killed."

In December 1967, an Army company of 130 men arrived in Vietnam. Nearly half of the company was African American, and most of the men were young, between eighteen and twenty-two years of age. The company was commanded by a captain whose hustle had earned him the nickname "Mad Dog." One of the platoons in the company was led by a twenty-four-year-old second lieutenant from Miami who liked the expression "I'm the boss" and who had failed to master the use of map and compass. The platoon contained only one NCO with combat experience.

In January, the company was assigned to an area in the northeast section of Quang Ngai province called "Pinkville," a name meant to invoke the density of Communist presence in the area. Much of the province had been designated a "free-fire zone" in which civilians were assumed to be sympathetic to the enemy and where a soldier could therefore shoot at will. It was believed that one of the local villages was home to a battle-hardened National Liberation Front (NLF) battalion.

By late February, the first platoon was "good and mad," having suffered seven killed and thirteen wounded by mines and booby traps. In *Interview with My Lai Veterans,* a 1970 documentary film, a GI was to cite the company's growing anger over the enemy's use of "sneaky stuff." By mid-March, the platoon had been reduced in number from forty-five to twenty-seven men. On the evening of March 15, the company captain ordered his men to attack the village housing the enemy battalion. Some of the men heard themselves ordered "to kill everything in the village"; others heard routine orders for a search-and-destroy mission. No orders were given for the handling of prisoners.

On March 16, at 7 a.m., the platoon commanded by the second lieutenant landed near one of the hamlets that made up the larger village. Having been informed that the villagers would be away at the local market, the men instead saw families cooking rice over small fires or nervously recovering from the artillery fire that had earlier "prepped" the area. No enemy fire was encountered, but, as the company broke up into small groups and made its way through dense undergrowth, using its weapons at will, it became hard to tell who was doing the shooting. A member of the second lieutenant's platoon arrested a civilian and then stabbed him in the back with a bayonet.

He then pulled the pin from a grenade and threw it and a middle-aged man down a well. A large number of villagers were herded into a central area. "You know what I want you to do with them," the platoon leader said to a private. A radio man heard a command to "waste them." The private eventually responded by emptying four or five clips from his M-16. Soon, there was shooting everywhere. The men shot cows, pigs, water buffalo, chickens, ducks, and hundreds of people.

Two additional platoons—the rest of Charlie Company—converged on the area. A member of one platoon later recalled cutting throats, cutting off hands, cutting out tongues, scalping. A third platoon, one sometimes accompanied by the company commander, stopped a male in his teens, ordered him to run, and then shot him when he refused. Members of the platoon pulled open a girl's blouse and fondled her breasts. A squad leader from the second platoon took a girl into a hut; she came out with no pants. A soldier with the first platoon opened his pants and threatened to shoot a woman's baby unless she agreed to give him a blow job.

"Push all those people in the ditch," the second lieutenant said, about the group of approximately one hundred villagers who had been rounded up by the side of a three-to six-foot deep irrigation canal. Platoon members helped their commanding officer push the prisoners into the ditch. Along with at least two soldiers under his command, he fired and reloaded until movement in the ditch had stopped. One of the men shooting began to weep, and attempted to give away his weapon. When a two-year-old boy crawled out of the ditch, the second lieutenant ran after him, threw him back into the ditch, and shot him.

A warrant officer looking down on the scene from a helicopter spotted an enemy soldier, the "only enemy person" he was to see that day. Observing the action at the ditch, he landed to see if he could help the wounded Vietnamese. He engaged in an argument with the second lieutenant and ordered the evacuation of some ten Vietnamese who had been cornered in a bunker. Returning to the ditch, he recovered the body of a small child, still alive, and flew it to a hospital. Three officers in overall command of the operation—a colonel, a lieutenant colonel, and a major-general—each observed the action in the village from helicopters; none gave a command for any of the firing to stop.

By 11 a.m., most of the shooting had ended. Three enemy weapons were captured in the village area; the company sustained no casualties. After nightfall, the NLF reentered the area and helped to bury the dead.

On March 29, 1971, Second Lieutenant William L. Calley was convicted of the premeditated murder of twenty-two civilians who had once lived in a hamlet in South Vietnam known as My Lai. The years between the event of the massacre and Calley's conviction can be divided into three phases: the official cover-up, which lasted until March 1969; the resurfacing of the My Lai story and the period of official Army investigations of it; Calley's court-martial. There was also a fourth phase, one consisting of the intense public reaction to the verdict, the ensuing intervention of President Nixon, and the further courts-martial of Calley's superiors, all of which ended in acquittal.

While the chain of command in which Calley occupied a place at the bottom did finally escape legal culpability, the key members of it were quite active in the original cover-up. As previously noted, three of those officers had even viewed the scene of the massacre from helicopters on the morning of March 16. None was inclined to take action in response to what had been seen. It was the warrant officer, Hugh Thompson, who forced the issue of an inquiry. Thompson was the helicopter pilot who had landed near the irrigation ditch in order to help evacuate wounded Vietnamese and who had engaged in a "heated discussion" with Calley over the behavior of his troops.

On returning to his operations area, Thompson immediately spoke to his section leader about what he had seen and done. The two men then took what they knew to their commanding officer. At this point, the various versions of the happenings at My Lai began to work their way up the chain of command, through a lieutenant colonel, John L. Holladay, a brigadier general, George H. Young, and finally to the commander of the Americal Division, Major-General Samuel Koster.

Generals Koster and Young decided to allow the unit under suspicion to investigate itself. They did so by turning over the investigation to Colonel Oran Henderson, Captain Ernest "Mad Dog" Medina's immediate superior. Medina was the commander of Charlie Company, the company in which William Calley commanded a platoon. The company formed part of Task Force Barker, commanded by Lieutenant Colonel Frank Barker. Charlie Company had been assigned in January 1968 to "Barker's Bastards," a five-hundred-man strike force responsible for challenging the NLF's 48th Local Force Battalion in the northern area of Quang Ngai province.

As Colonel Henderson began his investigation, the focus fell on whistle-blower Hugh Thompson. "We don't want Americans shooting Americans," his commanding officer had said to Henderson, as part of the order to investigate. Henderson took this to mean that General Young's concern was with the confrontation between Thompson and Calley at the ditch. Henderson's first act was therefore to question Thompson and his door gunners. The two gunners testified to seeing blood-filled ditches and at least sixty dead bodies. Yet Henderson would later deny any recollection of these talks. When he questioned Medina, on the same day, the captain reported that the dead civilians his men had come upon had been killed by U.S. artillery and gunships.

On March 19, Henderson gave General Young an oral report of his findings. He dismissed Thompson's claims as the observations of a greenhorn. Reporting to General Koster on the following day, Henderson offered him a list of twenty-six alleged civilian casualties, a list Lieutenant Colonel Barker had drawn up on a 3 x 5 card. The list gave a reason for each casualty, and noted the victim's gender and approximate age. But the focus again fell on the "machine gun confrontation problem" between Thompson and Calley, a problem which, Henderson said, had "apparently been whipped or put to bed."

Little more about My Lai surfaced until a year following, when a second whistle-blower came forward. On March 29, 1969, Ron Ridenhour sent a five-page letter describing the events at My Lai to congressman Morris Udall and a number of other Washington officials. A door gunner in Vietnam, Ridenhour had originally trained with members of Charlie Company. A month after the massacre he ran into one of his buddies from the company in Chu Lai. The private told him about My Lai, saying "We went in there and killed everybody." Ridenhour was appalled. In his letter he went on to write: "Exactly what did, in fact, occur in the village of 'Pinkville' in March, 1968, I do not know for *certain,* but I am convinced that it was something very black indeed."

Ridenhour made it his mission to bring the massacre to public attention. As a result of pressure from Udall and other congressional referrals, the Army began a "proper investigation" of the matter. The member of the inspector general's staff assigned the task, Colonel William Wilson, concluded that "there was big trouble." He also soon discovered some missing files. According to Hersh, clerks in the American Division headquarters remembered handling a thick file on the My Lai 4 investigations, including a letter from Koster to Henderson. Hersh's chapter "The Missing Files" is difficult to follow, since it replicates the stages in an inquiry where many of the players were trying to throw Wilson off the trail. Given the fact that the missing file was never discovered, Hersh concludes that "subsequent senior officers of the American Division" destroyed evidence in an effort to protect the reputation of their division.

Once Wilson had begun his investigation, there was, for the Army, no turning back. By August 1969, its Criminal Investigations Division had taken over the case. In September, Lieutenant Calley was charged with multiple murders of "Oriental human beings." Hersh broke the story in a *New Yorker* article in November. A week later, the *Cleveland Plain Dealer* published photographs of the massacre taken by Army photographer Ronald Haeberle. A few days after that, General William Peers accepted the appointment to inquire into the original Army investigation of the events at My Lai.

As a result of the findings of the Peers Commission, fourteen officers besides William Calley had charges filed against them. In each case except Calley's, the men were acquitted or the charges were dropped. Calley was sentenced to life in prison at hard labor. On the next day, responding to public outcry, President Nixon ordered Calley confined to his apartment rather than the stockade, pending his appeal. Five months earlier, the president had described My Lai as an "isolated incident." At a news conference following the release of his report, General Peers appeared to concur, stating that he had "no knowledge" of such behavior occurring on "other days" or at "other places."

It remained to Calley's defense team to make the case "that what had happened there was not unusual, but part of a pattern characteristic," as Michal Belknap writes, "of combat in Vietnam." And it was Calley's defense team that invoked a young man "commanded by somebody upstairs." *Newsweek* covered the massacre story with the question, "Calley Verdict: Who Else Is Guilty?" None of the higher officers were ever tried, and it was not until 2003 that the *Toledo Blade* broke the story about the Tiger Force. Founded in 1965, the Tiger Force was an elite Army unit that "engaged in a seven-month campaign of murder in Vietnam, during which they killed everyone they encountered in a free-fire zone, mutilated corpses, and kept strings of ears as souvenirs." These were the conclusions of a U.S. Army investigator, conclusions hushed up by the Pentagon when they reached the offices of the secretary of defense and the secretary of the Army. "The My Lai massacre," Patrick Hagopian concludes, and the cover up of other massacres like it, "was no isolated event."

Yet, as Nick Turse argues, "the exposure of My Lai paradoxically worked against bringing other war crimes to public attention. Atypically large as far as massacres by ground troops were concerned, My Lai dwarfed other mass killings, making many of the atrocity allegations that surfaced later seem small and less newsworthy by comparison. It was almost as if America's leading media outlets had gone straight from ignoring atrocities to treating them as old news, with only a brief flurry of interest in between." There was to be, in Daniel Lang's phrase, no "corporate searching" after the truth. Anyone interested in "The Real American War in Vietnam" might inquire instead into names and operations like Trieu Ai, Cam Ne, "cow cages," "black teams," and Speedy Express.

"The Real American War in Vietnam" is the subtitle of a book published by Turse in 2013, *Kill Anything That Moves*. In June 2001, Turse, then a graduate student, was conducting research in the National Archives when he stumbled across the records of the Vietnam War Crimes Working Group, a secret Pentagon task force set up after the My Lai massacre. The files "included more than 300 allegations of massacres, murders, rapes, torture, assaults, mutilations, and other atrocities that were substantiated by army investigators." Turse spent days copying the pages he had found, published an article based on the material, and then discovered that the records has been pulled from the archive shelves.

Taking Ron Ridenhour as his inspiration—he has received the Ron Ridenhour Prize for Reportorial Distinction—Turse went on to conduct over one hundred interviews with Vietnam veterans and came to a somber conclusion about the extent of American war crimes in Vietnam:

> The stunning scale of civilian suffering in Vietnam is far beyond anything that can be explained as merely the work of some "bad apples," however numerous. Murder, torture, rape, abuse, forced displacement, home burnings, specious arrests, imprisonment without due process—such occurrences were virtually a daily fact of life throughout the years of the American presence in Vietnam. And as Ridenhour put it, they were no aberration. Rather, they were the inevitable outcome of deliberate policies, dictated at the highest level of the military.

Turse focuses on casualties in the South rather than in the North. In the North at least 65,000 civilians were killed, primarily as a result of air raids. In the South, a country of some 19 million, a 1975 U.S. Senate committee estimated 1.4 million casualties, including 415,000 dead. In the years since that initial estimate, Turse points out, the figure has risen steadily to 2 million and beyond. Turse admits that "the scattered, fragmentary nature of the case files makes them essentially useless for gauging the precise number of war crimes committed by U.S. personnel in Vietnam." But the sheer number of South Vietnamese bodies killed or wounded argues for a war conducted with "impunity," a devaluing of Vietnamese persons coupled with command policies that created "a veritable system of suffering."

As his investigation neared its conclusion, General Peers did insist on one last act of candor. The Army's chief of information suggested that Peers, as he prepared for an upcoming press conference, change the word "massacre" to the phrase "tragedy of major proportions." For the occasion of the press conference, Peers acceded to the Army's request, but, in his final and published report, the word "massacre" was allowed to stand.

The denouement of Calley's story came quickly. As a result of a series of appeals, he was paroled in November 1974, four months after President Nixon had resigned from office. He then settled in Columbus, Ohio, where he managed his father-in-law's jewelry store.

The Other Side is the title of a book about the American enemy in Vietnam, one written by Staughton Lynd and Tom Hayden and published in 1969. The word "side" was to take on a curious standing in discussions of Vietnam, retaining for some its received meaning of "You're part of them, not us," while losing its definitional clarity for others. Just what "side," for instance, did the Army of the Republic of Vietnam represent? The weakness of the Army of the Republic of Vietnam (ARVN) had been made obvious as early as January 1963, when a force of 350 Viet Cong guerrillas stood its ground against an ARVN force four times in number and equipped with American armor, artillery, helicopters and fighter bombers. In *A Bright Shining Lie* (1988), Neil Sheehan gives the classic account of the debacle in his chapter "The Battle of Ap Bac." By the spring of 1965, Assistant Secretary of State William Bundy was seeing the ARVN as "outclassed." A year later Sheehan could write, "We are continually chagrined to discover that idealism and dedication are largely the prerogative of the enemy." By 1969 Jonathan Schell was questioning whether the Saigon regime deserved "the name 'government' at all. It would be more accurate to call it a conscripted army, and leave it at that—or, insofar as it exists in other ways for its people, to call it a public-relations firm."

During the late 1960s, Tobias Wolff served in Vietnam as a lieutenant in the Special Forces and as an adviser to an ARVN division operating out of the Mekong Delta. His memoir, *In Pharaoh's Army*, looks back on the officers "of rank in that unhappy army. All of them were political intriguers; they had to be in order to receive promotion and command. Their wages were too low to live on because it was assumed they'd be stealing, so they stole. They were punished for losing men in battle, therefore they avoided battle.

When their men deserted they kept them on the roster and continued to draw their pay, with the result that the losses were never made up and the units turned into scarecrow remnants hardly able to defend themselves, let alone carry the war to the enemy." As Michael Herr watched the South Vietnamese citizens of Hué retreat from the Communist onslaught, he was struck by the behavior of their South Vietnamese protectors: "Good little fighters, the A.R.V.N. . . . needed both hands . . . forcibly relieving refugees on the road of radios, wine, ducks."

One more example: in 2008, Andrew X. Pham published *The Eaves of Heaven,* a book he describes as his "father's memoir." It provides a penetrating account of life in South Vietnam's army. Born into a wealthy family in the North, Pham Nam Thong flees to South Vietnam in 1954. In 1961, he is conscripted into the ARVN. At his first training camp, he is served a mildewed rice soup. Then he discovers the diner where soldiers can buy a decent meal "at three times the market price." The money skimmed from the operation goes to the camp commander. By the time he is released from the army in 1967, Pham has come to believe that "entrenched corruption, outrageous inefficiency, and plain apathy permeated the upper ranks of the South Vietnamese Army."

One of the most significant weaknesses of the ARVN had to do with how it was originally structured. Basing its demands on the experience of the Korean War, the United States insisted that Saigon set up an army of heavy divisions to be used to block an invasion by the North. While the NLF and its guerilla arm, the PLAF, "went to great lengths to create a military force that was flexible and sympathetic to the lives of village families," the conscription policies adopted by Ngo Dien Diem in response to U.S. pressure created an army dissociated from local conditions. By the late 1960s, the ARVN's eleven infantry divisions fielded over one million men. Now part of what had by then become "one of the most maligned armies in modern history," soldiers of the ARVN also had begun to "redefine the meaning of the war" as a struggle for "their families' survival." Relying heavily on diaries, memoirs, letters, and oral interviews, Robert K. Brigham's *ARVN* (2006) turns on the profound irony that an army willfully deracinated ended up fighting for the most local of causes.

Such was the lot of many of the men American soldiers had been consigned to fight with. But what of the side Americans had been tasked to fight against? There is in any war, of course, a willful failure to empathize with the enemy, one based on the need to reduce him to a negligible and even a despised "other." But the events at My Lai suggest that this dynamic had extended itself beyond enemy soldiers to include much of the population of South Vietnam. For some American fighting men, all Vietnamese came to be seen as members of the "other side."

The difficulty, as ever, was how to see it feelingly. One could look and look and not feel anything, as Herr was to discover about the repeated viewing of dead bodies in Vietnam. "Even when the picture was sharp and clearly defined, something wasn't clear at all, something repressed that monitored the images and withheld their essential information." Herr writes *Dispatches* precisely in order to combat this numbness and dissociation, and the degree to which the book can be said to succeed depends on its power to move its reader to take responsibility for everything he or she sees—by way of Herr's prose—and to feel its force. "I didn't go through all of that not to see," Herr writes. And, having seen, there can be "no secrets about it or the ways it could make you feel."

Even Herr must acknowledge, however, that Vietnam confronts him with things from which he must "look away." My Lai inevitably raises issues about the limits of representation and about the danger of it all being converted into one more atrocity story, a horror to which we might become accustomed. Perhaps one most effectively represents a certain kind of horror by leaving it out. Hemingway came to believe as much and articulates the principle of selective omission in *A Moveable Feast* (1964), where he recounts that he once wrote an entire story about "coming back from the war but there was no mention of the war in it." "This"—the war—"was omitted on my new theory that you could omit anything if you knew that you omitted and the omitted part would strengthen the story and make people feel something more than they understood." Hemingway deploys his reticent omissions, especially in his writing about war, in order to encourage his reader to surmise the unnamed pain and emotion and therefore to "feel more."

It comes as something of a shock to realize that My Lai did not begin to take on a reality for the American public until the publication of Ronald Haeberle's photographs of the massacre in a November 1969 issue of the *Cleveland Plain Dealer.* It was the release of these images that led to articles about My Lai in *Life* and to mention of it on the evening news. And yet even Haeberle's vivid images somehow failed to move their audience, since the chief warrant officer who inherited the My Lai investigation from Colonel Wilson was amazed to discover that in the months before the images were published Haeberle had been incorporating his color slides of the massacre into talks given throughout central Ohio to Optimist, Kiwanis, and Jaycee clubs, as well as to groups of high school students. Despite the fact that these "pictures were the first hard evidence a massacre had taken place," there is no record of any aroused reaction from members of Haeberle's audiences.

Perhaps Shelley had it right when he wrote that "the deep truth is imageless," right at least in the sense that a literal visualization of a horror this deep can end up having the effect of bracketing it out. Two of the more compelling movies made about the war in Vietnam appear to come to this conclusion. While their politics could not be more different, both *The Green Berets* (1968) and *Apocalypse Now* (1979) culminate in scenes in which the filmmaker decided that an atrocity is better narrated than shown. And, in each case, the speaker on the screen finds himself up against the difficulty of trying to grasp the motive, the character—the sheer human reality—of the "other side."

Near the middle of *The Green Berets,* Colonel Mike Kirby—played by John Wayne, who also codirected the film—attempts to explain to a journalist (David Janssen) how hard it is to talk about Vietnam until having "seen it." He then proceeds to tell the reporter, who has just been traumatized by an incident of NLF torture, a story about a village chief the enemy did not kill. "They tied him to a tree," Wayne says, "and brought his teenage daughters out in front of him and disemboweled them. Then forty of them abused his wife, and then they took a steel rod and broke every bone in her body. Somewhere during the process, she died." Although Wayne prefaces his story with an appeal to the authority of visual evidence, the director chooses to convey this horror by way of an actor's voice rather than by shooting the described scene.

"I've seen horrors," Marlon Brando says to Martin Sheen, near the end of *Apocalypse Now.* He tells Sheen that horror has a face, that he must make a friend of it. Then he remembers the time of his service with the Special Forces, when they went into a camp to inoculate some children. "We went back to the camp, and they had come and cut off every inoculated arm. They were in a pile, a pile of little arms." Brando remembers weeping like a grandmother. "I wanted to tear my teeth out . . . And then I realized—like I was shot—like I was shot with a diamond, a diamond bullet . . . and I thought, my God, the genius of that, the genius. The will to do that. The perfect genuine complete crystalline pure will. Then I realized they were stronger than we"—that the "they" he and Wayne keep invoking without naming are "men filled with love."

I hope it will now be clear that in this chapter I am arguing that while the legal evidence generated by a trial can be invaluable as a guide to historical memory, the "evidence" created by the representations of art can also assist in the work of constructing a usable past. Hence the abundance of examples taken from novels, memoir, film, and—as we shall see—poetry, accounts that seek to widen the circle of concern and to invite their audiences to pass judgment not only on the players involved, but on themselves. And, despite all the challenges My Lai might pose to the representing imagination, each side involved in the story was to generate texts in which a reader can invest his trust.

On the American side, beyond the two books by Seymour Hersh, Michal Belknap's *The Vietnam War on Trial* has earned itself such a place. Belknap published his book under the auspices of a University Press of Kansas series called Landmark Law Cases and American Society. Contributors to the series are asked to omit formal citations and to supply instead an extensive bibliographical essay. In Belknap's case, the result is a sublimation of his wide learning and research into a gripping narrative of the massacre and, especially, of its legal aftermath. His book also begins with a chapter-length account of the war in Vietnam from 1945 to 1968 that is the single best short summary of the conflict I have read.

When Americans write and talk about the Vietnam War, they naturally deal with *their* experience of it. *The My Lai Massacre in American History and Memory* (2006) explores the limits of such an approach. "The story of the massacre progressively evolved into a story about Americans," Kendrick Oliver argues, "about the blame carried by Calley, Medina and their men, and about the wider distribution of guilt upwards, across the ranks of those who had managed the war, and horizontally across American society as a whole."

What might it mean to remember My Lai or the Vietnam War itself from *all* sides? In 2003, Christian Appy published a book attempting to do so. "Five years ago," he begins, "I began traveling the United States and Vietnam to interview people from all sides of a war that pitted two nations against each other, created bitter hostilities within both, aroused global alarm, and unleashed the most costly and ruinous destruction of any conflict since World War II. I wanted to explore the vast range of war-related memories that rarely appear together between the covers of a single book." The result was *Patriots: The Vietnam War Remembered from All Sides.*"

Appy eventually published fewer than half of the 350 interviews he recorded. His subjects range from Ta Quang Thinh, a North Vietnamese nurse serving in the South who, after being wounded, was carried north by a team of three men over a period of seven months; Yusef Komunyakaa, a reporter for the American Division who later won the Pulitzer Prize in poetry; Jo Collins, a Playmate of the Year mortared by the NLF when she flew in to visit troops at Black Virgin Mountain; and Truong My Hoa, the vice-chair of the Vietnamese National Assembly who was imprisoned for eleven years in a number of sites in South Vietnam and for one year in a tiger cage. As the voices on Appy's 573 pages offer up their memories, the effect is reverberative: echoes accumulate, tones interpenetrate, and any sense of side-taking gives way to a feeling of encirclement.

My account of the My Lai massacre thus far has dealt largely with the American side, in part because I believe it important to acknowledge what was done *by* us, or in our name. Oliver proposes a corrective to this approach, since, by virtue of it, "the actual victims of the massacre" have been routinely "displaced from the centre of debate and concern and thus rendered powerless to make their claims upon American memory and conscience stick." In the remainder of this chapter, then, I turn to words written by the Vietnamese.

From a Vietnamese perspective, three books are especially useful in representing the experience of individual citizens who found themselves taking or being forced to take sides during the war. The books are *Monkey Bridge* (1997), by Lan Cao; *A Viet Cong Memoir* (1985), by Truong Nhu Tang; and *When Heaven and Earth Changed Places* (1989), by Le Ly Hayslip.

Monkey Bridge explores the consequences of being "on the wrong side of a metaphor." The phrase appears early on in the novel and refers to the U.S. response to the Declaration of Independence issued by Ho Chi Minh in 1945. The United States choose not to hear or to respond to Ho's invocation of its own originating impulses and to side, instead, with the reoccupying French. Lan Cao's use of the word "metaphor" argues that the U.S. policy response involved a failure of imagination, a reading of history in which one nation refused to extend to another the right to self-definition on which it had been founded.

Monkey Bridge circles around "the official moment of collapse," April 30, 1975. In the chaos of American withdrawal and South Vietnamese surrender, a father gets left behind. Missing him at the appointed rendezvous, his daughter and granddaughter are forced to flee without him and to emigrate to the United States. The effort of the narrative becomes one of "fabricating continuity" and is conducted by the granddaughter, Mai, who becomes the teller of the story.

Baba Quan, we assume, has fought on the American–South Vietnamese side—why else would his daughter and granddaughter expect him to be transplanted with them? This belief is reinforced by the episode referred to in the novel's title, by what happened at Monkey Bridge. About midway through the story, we learn that Baba Quan, from his perch on a monkey bridge, a construction of bamboo, had once used this point of vantage to help direct a group of GIs out of a minefield.

The supposition about Baba Quan being on the American "side" turns out to be false. Near the end of the book, it is suddenly revealed that Baba Quan "*is a Vietcong*." Nothing in the novel has prepared us for this revelation; it comes as surprise rather than an expectation fulfilled. The omitted information has been, simply, omitted. It is, in sense, a trick. But if it is a trick, it is one that serves a brutally edifying purpose, since it confronts the reader with the difficulty of telling which "side" a Vietnamese might be on, as well as with the potentialities of temporarily crossing those lines, as Baba Quan does, at Monkey Bridge.

Truong Nhu Tang's title makes clear which side he was on: it is *A Viet Cong Memoir.* He even begins with the word "side," in his foreword, where he argues that while most stories of the war treat of "the military side" of the conflict, "there was another side of the war as well, one that the Vietnamese revolutionaries considered primary—the political side." As one of the founding members of the National Liberation Front, Truong will eventually rise to the position of minister of justice in post-1975 Vietnam. Then he will discover that the side he had been fighting for is not his side, after all.

Born into a wealthy family in Saigon, Truong is sent to Paris in 1945 to be trained as a pharmacist. There he meets Ho Chi Minh. Ho's strength and generosity strike him "like a physical blow." Converted to the nationalist cause, he begins to mobilize the overseas Vietnamese community. His wife leaves him; his parents disown him. Returning to Saigon in 1955, he quickly discovers the "shabby incompetence of the South Vietnamese political system." So he joins with doctors, factory owners, architects, and teachers to form an "extralegal" organization "largely nationalist rather than political," an organization eventually to be known as the National Liberation Front.

The NLF chooses to avoid "high level" warfare in order to prevent what it most fears, an invasion by the United States. Once the Americans do arrive, their entry provokes the movement of an increasing number of North Vietnamese troops into the South. This is the other invasion the NLF fears; as a "Southern revolution . . . generated of itself," it can have only a conflicted relationship with the aims and practices of the government in Hanoi. In *Viet Cong* (1966), Douglas Pike has argued that the NLF was largely a creation of forces in the North. Truong's book works to refute this claim, as it reveals the tensions and conflicts between forces of the North and South as they fought together on the enemy "side."

Truong was an urban intellectual. But what about the villagers in the South who joined in the "Peasant Insurrection," as David Hunt calls it. Basing its findings on 285 interviews conducted by the Rand Corporation from 1965 to 1968 in the Mekong Delta province of My Tho, Hunt's *Vietnam's Social Revolution: From Peasant Insurrection to Total War* (2008) presents a rich portrait of "the tangled feelings of individuals caught up in the revolution."

All of the interviewees were defectors and prisoners who had been associated with the National Liberation Front. "Interviewee no. 135, the Instigator," Hunt writes, "was born in 1936 in a middle peasant family in Tam Hiep village." He became politically active in 1959 and attended a training course for "the Destruction of the Oppression." His job was to recruit one "backbone element" per hamlet. He claims to have been given only five days notice of the uprising campaign against the Diem government. "During these five days I had to mobilize the Liberation Army forces in my hamlet to make machetes, wooden-fish, loudspeakers and a kind of bangalore made with hollow bamboo sticks filled with acetylene." In saying this, he plays down the fact that he and other local cadres had actually been organizing for "a whole year." He does so in order to bring his narrative of the Tam Hiep insurrection into conformity with official accounts later produced about the uprising. "Insurrection was in the air long before July 1960," when the order came from the top down, with the grassroots showing its own unique and powerful forms of initiative. "When the revolution came," Hunt concludes, "it took the form of a popular uprising that owed more to rural custom than to Mao or General Giap."

In trying to avoid a master narrative trapped in states and parties, Hunt's book is offered as a gentle corrective to David W. P. Elliott's massive *The Vietnamese War: Revolution and Social Change in the Mekong Delta, 1930–1975* (2003 and 2007). Elliott has priority over Hunt in that he actually conducted many of the Rand interviews on which both he and Hunt rely. And he takes a longer view, reaching back as early as the peasant uprisings of the 1930s.

Both Elliott and Hunt focus on the province of My Tho. Elliott devotes considerable attention to "the line of Party control," while Hunt attempts to reset the balance by homing in on the sometimes wayward and not always revolutionary motives of individuals caught up in war in the delta. The two studies converge on the belief that on both sides of the war "there was a vast difference between local realities and the prerogatives and beliefs of those higher up."

The arrival of American armor, planes, herbicides, and ground forces in 1965 created a crisis for the peasant insurrection. In 1964, it had looked as if the Saigon regime was about to collapse. A year later, the insurgents found themselves drawn in to a new, "total war." By 1967, villages in "the liberated zones lay in ruins, and villagers walked across a terrain littered with booby traps and unexploded munitions." By the time guidelines arrived for the Tet Offensive, the villagers of My Tho had already "concluded that there was no alternative to fighting the war to the finish" and surprised cadres by volunteering for the PLAF. They did not view Tet as "a 'step in a process.'" They looked forward, as Hunt maintains, "to a showdown that with one mighty stroke would put an end to their suffering. . . . Those who survived must have been heartbroken when it did not bring victory and peace."

During Tet the city of My Tho suffered the peculiar fate of being the native town of President Thieu's wife. In My Tho to celebrate the holiday, the president was accompanied by special detachments provided for his security. "Only on the second day of the offensive," Elliott relates, "when President Thieu was evacuated by helicopter, did the attacking forces become aware of his presence in the town." Aided by U.S. firepower, Thieu's security detachments saved My Tho from being overrun. At the end of a week, however, 25 percent of the town was burned and five thousand residences had been destroyed.

Truong Nhu Tang would survive Tet, and he too would suffer from the escalating violence after the American arrival. The most compelling chapter is *A Viet Cong Memoir* is called "Life in the Maquis." In it, Truong describes the six years—from 1966 to 1971—he spent organizing and hiding in the Iron Triangle. Continual land and air incursions by U.S. and ARVN forces require the maquis to be always ready to move; Truong carries only two pairs of black pajamas, a mosquito net, and a few squares of nylon cloth. The rice ration of twenty kilos per man a month leaves everyone "in a state of semistarvation." The cadres also eat elephants, tigers, wild dogs, monkeys, and even jungle moths. Most come down with malaria; for each of his years in the "septic jungle," Truong spends two months in hospital.

It is a life of "hiding and preparation." The NLF even devises a system of smokeless cooking in which fires are vented underground. Precautions are taken in order to avoid detection by the dreaded B-52s. At a kilometer, their bombs destroy eardrums; the shock waves can knock "their victims senseless." Evasion is aided by information forwarded from Soviet trawlers off the coast able to pick up the flight paths of the huge planes as they take off from Okinawa and Guam. Under bombardment, Truong writes, "one lost control of bodily functions as the mind screamed incomprehensible orders to get out."

And for all this—after the romance of founding and the deprivations of hiding out—Truong finds himself turned against because of his bourgeois past. Northerners begins treating members of the NLF "like uninvited guests." Increasingly harried about his "class deficiencies," Truong realizes that after Ho's death in 1969, "the ideologues were firmly in control." By the summer of 1970 he feels "locked in. France and the West had helped shape much of our political thinking, but it was a bitter paradox that France and the West had given us nothing to go along with it, no hope and no help toward adopting their own values to our society." Lost, he comes to believe, is the possibility of "a middle way."

In the peace treaty signed with the U.S. in 1973, no mention is made of Northern divisions still remaining in the South. And yet, as Truong points out, "Practically the entire North Vietnamese army was now inside South Vietnam—to stay." In May 1975, Truong watches the victory parade in Saigon but sees none of his divisions in it. Now "the true outlines of power revealed themselves." Truong sees that the Provisional Revolutionary Government founded by the NLF has been used as "the last linkup" the Northern Party "needed to achieve its own imperialistic revolution."

Despite his sense of increasing marginalization, Truong is offered the post of minister of justice, a job requiring him to preside over the detainment of perceived enemies of the state. Soon "everyone had some family member or other in camp." Two of Truong's brothers are told to bring food and clothing for a thirty-day stay. One month passes, and then another; it becomes clear that detainees will be held indefinitely. Arbitrary arrests accelerate throughout the countryside; one's name need merely appear on someone's list. People are snatched from their homes or offices; the arrests are "more kidnappings than legal apprehensions."

Truong resolves to escape. Through a doctor friend he makes contact with a wealthy businessman also looking for a way out. They find a thirty-five-foot riverboat. They set out, hit a sandbar, return to the river. On their second try, they are stopped by Thai pirates. The pirates take their weapons and money. Finally landing at an Indonesian oil-rig, they are then taken to a U.N. camp on Galang Island. Six months later, Truong makes his way to France, "the country where thirty years before my sense of patriotism was born and my political values shaped."

Truong argues that Americans need to understand "the Vietnamese who fought on the other side." But his narrative works to deconstruct any simple application of his chosen term. Thinking he was working for one side, Truong found himself coopted by another. And yet both sides were lumped together in the American mind as the enemy other; little attempt was made to address and sort out and therefore to exploit the complex and sometimes conflicting loyalties that existed, between 1945 and 1975, on Vietnamese ground. "Nixon and Kissinger suffered from a fundamental inability," Truong concludes, "to enter into the mental world of their enemy." More than this, they mistook a political for a military struggle. Truong concurs with the American negotiator who says to his North Vietnamese counterpart, "You know, you never defeated us on the battlefield." The point is deemed "irrelevant," however, irrelevant because the primary struggle, as Truong and his people saw it, was a political war waged against "the enemy's internal contradictions." That struggle succeeded in separating "American leadership from its internal support." The sides taken during that period of "ingrained distrust and ill will," Truong judges, have led to "effects" on the American body politic and "national psyche" that "may well be permanent."

Unlike the author of *Monkey Bridge*, Le Ly Hayslip works with expectation rather than surprise. When *Heaven and Earth Changed Places* consists of two intertwined narratives, the story of Hayslip's past in a village in South Vietnam, and the story of her return, in 1986, to the country she was forced to leave in 1970. Hayslip thereby grants a foreknowledge of narrative outcomes sufficient to enlist her reader as a concerned participant rather than as a merely surprised onlooker. By positioning her reader between a lost "then" and a fraught but promising "now," Hayslip also grants her the sense of being *in the middle* that is the core human experience described in the book. The freedom to move about in time generated by Hayslip's carefully chosen form also works to mitigate Bay Ly's (the name Hayslip gives her self-character) sense of being caught in an action that is foregone.

"For my first twelve years of life," Hayslip begins, "I was a peasant girl in Ky La, now called Xo Hoa Qui, a small village near Danang in Central Vietnam." She is born in 1950, the fifth year of the war against the French. At first, everything she learns about the war comes to her by way of midnight meetings held by North Vietnamese cadre leaders. She accepts what they tell her as true because it matches "the beliefs we already had." The core belief is that Vietnam is "a sovereign nation which had been held in thrall to Western imperialists for over a century." So, after the division of the country in 1954, and "because the North remained pretty much on its own, the choice of which side best represented independence was, for us, a foregone conclusion."

Yet Bay Ly's narrative will work to question this conclusion as she finds herself continually caught between sides. Near the end of her prologue, she turns to address the American GI and attempts to explain why he was so resented, feared, and misunderstood. "Because we had to appease the allied forces by day and were terrorized by Viet Cong at night, we slept as little as you did. We obeyed both sides and wound up pleasing neither. We were people in the middle. We were what the war was all about."

All this is by way of introduction; Hayslip then proceeds to take us, in excruciating detail, through the experience of being caught in the middle. At twelve, she plays war games; the children copy "what we admired." Some pretend to be Republicans, some NLF. The game soon becomes one played for mortal stakes, since the NLF occupies Ky La one day, the Republicans the next. Her family builds a bunker for protection from bombs, including space for "extra people" who may be running past. Since running things get shot at, she will learn when the time comes to stand still at the approach of Americans, "the way one learns to stand still in the face of an angry dog."

In her early teens, Bay Ly is inducted into a secret self-defense force and told she will be responsible for warning the NLF about enemy movements in the village. One night the Republicans bombard Ky La, and Bay Ly, hiding in a roadside trench, is discovered and arrested. The Republicans beat her and put her in tiger cage where she is compelled to relieve herself on the floor. After three days of beatings and interrogation, she gains release through family connections to the Da Nang police.

Six months later, the NLF stages a major attack against Ky La. The attack begins too soon, chaos breaks out, and the Republicans and Americans pound the area. "Two thirds of my village disappeared this way." Frustrated NLF members begin to take harsh steps to control the local population, including "special justice meetings" in which villagers are summarily accused and shot. As the war begins to devolve into a chain of vendettas, the "fear of the Viet Cong" becomes "almost as strong as our fear of the Republicans."

One morning in 1964, on sentry duty for the NLF, Bay Ly sees a "teeming mass" of Republicans approaching the village and manages to give a warning. "By giving my signal in time, I had prevented a Viet Cong massacre." At a midnight meeting in the swamp, she is honored for her bravery. "It was just like my old war games at school, except now everyone was on the same side."

The Republicans know that young women in the area have been acting as NLF sentries, and one evening, on a sweep through the village after an intense bombardment, Bay Ly is again arrested. She is tied to a post in an area swarming with ants and a sticky substance is applied to her feet. As the girls tied near her begin shrieking, Bay Ly tries to stand still, but her legs are soon swollen and purple. A guard returns, and drops a water snake down her shirt.

Bay Ly gives up no information and will eventually be released through a family connection to a Republican lieutenant and at the cost of half her dowry. But she has now earned herself the mistrust of the NLF. "Nobody gets out of My Thi so quickly," her father tells her, "even for a bribe." One morning on the way to hoe the fields she passes six Republican soldiers who then begin to follow her. As they do so, they spot two NLF fighters, killing one and wounding the other. "Now I had no doubt," Hayslip writes, "that my days with the V.C. were over. Not only had I mysteriously escaped the notorious My Thi prison, but I had just been seen leading a Republican squad toward a Viet Cong position. Nobody would be interested in my side of the story."

Guilt through inadvertence: Bay Ly's story devolves into one about the impotence of the individual, in a landscape of such brutality and confusion, to choose or to even define her *side*. Hayslip's narrative reveals instead that such wars always entail a third side, the complex in-betweenness of a typical civilian self. Bay Ly will be raped—twice—by the NLF in punishment for her alleged betrayal, and that is the end of her side-taking. "I no longer cared even for vengeance. Both sides in this terrible, endless, *stupid* war had finally found the perfect enemy: a terrified peasant girl who would endlessly and stupidly consent to be their victim."

Bay Ly does not yet know it, but her romance of emigration has begun. She will leave her village, move to Saigon, become pregnant, work as a prostitute. Ky Ly is destroyed by the Americans in order to create "a better 'killing zone.'" She finds her father living in a hovel with torn flesh. He has been tortured by the Americans. Some days later, he kills himself by drinking acid.

Throughout these excruciating revelations, Hayslip has been interposing the story of her return to Vietnam, one attempted in 1986. We do not learn until late in the memoir that before leaving her country in 1970 she had met and married Ed Munro, an American she meets in Saigon in 1969. What we do know is that at the beginning of the book she has said good-bye to three sons in San Diego and that the central purpose of her journey back is to "see my mother again."

The knowledge that Bay Ly has survived to live a prosperous life in the United States can work on the reader of her book in complex ways. It does little to alleviate the horror felt at her whipsawed life. But it does help to lessen, perhaps, the discomfort of an American reader, since, despite the depredations visited on Bay Ly and her family during the American War, it is also America that has remained open and free enough to take her in.

"I have not seen or spoken to my mother for almost a generation," Bay Ly thinks to herself, on the morning of her departure from Los Angeles. She and her mother have been estranged not only by time and distance but by the mother's opposition to her 1969 marriage. When Bay Ly finally arrives in Da Nang, her brother visits her, but her mother does not. The mother is worried she will lose her pension if she is seen "receiving money from the capitalists." Bay Ly's sister Hai has already spurned her out of similar fears. "For them," Bay Ly comes to realize, "the war has not ended."

A reunion is finally arranged, and, arriving at the appointed place, Bay Ly sees a tiny figure in baggy pants whose "bare feet stick out like old ginger." The approach is tentative, and before an embrace can occur the mother pulls a child between them, "like a bulletproof vest." Questions are exchanged; the two begin to talk. A meal is served, but no hugs take place. Finally, some gnarled fingers touch Bay Ly's elbow. The two women sit down side by side and proceed to have a talk. The mother accepts some candy from Bay Ly, and soon lumps of nougat are clinging to her toothless gums.

But Bon Nghe, the brother who had been sent North in the mid-1950s and who spent the war on the Communist side, refuses to accept anything from Bay Ly. "Bay Ly's a capitalist. I'm a Communist," he says. The mother then takes up Bay Ly's cause, arguing that "you've found common ground at this table, haven't you?" She reminds him that they both come from "Central Vietnam—*Trung* land—the land in the middle." The chapter ends with the brother sticking to his refusal and with the mother, "for the first time since our reunion," hugging back.

The brother will cling to his position. At the last family gathering, after a debate about the virtues of post-1975 Vietnam, Bon Nghe turns to Bay Ly and says: "You've seen both sides now—what both sides can do. Who do you think is right?" Her response to the question can put one in mind of how difficult it is to resolve the claims of love and freedom.

"'If you really want to know,' I say, . . . 'I think neither side really knows what it's talking about. Even Americans don't really know what freedom means, although they live it every day. You, Bon Nghe, and you, Ba Xuan— you love each other dearly but you talk like you don't know what love is all about.'" Bon Nghe is not convinced and presses her by asking, if neither side can provide a "perfect" world, "How are we supposed to choose?"

"We choose as we go along, little by little," Bay Ly answers. "We take some of this and leave a little of that." The answer, she has come to believe, lies in impure mixtures and ongoing compromises. The mother can therefore pay Bay Ly the supreme compliment, as she sends her back to America, of seeing that her daughter has "grown up to see the side of things that's hidden from most people," the side beyond taking sides.

In 1960, Robert Lowell published "For the Union Dead," a poem that looked into a hard and waning American future. Lowell stations himself in his beloved downtown Boston, now enduring urban "renewal." He see the big steam shovels gouging up the past, and remembers himself as a boy, nose pressed up against the glass of the aquarium, watching the "compliant fish." He goes on to remember the nation's wars, giving each its appropriate figure. At the center of these memories is the Civil War and the new "Civil Rights" war of the present moment, imaged by Lowell as black children on television, their drained faces rising like "balloons."

One of the things being shaken up by the current excavations is the St. Gaudens Civil War relief of Colonel Robert Shaw and "his bell-cheeked Negro infantry." The regiment's suicidal charge at Fort Wagner in South Carolina will be familiar to most readers of the poem, if at all, after seeing it depicted in the 1989 movie *Glory*. In thinking about Shaw, and the statue that commemorates him, Lowell begins to brood on the status and function of monuments. Shaw had been killed in the charge on Fort Wagner, and his father

> wanted no monument
> except the ditch,
> where his son's body was thrown
> and lost with his "niggers."

As the ditch becomes the central image in the poem, it also becomes a figure for the modern memorial. How many people have not suffered, in the twentieth century, a fate similar to Shaw and to his men, at the trenches of Flanders, or Katyn Forest, or Babi Yar? The ditch expresses something profound about how we create and remember the dead, and about the anonymity to which so many buried there have been consigned.

Then Lowell writes,

> The ditch is nearer.

How could he have known this? How could he have anticipated the ditch in which Schwerner, Goodman, and Chaney would be hidden in Mississippi, or the ditch in Vietnam that John Wade "finds himself at the bottom of?" To say "The ditch is nearer" is to foresee a future in which the country has turned itself into one vast mass grave, a country that has decided, as urban renewal becomes the central instance of the case, to destroy itself in order to save itself.

The first memorials erected at My Lai, in 1976, consisted of steles marking the ditch area and other sites where atrocities were committed. In the ensuing years a two-story museum was built on the site. The fields around the museum contain recreated burnt-out buildings and replicas of slaughtered animals. The museum displays reproductions of Ronald Haeberle's photographs as well as remnant objects like baskets and hairpins. On the second floor of the museum there is a stone stele into which are carved the names and ages at death of 504 Vietnamese killed at My Lai on March 16, 1968.

Some visitors to the My Lai Memorial have objected to the kitschiness of its visual replications and have called it "the My Lai Theme Park." Without making an actual pilgrimage to the site and without actually standing at the ditch, it is difficult to imagine the feelings being there might generate. The one ditch Americans are much more likely to visit and have feelings about is in Washington, D.C.

In order to experience the Vietnam Veterans Memorial, one approaches it from above, and then walks down, into the common grave. On the wall are the names of some 58,000 American dead, and the reader of the names can add his own to the assembled columns, since, in order to read the wall, he must stare into a polished granite surface that gives him back an image of his own face. Maya Lin's memorial thus responds to the call issued by Lowell in one of his last poems "to give/each figure in the photograph/his living name," and to include ourselves in, as well, as one of life's "poor passing facts." Of course the enemy dead go unnamed. But as we stand there, performing our reading, it is possible to imagine each country possessing somewhere, if only graven on surviving hearts, the names of the loved dead. To find oneself at the bottom of this ditch is to be invited, once again, to take up the work we are in, the ongoing act of nation-building that depends upon an honest effort to give each figure in the ditch his living name, and to acknowledge as well the lost names of all from every side who lie in unmarked graves.

CHAPTER

8

Columbia

"Then Rudd did the thing at the King Memorial Service," James Kunen writes, in *The Strawberry Statement,* his journal-like account of the developments taking place at Columbia University in April and May 1968. Kunen's "then" will prove telling. For those who lived through that New York spring, event followed upon event in a "then"-like sequence. Many of the surviving testimonies express a sort of baffled wonder at the unplanned. Any pattern of cause and continuity imposed by a historical retrospect must compete with the sense of it all having been one unlikely "then" after another. While much of consequence did result—the founding of Weatherman, a shift in patterns of university governance, the mobilization of the Harlem community—the Cox Report was to conclude that "the April uprising started and grew haphazardly." What happened at Columbia comprised an activity during which people were changed by doing.

The strike at Columbia turned on the irony that "the universities, starting as bases for protest," had by 1968 "ended up as targets for it." The words are William Sloane Coffin's, but they could have been written as well by Diana Trilling. Trilling lived with her husband, Lionel, in an apartment close to the Columbia campus, and her anguished memoir, "On the Steps of Low Library" (1969), serves as an elegy for a kind of academic life whose time now appeared to be ending. (Reading *The Armies of the Night* on the morning of April 23, "when the uprising began," she patterns her chapter after Mailer's "On the Steps of the Pentagon.") It is as if the wounding were occurring to her own body: "Touch a university with hostile hands and the blood you draw is prompt, copious, and real."

Trilling's memoir takes its place within a still-accumulating choir of recollection: F. W. Dupee's "The Uprising at Columbia" (1968), Kunen's *Statement* (published in part in *New York* magazine in 1968 and as a book in 1969), Susan Stern's *With the Weathermen* (1975), Tom Hayden's *Reunion* (1988), Bill Ayers's *Fugitive Days* (2001), Mark Naison's *White Boy* (2002), and Mark Rudd's *Underground* (2009). Each author confesses, in Mailer's phrase, to being "not central to the event," and, because of this admitted sense of marginality, each can also stand in for a latter-day reader whose felt distance from "the precise feel of the ambiguity of the event" can be bridged by way of an author's chosen words.

In the following chapter I have chosen to tell the story of the Columbia uprising in a chronological fashion, allowing the voices of my eight informants to surface whenever they have something arresting to say. The spine of the narrative relies on Robert A. McCaughey's "interpretive" but not official history of the university, *Stand, Columbia* (2003).

While McCaughey attempts to contextualize 1968 within a long tradition of "student misbehavior," his narrative proper begins with May 7, 1965, when campus protest "first turned confrontational." On that date a commissioning ceremony for the Naval ROTC was disrupted by "shouting students" protesting the presence of U.S. forces in Vietnam and of the Navy on campus. A number of those involved were members of the recently founded Columbia chapter of Students for a Democratic Society (SDS).

When Tom Hayden arrived at the University of Michigan in 1957, he found a campus suffering from a "congested loneliness." Hayden relieved his loneliness by joining the staff of the Michigan *Daily* and by befriending Al Haber, who, in 1960, set out to convert the trade-union affiliated SLID (Student League for Industrial Democracy) into an organization called Students for a Democratic Society. Haber's goal was to distance the new organization from the politics of the Old Left and to align its energies with those of the civil rights movement. In June 1960 Hayden traveled with Haber to the SDS convention in New York, and, in August, acting now as the editor of the *Daily*, he flew to the Democratic convention in Los Angeles, where he interviewed Martin Luther King. "Ultimately," King said to Hayden, "you have to take a stand with your life."

Under Haber's leadership SDS quickly grew into the most progressive student organization, and Hayden would serve as its first field secretary in the South. He worked with and admired Bob Moses for his "pattern of non-leadership," and he was arrested in a freedom ride on his twenty-second birthday. From his jail cell in Albany, Georgia, Hayden decided that he could be more useful by helping SDS to become a national force than he could by organizing in the South.

The result was "The Port Huron Statement," composed largely by Hayden in preparation for an SDS conference held in June 1962. Hayden's ringing, searching, declarative sentences take much of their inspiration from the optative mood of Emerson's prose. "Where do we find ourselves?" Emerson asks, in the opening sentence of "Experience" (1844), and the answer given is that we find ourselves "in a series of which we do not know the extremes." The best recourse for such a condition is to fare forward with hope, while acknowledging that we don't quite know whither we are tending. Heeding such counsel, Hayden wrote of the need for "an intuitive alertness to that which is capable of occurring, to that which is not yet realized, and passion for continuous unfolding." Since the civil rights and student movements "had taken all political intellectuals by surprise," the document argued that "politics should flow from experience, not from preconceived dogmas or ideologies." In *Democracy Is in the Streets* (1987), James Miller gives Hayden's "manifesto of hope" its most richly contextualized and sympathetic reading.

By the time Hayden arrived at Columbia, he had also organized in a Newark ghetto and paid a controversial visit to North Vietnam. Seemingly positioned at some abrupt edge, Hayden actually sought to face a number of constituencies. "Few could understand how I could seem at the time to support North Vietnam, plot disruptive confrontations, and work cooperatively with such figures as Averell Harriman and Robert Kennedy." Citing Kennedy's "Hamlet-like vacillation," Hayden continually signals his own. So he departs for Chicago, for instance, "trying to get along with all the forces heading there." The cumulative effect of such admissions is to convert *Reunion* into an uneasy affirmation, an elegy for missed opportunities, even a self-consuming artifact. "Why," Hayden asks, near the end, "Why did we, who were so able to shake existing institutions, leave so little behind?" It is his growing self-doubt and his ability to think against himself that Hayden's book most powerfully chronicles. His sense of having lost the political struggle leads not, however, to an emotion of defeat but to a questioning of the American myth that winning is the only thing. "I believe that as a nation," he concludes, "we have to develop wisdom from the experience of losing."

By the spring of 1967, Columbia's president, Grayson Kirk, had undermined his standing with his public by allowing the university's medical school to endorse a cigarette filter that claimed to reduce nicotine intake by 70 percent. The device not only failed to do so but created a taste that "compared unfavorably with smoking hay." It is in the context of this loss of face that the decision to proceed with building a gymnasium for Columbia College students in Morningside Park can best be understood. "All relevant elected officials at the neighborhood, borough, city, and state levels had signed off" on the park deal as early as 1961, but six years of delays had also allowed for a number of community officials to become opposed to the project as intrusive. The problem, as Trilling writes, was that Columbia had "for some years now been a constantly shrinking white island," and the gym was to extend itself out into predominantly black Harlem. Much was also made of the fact that "the facilities of the building were not to be used jointly but severally by Harlem and the University," with a front ("white") entrance for students, and a back ("black") door for residents of the neighborhood.

On February 8, 1968, earth-moving equipment arrived at the gym site, and two days later a demonstration brought construction to a halt. Columbia graduate student Mark Naison, an activist with CORE and a determined opponent of the war, had decided on "getting arrested on behalf" of an issue he cared about. After half an hour of chanting, Naison and some thirty protestors "approached the fence surrounding the construction site and tried to tear it down." Naison was among those charged by city police with disorderly conduct.

Columbia's membership in the Institute for Defense Analysis, not the gym project, had long been a more pressing issue for SDS. A twelve-university consortium, the IDA solicited faculty expertise on the use of air power in Vietnam and in the developments of weapons like Agent Orange. "IDA thus became," Mark Rudd maintains, "the shorthand symbol for Columbia's huge network of complicity with the war." On February 23, two hundred students marched on campus to protest the presence of recruiters from the Dow Chemical Company. A month later, the New York City director of the Selective Service was hit in the face with a lemon meringue pie wielded by recently elected SDS chairman Rudd. A week after that, SDS created a demonstration in Low Library, which housed the offices of the university administration, and Kirk resolved to punish a few of the participating students, including Rudd, whose names had been identified. Those singled out became known as the "Low Six."

Mark Rudd was a red-diaper baby, one of a group of Jewish undergraduates who hailed from New York City and its suburbs. He arrived at Columbia in the fall of 1965 and joined SDS the following spring. On Tuesday, April 23, of his junior year, he found himself presiding over a chaotic series of events. At a rally on behalf of the Low Six at the sundial, a campus landmark, Rudd had planned to instigate a march into Low in "an intentional mass violation of the rule against indoor demonstrations." As the rally began, he was handed a letter from the university's vice president, David Truman, proposing a meeting with the demonstrators in a theater on campus. Rudd read Truman's letter to the crowd, and then, not "sure what to do," found himself interrupted by a voice urging a march on Low. Rudd ran to the front of the now moving crowd. "Here I was, at the head of a demonstration about to burst into a locked building, or else run headlong into a mob of pissed-off right-wing jocks, and I had only the vaguest idea of what we were doing." Finding Low's doors locked, he then followed another cry, "To the gym site!" More talking at the site, and then a march back to campus. More talk, this time by two black student leaders, Cicero Wilson and Bill Sales, and then another yelled suggestion: "Seize Hamilton!" A march to Hamilton Hall, an entry, a confrontation with Dean Henry Coleman. Suddenly Rudd realized he had taken a "hostage"—a person, not a building. Coleman retreated to his office, and the occupation began. "Things were happening so fast by that point that I only dimly understood we had passed the point of no return." The three clichés in one sentence indicate not only Rudd's uncontrol of the unfolding outcomes but the limits of his narrative voice.

One irony of the week-long strike that ensued, in which five buildings were eventually occupied, is that Rudd spent little time in any of them. Events so far outran him that he found himself screaming, "I resign as chairman of this fucking organization!" By Friday he reclaimed his authority and was elected head of the newly formed strike coordinating committee. Rudd spent his days shuttling between buildings and meetings. To understand what life was like inside the newly "liberated" campus spaces, we must turn to James Kunen and his "Notes of a College Revolutionary."

Philip Beidler finds in Kunen's notes a "sense of generous recollection," while Trilling judges them absent of any "vestige of idea." "This book was written on napkins and cigarette packs and hitchhiking signs," Kunen informs us, and it maintains throughout a sense of spontaneous and un-self-important disarray. Kunen is wry and funny, with a clear sense of the absurdities of some of the event's abruptions. He claims no overview. Using a diary format, Kunen confines his awareness to the limited temporal horizon of the present tense. "Someone suggests we go sit down for awhile in Hamilton, the main college classroom building, and we go there." What he tells us is happening *now*.

One of the first things Kunen does in Hamilton is to leave: he doesn't want to miss crew practice. By eight that night he is back in Hamilton, trying "to meet some girls." On waking the next morning he is told that "the blacks occupying Hamilton with us have asked us to leave." So, "I get up and leave." With two hundred other students he rushes to Low and into President Kirk's office. He collects water in wastebaskets in preparation for a tear gas attack.

Windows play a central part in Kunen's entries; that night "one hundred and seventy-three people jump out the window" on news that the cops are coming. Kunen doesn't jump because he is reading *Lord Jim;* the police in any event fail to arrive. Later, "in through the window like Batman climbs Professor Orest Ranum, liberal, his academic robes billowing in the wind. We laugh at his appearance. He tells us that our action will precipitate a massive right-wing reaction in the faculty." Mark Rudd climbs in a window and urges the occupiers to leave for a sit-in in front of the building. "We say no, we're not leaving until our demands on the gym, IDA, and amnesty for demonstrators are met. Rudd goes out and comes back and asks us to leave again, and we say no again."

On the morning of Thursday, April 25, "I get up and shave with Grayson Kirk's razor." Kunen leaves Low to tell his crew coach he will be on the bus to a rowing competition at MIT the next day. At 2 a.m., he and thirty others sprint to Mathematics Hall. "We get inside and immediately pile up about 2000 pounds of furniture at the front door." Kunen then finds himself at a meeting about the police being on the way, a meeting chaired by "an Outside Agitator," Tom Hayden.

In late April Hayden happened to be in New York for a SNCC meeting. On the 23rd he received a call from "some black students at Columbia." They asked for his "advice and support," and Hayden hopped on the subway uptown.

"I had never seen anything quite like this," Hayden writes. "Various faculty and, as I recall, administrators intermingled with these 'revolutionary' students, perpetuating the traditional and casual mode of campus life just at the moment of its dissolution." He observed a new type of campus leader, "a nice, somewhat inarticulate, suburban New Jersey kid with blue eyes, sandy hair, and an easygoing manner." But Mark Rudd was also "committed to revolutionary destruction, sarcastic and smugly dogmatic." Feeling like "the (twenty-nine-year-old) old man of the student movement," Hayden offered Rudd his help.

"The next five days were an experience resembling the Paris Commune of the nineteenth century." Early on the morning of April 26, Hayden found himself, as did Kunen, part of the wave of students surging into Mathematics Hall; they entered with a key provided by a graduate student. By this point, four other Columbia buildings had been occupied, and "those of us in the five buildings now were on our own." Hayden was chosen to chair the commune in Mathematics Hall.

The students knew that a police raid was only a matter of time. Outside, counter-demonstrators, mostly campus athletes and fraternity members, were threatening violence. "We arrived at a consensus after about an hour that when and if the police came, we would block the entrances to the building but sit nonviolently when they entered." Liquid soap was spread on stairwells in order to impede a police charge. The enormous barrier of desks and chairs Kunen helped to assemble at the building's main entrance was tied in place with fire hoses.

The commune did not neglect its creature comforts. "A secret committee was swiftly appointed to slip in and out of the building," Hayden recalls, "to procure orange juice, bags of coffee, peanut butter and jelly, and if possible, salami and *The New York Times*. A stereo as well was imported, and soon the sounds of Dylan and the Beatles were floating around us. Dope smoking was banned, but not romance." At a Sunday meeting, Kunen found himself "concerned with the breast size of his revolutionary cohorts." The student radio station announced a wedding in Fayerweather, where the Episcopalian chaplain pronounced them "children of the new age."

Kunen's weekend passed relatively peacefully; on Friday he climbed out a window in Mathematics, on Saturday he rowed at MIT, and that afternoon he climbed back in. He therefore missed the confrontation with the Ad Hoc Faculty Group in Philosophy 301, where Mark Rudd declared any solution to the strike not involving amnesty for the occupiers to be "bullshit."

In the title essay of her 1968 *Slouching Towards Bethlehem,* Joan Didion notices "something important . . . the desperate attempt of a handful of pathetically unequipped children to create a community in a social vacuum. Once we had seen these children, we could no longer overlook the vacuum, no longer pretend that the society's atomization could be reversed. This was not a traditional generational rebellion. At some point between 1945 and 1967 we had somehow neglected to tell these children the rules of the game we happened to be playing." Didion is writing here about the lost souls in Haight Asbury, not the determined if wayward strikers at Columbia. But her analysis pertains, and perhaps more in its tone than in its argument. The real charge here being laid is against the parents ("Parents were missing," she writes in the first paragraph of the essay), not the children. The atomization of the sixties results from a failure of parenting, Didion concludes, a failure to pass along the rules of the game. The very choice of words like "rules" and "game," words she repeats throughout the passage, indicates Didion's acceptance of the arbitrary and conventional nature of the "values" that are passed from one generation to another, a transfer no less necessary, she also seems to believe, for all that. Being of a certain age, and already hard-pressed to protect her daughter from "the ambushes of family life," or to "give her home for her birthday," Didion includes herself in the group that has failed: "Maybe we have stopped believing in the rules ourselves, maybe we were having a failure of nerve about the game."

In his *A Fiction of the Past: The Sixties in American History* (1999), Dominick Cavallo appeals to "child-rearing practices" in an attempt to explain the sudden outbreak of radical activism among children of America's white middle class. "What distinguished the experiences of young people in the forties and fifties were the implacable intensity and limitless optimism with which their parents and others urged them to be autonomous." Reared in the ways of competitive individualism, and equipped with a "self-confidence nurtured by strenuous self-cultivation," these children moved into young adulthood possessed of values which then came into direct conflict with existing social realities, and rebellion was the result. In Didion's terms, the parents of these children had fed them on ideals while omitting to fill them in on the fact that American life was a highly structured game. From either perspective, the uprising at Columbia presents a unique case of the Failure of the Parents, one in which many faculty and virtually all of the university's administrators, unlike Didion, failed to *imagine with* the young.

Part of the problem arose from the fact that the more the actual adults involved insisted on sounding and acting like "adults," the more they missed the point. Diana Trilling's "I am a mature woman" can be taken as an extreme instance of the case. A primary concern in her essay is to evince probity, retain distance, uphold reason, burnish intellectual credentials. But the unlooked-for result, as Robert Lowell puts it, is a document of "unseeing didacticism." "Fussing at thought," Lowell objects, matters more to Trilling than any quest for empathy.

"Columbia is my husband's university which he first came to as a freshman of sixteen and never left except for a distant year at Wisconsin and a recent year at Oxford, and I live close to the campus." This is the husband who authored *The Liberal Imagination* (1950), and it is the word "liberal" that his wife is most concerned to defend. She deploys the word as if it announced its own authority, deploring a revolution "antiliberal in its lawlessness and its refusal of reasonable process." The revolution at Columbia was against many things, but "liberalism" surely ranked low on anyone's list. That liberalism had failed was, however, not entirely beside the point, since it was the most liberal Washington administration since Roosevelt's that those protesting the war found themselves arrayed against. Locating her analysis within an Old Left context, Trilling does prove willing to remind her reader of liberalism's ongoing failure to "oppose" Communist dictatorship, but the issue belongs to the debates of the 1930s. She thus reduces the event to a struggle over "being deprived of a definition" of an increasingly irrelevant word.

Trilling is unable to see what Mailer, Kunen, and Hayden can see—that the culture had entered the realm of the *carnivalesque*. Perhaps only an imagination possessed of a ludic sense could engage in this play for mortal stakes. One word being deprived of a definition was the word *administrative*, at least when lived out by institutional leaders who saw themselves as the knowing parents of their uninformed client-children. These "children" were in fact engaged in a critique of their elders' refusal to engage in what Thoreau calls "thinking." "With thinking," he argues in *Walden*,

> we may be beside ourselves in a sane sense. By a conscious effort of the mind we can stand aloof from actions and their consequences; and all things, good and bad, go by us like a torrent. . . . I only know myself as a human entity; the scene, so to speak, of thoughts and affections; and am sensible of a certain doubleness by which I can stand as remote from myself as from another. However intense my experience, I am conscious of the presence and criticism of a part of me, which, as it were, is not a part of me, but a spectator, sharing no experience, but taking note of it, and that is no more I than it is you.

Thoreau here presents thinking as ecstatic—"being beside ourselves" is the very definition of the word "ecstasy." But it is a "sane" ecstasy; thinking involves a sense of being carried away while remaining centered enough not to get lost in the transport. So while there is a pleasure in thinking, it is not simply self-pleasing, or self-regarding, since thinking also stands off from all the intensities of experience and engages in a "criticism" of them. Not criticism as depreciation or running down, but rather as an awareness, an acknowledgment. So, according to Thoreau, true thinking is double, and self-observing, while remaining in some way playful. It is the kind of thinking exemplified in *The Armies of the Night,* where Mailer addresses himself in the third person not in order to enhance his stature but so as to situate it, critique it, and gently mock it. At some profound level, thinking protects the self against believing its own act, and hence from making hubristic errors. As a part of the thinking self stands off and watches the "I" thinking, it remains aware of the passing "authority" of any one thought, a process also foregrounding the contingent nature of authority itself.

The word "authority" proved as important to President Kirk as the word "liberal" did to Diana Trilling. "Our young people, in disturbing numbers," he declared on April 12, "appear to reject all forms of authority." He called the students "transitory birds." Some faculty members proved even less politic, as when Professor Herbert Deane gave Kunen his title: "Whether students vote yes or no on a given issue means as much to me as if they were to tell me they like strawberries." Even the "mature" Trilling saw that Kirk's failure of language expressed a larger failure of imagination, one that turned on his chosen god-term. The president displayed an "inability," she wrote, "to address the campus except in the language of traditional authority."

As Trilling concludes, "the chief parental figures on the campus, the Columbia administrators were fathers in an anxiety dream." Informed of the occupation of Hamilton Hall, Kirk's "first inclination was to call in the New York City Police." David Truman succeeded in talking him down. Aware that ordering police onto campus would "in all probability destroy my usefulness hereafter as president," Kirk insisted on playing Creon, opting for an *Antigone*-like scenario that upheld the principle of his rule but which also spelled his own doom. Yet he also remained naive about the use of force, unaware of how little control he would have over the actions of the police once they had been summoned. And neither Kirk nor Truman "was present, observably present, on the campus," Trilling remarks, "when the police went into action."

How could Kirk have acted differently? The behavior of Kingman Brewster at Yale provides a counterexample. In 1968, when John Lindsay called Brewster for advice on the situation at Columbia, Brewster gave a Kirk-like response, telling New York's mayor that "the very future of the American university depended on punishing the strikers." Two years later, when the troubles came to Yale, Brewster acted quite differently, in part, no doubt, because he had learned from Kirk's example.

I was a graduating senior at Yale in the spring of 1970 when students began to agitate over the New Haven murder trial of Black Panther Bobby Seale. Brewster adopted a "loose bag" approach, falling back before student demands and incorporating as many as he could. He had the wit and the imagination to imagine with the young. After eleven of Yale's twelve residential colleges voted to go on strike, Brewster addressed a full faculty meeting and said, "I am skeptical of the ability of black revolutionaries to achieve a fair trial anywhere in the United States." In response, Vice President Spiro Agnew issued one of his calculated putdowns: "I do not feel that students of Yale University can get a fair impression of their country under the tutelage of Kingman Brewster."

Despite posters reading "Come to New Haven for a Burning on May Day," Brewster declared that the gates of the university would remain open. The *New York Times* then declared Yale a threat to the justice system of the United States. Chaplain William Sloane Coffin was so angered by an editorial titled "Murdering Justice" that he called *Times* columnist James Reston and said, "Frankly, you've got a horse's ass covering the thing up here." Coffin's longtime civil rights and antiwar activism positioned him so far ahead of all but the most radical students that none among them could claim that their parental figures had failed to imagine them. "Above all," Coffin writes in *Once to Every Man* (1978), Brewster "wanted to avoid what had happened at Columbia, Harvard and Cornell, where the universities, starting as bases for protest, had ended up as targets for it." So when over fifty thousand people poured into New Haven on the first weekend of May, the university stood ready to house and feed them, student marshals helped control crowds, the New Haven police chief maintained firm control over his men, and no one was seriously injured in the three days of demonstrations against the Seale trial that eventually merged with the nationwide reaction to Nixon's "This is not an invasion of Cambodia" speech.

As for the Columbia faculty, it found itself caught between an unpredictable student body and an intransigent administration. Those who formed the Ad Hoc Faculty Group on Thursday, April 25, called for a suspension of the gym project and agreed to interpose themselves between the police and the students. But the AHFG by no means represented the majority of Columbia's faculty, a teaching staff divided into sixteen separate entities, groups that usually communicated through their deans.

In "The Uprising at Columbia," F. W. Dupee supplies a good-natured account of one teacher's dilemma. A professor of English, Dupee was teaching a Shakespeare course in the spring of 1968. Once the strike started, he joined one of the buffering faculty patrols. "Politically, the patrolling was a delicate business. Physical nearness to the rebels brought us closer to them in sympathy, hardship for hardship, danger for danger." Faculty patrollers had become, he realized, "cop watchers." Dupee anticipated the coming raid, and resolved to put his body in the way. "It was as if I were two distinct persons, one of them almost stifling in the 'blackout' of his usual style, character, profession, identity; the other vaguely exulting in the strange feeling of freedom consequent upon the same feeling of loss." Dupee admits his liability to doubt, his capacity for self-surprise, and therefore to the possibility of *thinking* as Thoreau understands it—of being beside himself in a sane sense. Whatever blackout of identity he may have experienced, Dupee retains a strong enough sense of his usual style, however, so as to refrain from narrating the eventual bust. That story belongs, he knows, to the students. Instead he cuts away from the scene of violence and chooses to end his essay by jumping ahead to May 3, the day he returned to teaching *The Winter's Tale* in a room filled with students on crutches or wearing bandages and a teacher with a black eye.

Another faculty interposer stood on the morning of April 30 before the south entrance to Fayerweather Hall. Police had already entered the north entrance of the building, this unnamed "instructor" remembers, so a charge against "those of us who had placed ourselves at the south entrance . . . was clearly *unnecessary*." Uniformed police charged the faculty line nevertheless, and the instructor was thrown over a hedge. "Upon landing in the grass I was repeatedly kicked in the side." Crying out, "For God's sake how do I get out of here," he is answered with the words "Mother Fucker," and is again kicked and pushed to the ground. Similar testimony can be found in the 372 "Eyewitness Statements" quoted in *Police on Campus,* a report coauthored in 1969 by six scholars and lawyers on behalf of the New York Civil Liberties Union.

Faculty who stood with students took up their posts out of a variety of motives, and many, like Dupee, were deeply watchful selves. But far too many of the adults at Columbia spoke out against the bad behavior rather than attempting to imagine the sources of it, as when President Kirk was quoted as saying, on the front page of the *New York Times,* and with the newspaper's tacit approval, "My God, how could human beings do such a thing?" Noam Chomsky might have responded, "Only one totally lacking in judgment could find himself offended by 'student extremism' and not, to an immensely greater extent, by the events and situations that motivate it." By focusing on behavior rather than on the feelings sending it up, Kirk missed something important about the movement and betrayed as well a weak grasp of the fundamentals of parenting. As Todd Gitlin argues, "We are once and for all a *youth* movement, aiming to reform our elders, and if they will not reform, there is no alternative but to throw ourselves down on the floor and scream—to act, in fact, 'like children.'" The goal of such a movement lay in the call to mothers and fathers to become better parents. But adults can only successfully respond to such a call, Didion writes, if we have consented "to keep on nodding terms with the people we used to be." The people we all used to be, of course, were once "the young," and so the call, as ever, is to remain on nodding terms with the romantic hopes and dreams, however unfulfillable in the real world, of one's youthful self.

Something had been lost, surely, some faith in traditional "authority." Richard Hofstadter spoke to the dimensions of the loss in his 1968 Columbia University commencement address. "Here at Columbia, we have suffered a disaster whose precise dimensions it is impossible to state, because the story is not yet finished, and the measure of our loss depends upon what we do." Looking back across more than four decades, the "disaster" at Columbia appears to have been, in Mailer's formulation, a case of gain-through-loss. For what Columbia did in the following decades was what its brother institutions also did: it began to admit women; it altered its relation to the surrounding neighborhood; it divested in South Africa; it more actively recruited minority students; it created new systems of student participation in university governance; and it renewed its curriculum, participating in the dramatic expansion of the canon that was the central intellectual event of the aftermath years.

If it also found itself a "university in ruins," this was a fate Columbia shared with every other institution of higher learning and one that resulted from the end of the Cold War and the shift of federal resources away from university enterprises. As Bill Readings has shown, such diminishments were the result of global flows of power and capital that any nation's universities were largely powerless to resist. In his address, Hofstadter had spoken of the university as a "community" and "a kind of free forum," thereby affirming its traditional place and role. But "the realization of 1968," Readings reminds us, "is that the functioning of the University, the question of its role, is not a self-evident one."

And so the bust came. The action that began early on the morning of April 30 would prove to be the largest police arrest in the history of American campuses. The police faced some twelve hundred occupiers in five buildings; it was agreed that they would enter without their guns and wearing their ID badges. Mark Rudd was not in a building when the raid began, and, missing it all, he found himself on Broadway, "beside myself with anger and despair." In what he calls "a puny gesture," he chucked a brick through a post-office window.

While injuries were reported at Hamilton, Avery, Low, and Fayerweather Halls, it was in Mathematics, the "last building to fall," that things became most violent. At two in the morning, water and phone service to Mathematics were cut; both Hayden and Kunen were inside.

"A girl comes up to me with some paper towels. Take these, she says, so you can wipe the vaseline (slows tear-gas penetration) off your face when you're in jail." Kunen follows her advice, and then takes his place at the first barricade. He joins in singing "We Shall Not Be Moved" and realizes "that something is ending."

Kunen watches the police cut through the ropes and hoses. Then "they pull us apart and carry us out, stacking us like cord wood under a tree. The press is here so we are not beaten." Kunen glances up to see "kids looking down at us from every window in the building." The police, he thinks, will have to ax every door to get at those offices, and "They do."

At the 24th precinct, while being booked, Kunen meets Angus David, "who was on the sixth floor of Math and refused to walk down. He has been dragged down four flights of marble stairs and kicked and clubbed all the way. A two-inch square patch of his hair has been pulled out." At the tombs, Kunen shares a cell with protestors from Avery Hall. "They tell us how they were handcuffed and dragged down stairs on their stomachs. Their shirts are bloody."

Kunen's deadpan account of the bust can be compared with student testimonies from *Police on Campus*. One of these eyewitnesses was a student Kunen had seen looking down from the sixth floor of Mathematics. He recalled being "hit on the head and, while on the floor, kicked and hit out of the room." Another student waited in Room 611, while the police chopped through the door. After saying "I'll walk," he was "lifted by the hair by one policeman, struck several times on the back and sides," and finally found himself at the door of the room. After exiting the room, he was accused of hitting a cop, forced back in, and struck with nightsticks that fractured his jaw. The most serious injury of the entire action was suffered, however, by a policeman left permanently disabled by a student "falling or jumping on his back" in Fayerweather Hall.

Perhaps the most grievous injury suffered by a faculty member was not a bodily one. It occurred during the second wave of protests, in late May, when the papers of Professor Orest Ranum were burned during the reoccupation of Hamilton Hall. Ranum was the man who back in April had climbed, "like Batman," through a window in Low. His field was French history; in 1968 he published *Paris in the Age of Absolutism*.

An outspoken critic of the student strike, at one point Ranum referred to Mark Rudd as an "Ahab" forcing his crew to man a doomed *Pequod*. The fire that destroyed his papers remained something of a mystery until 2009, when Rudd revealed his knowledge of it in *Underground*. Just before the police broke into Hamilton, Rudd's friend John Jacobs told him he wanted to set a fire upstairs. "Okay, go ahead," Rudd answered. "I didn't know he was going to target Professor Ranum, but I suspect he knew exactly whose office he was breaking into. JJ hated hypocritical liberals, and the professor, who had tried to stop the original occupation of Low by saying he was sympathetic to our ends but not our means, had become an opponent of the strike." In the fire, McCaughey estimates, ten years of research were destroyed.

Hayden provides a muted account of the bust. He deals mostly with the anticipation of it, the lighting of candles, the locking of arms, the "visualizing" of police anger. When the violence comes, he gives it a paragraph. The police do their work with "ruthless efficiency." A paragraph later, he breaks off his Columbia narrative. "I took leave of my new friends the following day and tried to resume my focus on preparing for Chicago." He makes no mention of the fact of any arrest. "Like the Lone Ranger," Kunen writes, "he didn't even wave good-bye, but quietly slipped away, taking his silver protest buttons to another beleaguered campus."

"In any retelling of the events at Columbia," Mark Rudd argued forty years later, "the African-American students should have been central." Rudd did not, however, directly experience one of the key moments in the strike, when white students were asked to leave Hamilton Hall. Mark Naison was among those expelled, and his memoir *White Boy* not only brings black students to the center of the story but chronicles Naison's ability to carve a workable future out of that bitter spring.

Naison was born in the Crown Heights section of Brooklyn in 1946. In 1959 he enrolled in Wingate High, where he became caught up in "an uneasy experiment in racial diversity." Seventy percent of the Wingate student population was Jewish, ten percent Italian, and the rest made up of black students whose families had begun pushing out of a decaying Bedford-Stuyvesant. These black students "carried themselves very differently from the black kids I grew up with," Naison recalls, displaying a racial cohesion, a street slang, and a stylish mode of dress. After their son was drawn into a fight with a "lanky six footer," Naison's parents transferred him to Erasmus Hall, then the largest high school in the country.

The irony of Naison's removal is that he himself was determined to stay. From an early age, Naison had found a kind of freedom in playing out his identity along the color line. As a boy, he became a sports fan and athlete,

partly in reaction against his parents' intellectualism. He was fascinated by
rock and roll. Both passions, he came to see, were integrated activities, "open
to people of every background who possessed the requisite talent. For our
generation, part of becoming American was becoming culturally 'black.'"

When Naison entered Columbia in the fall of 1962, his class of 660
contained six African Americans. Reading James Baldwin's *Another Country*
(1952) made him realize that "none of my black teammates"—Naison had
maintained his devotion to basketball—"had ever talked to me honestly about
how racial discrimination affected them." In his sophomore year, Naison
joined CORE and began organizing in Harlem, where he found "admirable
people trapped in intolerable conditions."

In his senior year, Naison "became romantically involved with an African-
American woman and found myself violating one of the most powerful racial
taboos in the United States." Despite the stiff resistance of his parents, he
and Ruthie remained companions for six years. During that time Naison
was fully integrated into Ruthie's family.

As the Black Power movement gathered steam, Mark and Ruthie began
to feel an increased sense of "social responsibility" and so also began to
comport themselves "as a team of social workers." At the same time, the
emergent premium on "blackness" began to exclude Naison, and he came
to long for an "interracial DMZ." The metaphor of a demilitarized zone
suggests that, for Naison, issues of racial justice were becoming entangled
with his growing sense of resistance to the war.

In the fall of 1966, Naison began graduate work in history at Columbia.
His master's thesis focused on an interracial sharecroppers' union founded
in Arkansas during the Depression. At the same time, he "started working
with several community organizations seeking to prevent Columbia from
constructing a new gymnasium in Morningside Park." The fear was that the
project might be the first step in a university strategy to transform Harlem
into a middle-class neighborhood. He threw himself into radical politics
and joined SDS.

So it was that Naison eventually found himself among a group of students trying to tear down a chain-link fence at the gym construction site.
He was also at the sundial rally for the confused series of marches ending in
the occupation of Hamilton Hall. Once inside, Naison joined in the initial
salvo of speeches "describing the many unsuccessful efforts by community
organizations and CORE to prevent Columbia from displacing low-income
residents in Morningside Heights."

While for Mark Rudd the "gym issue" may have been a "manufactured" one, an admission he made in a speech given in Boston in the fall of 1968, the situation was quite real for Naison, growing as it did out of a lifetime of being "race conscious." It therefore came as a considerable shock when, returning to Hamilton after a dinner run, he found that all the white occupiers had been expelled. Back at his apartment, he learned that Ruthie had been asked to join the Hamilton demonstration—without him. "I felt devastated by her departure."

Part of Naison's appeal comes from his refusal of bitterness when it offers itself as a convenient emotion. Admitting to the resentments that are experienced, he refrains from generalizing them into a dismissive critique. In the days that followed his expulsion, Naison joined the logistical force bringing food and messages to the occupied buildings. "The racially bifurcated character of this protest raised some difficult issues for me," he writes, especially since he realized it had the power to shatter his relationship with Ruthie. "I respected the Black Power movement but also regarded it with profound ambivalence." The peculiar value of Naison's memoir lies not only in his honest admission of a radical ambivalence—his own way of being beside himself in a sane sense—but in its depiction of the strike at Columbia as a poignant chapter in the history or race relations in his country.

The administration eventually made "a separate deal" with the black students in Hamilton, and they exited the building through underground tunnels and emerged unharmed, "just before the New York police moved in on the other four buildings." When the occupiers were "violently dispersed . . . , almost no African-Americans became involved in the mayhem." The Columbia administration, Naison reasoned, had ended the occupation without provoking riots in Harlem, and, in so doing, had managed to divide the student community along racial lines. "Separate treatment of blacks," Dupee speculated, also had something to do with their having left Hamilton "neat as a pin."

Despite the divisions resulting from the strike, Naison remained committed to living his life in "multiracial settings." In doing so, he had to resist an SDS in which "guilt about whiteness" had become a "primary motivating force." Trapped in "an ideological and emotional whirlwind," his closest friends adopted a new political strategy assuming the possibility of black-led revolution and began calling themselves Weatherman. Naison and a female member of the collective posed as husband and wife in order to rent a group house in Brooklyn's Prospect Park. "Machismo and physical aggressiveness" became increasingly fashionable within Weatherman, and "the women," Naison notes, became "the driving force in this transformation."

Deciding that monogamy must be "smashed," the collective judged Mark and Ruthie's relationship to be in violation of the new policy. After barely surviving a group criticism session, Naison decided that he was finally out of Weatherman. "It was time for me to face the limits of my political commitments and advance the causes I espoused in ways that seemed more practical and safe."

Naison turned back at the moment when many members of SDS did not. In the summer of 1969, as a result of a doctrinal dispute at its national convention, a group including Bill Ayers, Bernadine Dohrn, John Jacobs, and Mark Rudd split off from SDS and formed Weatherman. In defining its mission as "revolutionary anti-imperialism," Weatherman's advocacy of armed struggle reached beyond national boundaries, as Jeremy Varon has shown, linking up with movements like West Germany's Red Army Faction. Weatherman thus set out to become "a fighting force" in a world "on fire." "We meant to learn to fight through fighting," Ayers writes in *Fugitive Days*, "moving from small to large, developing skill and experience, growing in strength and power through the practice of revolution."

"A striking number of Weathermen participated in the rebellion" at Columbia, Varon points out, "whether as students or as agitators from the outside." "Weatherman grew directly out of Columbia," as Mark Rudd later claimed, but its cells could soon be found "almost everywhere." "At the close of the sixties," Susan Stern remembers, "SDS was like a big family spread across America. You could travel almost anywhere, and you would have an enclave of friends who would welcome you. You always had a place to crash, some food, some dope, and some sex." Stern stayed with Weatherman as it moved underground following the Days of Rage action in Chicago, in 1969, and her "Personal Journey of a Revolutionary Woman" provides a vivid account of living out that choice.

The tension between being both a "revolutionary" and a "woman" runs throughout Stern's narrative. Her sexual appetites and her desire for an exclusive partnership with a man continually came up against the call to smash monogamy. Moving into a Weather house in Seattle, she agreed to do so only if allowed to continue sleeping with her boyfriend, Garrity, who lived across the street. Unable to ignore the claims on her of "a body named Susan Stern," her *With the Weathermen* testifies to the persistence of female will in a movement seeking to transcend traditional identity formations.

"The inexperience of the women" as actors and leaders emerges as one of Stern's most urgent subjects. "Part of the problem with Columbia SDS, and everywhere else, was that it was operating at 50 per cent of its potential. Women were almost systematically excluded from anything but a secondary role."

As early as 1965, in the year she divorced her husband, Tom, Casey Hayden had made similar claims about her work for SNCC in a "memo" called "Sex and Caste." "There seem to be many parallels that can be drawn between treatment of Negroes and treatment of women in our society," she wrote, conditions which force them to "work around or outside hierarchical structures of power." In *Ready from Within* (1986), another activist, Septima Clark, was to identify "the way men looked at women" as "one of the weaknesses of the civil rights movement." And Marge Piercy, in her 1969 essay "The Grand Coolie Damn," observed that if in the movement "the rewards are concentrated at the top, the shitwork is concentrated at the bottom," with that work being done by a "largely unpaid, largely female work force." She wrote of herself as a "house nigger" and a "slow learner," and of the common practice of "fucking a staff into existence." "A man can bring a woman into an organization by sleeping with her and remove her by ceasing to do so." "Only a woman willing and able to act like a stereotyped American frontier male," Piercy argued, "can make herself heard."

Bernadine Dohrn was such a woman. A cheerleader at her Milwaukee high school, Dohrn received a J.D. from the University of Chicago Law School in 1967. At the 1969 SDS convention, she led the walkout resulting in the formation of Weatherman. Dohrn was a charismatic speaker and the leader of the women's phalanx as it charged through the streets of Chicago. She soon made the FBI's Most Wanted List; J. Edgar Hoover called her "la Pasionaria of the Lunatic Left."

Stern met Dohrn in New York in the fall of 1968. "She was not so much beautiful as she was commanding; there was something in the way she carried herself that exuded authority." Stern was awed by the way Dohrn "spoke and moved; such control, such self-assurance, such elegance. She immediately became a symbol of what I hoped to become. At the same time I felt helplessly inadequate in the face of all that splendor."

Stern never overcame her felt sense of inadequacy, despite her assault on a policeman in Chicago and the repeated sexual buccaneering that earned her the ultimate sanction: she was too "individual." She often go-go danced in order to support her commune. "My lips were parted for the revolution; my heart beating, my blood racing, and my tongue ready to pour out endless homage to it. And I didn't understand a damn thing about the revolution, and failed it miserably." At one point, on a Seattle bedroom wall, Stern painted "an eight-foot tall nude woman with flowing green-blond hair, and a burning

American flag coming out of her cunt." By way of this self-portrait, Stern imaged herself as "tall and blond, nude and armed, consuming—or discharging—a burning America."

Stern's power as a writer comes from her uncensored physicality; her body is both the crossroads of her experience and the calendar on which change is registered. It never leaves her alone; at her 1970 trial for conspiracy, a swollen Bartholin gland caused her such pain that she could not sit up in the courtroom. Bill Ayers's *Fugitive Days* operates, by contrast, more on the level of metaphor and idea. What he shares with Stern is a hysterical style.

"I ran and I ran," Ayers writes, about the Days of Rage, echoing Stern's "I ran and ran." "Wait a minute," his opening sentence pleads, as if he might stop time and go back to the moment before he receives the telephone call about the explosion, the call bringing the news that his girlfriend, Diana Oughton, and friends Ted Gold and Jerry Robbins have been killed while building a bomb in a Greenwich Village townhouse. Now the real running begins; "I am running for my life, but I don't know where I'm going." Ayers's narrative never recovers from its initial breathlessness. But the 1970 explosion in New York City simply reinforces a process long since under way, his response to a movement which "swept us away completely because it demanded everything of us, and because it offered everything to us—high purpose, real work to do, love, dreams, hope." Being so caught up, so swept away by a force greater than himself, Ayers trades the fact of agency for a sense of urgency; his is a world of "zinging" incentives, "crystal chaos," chest-striking "thunderbolts." He seeks above all "to hold on to this heightened feeling of ruin."

The infrequency of time markers in their prose, combined with an unvarying melodramatic tone, leaves Stern and Ayers stranded in a sense of the continuous present. *"There seems so little continuity in my story,"* Ayers admits. Whether or not this is conscious achievement, it makes for an exhausting reading experience. But it is also an illuminating one, since it suggests how little politics really matters to either writer and conveys instead the longing for that "elusive moment" each is seeking, an ingathering of time and history in a continual "high." The impulse in both narratives is to resist mindfulness and to reach beyond thought toward the condition of racing blood.

But Stern is much more forthcoming than Ayers, willing to reveal her doubts and failures and to be concrete. While reading her, we come to know her specific location and its material conditions, the way people talk, the extent of her awkward urges. Ayers is more likely to retreat into an inexpressibility topos, as in "I cannot reproduce the stifling atmosphere that overpowered us." This inability to "reproduce" experience lends *Fugitive Days* a sense of missed opportunity and may also account for its mixed reception on publication, when a number of critics judged it to be at once idealizing and evasive.

Stern's story ends badly; after her first trial in 1970, she will undergo a series of arrests and releases on charges varying from assault to jaywalking. She began writing her memoir in 1972 while being held in jail for contempt of court. After her release she did months of research throughout the country, locating leaflets and newspapers and conducting over thirty interviews. She even read *The Strawberry Statement.* Doubleday published her book in 1975; a year later Stern was dead at thirty-three, suffering irreversible brain damage following cardiac arrest. According to her death certificate, Stern's heart attack occurred after "drug & alcohol ingestion."

Ayers stayed underground until 1980. Over the years he participated in the bombing of the New York City Police Department headquarters, the Capitol building in Washington, and the Pentagon. By the time he and Dohrn emerged from hiding they were the married parents of two children. A year after resurfacing they adopted Chesa Boudin, whose parents were serving life sentences for attempted robbery and murder. Federal conspiracy charges against Ayers and Dohrn were dropped because of governmental misconduct arising out of the FBI's COINTELPRO operation. Ayers went back to school, earning an Ed.D. from Columbia in 1987. He became a professor of education at the University of Illinois in Chicago and was named its Citizen of the Year for his work on public school reform. Dohrn became an adjunct professor at the Northwestern University School of Law. In 2002, Chesa Boudin, raised by Ayers and Dohrn, was named a Rhodes scholar.

A decade before Ayers and Dohrn returned to the world, Mark Naison began the shift so many activists of his generation were thereafter to make, away from dreams rooted in utopian universals and toward a recommitment to the local. Hired by Fordham's Institute for Afro-American Studies in the spring of 1970, he set out to make a career there. The only white member of the institute, Naison resolved to finish his dissertation and to abandon armed struggle. It was time, as one of his advisers told him, to become a "*helpful*" figure" instead of a "*machismo*" one.

Over the next thirty years, Naison dove deep into the great adventure of bringing a repressed or forgotten past back into the classroom. The incorporation of African American history and literature into the national narrative was a work that caused the canon to expand, not to explode. Interests were, of course, inevitably threatened, and Naison's program eventually encountered the "growing hostility of Fordham's faculty." In response, he and his colleagues instituted a "tough new writing policy." With term papers, "literary quality" was now to be factored into a final grade. As all this happened, the burning of the South Bronx began, and Naison watched an entire region of the city disappear.

After his eventual separation from Ruthie, Naison met and married Liz Phillips, a white woman. As the country began its swing toward the right, in the seventies and eighties, enrollments in his program began to drop. Financial aid was frozen for minority students. In 1976, after fighting off efforts to dissolve the institute back into existing departments, Naison saw it become the department of Afro-American Studies, the only independent black studies department at a private university in the New York City area. In 2005, he published *Communists in Harlem in the Depression*. For a while, it looked as if Fordham was doomed to become "a white island in a black and brown sea," but, in the nineties, after a more proactive admissions policy and some inspired hires, as well as renewed community outreach, Naison once again found himself surrounded by students of all colors "who were risk-takers and adventurers."

One consequence of student "battles," James Patterson notes in *Grand Expectations,* was that "Black Studies programs began to proliferate." For a historian who also characterizes student activists as "spoiled brats," this is no small admission. Naison's memoir gives life to Patterson's claim, and reminds us of one of the clear social goods to come out of the sixties. African Americans had won full legal equality in 1964 and 1965, with the passage of the Civil Rights and Voting Rights acts. They had done so largely through their own efforts, and with some white help. But the much more complicated goal of social equality lay generations in the future. It was a work that could only proceed after the nation had consented to participate in a vast project of historical recovery, one spearheaded by humanities departments like Naison's. His is a story of the gains that resulted from campus unrest, of a man who opened himself to the experience of violent radicalism and who integrated it into a commitment to the immediate problems of his home ground as well as to the opportunities for soul-making available within any academic career.

9

Nixon and Occupatio

"I was born in a house my father built," *RN* begins. The theme of self-making and the self-built threads its way through much of what Richard Nixon did and wrote. In his ongoing act of self-fashioning through words—no American president since Theodore Roosevelt had been so prolific an author—the place of origin, figured in the opening sentence of the memoirs as a house, plays an inescapable part. Nixon was above all a Californian and, more specifically, a product of the working- and middle-class suburbs of Los Angeles. It was to California that he was forced to return, after the three crucial setbacks of his adult life, and it was his struggle to transcend these origins that also endowed him with a capacity to empathize with those he attempted and failed to leave behind.

This story can be refigured as "the loss of the East." The first loss occurred in 1930, when, after being accepted by Harvard and Yale, Nixon found he could not afford the Ivy League and so settled instead on Whittier College. (During the House Un-American Activities Committee hearings, Alger Hiss said to Nixon: "I graduated from Harvard, I heard your school was Whittier.") Seven years later, in the months following graduation from law school at Duke, a failed New York job search ended in a decision to head home. "He really had no choice but to return to Whittier," Herbert Parmet writes. In 1961, after the loss to Kennedy, Nixon sold his Washington, D.C., home and moved, before setting up house with Pat near Bel Air, into a bachelor apartment on Wilshire Boulevard. "It was not an easy time," the memoir admits. Finally, in August 1974, in the final act of the Watergate scandal, the helicopter "began to rise" off the White House lawn. It flew low "next to the Washington Monument," Nixon continues. "Another swing," he writes in the final sentence of *RN,* "and we were on course for Andrews, where *Air Force One* was waiting for the flight home to California."

No one who has not made the transit from West to East can fully understand the persistent sense of out-of-placeness and even impostorhood such a motion can entail. Like Nixon, I too headed east as a young man. Arriving in New Haven in 1966 with a three-piece herringbone suit purchased at May Company, I found a student body in rebellion against the very "coat and tie rule" that had marked Yale as desirable and distinct. One felt the twoness: a Californian, a Yalie. At Virginia, in my first teaching job, I decided to begin reading the writers from my home state. The book I eventually published may have won the university's 1987 book prize, but by then I had been denied tenure, for many reasons, surely, but in part because for some of my colleagues a literary history of California did not quite fit in. They looked on Steinbeck, Chandler, and Snyder, in Edmund Wilson's dismissive title, as *The Boys in the Back Room.*

"I am part of that," Nick Carraway says in *The Great Gatsby.* By "that" he means the Middle West, the place he came from. Nick's journey, like Nixon's, and my own, reverses the American myth of "westering." In that story, as in *Two Years before the Mast, The Overland Trail, Roughing It,* and *On the Road,* the eastern "greenhorn" heads west in order to renew his health, gain an education, and grow into manhood. For a Californian, or a Minnesotan, the pattern is necessarily reversed. To be born *west* is to be required to go east, where one is then tested by the "establishment." (As early as 1952, H. R. Haldeman saw Nixon as "fighting against odds, and the establishment.") To go east can also prove, as it did for Nick Carraway, an experience of disillusionment. "When I came back from the East last autumn," he tells us, "I felt that I wanted the world to be in uniform and at a sort of moral attention forever." Nick returns west voluntarily, while Nixon did not, and, by the time of his last forced return to California, he had become the source of the very disillusionment from which Nick feels it necessary to flee. For all Nixon's success at triumphing over the East, he remained, finally, a man of the West, a perpetual outsider even as he occupied the very center of American power.

As he attempted to make his way beyond his home place, Nixon remained firmly identified with it, especially since "the crisis of the self-made," as Garry Wills calls it, describes quite accurately the experience that unfolded in Southern California during the decades in which Nixon rose to power. Between the years in which the region had been settled and built up, and the year of Nixon's election to the presidency, a huge and terrifying shift had occurred, one that threatened much of what had been gained by the "first home producers," like Nixon's father, who had constructed in the various towns that made up Los Angeles their version of the good life.

Nixon's maternal grandfather left Indiana for California in the 1890s and helped found the Quaker colony of Whittier. Intending to build his own home there, he brought with him doors, window frames, and lumber. In Whittier he built his house and planted an orange grove. The pattern repeated itself in the next generation, when Frank Nixon married Franklin Milhouse's daughter Hannah, bought a lemon ranch in Yorba Linda, and built a two-story frame house. "Our life in Yorba Linda was hard but happy," Nixon maintains, and the word "hard" reverberates through the chapter he titles "Early Years." It was in that house that the young Richard was sometimes awakened "by the whistle of a train," and then "dreamed of the far-off places I wanted to visit someday."

When Richard was nine, Frank Nixon moved his family to Whittier and built a second house, a clapboard on South Painter Street. A few years later he opened a gasoline station and did well enough to have an old church building moved to his lot and converted into a general store. Hannah Nixon supplied the store with homemade pies priced at thirty-five cents each. The family kept so busy that it rarely met for meals. Richard worked in the store through college, rising at 4 a.m. to drive into Los Angeles and select produce at the farmer's market. "My father had a deep belief in the 'little man' in America," Nixon later recalled, and "for those who were willing to work hard, California in the 1920s seemed a place and time of almost unlimited opportunity."

The Nixon family story can stand in for the larger story told by Becky Nicolaides in *My Blue Heaven: Life and Politics in the Working-Class Suburbs of Los Angeles, 1920–1965* (2002). The end date of her study is overdetermined rather than arbitrary; it is the year of the Watts riots. Nicolaides opens her book with the following scene: "On a warm August night in 1965, the white residents of South Gate stood guard over their beloved homes. Yards away across the railroad tracks in Watts, African-American anger was raging in one of the worst urban riots of the decade. Fires were searing, store windows were shattering, and unsuspecting whites found themselves the targets of violence. In South Gate, residents puzzled over this outburst. Why, they wondered, such an uncontrolled display of anger? In their minds, nothing warranted such behavior." In *Five Fires* (1997), I wrote about the swift transit, in South Central, from a sense of somnolence to the fact of violence. Watts, like Lynwood and Compton, towns where my parents grew up and where I was born, appeared outwardly, until the mid-sixties, to be calm and even boringly stable places. How was it that an uprising began in a city in which many blacks had been able to purchase modest single-family homes and in a "riot area" which the McCone Commission report described as having streets "wide and usually quite clean," with "trees, parks, and playgrounds"? One answer, as we have seen, was supplied by Nathan Cohen's analysis of "the structure of discontent," concluding that discontent increases as social contact increases. Rising incomes and expectations among blacks intensified frustration and anger. Watts had the highest population density of any area in Los Angeles County, and African Americans struggling to move out from it quickly came up against all that they did not yet possess. In the cruel logic of Cohen's well-supported conclusions, to rise, it began to seem, was also to fall.

There were of course specific local causes behind the rebellion in Watts. Since the passage of *Brown*, Los Angeles communities had been engaged in massive resistance to school desegregation. Jordan High School in Watts was 99 percent black in 1963, while South Gate High, only a mile away, was 97 percent white. When civil rights groups demanded that school boundaries be redrawn in order to achieve integration, white residents organized the South Gate Education Committee and presented the Board of Education with 17,500 signatures decrying "social experimentation." Appropriating the language of the rights movement, the SGEC claimed to be upholding "the 'rights' of the suburb's children." The campaign succeeded, and South Gate's schools remained unintegrated. Meanwhile, the Rumford Fair Housing Act, passed in 1963 in order to end discrimination in housing throughout California, was repealed a year later in a statewide initiative. In South Gate, 87.5 percent of voters supported Proposition 14. In that year, in the once solidly Democratic 23rd Congressional District, which included South Gate, Compton, Lynwood, Bell, Vernon, and Downey, a Republican candidate won 55 percent of the vote. So began a shift in voting patterns that would reveal South Gate to be "a haven of the 'silent majority.'"

Four years later, South Gate would vote 48 percent for Richard Nixon, 40.7 percent for Hubert Humphrey, and 11 percent for George Wallace. South Gaters meant to defend the right "to control the integrity of their property and their capacity to benefit from its value," but white flight had already begun, and, by 1990, the city would be 83 percent Latino, and many people there, like the enterprising settlers of the 1920s, would again be living in garages.

So the structure of white discontent took a shape not unlike the structure of black discontent: somehow to win was also to lose. Those men standing in front of their hard-won homes, looking up at a sky filling up with smoke, were men who would from that day forward become, as Joan Didion calls them, "the secret frontiersmen" of an emerging social movement. They were fighting, they believed, for their way of life, and their defeat only led them on into a cultural holding action I have called the "Reaction."

South Gate is located about seven miles west of Whittier and never aspired to the gentility that marked the Quaker settlement, a place my father recalls as being a sort of "snob-hollow." Nicolaides describes instead a pattern of settlement and development in which immigrants from the Middle West and the Great Plains bought generously sized lots, slowly built their own houses—sometimes living in a garage while doing so—turned their homes into sites "of domestic production," raised produce and animals in the back yard, found jobs in the town's tire and chemical factories, or nearby, in the Central Manufacturing District, and gradually established a way of life not dependent on welfare capitalism. None of these homes was especially expensive or fancy; in 1924 a two-room house and a garage on a 60' x 130' lot was offered for $1,200. This was a working class world in which "the center of gravity . . . had shifted away from the workplace to life outside of work." Nothing signified identity so much as one's home, and it was, in most of the towns in the region except for Watts, a white identity, one shored up by deed restrictions "against occupancy by non-Caucasians." The mentality that grew up in such places is described by Nicolaides as one embracing "self-reliance, independence, Americanism, familism, and racial separation."

In 1926, when my father was two years old, his family moved from Manitou, Oklahoma, to Lynwood, California. Lynwood borders South Gate on the west. The Wyatt family settled on an acre of land not far from the Los Angeles River. A relatively wealthy man, my grandfather contracted out the building of a white stucco three-bedroom house. Three years later he lost his bank in the Wall Street crash. Then he did what his neighbors in South Gate did: he lived off his land. The orchard behind the house provided apricots, peaches, plums, lemons, and persimmons. My grandfather built 24' x 24' redwood coops and started raising chickens. When the business failed, he turned to raising worms. Like Nixon driving to the produce market, my father's brothers did a circuit once a week, selling cans of red worms to hardware stores all over Southern California.

The six Wyatt children stayed close to home, settling in the nearby towns of Compton, Lakewood, and Long Beach, or moving a little further away, as my father eventually did, to San Bernardino. After my grandfather's death in 1939 my grandmother stayed in the house on "the Acre," as the family called it, until the early 1950s, when she sold the land to the state. Today, the Acre is under the Long Beach Freeway.

My father remembers quite well the day the Watts riots began. He was at the Los Angeles Furniture Mart, a few miles northwest of Watts as the crow flies. He looked out the window from a high floor and "saw something that has never been understood—I saw a very organized method of burning down a city. If you drew a forty-five degree line across Watts and extended it north, it would hit Beverly Hills. I saw a fire start here, and everybody rushing to that. And then there was big jump, and it would start over there, but in that same forty-five degree line. And then they came back, and started another one by the first one."

On reading this, one might take my father to be one of the resenters. As far as I can tell, however, his observations are voiced more out of awe than bitterness. They do express a casual and lifelong racism that also coexists with a much more powerful and lifelong commitment to social justice. My father knew as he watched the smoke billowing up that he had nothing personally to fear, apart from the question of which might be the safest road home. By the time he looked out the Furniture Mart window, he had moved his family out of Los Angeles. But my maternal grandmother was still living in Compton, and my father's brother Bill owned a very successful manufacturing company, Wyatt Automatics, in South Gate, so the family was not entirely out of harm's way.

My father was, I suppose, the "little man" Nixon writes about, an artist who started business after business, went bankrupt twice, and kept making a modest living with his hands until retiring in his early seventies. Given the threat to his family's home place that the riots represented, as well as the complete loss of those landscapes as white flight transformed them into "South Central" during the 1970s and 80s, the question becomes: Why did he not also become one of the foot soldiers of the Reaction?

As with so much in life, it comes down to how one takes things. My aim is not to analyze the sources of resistance that prevented my father, a lifelong Democrat, from becoming a Republican. It is rather simply to point out that the politics of resentment, a politics fed in California, as elsewhere, largely by racial fears and anxieties, was something it was possible to resist. Nixon saw that the growing resentment was founded on something valuable and real, a cherishing of home and of a sustaining, if limited, "way of life." His decision to capitalize on these feelings rather than to counter racial tensions was, as well, his own free choice.

But of course the choice was conditioned by Nixon's repeated "loss of the East," and by a liability to resentment that had started long before that. As the biographers agree, Nixon was from an early age "painfully conscious of slights and failures." "What starts the process, really," Nixon once told an aide, "are laughs and slights and snubs when you are a kid." Stanley Kutler sees a Nixon who "thrived on conflict, conflict that ineluctably resulted from a lifetime of accumulated resentments." In 1950, Senator Robert Taft applied the word that would stick: "vindictive." Nixon's genius was to merge his private history of humiliation with the sense of loss and bewilderment felt by the "little people" from which he sprang, "all those," as Joan Didion writes, "who have felt themselves not merely shocked but personally betrayed by recent history."

In order to speak to this sense of betrayal in 1968, "the code phrase 'crime in the streets' that had been coined to encourage white backlash in the Goldwater campaign of 1964 now was refined to 'law and order.'" The phrase functioned as a metonymy: on hearing it, the mind was meant to take "law and order" as standing in for its anxieties about race. The sequence of association is made apparent in Nixon's August acceptance speech, in which a sentence citing "unprecedented lawlessness" is followed by one about "unprecedented racial violence." By invoking "law and order," Nixon was able to address the fears of his constituents without speaking directly about them. After making the error of taking the president "literally" during their first interview, Henry Kissinger "learned that to Nixon words were like billiard balls; what mattered was not the initial impact but the carom."

"To deny that he was saying what he was saying," Stephen Ambrose writes, was a favorite Nixon tactic. In classical rhetoric this device is known as *occupatio,* a move in which a speaker emphasizes something by pretending to pass over it. Nixon's October 26 statement about the Johnson administration's attempts to begin peace talks provides a striking example of the device in action. "I am . . . told that this spurt of activity is a cynical, last-minute attempt by President Johnson to salvage the candidacy of Mr. Humphrey. This I do not believe." For a master of occupatio, there is a calibrated slippage between expression and intent.

Nixon's habit of playing devil's advocate with himself became his own private form of occupatio. William Safire noted the pattern in Nixon's speech: Nixon "would argue against his finer impulses from time to time, using whatever aide was present as a sounding board, and in that convoluted way talk himself around." A famous instance of the case is Nixon's proposing to offer payoffs to the Watergate burglars in order to keep them quiet, and his then saying, as if directly to the taping system hidden in the Oval Office, "But that would be wrong."

Or, at least, this is the myth that has come down to us. Fred Emery corrects the record, while further complicating it. Nixon's then chief of staff, H. R. Haldeman, having just listened to the March 21 tape, came to Nixon and told him that "if [John] Dean ever testified about the [E. Howard] Hunt payoff, Haldeman would testify that Nixon had said, 'but that would be wrong.'" Here, Haldeman adopted his boss's verbal habit, supplying him with a nice bit of occupatio. In fact, "Nixon had not said this, at least not in regard to the payoff; he had said, 'it would be wrong' about eventual clemency, as Nixon well knew, and as Haldeman's own notes of the tape faithfully record." To whom, then, were such proposings and un-proposings addressed? And which phase of the transaction expressed what was really wanted—the fantasy entertained, or the eventual repudiation of it?

Occupatio is a time-honored rhetorical strategy that announces itself fairly openly to be a calculated act of persuasion. There is nothing venal about using language in this way; one could in fact argue that it displays a sophisticated understanding that to speak any "meaning" in words is to engage in an act of displacement. The practice became complicated in Nixon's case, however, when it was routinely deployed to further his pretension to straight shooting. The experience provided by his memoir is a case in point. To read *RN* is to become immersed in a plain style so unwilling to question or to play with its own tones and assertions as to make one wonder whether Nixon has any awareness of its highly skilled rhetorical manipulations.

Nixon writes, for instance, that in June 1968 his campaign advisers analyzed his "performance" in formal and informal situations and "decided that the more spontaneous the situation, the better I came across." Yet virtually all of his encounters with the public were staged. Some twenty pages after making the claim about spontaneity, Nixon describes a four-hour telethon held the day before the election. "Bud Wilkinson acted as moderator, reading the questions to me as they were phoned in from across the country." His advisers had opposed the telethon as a costly and tiring effort, but, Nixon concludes, "it was my best campaign decision. Had we not had that last telethon, I believe Humphrey would have squeaked through with a close win on Election Day."

As Jules Witcover recounts, the telethon was anything but spontaneous. Questions phoned in were passed to Nixon staffers, "who then put them aside and substituted others written by the staff and on the same subjects in ways that would best serve the candidate. The substitute questions were then presented on the air by friendly moderator Bud Wilkinson, attaching to them the names of the posers of the original questions."

To call this "lying" is to miss the point. Nixon did not consciously set out to tell untruths. The practice of the years had developed in him an acute sense of what might be at once self-promoting and self-protective. His assumption that he meant well, and that he was a man in the arena "standing up for what he believed," simply tabled the question of mendacity. This performance connected with a "something unadmitted" in much of his audience, a swelling rage that excused—that did not even apprehend—Nixon's failures of feeling. Thus, as Melvin Small argues about Nixon's 1952 Checkers speech, "most political commentators missed the fact that the performance they perceived as mawkish and maudlin played very well with the average American viewer." This viewer did not object to mention of Pat's "respectable Republican cloth coat" or to "our little girl" Tricia and her "little cocker spaniel dog." The imagined listeners heard a man "who shared their own feelings, thought as they thought, and valued what they valued."

The differing responses to the Checkers speech, and to Nixon's entire career, form part of America's long and complex history with the "sentimental." According to James Joyce, sentimentality is the desire to enjoy without acknowledging the immense debtorship for a thing done. The thing done, in this case, would be the having of a feeling. But having feelings is a risky business, one often fraught with soul-stretching pain. Avoiding this, while knowing it to be a supreme part of being alive, a sentimental person lays claim to emotions that are unfelt; he wishes to "enjoy" the claim of being capable of something he has refused to pay the price of acquiring.

Nixon may have set out to perform sincerity in the Checkers speech, but the sheer excess of its language and emotion argues for a man who had suspended disbelief in the artificiality of the performance. The entire career can be seen, from this perspective, as an act of occupatio, and the question becomes to what extent Nixon himself was taken in by it. This self-alienation passing itself off as integrity proved in any case to have broad and revealing appeal. As Norman Mailer observed while watching Nixon's arrival in Miami, "there had been a gap between the man who spoke and the man who lived behind the speaker which offered every clue of schizophrenia in the American public if they failed to recognize the void within the presentation."

The gap between the man who spoke and the man who lived behind the speaker surfaced repeatedly in Nixon's lifelong habit of referring to himself in the third person. "I see another child tonight," he ventured, at the end of his 1968 acceptance speech, and of course the child is Richard Nixon, a "he" who "stands before you." Thinking back on his unlikely alliance with Henry Kissinger, he writes of "the grocer's son from Whittier." The "diary" he kept in the Oval Office slips easily between the word "I" and phrases like "the effort to get the President." Perhaps Nixon's most notorious public usage of the third person occurred in his press conference after losing the race for the governorship of California, when he reassured the press that "you won't have Nixon to kick around anymore."

During the 1968 campaign the phrase "law and order" was most strongly associated with George Wallace, the third-party candidate from Alabama. Wallace provided Nixon with cover on the right until he was able to recruit his own surrogate for him in the person of Spiro Agnew. Not himself much interested in speaking in code, Wallace promised to greet "anarchists" with "a good crease in the skull." The historian Alan Brinkley later played down the subject of Wallace and race: "Very few people were willing to take literally what he was talking about, which was law and order, long-haired demonstrators, pointy-headed intellectuals and bureaucrats—a cruder form of the right-wing rhetoric of the next twenty-five years. Race was certainly part of the message, but it wasn't the whole message." It was nevertheless difficult at the time to dissociate the man who spoke of "the so-called civil rights laws" from the governor who in 1963 had stood in the schoolhouse door as admitted black students attempted to attend class at the University of Alabama. Wallace was simply acting on his 1958 pledge: "I'm not going to be out-niggered again."

At a Wallace rally in Baltimore, Garry Wills watched a man skilled at connecting with a "vague unlocalized resentment." Wills sensed in the crowd an upwelling of status anxiety; the kids in the street were making a "mockery" of one's little life. "The desire for 'law and order' is nothing so simple as a code word for racism; it is a cry, as things begin to break up, for stability, for stopping history in mid-dissolution." The people cheering for Wallace are angry not "that kids are screwing in the parks, but that they *proclaimed* they were doing so." "Why *not* get away with it," such behavior asks. "And the parents had no answer. That was what brought out cruelty in the solid burghers of America"—to have their lives disdained. "They had 'done everything for their children'—except answer them. And that failure was enough to undo all they had done. They are angry not so much at their children as at themselves for failing the children." And the children, "taught to doubt, far from defending their parents' way of life, question it with new rigor, mercilessly. Under that questioning, these parents fall back on a mindless faith in George's 'good old America.'"

Wallace may have promised a "cosmic spanking," but it was Maryland governor Spiro Agnew who administered it. Agnew had entered 1968 as a supporter of New York governor Nelson Rockefeller. A rich man who "bought" the ideas of others, Rockefeller's most expensive gift to the nation would prove to be his in-house foreign affairs intellectual, Henry Kissinger. In 1968, Rockefeller proved the consummate waverer, declaring his availability, dropping out of the race, and then jumping back in again. As the head of a draft Rockefeller movement, Agnew summoned reporters to Annapolis on March 21 in order to have them share in the excitement of his candidate's announcement. Rockefeller appeared on screen and then said, "I am not a candidate campaigning directly or indirectly for the presidency of the United States." Stunned and embarrassed, Agnew quickly shifted his support to Nixon, who had sent a consoling emissary to Annapolis after Rockefeller's March "surprise."

Three incidents made Agnew an appealing pick as Nixon's eventual running mate, and they all had to do with his "speaking back" to black power. As Dan Carter writes in *The Politics of Rage* (1995), Agnew quickly learned that "the trick, for candidates who hoped to benefit from the 'Wallace factor,' was to exploit the grievances he had unleashed while disentangling themselves from the more tawdry trappings of his message."

In August 1967, the black activist H. Rap Brown encouraged a crowd in Cambridge, Maryland, to "get your guns" and "to take some of them with you." Police fired pellets into the crowd, wounding Brown. The all-white fire department then refused to fight the fires that broke out in the black section of town. On arriving in Cambridge, Agnew ordered Brown's arrest and said, "I hope they pick him up soon, put him away and throw away the key."

On March 27, 1968, some two hundred students at Bowie State, a traditionally black college in central Maryland, led a boycott of classes to protest dorm and classroom conditions as well as the refusal of tenure to a popular professor. The governor's emissary "responded to demands for Agnew's presence by pulling out a cigarette lighter and offering it to the students to burn the place down." Two days later, Agnew met with Nixon in New York, who was impressed with his "strength."

Less than two weeks after that, the shooting of Martin Luther King Jr. was followed by rioting in Baltimore. As National Guard and federal troops moved into the city, Agnew belatedly sent Coretta Scott King a message of condolence.

Then, on April 11, Agnew summoned Maryland's black leaders to Annapolis. Many of them, like Parren Mitchell, head of Baltimore's poverty program, had gone days "without sleep, walking streets at war, trying to calm them." When Agnew entered the room he was surrounded by fully uniformed state troopers, one carrying a riding crop. He was still aroused by the opening of a SNCC office in Baltimore and its director's "calling the city's war on crime a war on the black man." "Some of you here, to your eternal credit," Agnew told his audience, "quickly condemned this demagogic proclamation. . . . But when white leaders openly complimented you for your objective, courageous action, you immediately encountered a storm of censure from parts of the Negro community. . . . *And you ran.*" By the time Agnew had finished speaking, four-fifths of his audience had walked out of the room.

In their captivating political thriller *A Heartbeat Away* (1974), Richard Cohen and Jules Witcover title their second chapter "Creature of Suburbia." Agnew left Baltimore for the suburbs in 1947. "The Baltimore County to which Spiro Agnew moved, and in which he charted and achieved his first political success, was a white noose—96 per cent white—around a black inner city." As he rose to power, becoming County Executive in 1962, Agnew understood that his future lay in representing the interests of the noose.

Soon after Agnew took power in the county, a partner in a local engineering firm named Lester Matz began funneling money to Agnew through a go-between called "the Close Associate." Matz even drew up a chart "listing how much money the engineers receiving county contracts could be expected to kick back." Matz paid Agnew 5 percent on engineering and 2.5 percent on surveying contracts. When Agnew was elected governor in 1966, the practice continued. In the summer of 1968, Matz delivered a manila envelope containing $20,000 to the governor's office. On one occasion after Agnew became vice president, Matz brought $10,000 in cash to the White House. The money was meant to cover percentages due on contracts awarded by the state during Agnew's time as governor. When "the Close Associate" pressed Matz for a contribution he too could pass on, Matz complained to Agnew, who replied, "Say you gave at the office."

Agnew appealed to Nixon as a Reactive Self. The Reactive Self operates in response to a perceived outer threat. It defines itself as against, not for. Both Nixon and Agnew set out to appeal, as Nixon admitted, to people who were "unhappy about something," where the "something" was not looked for within. One of Nixon's favorite formulations was the "those who" construction, a claim in which a vague, unnamed set of others is held responsible for provoking his and his audience's felt sense of indignation.

This motion of mind is comparable to Max Scheler's concept of "ressentiment." Scheler argues that the self can move toward the other with love or with fear and resentment. The movement with love does not express a need or a lack but a superfluity, a confidence that through loving "even the least of these," one can connect with a sense of more abundant life. The movement of ressentiment expresses a sense of inner lack, one projected outward onto the other, who is then blamed as the cause of the frustration. In the history of the United States, the role of the other has often by played by someone black.

In 1968, Ernest Gaines published a collection of short stories called *Bloodline*. In one of the stories, a habitual offender in the local jail named Munford Bazille tells a newcomer about his fifty years of getting in trouble, being caught, and having white people get him off. "I kept on getting in trouble, and they kept on getting me off. Didn't wake up till I got to be nearly old as I'm is now. Then I realized they kept getting me off because they needed a Munford Bazille. They need me to prove they human—just like they need that thing over there. They need us. Because without us, they don't know what they is—they don't know what they is out there. With us around, they can see us and they know what they ain't. They ain't us. Do you see? Do you see how they think?" Gaines makes the case that Scheler might have made: that a resentful "white identity" can only come into being and know itself through an act of negation, by defining itself against the black other.

Another aspect of Nixon and Agnew's sense of grievance expressed itself through the "They All Do It" response. The response kicked in most forcefully when either man found himself in legal trouble. In 1977, looking back at Watergate, Nixon conceded that he had played it "exactly how the other side would have played it." In *RN*, as he narrates the Watergate story, Nixon writes often of the "double standard," a media tendency to excuse, say, a break-in of John Kennedy's doctor's office in 1960 and to condemn the burglary of the offices of Daniel Ellsberg's doctor. It was the press that insisted on seeing him as "a willful deviant from past practice."

Early on in *Go Quietly . . . or Else* (1980), Agnew quotes his comments before the judge in the case of *United States of America v. Spiro T. Agnew*: "My acceptance of contributions was part of a long-established pattern of political fund-raising in the state." He proceeds to depict his ouster from the vice presidency as masterminded by "left-wingers" who, in order "to make their revolution a success . . . had to get rid of me first." He did not choose to resign but was in fact frightened into doing so by "an indirect threat from The White House that made me fear for my life." Told by Nixon's chief of staff, Alexander Haig, that "the President has a lot of power," Agnew feels a chill. "I interpreted it as an innuendo that anything could happen to me; I might have a convenient 'accident.'" Such "threats" are what made him resign, and he thereafter consents to admit to "tax evasion." Even then, he is forced to lie, to *pretend* to be guilty: "I had to twist the truth to make it possible for the judge to accept the settlement."

Agnew's bid for innocence is purchased at the price of giving up any claim to be a volitional self. He does not act out of a set of affections or principles but in response to conspiracies and intimidation. Not being responsible for the outcomes in his life, he also cannot be wrong. He therefore chooses to describe his actions, as Nixon does when describing Watergate, not as venal or immoral, but as, simply, "stupid."

The use of the word "stupid" to cover these cases expresses something common to both men, a "striking unwillingness readily to acknowledge error or misjudgment and correct it." As a consequence, each man transforms the account of his downfall into a process narrative, attending closely to the complicated procedure whereby he reacts to the "enmity" coming at him. In a volume of 1,078 pages, "the Watergate break-in" first surfaces in *RN* on page 625. Over 400 pages of the book are thereafter dominated by Nixon's response to the last of his crises.

In the span of these pages, Nixon owns up to an astonishing range of feelings: "confusion," "ambivalence," "outrage," "guilt," "anguish," "sadness." The language of feeling proves, however, a tantalizing but finally dropped stitch, one all too easily lost in the twists and turns of Nixon's account. Wills had noted in Nixon's campaign speeches an "unwillingness to build toward a climax," and, despite the richness of his material, the same reluctance manifests itself here. The reader will look long and hard for a Watergate recognition scene. Tracking becomes the task, as move follows countermove. A deeply dismaying and perhaps even a tragic episode in the nation's history is thereby reduced to a problem of management. "As soon as Dean's testimony was over, I once again made the mistake I had been making since the Watergate break-in: I worried about the wrong problem." *Wrong*, Nixon means, insofar as his behavior did not succeed in extricating him from the mess. The language of his memoir thus only perpetuates the original crime: it is not the language of confession but of continued cover-up. Despite its frequent admission of mistakes and stupidities, *RN* remains the self-defensive testimony of a Reactive Self. As Jeffrey Kimball concludes, "Nixon never had truly understood or acknowledged his responsibility in the unfolding calamities of his life or his country's, and therefore he underwent no redeeming transformation."

Of Nixon's 1968 campaign itself, there is not much to say. He appeared with Agnew only once, and let him do the heavy lifting. It was Agnew who denounced students as "spoiled brats who never have had a good spanking," and who explained, about not visiting the ghetto, "If you've seen one city slum, you've seen them all." When Agnew referred to a reporter as "the fat Jap," Nixon nailed the behavior while attempting to excuse it: "He naively used inflammatory codewords."

After being taken to task for suggesting that the best use of the *New York Times* was at "the bottom of a bird cage," Agnew declared that "I do not intend to play games with the secret meanings of words nor practice the gentle art of platitude. I do intend to rely on dictionary definitions." Of course playing with the secret meanings of words, while pretending to stick to dictionary definitions, was what the campaign was all about. No one was better equipped to finesse the gap between what was literally said and what was figuratively meant than William Safire, the Nixon speechwriter who also fed Agnew language during the campaign. Safire eventually retired into a column in the *New York Times Magazine* about lexicography in which he celebrated the boundlessness of "dictionary definitions," but in 1968 he was happy to supply Agnew with coy put-downs and catchy alliterations like "positive polarization."

Meanwhile, Nixon ran "the most controlled and protected candidacy in American political history." He paid only two visits to black communities. A Chicago rally held a week after the chaotic Democratic convention was by admission only, and the longhairs who managed to sneak in were redirected down a hallway exiting to the street. Nixon allowed the public to believe that he had a "secret plan" to end the war. Rejecting the 1960 strategy of visiting all fifty states, he decided not "to make that mistake again." He campaigned largely in the Big Seven: New York, Pennsylvania, California, Texas, Illinois, Ohio, and Missouri. "The candidate should take time to think," he said. "Every three weeks I go to Florida for a few days. That's how I keep the tan."

The recessive quality of the Nixon campaign reflected his sense that the audience to which he spoke was a "silent" one. Safire had appropriated the phrase "silent center" from Illinois senator Paul Douglas, and during Nixon's campaign and presidency the word "silent" would become perhaps the most resonant term. In his 1968 Labor Day statement, Nixon invoked "the silent Americans" who have "a legitimate grievance that should be rectified." He first used the word on May 16, when he spoke of "the silent center, the millions of people in the middle of the American political spectrum who do not demonstrate, who do not picket or protest loudly." The trope of silence argued that in not speaking this so-called majority was also somehow expressing itself, and that it had found in Nixon its discerning auditor.

As he helped Nixon write a new introduction to *Six Crises* (1962) in the spring of 1968, Safire had urged on him "fairly frank language." But by November 1969, when Nixon gave his "Silent Majority" speech, any will toward frankness had given way to an endless work of encoding and decoding. Nixon was right: he had proven more adept than any recent politician not only at hearing the meanings in the silence but in playing games with "the secret meanings of words" so as to give that silence a voice. A speech in which Nixon outlined his "plan for peace" in Vietnam is thus remembered instead for a one-sentence plea: "And so tonight—to you, the great silent majority of my fellow Americans—I ask for your support." The resultant outpouring was, Nixon writes, "the biggest response ever to any presidential speech. . . . [F]or the first time, the Silent Majority had made itself heard."

As he crosses the Potomac in *The Armies of the Night*, Norman Mailer is moved by the sense that he, himself, "had grown." Less than a year later, in Miami, he wonders whether Nixon has grown as well. There he sees "a man who had risen and fallen and been able to rise again, and so conceivably had learned something about patience and the compassion of others." Gazing at the candidate's "lovely looking" daughters as they arrived in Miami, Mailer comes to wonder whether "the remote possibility of some reappraisal of Richard Nixon was now forced to enter the works." He sees and thinks these things, of course, before the events of the six years to come, or before the massive public relations campaign launched by Nixon during his retirement. Still, a question lingers in the air, one posed by an unlikely source. On the last page of *White House Years*, Henry Kissinger asks: "What would have happened had the Establishment about which he was so ambivalent shown him some love?"

What would have happened cannot be known, but, in concluding this chapter, I can perhaps at least give it over to two men, essayist Richard Rodriguez and speechwriter Raymond Price, who have each found a distinctive and compelling way to show Nixon something like love.

In *Brown: The Last Discovery of America* (2002), Rodriguez finds himself identifying with Nixon's history of earnest striving. Rodriguez begins his essay on Nixon, titled "Poor Richard," by comparing himself to Benjamin Franklin. In his early reading, Rodriguez admired Franklin and his "vertical yearning." "Ben's ambition magnified my own." He also taught him to buy a black suit and to attend self-improving lectures.

But Richard Rodriguez is not "poor" in the way Franklin's Richard is poor. He is both "brown"—Mexican-American—and Californian, a figure of the edge. "I wore a black suit as Nixon wore a black suit." With "unease, yes, but also optimism." In school he, too, is a creature of "fawning ambition." As he reads deeper into the American novel, with its fantasy of the city in the distance and the "lukewarm cocktail," Rodriguez begins to see that "for all our professed admiration of the ascending narrative line, Americans often resent the awkwardness of arrival." Nixon continued to appeal because he so clearly had not and never would quite arrive, and, even when it seemed that he had done so, he did so awkwardly. And therefore Kennedy, clearly at home with himself and born into the money the striving self has been taught to want to acquire, must necessarily win. "Gold-dusted and ghost-written," in the televised debates Kennedy "appeared completely natural. Nixon perspired."

Rodriguez sees what Alger Hiss saw as he squared off against Nixon at the HUAC hearings, although unlike Hiss, he does not disdain it. "Harvard College will always beat Whittier College in America. The game is fixed and there is nothing to be done about it." Nixon finds himself "humbled enough by national defeat to lower his sights to California," and losing again there, sneers at the gang of reporters. But Rodriguez finds something more in Nixon's loss of control: "His pettiness showed that he cared."

Nixon's effortfulness consoles Rodriguez; "I thought I was the only one in the world who had to try so hard to become." In *The Ends of Power* (1978), H. R. Haldeman was to write of his former boss as "the poor boy (he never let you forget it) from a small California town." Like Nixon, Rodriguez clings as well to his history of trying, and values his success as something earned, not given. But he does learn enough about masking his efforts to take the advice from a college friend—lose the black suit. And then—shockingly—the Nixon of the black suit becomes the "brown" president.

Affirmative action has been Rodriguez's white whale, the object of a life-long quarrel. He chooses less to argue against a policy than to set the fact of it and its effects against a set of lovingly tendered memories of a private world that vanishes once the tampering begins. Rodriquez sees affirmative action as not only invading his home space but as converting its intimacies into quantifiable deficiencies. "In college, because of Lyndon Johnson, I became a 'minority student.' But it was not until Richard Nixon's administration that I became brown. A government document of dulling prose, Statistical Directive 15, would redefine America as an idea in five colors: White. Black. Yellow. Red. Brown." How, "after all that Richard Nixon had written about how hard work wins the day in America," how could he now preempt Richard Rodriguez's novel of success by affording him "a way to cheat?" What if one had wanted to win, on his own, "the prize of admission?" Garry Wills gives the question a more reductive cast: "The deserving rise; if the undeserving are also helped, what happens to the scoring in this game of spiritual effort and merit badges?" Even if one approved of the motives sending up Directive 15, "the saddest part of the story," Rodriguez argues, "is that Nixon was willing to disown his own myth for political expediency."

"Having betrayed his own memory of himself," it was perhaps inevitable that he "betray his public annals"—that he make the tapes. Yet "the tapes seem to me the least authentic version of Nixon extant." Who among us would willingly consent to be judged by our off-the-record talk? It is the composed self that matters, the face we prepare to meet the faces that we meet. "From his books," Rodriguez writes, "I am convinced Nixon was not a coarse-grained man." The tapes were in fact an act of imitation, one more failed effort to arrive:

> Poor Richard. It is as though the Nixon on the tapes is talking the way he thinks "they" talk.
> They don't.

At the Nixon Library in Yorba Linda, Rodriguez wanders the gardens and notices the effort to "Republicanize" the borders of lavender; they are side-walled and topped like a privet. The library collects everything but "assigns no value." There is the presidential limousine, the inaugural Bible, the Refusal to be Deposed. "I suppose you would say it is tasteless." Even so, Rodriguez discovers, "I prefer the plain precepts of Whittier College to the noblesse oblige of Harvard. I hate it when Harvard wins. The winners win."

I imagine my father walking those gardens, during the years of his retirement, although it is not a visit he would have been likely to make. Despite the many setbacks in his working life and the loss of his home place to the frightening dynamics of the inner city, Dad never had time for the politics of resentment. His feelings about Nixon were also complicated by the fact that as a young man with dark and receding hair he had once been mistaken for the senator from Whittier.

During the final twenty years of his working life, Dad ran a successful business manufacturing acrylic flowers. In his Costa Mesa warehouse, he and his two "illegals" cut the clear plastic on band saws, polished it in a huge sander, and then glued the airbrushed lilies and roses into striking bouquets.

Then he got up early every Saturday and Sunday morning and queued up his van at the Orange County Swap Meet, where the gates opened at six and he laid out his wares in a space on the huge asphalt lot.

Dad dissolved the business in 1997 and retired to Laguna Beach. He found an apartment on Cliff Drive with a pool and a view of the ocean. His rent was thirteen hundred dollars a month, about five hundred dollars more than he netted from Social Security. There was no pension and no life insurance. He lived simply, averaging forty dollars a week on groceries. He did "esoteric" portraits, for two hundred and fifty dollars each, and, along with the reduction in rent he received for maintaining the apartment's huge complex of flower beds, he was able to get by.

He had a good three years there, before he packed up his 1992 Corolla and headed east. We knew he would come east sooner or later; there was nowhere else to go. And so now he lives across town, in Charlottesville, and, despite once having been forced off the Santa Ana Freeway by a car full of black guys who said to him, as he pulled over, "We know where you live," and having been robbed at knifepoint in his house on Charlottesville's Cleveland Avenue by a black man who came in through an unlocked sliding glass door, he still votes Democratic and campaigned his heart out for Barack Obama.

Nixon is buried in Yorba Linda; Dad will be buried in Charlottesville. Does it really matter, finally, where one ends up? Rodriguez notices that for Nixon "the Resting Place is not far from the Birthplace, across a small pathway." So much distance traveled, in terms of years and effort, between the setting out and the final arrival, and yet virtually none at all between the actual starting and ending points. But the irony of the closed circle reveals little. Rodriguez himself has stayed close; "for the greater part of my life my address has been within walking distance of the Pacific." It is not the conquest of the East that mattered, the triumph over geographic space. "All serious daring," as Eudora Welty puts it, "starts from within." The library at Yorba Linda houses the artifacts and tends the graves. It is a *spot*. But for Rodriguez, at the end, it becomes a platform for a recognition scene between one mental traveler and another, as one writer brings another close, acknowledges the limits of the imagination, and then lets him go:

> One can imagine a version of Richard Nixon here in Yorba Linda. Young. Awkward. Self-effacing. Embarrassed. Friendly. But one cannot imagine the man who became great and dark-minded. For it was in his mind the suit lodged.

"You do like California, don't you?" Nixon asked Raymond Price, on the morning of his last full day in office. Price replied that he did. In the years to come he often found himself there, assisting Nixon with his memoirs. So it was back to that—back to the back room. In the meantime, however, Price had operated at the heart of power, as one of Nixon's three main speechwriters.

"I liked and admired him," *With Nixon* (1977) begins. "I still do." Actually Price opens his book a page before that, with the moment of "farewell," the helicopter positioned for take-off on the South Lawn. He notes that the departing president is still "erect." In beginning with this sense of an ending, one through which the book will frequently circle back, Price suffuses the entire performance with a gentle, persistent nostalgia. And, by continually returning to the endgame of the Nixon presidency, Price also creates a narrative structure in which Watergate is the central refrain.

A call comes in February 1967: would Price like to join the Nixon team? Price meets Nixon for lunch at his New York apartment. He glimpses the man's "human side" in his banter with his butler, Manolo. They talk for three hours, and Price comes to appreciate Nixon's "intellectual range, the quickness and facility of his mind." He also makes note of his habit of referring to himself "dispassionately" in the third person. After spending a week reading up on Nixon and talking to friends, Price signs up with the campaign and finds himself installed in a comfortable corner of Nixon's law offices.

Price begins with an end and a beginning. While the reader might then expect him to proceed with an account of the run for the presidency, he gives the campaign only brief mention. Chapter 2 in fact opens with a meditation on the identity of a man Price has now known for over ten years. In trying to fathom the "air of mystery" around Nixon, Price turns to William Safire's comparison of the president to a "layer cake."

According to Safire, the top layer of the cake is the "progressive politician." Below that, one slices into the unnecessarily pugnacious man. Then comes the poker player with the long record of winning and losing, and further down, the hater, the impugner of motives. Four more layers follow: the realist; the observer-participant; the calculating risk-taker; and, finally, the solitary swimmer (swimming alone was Nixon's favorite pastime), the loner. Price reads the metaphor as arguing that the only way to slice the cake is "vertically, not horizontally."

While Price frequently invokes Nixon's "complexities," a layered self is hardly complex. The logic of the metaphor argues instead for an unintegrated identity. However many layers are involved, they are simply stacked one on the other, and the whole thing is held together by gravity, and by icing.

The layer cake metaphor tells us nothing more than does Price's own sense of Nixon as man with a "light side" and a "dark side," parts of the self that "over the years . . . have been at constant war with one another." Price sees the light side as "by far the larger part," while the dark side "grew not out of his nature, but out of his experiences in public life." The dark side is the Reactive Self, one not chosen but caused by Nixon's having had "his trust too often abused." The best advice Price gives Nixon, when in 1975 they confer on the writing of the memoirs, is that "instead of being embarrassed" by his dark side, "he should acknowledge it."

Price was a good fit for Nixon because he understood and to some degree shared the attitudes of his base. Deeply skeptical of "the media" and "the trendsetters," he saw Nixon as the champion of "new forces that sprang essentially from the nation's heartland." The point of the Nixon revolution was to "shake the snobbish assumption of natural superiority that lay in the fashionable East." By the time of the 1972 campaign, Nixon was coming off "as almost aggressively square," and saw himself as standing for "patriotism, morality, religion."

"At the heart of . . . ," Price often writes, as in "At the heart of the social issue was fear." He reads the "eruption of resentment" as an expression of "injured pride." In 1972, Nixon's overwhelming support from Middle America is "a crying out for some measure of respect for their own values, their own interests, their own right to belong."

As for the other "side" in this "bitter" division, Price summons a less kindly rhetoric. They are "mobs in the streets" who indulge in "orgies of mindless violence." At one point, he resorts to a "those who" construction: "violent protest was romanticized by those who saw themselves marching in the cultural vanguard." "Great universities," he complains, have been brought "to their knees." The sixties are, finally, a "mess."

As the "basic collaborator" on Nixon's first inaugural address, Price chose to describe the cultural divide as "a crisis of the spirit." In the speech as given the word "spirit" appears six times. Perhaps this was in response to Billy Graham's urging on Nixon a "strong spiritual emphasis." By the time Nixon flew his team of speechwriters to Key Biscayne, he had in any event embraced the idea: "We've got to write the section about the spirit of America, about confronting ourselves, in a way that we don't condemn everybody." Something had gone "dark" within many Americans, Nixon believed, and "spirit" was as good a word as any to cover the case.

Price was more concerned about the *volume* of noise. In 1969, after the president affirmed that "under no circumstances will I be affected whatever" by the fall Moratorium against the war, he received a letter from a student asking him "to take note of the will of the people." Price drafted Nixon's reply, one in which he argued that "to allow government policy to be made in the streets would destroy the democratic process. It would give the decision, not to the majority, and not to those with the strongest arguments, but to those with the loudest voices." The point had already been made, in his first inaugural address, and in lines composed by Price:

> To lower our voices would be a simple thing.
> In these difficult years, America has suffered from a fever of words; from inflated rhetoric that promises more than it can deliver; from angry rhetoric that fans discontents into hatreds; from bombastic rhetoric that postures instead of persuading.
> We cannot learn from one another until we stop shouting at one another—until we speak quietly enough so that our words can be heard as well as our voices.

It was this "theme," Price tells us, "most widely bannered in headlines the next day."

In meeting this crisis, Nixon did many good things. His administration saw the passage of the Clean Air Act and the establishment of the Environmental Protection Agency. The Selective Service was abolished; OSHA, the Consumer Product Safety Commission, and Amtrak were inaugurated. Funding for the NEH and the NEA increased six-fold. Executive Order 55 promoted minority hiring, and by 1974, when Nixon left office, the formal desegregation of the nation's schools was largely complete, although housing patterns and class differences would keep de facto segregation in place in the years to come. His domestic adviser John Ehrlichman put it rather cynically when he said that "non-conservative initiatives" were "deliberately designed to furnish some zigs to go with our conservative zags."

For all his progressive domestic reforms, Nixon "successfully avoided the appearance of liberalism while wooing conservatives, especially southerners." He maintained a willful gap between acts and words. As a word-man, Price often pondered this gap, although it was "the fashionable liberal's . . . fascination with words" that most arrested him. The liberal, Price argues, "can accept *acts* that contravene his ideals more readily than he can accept *words* that contravene his ideals." The reaction to the language of the Oval Office tapes was for Price a case in point. After their public release in April

1974, "those with a monopoly of the means by which words and ideas and perceptions of the truth reach the public" engaged in a "concerted onslaught" against the Nixon administration. "As nearly as I can discern it," Price concludes, "a brilliant, complex, dedicated, often devious, sometimes duplicitous president was driven from office not for what he did, but for what, in the protected privacy of his own resentment and rage, he said." Price persists in the assumption that acts matter more than words, ignoring the fact that a president's speech acts are performative in a unique and powerful way.

What the president can be heard as saying on the tapes is striking enough. The edited transcripts released by the White House are full of the phrase "expletive deleted." They are shocking not so much for their criminality, as in the "smoking gun" recording of June 23, 1972, in which Nixon instructed H. R. Haldeman to have the CIA stop the FBI investigation of the Watergate burglary, thus providing the evidence that Nixon had in fact engaged in obstruction of justice. Just as demoralizing is the sheer inarticulate banality of the language, as in an aside made on the same day: "The arts, you know—they're Jews, they're left wing—in other words, stay away."

Price's last service to the Nixon presidency was to assist in the composition of the resignation speech. He actually wrote two speeches, one in which Nixon resigned, and another in which he did not.

Feeling tired and stale at the end of 1973, Price had written a memo to the president stating that "I no longer feel able personally to argue our Watergate case." He wanted to resign, but he hoped that the president would not. "Even if he were guilty, I wanted him to win the fight." Price's attitude throughout *With Nixon* is of a man who takes a pragmatic rather than a moralistic view. Thus he can say, "I care less about whether a president breaks a law than I do about whether he keeps the peace." In the event, chief of staff Alexander Haig did not pass along Price's memo, and Nixon, at a December dinner, gently pressured Price to stay on in order to work on the State of the Union address. "There was no way out," he realized. "I was aboard for the duration."

"We need a resignation speech," Haig finally told Price, on August 1, 1974; he had just read the transcript of the June 23, 1972, tape. What had been said, it turned out, was "a disaster," Price writes, "the smoking pistol that tied Nixon directly, and at the very outset, to the cover-up." Brooding over the meaning of words he has still not yet read, Price goes on to argue that the entire affair is still *only* a matter of things said. Nixon now has to resign because of the "Profumo factor," a reference to a British politician forced from office "not for what he had done but because he lied to the

House of Commons about it." Then Price gets his hands on the transcript, reads it, and finds it "worse than Haig had described."

Still, Nixon resists, and proceeds to have Price write a speech in which he will explain the tapes "but without resigning." Although Price thinks this move a "disastrous mistake," he accepts the charge. That night, he completes a draft of the speech requested as well as a further draft, "Option B," a speech in which a resignation is announced.

When it came to the question of giving up the presidency, both Johnson and Nixon long entertained the thought before finally agreeing to having it put in words. And by dividing up the task among a number of speechwriters, Johnson had meant to keep alive his hopes of clinging to office. Only after Clark Clifford insisted on a "peace speech" rather than a "war speech" did Johnson come to accept the need to accompany such an approach with the announcement that he would not seek or accept the nomination. Of course, as we have seen, Horace Busby had written a statement to this effect as far back as January, and Lady Bird had even weighed in on its grammar. By the time Johnson gave his March 31 speech, all the options had narrowed down to one, with far too many collaborators in the process for there to be any turning back.

Nixon, in contrast, worked primarily with one man on his parting speech, and ended up writing much of it himself. While Price's "Option B" served as a basis for the speech delivered on August 8, 1974, it was not quite the farewell speech Nixon decided to give. In the speech as given the president indulged in his habit of placing "the noblest possible interpretation" on his decision to resign, representing it as "what was best for the Nation." "The interests of the Nation must always come before any personal consider-ations," he repeated. "The interests of the Nation" are invoked three times, as if altruism rather than sad necessity were the force at work. The speech as given reflects Nixon's final instructions to Price not to write a "speech proclaiming a guilt that he did not feel."

Price's "Option B" counters this missed opportunity with something close to an outright confession. In doing so, it remains faithful to Price's best imaginings of the president:

> Last week, in my review of the tapes to be turned over to the Special Prosecutor, I discovered one that indicated my own knowledge of the Watergate cover-up was greater than I have previously indicated, and that it came sooner—in fact, that I did learn shortly after the break-in that it was a potential source of severe embarrassment to the Administration and to my campaign committee, and that I did,

at that time, approve actions which I hoped would have the effect
of covering up the connection.

In a single sentence, Price cuts through two years of circumlocution to
achieve a model of frank speech. The emphasis falls on Nixon as agent rather
than victim: "I discovered . . . I have previously indicated . . . I did learn
. . . I hoped." By publicly uttering such a sentence, Nixon could have passed
a Last Judgment upon himself that might have helped to bind up many of
the nation's wounds. It is terribly sad, and terribly fitting, that in finally
rejecting the imaginings of the man he called the "voice of my conscience,"
Richard Nixon ended his public career by choosing not to say what is here
so simply and honestly said.

CHAPTER

10

Chicago

On the evening of Wednesday, August 28, 1968, Tom Hayden found himself in Chicago's Grant Park, disguised in a false beard and a football helmet. A few hours earlier his friend Rennie Davis had been clubbed to the ground by Chicago police. Hayden then urged the assembled demonstrators to break into small groups and to make their way to the Conrad Hilton Hotel. Blocked by police lines preventing direct movement toward the Hilton, the crowd of some five thousand began working its way north and then west across an open bridge, at which point it looped south toward the hotel. "It was nearly dark, the city lights turning on," Hayden remembered, when they reached the corner of Michigan and Balbo, "where all the swirling forces were destined to meet." The Battle of Michigan Avenue was about to begin.

Hayden had come to Chicago for a "giant antiwar march" and to protest business-as-usual at the Democratic convention, which would eventually nominate Hubert Humphrey as its presidential candidate in the waning hours of Wednesday night. Planning for the action had begun in December 1967, when Hayden and Davis met with the administrative committee of the National Mobilization to End the War in Vietnam, known as "the Mobe." The Mobe would be joined by the guerilla theater of the Youth International Party, the Yippies, headed by Jerry Rubin and Abbie Hoffman. The Yippies planned a Festival of Life as a contrast to what it called a Convention of Death.

Arrayed against the planners was Richard Daley, the longtime mayor of Chicago. Daley had been angered and embarrassed by April riots in the city following the shooting of Martin Luther King Jr., disturbances in which eleven blacks had been killed and ninety policemen injured. He had tried and failed to quell the violence by issuing a "shoot to kill" order.

Demonstrations and marches required permits, and by June it had become clear that the city intended to grant none. Police officer Will Gerald admitted as much: "Mayor Daley was pissed in April—that led to what happened during the peace march, and what took place on the streets during the convention." As Daley continued to build an "iron curtain" around the event, Hayden found himself confronting the "bitter evidence," as he wrote in *Reunion,* that "America was turning out to be more like Mississippi than not." More driven by a racial politics, he meant, than either South or North wished to acknowledge.

Daley had been elected mayor in 1955. He lived simply in a modest brick bungalow in the Bridgeport neighborhood of Chicago's South Side. He ran an efficient urban political machine, one that depended on personal loyalty and the dispensing of favors. Chicago, he believed, was his city; and what was at stake for him, as David Farber argues in *Chicago '68* (1988), was the issue of "jurisdiction." Daley and his people saw Chicago's urban space "as a concrete sphere of activity," as local and indigenous, while for the incoming protestors it served more as a realm of "symbolic confrontation." For the Mobe and the Yippies, the goal of the protests was "to create a visual image of the State in action." Daley wanted to keep trouble out of his town. The "police riot" that resulted was, in William Styron's words, "the triumphant end-product of his style."

The Mobe's organizers vastly overestimated the hoped-for turnout, informing the city to prepare for two to three hundred thousand protestors. In the event, no more than ten thousand showed up, and half of that number lived in the metropolitan area. "My God," Hayden said to himself," on Saturday morning, "there's nobody here."

The people who gathered in Chicago's Grant and Lincoln Parks were outnumbered by an on-duty police force of 11,900. During the week of the convention, each man was to work a twelve-hour shift. All police on crowd control wore helmets and carried nightsticks, service revolvers, and cans of Mace. The batons and Mace were to be used only when necessary "to make the arrest." Officers were ordered never to strike a person in the head with a baton.

The police were backed up by over five thousand members of the Illinois

National Guard. Each Guardsman was equipped with an M-1 rifle. Some six thousand Army troops, including members of the 101st Airborne, were massed in Chicago's suburbs. Up to a thousand undercover agents—from the FBI, CIA, and Army and Navy Intelligence—also blended into the crowds.

"We wanted to have legal and undisrupted demonstrations," Rennie Davis later said, but having them depended on receiving city permits. Only one permit finally would be granted, for a Wednesday afternoon rally at the Grant Park bandshell. Mobe leaders went to court on August 18, charging Daley and city officials with conspiring to deny the antiwar group its right to assemble. On Friday, August 23, three days before the official opening of the convention, U.S. District Court judge William J. Lynch ruled against the plaintiffs.

Meanwhile, according to *Rights in Conflict* (1968), the official report on Chicago issued by the National Commission on the Causes and Prevention of Violence, "the general media published an elaborate array of potential threats to the city and to the delegates." The Walker Report, as it came to be called, cited rumors that natural gas lines were to be dynamited and sewers flooded with gasoline. Some 230 "'hyper-potent' hippie males" had been organized "into a special battalion to seduce the wives, daughters, and girl-friends of convention delegates." Talk on the street had it that mortars had been emplaced in order to bombard the International Amphitheatre, where the convention was being held, from several miles away.

Much of the preconvention publicity issued on behalf of the demonstrations was incendiary. Davis spoke of "turning delegates back into the Amphitheatre as they attempt to leave," while Rubin urged protestors to bring smoke bombs and "crud to throw." The Chicago *Seed* issued a prediction that "cars and buildings will burn."

Mobe and Yippie organizers attempted to anticipate the city's heavy response. A legal defense committee was established and bail bond funds were solicited. A hospital in the city's Near North Side neighborhood agreed to deal with the possibility of mass injuries. "Movement centers" were set up in storefronts and church basements, and marshals were recruited to monitor the activities of demonstrators. One marshal-in-training wrote his girlfriend, "I realize at this time that there are very good chances that I may be injured or arrested because I am here."

One big problem remained: the demonstrators had no place to sleep. By law Chicago parks were to be vacated by 11 p.m. In refusing any permits for visitors to gather in its parks, the city therefore assured a clash over the timing and issue of curfew.

The "siege of Chicago," as Norman Mailer called it, began on Friday, August 23, and lasted for a week. The first major incident involved the release of Pigasus, the YIP candidate for president, in the Civic Center Plaza. The pig was promptly locked up by the Chicago Humane Society and six persons were arrested. The final incident of violence involved a police raid on hotel rooms occupied by McCarthy supporters early on the morning of August 30. The convention itself began on Monday, August 26, and ended, with Hubert Humphrey's acceptance speech, on Thursday night.

At the center of the space being contested in Chicago was the Conrad Hilton Hotel, located on the corner of Michigan and Balbo Avenues. The Humphrey and McCarthy campaigns were sequestered in the hotel. The Hilton faced Grant Park, a rectangular "alternation of lawn with superhighways" running along the east shore of Lake Michigan. Two miles to the north of the Hilton was Lincoln Park, where YIP established its headquarters. The convention site, the International Amphitheatre, was located across from the Chicago stockyards and five miles south of the Hilton.

"In Chicago," Mailer was to write, "there was no symbol," no "chalice to hold his fear" like the Pentagon. Perhaps this was because "the fight was over space," as John Schultz maintains in *No One Was Killed* (1969), and Mailer, as a credentialed journalist, found himself more inside than out. Had he spent more time on the streets, he might have seen how the fight also came down to simple things that acquired the status of symbols: a pig, a flatbed truck, an equestrian statue, a flag, a hotel window. In the swirling welter of charge and countercharge, these objects provide, for a latter-day understanding, a few nodal points in the flux.

Given the immense scale of the event, anyone entering into that seven-mile space in those seven days found himself or herself sometimes in and sometimes out of the action, positioned on a continually sliding scale between spectator and participant. Mark Lane calls himself a "quasi-demonstrator," split between what he "experienced" and what he "saw." Just where was the heart of the "event"—on the convention floor, at police headquarters, or the sidewalk in front of the Hilton? Any answer is mediated by the surviving accounts, most of which side with the demonstrators, books like Schultz's *No One Was Killed*, Lane's *Chicago Eyewitness* (1968), David Lewis Stein's *Living in the Revolution* (1969), and Hayden's *Reunion*.

In *Battleground Chicago* (2004), Frank Kusch provides the best guide to the police experience of convention week. Kusch conducted eighty interviews with Chicago cops, and he quotes liberally from them. None of his informants has yet published a full-fledged account of his own. Scores of writers also descended on the city, including Jean Genet, William Burroughs, Gore Vidal, William Buckley, Elizabeth Hardwick, Allen Ginsberg, Terry Southern, and William Styron, and a number of them have left brief and pungent accounts of their time there.

The fundamental human experience called up by that August week was the facing of fear. The fear was primarily of the physical risk of being hit by something thrown by a demonstrator or swung by a cop. It was the kind of fear the marshal-in-training shared with his girlfriend. "I was very afraid," David Lewis Stein writes, about the moment in Grant Park when the Yippies began to lower the flag. "I was still terrified of those night sticks, of being beaten and left bleeding in the gutter." The physical fear was accompanied for some, as Mailer admitted to himself, by "another fear," a "conservative" fear, "his reluctance to lose even the America he had had." The country had allowed him to write. "He had lived well enough to have six children, a house on the water, a good apartment, good meals, good booze, he had even come to enjoy wine." Was some step now required that would force him to risk losing all that? In the size of his fear—of disruption, reaction, exile—Mailer discovers how large a loss that would be. "He liked his life. He wanted it to go on, which meant that he wanted America to go on—not as it was going, not Vietnam—but what price was he really willing to pay?"

It turns out that Mailer will not risk all that much. As with the March on the Pentagon, he turns out to be mostly a spectator "not central" to the event. He arrives late for the confrontations at Lincoln and Grant Parks; he misses the moment. But he continues to provide an essential brooding presence as he stands in for any thinking American not present to the event who likes his life and who also remains committed to taking Chicago in.

"In" was to become the pivotal word, a preposition measuring one's distance from the urgencies of the event. What happened outside on the streets was to assume greater importance than what happened inside under a roof—except when the distinction between in and out collapsed, as it did with the window of the Haymarket Lounge. As Mailer admits, to give an account of the Democratic convention is not, however, to render "a description of the event. The event was a convention which took place during a continuing five-day battle in the streets and parks of Chicago."

For John Schultz, "the Chicago cop, in his skyblue short-sleeved shirt and skyblue helmet, was already"—by Monday—"the most constant image in all the activities of Convention Week." Schultz experiences the police as performing a repeated act of blocking: "They simply stood there and blocked my dreams." "Blocked" is the title of the opening section of *No One Was Killed*, and as the book unfolds the word acquires considerable force. That being blocked by police was a common and even perhaps the generic experience of the week is supported by numerous accounts, including the Walker Report. "Discovering that lines of escape were blocked, many demonstrators panicked and began to run in all directions." While the sentence describes the clearing of Lincoln Park on Monday night, it could be applied to most of the confrontations between the crowd and the police.

On Wednesday night, as he joins the attempted march from Grant Park to the Amphitheatre, the full force of Schultz's verb is realized. All but one exit from the park is blocked by police, and as demonstrators are forced north into a massive U-turn ending up in front of the Hilton, the tensions of the week achieve critical mass. "No one should know better than the cops on the line what happened," Schultz maintains, "when they blocked all access."

Schultz attends to the emotions felt on both sides of the police lines. He feels his anger as "a flagrant gift." But by ramming into the crowds, by "clubbing, clubbing, clubbing," the cops have also "made a mistake. They had raised the most important issue: the issue of bravery." Schultz's bravery consists in his continuing to remain in the parks and the streets, but it is also the bravery of the professional writer who places himself "here because I have found and am following the movement of a story." By doing so, he purchases the right to fault the Walker Report, another version of the story, for having "winnowed out all the terrible dignity of human motive and decision." McCarthy campaign worker Ben Stavis insists on the word "dignity" as well. "That no one was killed does not, of course, reflect on the professional restraint of the Chicago police. It stems from the unusual dignity of the demonstrators while being gassed and clubbed."

The Walker Report characterized what happened in Chicago as a "police riot." Careful with words, Schultz objects to this description. To give the event such a label "is to shirk what happened," since "the Chicago police were acting under orders." They had not lost control but were fulfilling the expressed will of the mayor. As police officer Hank Peterson later concluded, "I think that this was planned from the beginning. . . . [I]t was no secret that the city—I mean, boss Daley—wanted to see a situation where we were going to beat the hell out of demonstrators." Schultz concurs: "There was no breakdown in police discipline during Convention Week." In a famous slip of the tongue, Mayor Daley reinforced such impressions when, in September, he maintained that "the police isn't there to create disorder; the policeman is there to preserve disorder."

Schultz also read the week's events as inflected by race and class. "This was white family war, family rage, family fight over family destiny." As Joan Didion and Garry Wills were also to observe, the late 1960s involved a war of parents against children. Elizabeth Hardwick read the official response to the demonstrators as the expression of a "sordid, parental self-protection." "That was the true menace of Chicago," Wills argues, in *Nixon Agonistes.* "These *were* our children in the streets—indicting us." That they were mostly white children, the black presence on the streets of downtown Chicago during convention week being minimal at any one time, only drove home the case.

Anxieties about class complicated the sense of white dismay. As he followed the "events at the flagpole" on Wednesday afternoon, Schultz sensed an opening in "the gates in the complex sewer system of American rage that drains out of the above-ground status scramble." In a country where "self-importance is measured only by the diminishment of another person," the kids in the street appeared to care little for the pleasures of othering, except in their taunting of the police. And a gathering culture of "ressentiment" would more than match the behavior of these "children" as it continued to "other" them.

By 1968, Tom Hayden had become "an improbable shadow ambassador" from left to liberal America. The same man who had made unauthorized trips to Hanoi was now holding private meetings with Robert Kennedy and Averell Harriman. Seeking for a marriage of militance and breadth, Hayden hoped for a coalition "uniting the mildest liberal critics of the war with the most militant members of SDS." By the time he arrived in Chicago, he had also come to sense that the American people had to be "forced into a moral squeeze" if change were to occur.

One of the recurring themes of 1968 is the leader who becomes a follower. While it may be convenient to think of Davis, Hoffman, Rubin, David Dellinger, and Hayden as out in front of the crowds they meant to exhort, Schultz probably has it right when he claims that "they did not comprehend the failed situation into which came new energy." As Mailer had discovered nine months earlier, at the Pentagon, and as Schultz was to reframe the insight, "I had learned at last not to anticipate anything. By this time, the principle was established in everyone's deepest mind of not being bound by resolutions but going with the movement of whatever was happening."

Nevertheless, Hayden's experiences in Chicago assume, in retrospect, a significant shape—a danse macabre between an activist and the police. Hayden's primary human contact would turn out to be with the two plainclothesmen assigned to tail him and Davis during convention week, Ralph Bell and Frank Riggio.

"Have you met yours yet?" Davis asked Hayden, on Saturday morning. Hayden had already noticed a man with a gun standing outside his apartment. Now there was a "beefy, casually dressed man with crossed arms, menacing eyes, and greased hair" guarding Davis's office. The men had been tasked "to follow us," Hayden writes, "at the fairly claustrophobic distance of about ten feet wherever we went."

The first major action of the week came on Sunday in Lincoln Park. On Saturday Allen Ginsberg had released a statement warning that "city police insist they'll bust anybody sleeping in Lincoln Park after 11 p.m.," and on the next day and at the appointed hour the blue helmets began moving through the park. Given fair warning, and in a pattern that would be repeated, most of the crowd surged out of the park and onto city streets. "When they approached an intersection that was blocked by police, they would simply turn and move down another street." Bottled up by a police line at the Michigan Avenue Bridge, the crowd dispersed, smashing car windows and breaking off aerials as it retreated.

Meanwhile, back in Lincoln Park, a thousand demonstrators fell back before police skirmish lines. Some in the crowd threw rocks and bottles and yelled "Hell no, we won't go," "Pigs, pigs, pigs!," and "Mother fuckers!" When the police charged, the crowd would fall back, and then press forward again. Officer Al Ogilvie noticed something new: "The thing about this crowd was that since it thrived on confrontation it behaved in a way much different than any other crowd I've ever seen. . . . [T]he police would break people's heads but the crowd would not run away. [It would] regroup and surge back." Hand-to-hand fighting broke out; in a scene often repeated—the Walker Report was to carry an entire section devoted to police violence against the press—a Chicago reporter was knocked to the ground and beaten. At the Eugenie Triangle, cars were brought to a stop and drivers began honking their horns in "an incredible cacophony." For Hayden, back in Lincoln Park, the tear gas fired by police turned the "balmy night air into a jolting, choking, inescapable darkness."

Hayden had managed to shake Bell and Riggio earlier that day while letting air out of one of their tires. When the two plainclothesmen attempted to shove him inside their unmarked car, a crowd gathered and began chanting, "Let him go, let him go!" Hayden escaped, and was thus free to maneuver against the police later that night and to grab a few hours of sleep on a couch at a friend's apartment.

On Monday afternoon, as he met with a group of marshals in Lincoln Park, Hayden noticed police officers taping over their badges. Then he saw a police wagon and a car approaching. "I'm going to be arrested right now," he thought, as Bell and Riggio jumped out. "I oughta kill you right now," Riggio said, as they drove him downtown.

Quickly bailed out, Hayden spotted a "new man with a gun" as he left the police station. He was the original tail, the one first seen on Sunday morning. After losing him in traffic, Hayden cruised by Lincoln Park as curfew approached. In the park, demonstrators threw up a barricade while Allen Ginsberg squatted on the ground chanting "om." When a single squad car detoured through the park behind the barricade, it was swarmed by the crowd and its windshields were smashed. Some fifty officers charged forward to the cries, "There's a squad car trapped!" Tear gas and smoke bombs were released, the police advanced, and some in the crowd heard them chanting, "Kill, kill, kill!"

Hayden, meanwhile, was down on Michigan Avenue. He ran into some journalists who "invited" him into the Hilton. But a hotel officer grabbed his arm and said, "We don't want this man in here." As they argued at the door, Riggio appeared. Then "out of nowhere came Bell, charging like a linebacker, . . . beating my head, dragging me through the kicking boots of other police, twisting my arm in a karate hold, and slamming me into a police car." Arrested for a second time, Hayden found himself in detention with Bill Ayers. Bailed out at 3 a.m., he came to realize that "I could not be me, not on the streets of Chicago."

At this point Hayden turned to disguise. The Hayden who emerged on the streets on Tuesday afternoon wore a false beard, sunglasses, neck beads, and a yellow-brimmed hat alternated with a football helmet. His day would pass peacefully, ending in a surprise at 2 a.m., when police announced that demonstrators would be allowed to sleep in Grant Park. An hour later, he watched jeeps screened with panels of barbed wire make their way down Michigan Avenue: the arrival of the National Guard.

As James Miller writes, "Wednesday was the big day." If American history can be understood to converge on a number of key dates, then Wednesday, August 28, 1968, is surely one of them. It was the day, to use Hayden's verbs, when hope was "blocked" and "crushed" by fear. The nouns matter, as well. If, as Richard Rorty argues in *Achieving America* (1998), American life wavers between the politics of hope and the politics of fear, then that day in Chicago helped tip the balance toward fear, in Mailer's accurate prediction, for the next "forty years." And even the candidate who eventually

ran and won on a platform of hope and change in 2008 was soon to find
those aspirations blocked by the enduring politics of Reaction as well as by
his own diffidence.

The commotion began at the flagpole in Grant Park during the officially
sanctioned Mobe antiwar rally. By now, Hayden records, "many of the delegates were joining our nightly protests as they returned to the hotels"; the *in*
was becoming confused with the *out*. As the rally went forward, news came
over the radio that the convention had rejected the peace plank. "A shirtless
longhair" began to lower the flag, Hayden recalls, and police rushed forward
to arrest him. What Hayden did not know, or does not choose to mention,
is that the group which completed the lowering of the flag and then raised
something red in its place contained at least one undercover police officer.

When Rennie Davis took the microphone to announce that the rally had
secured for itself a legal permit, the police charged again. As Davis lay on the
ground with his head "split open," a man stood over him with a microphone
and a tape recorder. He was from Naval Intelligence. At the hospital, staff hid
Davis under a sheet and rolled him out to a getaway cab when police tried
to arrest him. The afternoon waned; David Dellinger called for a nonviolent
march to the Amphitheatre. When Hayden got up to speak, he urged the
crowd to "avenge" Rennie. "Tom had walked a thin line for several days,"
Dellinger remembered. "Now he had crossed over to the other side."

Over six thousand journalists were at work in Chicago during convention
week. After Mayor Daley complained to Walter Cronkite that cameras never
showed police reasoning with the marchers, the president of CBS News
responded, "The pictures and sound of the Chicago Police Department in
action speak for themselves." For most Americans, Chicago was a thing
seen. The Walker Report begins by acknowledging that "what 'the whole
world was watching,' after all, was not a confrontation but the picture of
a confrontation." For most onlooking Americans, Chicago came down to
seventeen minutes of film shot between 7:57 and 8:14 p.m. on Wednesday
night, to the picture of what quickly came to be known as the Battle of
Michigan Avenue.

As the violence at the Grant Park bandshell subsided after the clubbing
of Rennie Davis, some five thousand marchers attempting to leave the park
found all exits blocked except to the north. "We had a feeling of being trapped
by cops," one remembered. Others were forced up against National Guard
troops at Congress Avenue. The Guard fired "a little tear gas" to push them
back. Most of the gas blew back toward the Hilton.

As darkness fell, the word was passed: "Two blocks north, there's an open bridge; no gas." Scores of demonstrators began crossing the Jackson Boulevard Bridge, which led west toward Michigan Avenue. "Just as we crossed," David Lewis Stein recalls, "a covered wagon drawn by mules, the Poor People's Campaign Train, came jogging along Michigan Avenue. . . . It was a magic moment, the ghost of Martin Luther King rising up to lead us."

The Hilton now lay two blocks to the south. When the crowd reached the northeast corner of the Hilton, at the intersection of Michigan and Balbo, it began to bunch up against the police lines that had been set up around the hotel. Behind these lines the police were attempting to contain another two to three thousand demonstrators who had gathered at the intersection earlier in the evening. Debris was being thrown from the Hilton's upper floors.

Balbo runs east–west; Michigan Avenue runs north–south. It was from the west that the inciting charge would come. Some fifteen minutes before eight, a reserve police platoon began to move east on Balbo, from behind the Hilton, in response to the call, "Police officer needs help." Rocks and bottles rained down on them and "forced the officers to defend themselves from injury," a deputy chief later reported. "To many other witnesses, it seemed that the police swept down Balbo and charged, with clubs swinging, into the crowd without the slightest pause."

Pushed up against the Hilton by the police moving down Balbo, Stein imagined the situation, for a moment, from their point of view. "Michigan Avenue looked as if it was filled with writhing, screaming, hysterical people. I think if I had been a cop about to march into that mob, I would have been afraid for my life."

Bodies began falling over each other as the crowd attempted to "reverse gears." Demonstrators piled up against the police lines to the south, and nightsticks began forcing the crowd back on itself. "There was no place for them to go," a McGovern worker said. Individual policemen began breaking formation, and soon "all the policemen from the original line at Balbo were just swinging through the crowd."

The pressure was especially great up against the plate glass window of the Hilton's Haymarket Lounge. One policeman rescued a ten-year-old girl from the press of the crowd; another "calmly walked" the length of the barricade and sprayed people with Mace. "The police were angry," one witness later recalled. "Their anger was neither disinterested nor instrumental. It was deep, expressive and personal. 'Get out of here you cock suckers' seemed to be their most common cry."

Hayden found himself at the hotel window. "Then, as people started staggering backward, someone kicked in the window behind us, and we fell through the shattered street-level opening to the Hilton's Haymarket Lounge." Nora Sayre watched "a little old woman" pat "a rebel on the chest, murmuring, 'Knock the socks off them.'" Then the police rammed their blue barricades "against the building with such force that many next to me, including the old woman, were thrust through the hotel's plate glass windows." Mark Lane watched a woman fall through onto the glass. "The police continue to charge, clubs flailing. They run through the broken window and beat the woman on the floor." After campaigning for McCarthy all spring, David Mixner also found himself at the window. He spent over three months on crutches from injuries sustained there.

A startled William Styron, on assignment with *Esquire,* witnessed the scene as a silent movie from inside the hotel: "Half-blinded from the gas I had just caught on the street, I watched the unbelievable melee not from the outside this time but in the surreal shelter of the Haymarket bar, an hermetically sealed igloo where sound-resistant windows offered me the dumbshow of cops clubbing people to the concrete. . . . [A]n explosion of glass at the rear of the bar announced the arrival of half a dozen bystanders who, hurled inward by the crush outside, had shattered the large window and now sprawled cut and bleeding all over the floor of the place while others, chased by a wedge of cops, fled screaming into an adjacent lobby." Hayden summed it up: "Now, the *inside* of the Hilton was a battleground."

Norman Mailer watched the scene "in safety from the nineteenth floor." Out of what he saw he produced one of his trademark compound similes: "The police attacked with tear gas, with Mace, and with clubs, they attacked like a chain saw cutting into wood, the teeth of the saw the edge of their clubs, they attacked like a scythe through grass, lines of twenty and thirty policemen striking out in an arc, their clubs beating, demonstrators fleeing. Seen from overhead, from the nineteenth floor, it was like a wind blowing dust, or the edge of waves riding foam on the shore." Mailer's comparisons register the fact of a felt distance; here the poetry is in the pattern, not in the pity. Like a god looking down, he can even call it "beautiful." What is seen unfolds as a process governed by chain saw, scythe, and, finally, wind and wave. In Emerson's words, "Things are in the saddle,/And ride mankind." Human agency is subsumed first to its tools, and then to mere natural processes. Still, there is a sense of a harvest being brought in, a reaping of what has been planted, and Mailer has his vision: "It was as if the war had finally begun, and this was therefore a great and solemn moment, as if indeed even the gods of history had come together from each side to choose the very front of the Hilton Hotel." But a war over what, and between whom?

Few Americans were permitted such an overview. Nor was it possible for them to witness the seventeen minutes as they were happening. The first network coverage of the event did not appear on television screens until 9:30 p.m.; it took that long for the footage to be readied for broadcast. It was in response to these delayed visuals that Senator Abraham Ribicoff made his charge from the convention podium that "with George McGovern, we wouldn't have Gestapo tactics on the streets of Chicago." Mayor Daley then drew his finger across his throat, rose to his feet, and shouted, "Fuck you, you Jew son of a bitch, you lousy motherfucker, go home." It turned out that Daley spoke for at least some members of the silent majority. When the early numbers began coming in, as they did in a *New York Times* poll taken shortly after the convention ended, the one thousand people interviewed "overwhelmingly supported the police." Or, as Mailer saw, at the moment of impact, "the true feelings of the people, said the policemen's clubs, were with the police."

Once again, the moment had been met with "the true feelings of the people." But did the Movement cause the Reaction? There was, surely, a failure of empathy on both sides. David Farber cites the continual baiting of police as the most obvious evidence of the demonstrators' "inability to see the other in its own terms." It is one thing, however, to call up an "other," and quite another to cite that other as the motive force of one's own actions. Yet Chicago presented anyone who wished to reach for it with a ready-made "You made me do it" response.

"Almost every society seems to live with suspicion and contempt between ordinary people leading complacently ordinary lives and the politically, intellectually, and culturally 'advanced' elements of the population. The war in Vietnam," Thomas Powers argues in The War at Home, "brought these two classes, always vaguely hostile, to the verge of collision." Anyone reading this book probably counts him or herself as one of the "advanced." But being advanced only increases the responsibility to "see the other," as Farber puts it, "in its own terms." And yet "the hardest part of writing about the sixties," Farber concludes, "was getting the 'silent majority's' perspective straight."

In his essay "The Silent Majority and Talk about Revolution" (1994), Farber argues that Nixon understood his country as divided between "those who speak and those who are silent." As early as 1948, Nixon had found Alger Hiss "too mouthy." One problem in getting the silent majority's perspective straight lies in the fact of its having left little behind in the way of a written record. Some of the most powerful testimony from the right to come out of Chicago came from the police response to the Walker Report. Officer Ernie Watson provides one example. "It was a piece of garbage. They must have paid a lot of people to lie or slant the truth. It was a communist rag." Officer Terry Novicki made more of an attempt to respond to the charges of a police riot: "And some guys lost it. I came close, and I just gritted my teeth, but imagine some punk yelling to you that they'd like to screw your wife; it's all you can do not to kick their brains in." Imagining a self in that position is, for every American, part of the ongoing work we are in.

"Did the radicalism of Chicago elect Richard Nixon?" After struggling with this question for twenty years, Tom Hayden could find no "neat" answer. He admits to not wanting to take any blame for Nixon's victory, while also allowing that a Humphrey administration would have spared the nation the traumas of Watergate.

Hayden concludes that one's response is one's responsibility. The demonstrators did what they did; the police and the Democratic Party did what they did. It will not do, in any of the cases, to say that the thing done was done "in response." "To blame the protestors in Chicago, and the student radicals in general," Hayden comes to believe, "unfairly absolves the Johnson White House and the Democratic leadership from primary blame for their own self-destruction. Our cause was both just and rational, even if all our methods were not. Our values were decent ones, even if we could not always live up to them. We were not responsible for the killing in Vietnam or the segregation in Chicago."

Of course a reaction—"a visual image of the State in action"—was what the protestors meant to provoke. The politics of symbolic action depended on an action-reaction dynamic. The protestors got what they asked for—and more. In succeeding, they failed. The tragedy of the psychodrama in Chicago lay more in the long-term fallout than in the immediate damage done. After Chicago, the two sides of the social divide began to harden in their attitudes, a polarization marking the beginning of the end of political dialogue.

Yet in saying all this, something isn't answered; it isn't even asked. What lay beneath the strength and violence of the Reaction? In The Emerging Republican Majority (1969), Kevin Phillips attempted a preliminary and still compelling response. In an impressive collection of maps and tables, Phillips quantified the shift to the right that began in 1968. The shift, he argued, turned on the issue of race.

In 1964, white men voted Democratic at a rate of 60 percent. Four years later, that number had dropped by almost twenty points, to 41 percent. And "the principal force which broke up the Democratic (New Deal) Coalition," according to Phillips, was "the Negro socioeconomic revolution." American politics, he concluded, "cleave along distinct ethnic (in this case, racial) lines." As Maurice Isserman and Michael Kazin report, "Nixon read the book over Christmas 1969 and took its prescriptions to heart."

But what did America's racial lines have to do with Chicago, an event made up largely of white-on-white violence? The largest contingent of African Americans on the city's streets were members of the police force itself, one-quarter of which was black in 1968. So how might race be understood to play a role in this "white family war?"

It can be understood to play a role if we read Chicago as a crucial chapter in the growth of American "ressentiment," a complex of emotions which can be aroused by any number of "others" but which, for a certain kind of white imagination, always circles round to the foundational fact of the black "other" it has created and spurned. Chicago was an immense diversion away from this history—even a kind of strange relief, for some—as the phrase "law and order" found itself temporarily redirected at the nation's white children rather that at its black underclass. In the years to come, the white family war was to resolve itself by absorbing its resentment over the acting-out of its white children into a growing fear of inner city crime.

The issue of race had been there from the beginning. As we have seen, Daley prepared for the August convention in reaction to the black uprising of the previous April. The proximate cause of that month's rioting had been the murder of Martin Luther King Jr., but the Chicago Riot Study commissioned by Mayor Daley and submitted to him on August 1, looked beyond the immediate moment and claimed that "for the majority of blacks the riot was a spontaneous overflow of pent-up emotion." The damage done on Roosevelt Road and West Madison Street was serious enough to prompt President Johnson to send federal troops into the city and the mayor to issue his famous "shoot to kill" order.

Behind the riots of April 1968 lay Daley's experience of King's "War on the Slums" in 1965 and 1966. Bayard Rustin had warned King, "You don't know what Chicago is like. . . . You're going to be wiped out." The prolonged efforts to secure open and affordable housing for Chicago's poor culminated in the summer of 1966, when King, arriving at Marquette Park for a march on four realty offices, stepped out of a car and was struck by a rock on his right temple. As he picked himself up and kept walking, "hostile whites" continued to trail and harass the marchers. King remarked that he had "never seen anything so hostile and so hateful as I've seen here today." Later that year, after the city failed to implement an agreement on housing policy struck with the Southern Christian Leadership Conference, King threatened more demonstrations. Such comments, Mayor Daley responded, might well produce a "white backlash" against Democratic candidates in the fall elections.

When the mayor found himself faced with a major incursion into his city in August 1968, there was therefore an intention already at work, one directed against a fear having little to do with the antiwar movement. Chicago police officer Tom Freeborn makes the connection explicit while speculating on why those arrested during convention week experienced so little post-arrest violence. "Nothing happened to them *because it was a show—a sham for [police chief James] Conlisk and Daley* that we were not going to let this generation and the Negroes run free in his city and embarrass *his* city."

"And the Negroes." Freeborn's phrase effects a powerful segue, a deferral to the abiding subtext. Between 1940 and 1960, the black population of Chicago tripled, from 8 to 23 percent. The figure rose to 30 percent by 1970. Thirty years later, Chicago's non-Hispanic white population totaled only a little more than 30 percent. In 2000, the entire Chicago public school system was 9 percent white, and not a single high school in it had a majority white population.

"White flight" we call this, but flight from what, exactly? From falling home prices, urban decay, failing schools, and above all, perhaps, from crime. Yet none of these outcomes was inevitable, in Chicago or elsewhere, and each development can in fact be traced to a kind of collective, self-fulfilling prophecy that led to a failure of nerve, and where the nature of the flight was somehow linked to and driven by something as primitive and underexamined as the opposing term in the binary—to "black arrival." Perhaps only a novelist devoted to passing "Chicago through his own soul" could do justice to this powerful dynamic. Saul Bellow makes such an attempt in his eighth novel, a book devoted to excavating the "dark" secret in the white American unconscious, a figure he conjures up in the character of Spofford Mitchell.

As early as "Looking for Mr. Green" (1951), Bellow had sent his imagination into the black neighborhoods of his city. George Grebe is employed to deliver welfare checks in Chicago's Negro district, but he cannot find his man. Nor can he decipher the graffiti on the ghetto walls. "So the sealed rooms of pyramids were also decorated, and the caves of human dawn." In

1970, Bellow relocated this project to New York, where a curmudgeonly Mr. Sammler comes up against the fact of rising urban crime rates and engages in a kind of psychic struggle with a black pickpocket on the subway. His last serious attempt to take on the beauty and dread of an increasingly racialized city life occurs in The Dean's December (1982).

Set during the early years of the Reagan administration, Bellow's novel is actually a tale of two cities: Albert Corde, a dean at an unnamed college in Chicago, finds himself in Bucharest in support of his wife, Minna, whose mother is dying. As he naps in the chilly apartment and helps in attending to hospital and funeral duties, he reflects back on a career in journalism and the trouble it has stirred up. Corde, it turns out, has published an article in Harper's about the conditions in the Cook County Jail and about a black-on-white rape and murder case. After Corde's provost accuses him of embarrassing the college, the ensuing brouhaha will lead Corde to resign and Bellow's reader into a strenuous experience of self-encounter with his or her feelings about race.

Corde's study of William Blake has taught him that "cities were moods, emotional states, for the most part collective distortions, where human beings thrived and suffered, where they invested their souls in pains and pleasures, taking these pleasures and pains as proofs of reality." Bellow's shadowing of Chicago with an Eastern European capital does call up the simultaneity, in 1968, of the stateside police riot and the Soviet invasion of Prague, which began on the Wednesday before convention week.

In 1968, the impulse toward reform and even revolution reached far beyond the United States. In Czechoslovakia, it was the Writers Union that led the way when Ludvík Vaculík spoke against the repression of intellectuals and writers by the Communist Party following the Six Day War. In June 1968, Vaculík issued his manifesto "2000 Words," calling for the repudiation of those who were misusing power and urging Czechs to defend themselves against any invasion by foreign forces. When the troops and tanks of four Warsaw Pact nations entered Prague on August 20, they did so in part because of Leonid Brezhnev's agitation over Vaculík's defiance. The only Eastern European head of state to denounce the invasion was the Prime Secretary of the Romanian Communist Party, Nicolae Ceausescu.

Corde finds himself in Ceausescu's Romania over a decade after the events of the Prague Spring. In both Eastern Europe and Chicago the revolutionary tide has ebbed, with each culture devolving back into its preferred default position, a "penitentiary" versus a "pleasure society."

The dean's articles have brought to light a story everyone knows but wants to forget. He had wanted simply to "find out what Chicago, U.S.A., was built with." But the frankness of his words unsettles American bureaucracies and complacencies in the same way that Vaculík's had threatened Brezhnev. Corde had described "broad-daylight rapes and robberies, sexual acts in public places, on the seats of CTA buses, on the floors of public waiting rooms, men on Sheridan Road spraying automobile fenders with their urine." This is the sort of material that grounds Bellow's rant about the breakdown of civility and civilization in *Mr. Sammler's Planet* (1979). But Corde's tone is rueful rather than angry, just as Bellow's elected form in *The Dean's December* replaces a jeremiad with an anguished and ongoing attempt at dialogue.

The "most controversial part" of Corde's article involves the case of Spofford Mitchell. It is a story that emerges through a dialogue between Corde and Chicago public defender Sam Varennes. In the novel, the story comes out during a long bout of remembering carried out in Bucharest. Before providing Corde's remembered version of his conversation with Sam Varennes, Bellow gives his reader the facts of the case:

> The victim was a young suburban housewife, the mother of two small children. She had just parked in a lot near the Loop when Mitchell approached and forced her at gunpoint into his own car. . . . He drove to a remote alley and assaulted her sexually. Then he locked her into the trunk of his Pontiac. He took her out later in the day and raped her again. . . . Towards daybreak of the second day, for reasons not explained in the record, Spofford Mitchell let Mrs. Sathers go, warning her not to call the police. . . . As she turned away from the third or fourth closed door, Mitchell pulled up and reclaimed her. He drove to an empty lot, where he shot her in the head. He covered her body with trash.

Bellow allows his reader to experience the shock of reading this passage before complicating that response with the quoted dialogue that follows it. In that dialogue, two men speculate on intention and feeling. They move away from the thing done to the how and the why of it. "I'm trying to guess whether he understood her emotions," Corde ventures. Like John Schultz on the streets of Chicago, Corde is attempting to find a language that will not winnow out all the terrible complexity of human motive and decision. The drive toward understanding may be a laudable thing, but the reader already knows how he or she has reacted to "the facts" of the case before entering into the question of "what might the real content of these facts be?"

The gift of the novel is to show us how an unexamined response to such "facts" provided the essential fuel, after 1968, of the Reaction.

In the pages that follow, Corde rereads a long passage from his article and then sets it aside, trying to imagine a "new version, wider in perspective." He remembers that while talking to Varennes he had said and thought many perhaps unpublishable things: that America no more knew what to do with its black underclass than it knew what to do with its children; that when Sally Sathers stares at Spofford Mitchell with terror, she sees a man "filled with a staggering passion to *break through*"; that the worst slums are those we carry around inside us, "every man's *inner* inner city." These, again, are thoughts Corde only shares with himself, as if trying them out, testing their validity. Such "whirling" thoughts cannot be accommodated by journalism—they appear nowhere in Corde's published article—but only by the deft management of time, recollection, and careful movement in and out of characters' voices and minds possible in a novel. In the tradition of the great social realists, Bellow invites his reader, by way of Corde's continual self-interrogations, to face up to the contents of his or her own political unconscious.

Immediately before giving the "facts" of the Spofford Mitchell story, Bellow inserts a paragraph which it may be easy to overlook but which has a serious bearing on the aura around the case. It reads as follows: "The Mitchell case was not exceptional. There were thousands of similar crimes in police files across the country. But there were special circumstances which made it important to Corde." The prose here makes a truth claim difficult to verify. Despite its heavy reliance on the science of statistics, the field of criminology has very little hard data to offer a person interested in the question of black-on-white crime. Yet of course it is the rumor of such crime, a rumor here casually forwarded by Bellow's prose, that grounds political attitudes in many American minds and makes them subject to being manipulated by the rhetoric of "law and order."

Crime statistics come in two forms: from the Uniform Crime Reports (UCR) system, numbers gathered by criminal justice agencies; and from the NCVS, the National Crime Victimization Survey conducted by the Bureau of the Census. UCR data includes only offenders whose crimes have come to the attention of a law enforcement agency. It tracks eight offenses, including murder, forcible rape, robbery, and aggravated assault. NCVS data comes from self-reporting, interviews conducted annually of some 75,000 persons.

A number of anomalies result from the comparison of these statistics. In simply placing the two sets of numbers side by side, it becomes clear that "fewer than half of all victimizations are reported to the police." The crime of rape is particularly subject to vagaries in reporting, with criminologists concluding "that most rapes go unreported." Moreover, according to the criminal justice scholar Coramae Mann, "reporting practices for certain crimes, such as forcible rape, have been found to differ in accordance with racial status. White rape victims tend to report black offenders more often to the police than they do white offenders."

In his essay "Race and Crime Trends in the United States, 1941–1990" (1995), another criminologist, Gary LaFree, points out that the UCRs collect two kinds of information: "total crimes *known to police* and total arrests." Only the second set of figures—for total arrests—reports the suspect's race. But the measure of arrests data only record the race of the offender, not the race of the victim. Nowhere in the measure of arrests data can one find a category called "black-on-white" (or "white-on-black") crime. In relying solely on these numbers, it is simply not possible to know with any degree of accuracy who does what to whom.

As David Jacobs and Daniel Tope argue, in "The Politics of Resentment" (2006), "although few crimes are interracial, the conventional wisdom sees violent street crime as almost entirely the responsibility of underclass minorities who, it is erroneously believed, often victimize whites." Violent crimes, they reiterate, "are almost always intraracial." In 1986, there were 90,439 known forcible rapes in the United States. Among white rape victims, 81.5 percent perceived their attackers as white; 11.3 percent perceived them as black; and 7.2 percent perceived them to be members of other races. These numbers might seem to stabilize what remains, in fact, an open question, but rather than nailing down the facts about interracial rape, they serve instead to point up the persistent gap between what actually happened, what was reported, who was arrested, and what victims "perceived."

It is such sets of numbers, perhaps, that "Dr. William Wilbanks, a criminologist at Florida International University, had to sift carefully through . . . to find that in 1988 there were 9,406 cases of black-on-white rape and fewer than ten cases of white-on-black rape." The quotation is from Jared Taylor's *Paved with Good Intentions* (1992). The footnote in support of Taylor's claim cites an article Wilbanks "submitted for publication to *Justice Professional* (November 7, 1990)." Taylor's sentence has had a long half-life. It is quoted in a 2002 article in the *Virginia Quarterly Review* and appears verbatim on websites with names like "Our Race Is Our Nation" and "Obamanation."

A reader of Taylor's book will find it difficult to determine where he and Wilbanks find the numbers backing up their claims. Yet the importance of "crime" as a political issue in the 1968 election and beyond remains an indisputable fact. Nor did the electorate simply imagine the problem into being. Every available set of statistics does show—and the fact surely underwrites the shift to the right identified by Phillips—a rapid rise in violent crime beginning in the mid-1960s and, from then on, both "differentially high offending rates by African Americans for serious violent offenses and the presence of differentially high arrest rates for African Americans, especially for rape offenses." What to make of this emergent problem—how to feel and think about it—remained, as ever, a moral conundrum.

"I became a rapist": Eldridge Cleaver's Soul on Ice pivots on this shockingly direct statement. The sentence abrupts into the essay "On Becoming" as the result of a careful process of self-scrutiny. In it, Cleaver achieves the recognition scene that is one of the most useful products of serious thought. By doing so he also provides the "version wider in perspective" sought by Corde as he thinks back on the case of Spofford Mitchell.

Cleaver begins his autobiographical essay with Brown v. Board of Education, a cultural event requiring him to "take stock." Imprisoned for possession of marijuana at the time of the Supreme Court decision, he decides to pursue this stock-taking "through reading." It is then that he encounters "The Ogre." She has her claws "buried in the core of my being." He comes to see that he must confront her power over him, or be destroyed. "I, a black man, confronted The Ogre—the white woman."

A prison guard enters Cleaver's cell and tears down the photograph on his wall. "Get yourself a colored girl for a pinup—no white woman—and I'll let it stay up," he says. Cleaver is suddenly overcome by a terrible feeling of guilt. "Did I really prefer white girls over black? The conclusion was clear and inescapable: I did."

Most of his fellow black inmates admit to the same preference, and together they go on to notice how "a black growing up in America is indoctrinated with the white race's standard of beauty." Then Emmett Till is murdered, and Cleaver finds himself staring at a magazine picture of the white woman with whom Till was said to have flirted. He feels her appeal. And he flies into a rage "at the history that had placed those tensions of lust and desire in my chest." After reading Marx and struggling to understand his "critique," Cleaver decides to adopt a "ruthless attitude toward white women." This brings him to utter his startling sentence: after his release from jail, "I became a rapist."

Imprisoned once again, and for a rape he has in fact committed, Cleaver takes a long look at himself and admits that he has been "wrong." "That is why I started to write: to save myself. . . . I had to seek out the truth and unravel the snarled web of my motivations."

In his willingness to deploy words like "wrong," Cleaver becomes another example of a writer thinking against himself. (It is the argument of this book that this is what thinking *is*.) Cleaver makes his thinking against himself his conscious subject, while again attempting to resolve the inner tensions. Bellow refines the process even further, leaving Corde suspended between the voices that articulate him.

In choosing to represent Corde's inner argument as ongoing and open-ended, Bellow enacts the inevitably divided mind of a mature political self. It is not that one side of that mind is blue or red, left or right: the voices that speak through Corde cannot be reduced to a simple polarity. Instead, they express the interplay between hope and fear that is part of the American inheritance.

Cleaver's essay has much to teach us about how one significant inheritance continues to shadow contemporary life. "On Becoming" provides a crucial chapter in the history of lynching, and it does so by striking back at its logic in the most literal way. Lynching was above all a response to a *rumor,* to the fantasy that black men wanted white women and therefore had to be preemptively punished for doing so. This is why "Dry September" (1931), Faulkner's great lynching story, begins with the words "Through the bloody September twilight, aftermath of sixty-two rainless days, it had gone like a fire in dry grass—the rumor, the story, whatever it was." The rumor, of course, is that Will Mayes has molested Minnie Cooper. And he will be duly lynched, despite the admission by the leader of the lynch mob that it is of no consequence to him whether or not a rape actually occurred. Cleaver answers this stubbornly persistent rumor by saying, in effect, "All right, you have imagined the Black Beast, and I will act the part."

Just as the Black Beast takes up residence in the white mind, so the white Ogre has been implanted in the black one. Both are projections, acts of mental colonization, although the cultural power of each figuration necessarily differs. The projections are experienced as natural forces, a "whatever" shaping attitudes and compelling conduct with the unstoppable force of the weather.

Bellow's Spofford Mitchell, then, is a black version of the Ogre, an image that has been implanted in the white unconscious and that operates to structure its behavior in complex ways. The point in confronting one's "Spofford Mitchell" is less to empathize with him as a fictional character than it is to recognize him *as* a fiction and to acknowledge one's susceptibility to the anxieties he represents.

Bellow initially equates this work of acknowledgment with an act of seeing. Eyesight as insight is a pervasive metaphor in Bellow's novel; he places an immense trust in all that can be delivered by the verb "to see." Corde wants to "see at first hand the big manifestations of disorder." In the American moral crisis, "the first requirement was to experience what was happening and to see what must be seen." But in his struggle to become "a moralist of seeing," Corde must also admit that "the facts were covered from our perception." The increase in theories and discourse, as well as the "false representations of 'communication,'" have led to horrible distortions of the public consciousness. And there are the abiding "distortions of the atmosphere" itself that must also be taken into account, the simple limitations of the organs of sight when faced with the complexity of the world. Corde acknowledges this at the end, as he joins his astronomer-wife in the lift at the Mount Palomar observatory. "Through these distortions you saw objects, forms, partial realities. The rest was to be felt."

So feeling must come in aid of seeing. It is every reader's "snarled web" of feelings that is exposed and tested by the Spofford Mitchell story. One's acknowledged response to that story can then produce a Cleaveresque moment of self-recognition. Corde leads the way in this activity; against the "theorizing," Bellow repeatedly assigns his character the phrase "Corde felt." "And he felt" is one of Mailer's favorite constructions as well; in *Miami and the Siege of Chicago* the confirming existential event is the return of feeling after bafflement or torpor. Once we have had our feelings, Bellow's novel then requires us to think about them. Only thinking can allow us to sort out the programmed feelings, to distinguish those based on rumor and false consciousness from those that are deep and true. "These times we live in give us foolish thoughts to think," Corde says to himself, "dead categories of intellect and words that get us nowhere. It was just these words and categories that made the setting of a real depth level so important."

One way to "retrieve reality" from "the trash" is to "represent it anew as art would represent it." Corde is not at all sure that his *Harper's* article is not another piece of trash. "Nothing true—really true," he concludes, "could be said in the papers." A journalist's language is subject to "the right clearance," where the censoring power is nothing so obvious as a managing editor or an interfering provost but, instead, the received rhetorics of what has come to be called "communication." Corde's growing ambivalence about the practice of journalism leads him to call it "a bad profession." It is bad because too much of it reinforces the prevailing rumors instead of uncovering the processes by which those rumors colonize the soul.

Like Cleaver, Bellow knows that the only way forward is through the analysis of painful self-critique. For example: Corde quotes himself on "pity" and "love," feelings he has assigned to the nurses and attendants in the County Hospital, and then dismisses his fine words as "stuff." The accuracy of the dismissal matters less than does the revisionary motion of mind. The offered experience asks the reader to remain with the shifting "tensions" of a mind feeling and thinking. Such an artistic structure could have contained any subject, but it is Bellow's gift to us that he chose to devote it to the excavation of a rumor—and the consequences to our politics of believing it—so deeply buried in the core of his city's and his country's being.

If Chicago '68 was a "white family war," as John Schultz claims, then to turn from what happened there to *The Dean's December* might seem a digression. The connection between the novel and the event lies in the fact that Chicago worked in many minds to justify the movement toward Reaction. The silent majority and the supporters of "law and order" went on to prefer a politics of fear to a politics of hope, and, in the years to come, America's white family was to become increasingly divided. But it remained united, as Bellow's novel reveals, by the inescapable legacy and ongoing struggle between the two voices within, voices prompted to brood on race by the shifting and ambiguous patterns of urban crime. There was the loud, clamorous, easily offended voice of resentment, and the still, small attentive one that spoke of enduring affinities. Whichever voice one chose to listen to, or whether one chose even to acknowledge the presence of the two voices at all, remained a matter of individual choice, but, for any white American reading *The Dean's December*, it was no longer possible to believe that double consciousness stood only on the far side of the color line.

11

Kissinger and the Dragon Lady

As Richard Nixon writes in *RN*, he and Henry Kissinger saw themselves as people who "made history." The phrase refers to their power to shape events on the national and international stage. But Nixon and Kissinger made history in another sense—by writing it. They did so in memoirs of almost crushing length; Kissinger's *White House Years* (1979) exceeds *RN*'s 1,120 pages by 300 more. Having myself published a memoir, it is difficult for me to disagree with *RN*'s opening claim that "memory is fallible and inevitably selective." Nor is it hard to understand the memoirist's desire to protect the people he has loved and worked with from gratuitous exposure, and therefore to grant him the right to tactful omission.

We've seen that when Hemingway wrote about the art of omission in *A Moveable Feast* (1964), he maintained that as a writer "you could omit anything if you knew that you omitted and the omitted part would strengthen the story and make people feel something more than they understood." Omission used in this way is an art of inclusion; through the continual repetition of abstract nouns like "it" and "something," for instance, Hemingway's prose draws attention toward the presence of something indicated but not named. As a result, the reader is made increasingly aware that Hemingway's characters are shadowed by feelings and forces they cannot or will not artic-ulate. Omission might in fact be said to be Hemingway's subject, where the word refers to the self as an iceberg, supported and directed and haunted in its movements by all that is being kept beneath the surface of what it consciously understood. The point of reading Hemingway, then, would be to recognize oneself as also possessing such a self.

In setting out to read Nixon's and Kissinger's memoirs, I approached them as I had every other book read for this project, as a set of truth claims inseparable from the rhetorical and narrative devices by way of which the claims were being made. I knew that each man was obsessed with secrets, with the plugging of "leaks." I knew that each saw himself as a pragmatist, a practitioner of realpolitik, and a world-historical figure. I was not prepared, however, for the sheer audacity of each performance, the brazen evasion of responsibility for outcomes each man had so openly sought. And here the very length of the performances became an indictment of them. "Each man" deploys "overwhelming detail," as Stephen Ambrose maintains, "not so much to elucidate and enlighten as to confuse and contradict." Inclusiveness here functions to direct attention *away* from what is being omitted. What I came to feel then, in reading these books and in setting them alongside the many competing accounts, was not Hemingway's "something more" than I understood—I was not being asked to feel anything this self-revealing or complex—but rather an escalating rage at two men who had become "convinced that consistent lying," as William Safire writes, "can be the right thing for the country."

The big lie each book tells about the fall of 1968 has to do with the manipulation of the Paris peace talks by the Nixon campaign. The negotiations over peace talks mattered because—once formally under way—the talks promised not only to bring an end to the war but to determine the outcome of the 1968 election. Preliminary discussions between the United States and the North Vietnamese had begun in the spring of 1968, and the Johnson administration pushed hard for the opening of formal talks before the first Tuesday in November. In the event, the South Vietnamese president, Nguyen Van Thieu, refused to sit down at the table and did not send representatives to Paris until two weeks *after* the American election, a concession made only once he had received a "strong word" from the president-elect. The promise of a bombing halt and of the start of official talks had helped Hubert Humphrey narrow a fifteen-point gap in the polls into an almost even race by late October. When the talks failed to begin, Nixon went on to win by a narrow plurality of 43.4 to Humphrey's 42.7 percent, with George Wallace garnering the remaining votes. The story about why Thieu refused to sit down at the table is one both *RN* and *White House Years* choose to omit.

Kissinger begins his memoir by describing his wonder at being asked to serve in the Nixon administration. Finding himself at the January inauguration ceremony, his "feeling of surprise at being there was palpable. Only eight weeks earlier the suggestion that I might participate in the Inauguration as one of the new president's closest advisers would have seemed preposterous. Until then, all of my political experience had been in the company of those who considered themselves in mortal opposition to Richard Nixon."

Kissinger then backs up to fill in the events of the preceding months, representing his relationship with the president-elect as starting with "The Phone Call." At lunch with his patron Nelson Rockefeller on November 22, 1968, he is interrupted by Nixon's appointment secretary and a request that Kissinger "meet with his chief." Kissinger again strikes a tone of wonder: "No one at the lunch could conceive that the purpose of the call could be to offer me a major position in the new Administration." In due course, and despite Nixon's having "screwed it up again," as his campaign manager (and later attorney general) John Mitchell puts it—the president-elect has somehow failed to convey to Kissinger during their meeting that he wishes him to become the new national security adviser—Kissinger joins the White House team.

The phone call episode is followed by a section titled "Meeting Richard Nixon." In it, Kissinger moves back another step in time. Beginning by saying, "I did not know the President-elect," he then proceeds to detail their one meeting prior to the fall of 1968, at a 1967 Christmas party in New York. There Nixon complimented Kissinger about his first book, a "few strained pleasantries were exchanged," and "we . . . went our separate ways." So "the grocer's son from Whittier and the refugee from Hitler's Germany" began their "partnership," as Nixon calls it, a trading in sycophancy that was to culminate in the Lincoln Sitting Room on August 7, 1974, where Kissinger, the "not very orthodox Jew," knelt in prayer beside the weeping president. "You made the tough decisions," he said to Nixon, once the two men were back on their feet. Nixon had by then converted Kissinger into his Boswell and would pay the price of doing so, since, despite the president's last request to him—"Henry, please don't ever tell anyone that I cried and that I was not strong"—Kissinger alone can have been the source of this story.

Kissinger's account of his "contribution to the American political process" in 1968 abbreviates a complex novel into a very short story. During the campaign, he admits, "several Nixon emissaries—some self-appointed—telephoned me for counsel." Agreeing to answer specific questions on foreign policy, Kissinger avers that only one question was ever put to him by the Nixon organization. Mitchell asked him if he "thought the Johnson Administration would agree to a bombing halt in Vietnam in return for the opening of negotiations before the election." Kissinger replied he thought it highly probable that the North Vietnamese wanted a bombing halt on these terms, and thereafter "Mitchell checked that judgment with me once or twice more during the campaign."

This minimalist version of his early contacts with Nixon and his people only throws into greater relief Kissinger's habitual use of overwhelming detail. A gifted, sometimes eloquent, and often witty writer (Richard Helms's "smile did not always include his eyes"), Kissinger's calculated omissions create a romance in which an "arrogant" Harvard intellectual finds himself magically transported into doing service in the opposition camp. But Kissinger had in fact worked very hard in order to be "there." His activities as a "willing collaborator" in the Nixon candidacy lie at the heart of one of the great twice-told tales of 1968. In 2000 Christopher Hitchins opened *The Trial of Henry Kissinger* by describing the story as "an open secret that is too momentous and too awful to tell." To describe it in this way was to concede in advance what once again proved to be the case—that the more this story is told, the more it somehow fails to register as the crowning scandal of a scandal-ridden year.

More than two months before "The Phone Call," on September 12, 1968, Nixon notes in *RN*, "Haldeman brought me a report from John Mitchell that Rockefeller's foreign policy adviser, Henry Kissinger, was able to assist us with advice." Nixon's memoir makes four references to contacts between Kissinger and the Nixon campaign during September and October. In *The Price of Power* (1983), Seymour Hersh maintains that contact with Kissinger began "a few weeks after the convention," when Richard Allen, Nixon's coordinator for foreign policy research, asked him to serve as a member of the candidate's foreign affairs advisory group. "I can do you more good by not coming out for you publicly," Kissinger replied. Kissinger had in fact already helped Allen draft the Vietnam plank at the Republican convention, while also writing in the same month a letter to Averell Harriman complaining, "I am through with Republican politics. The party is hopeless and unfit to govern."

On September 26, Kissinger called John Mitchell and told him "something big was afoot regarding Vietnam." Mitchell now had a direct link to Kissinger, one he kept secret from Allen. Twelve hours before announcement of the bombing halt, Kissinger phoned Allen with "important information." Calls to Allen were made from "a public telephone so the Democrats would not find out"; the two sometimes spoke in German in order to maintain secrecy.

John Mitchell later said, "Henry's information was basic. We were getting all of our information from him."

"Kissinger's offer to report secretly on the peace talks for Nixon," Hersh writes, "would have astonished his friends in the Paris delegation, who continued to trust him in the weeks before the election as if he were still a part of the team seeking a settlement of the Vietnam War." Beginning in 1967, and working through two French intellectuals, one of them a close friend of Ho Chi Minh, Kissinger had assisted the Johnson administration in discreet exchanges of messages between Hanoi and Washington. Kissinger also nudged the administration to take a fresh approach to a settlement with the North Vietnamese, one that achieved full expression in Johnson's so-called San Antonio formula, in which the president uncoupled the possibility of a bombing halt from an unconditional withdrawal by the North. When in Paris, Kissinger was kept abreast of developments in the talks by David Davidson, aide to Harriman, leader of the U.S. delegation.

Regardless of which American side Kissinger was working for, his most useful contacts were with the North Vietnamese. It was, however, impossible to manipulate Hanoi; there was nothing either he or the Nixon camp could offer them. The best he could do was to signal whether formal talks might actually begin. While Mitchell deemed such information "basic," it provided only tactical support for a much more daring strategy, one involving the South Vietnamese. Whether or not the North agreed to sit down, the talks would mean little if the South Vietnamese refused to participate. In the best of all worlds for the Republicans, the North would agree and the South would resist, thus dashing both the hopes for settlement and the momentum they might have given to the Humphrey campaign. In this endeavor, the Nixon camp sought out another international operator, a native-born Chinese woman known by some, like Clark Clifford, as the Little Flower, and by others, like H. R. Haldeman, as the Dragon Lady.

Anna Chennault published her memoir a year after Kissinger published his. Hidden in plain sight in this very public work of self-fashioning is the fascinating story of how a Chinese immigrant helped to delay the Paris peace talks and therefore to ensure the election of Richard Nixon.

The Education of Anna (1980) combines the traumas of The Joy Luck Club with the tone of Gone with the Wind. Born in Peking in 1925, Anna Chen saw her middle-class life broken up by invasion and civil war. She lost track of her four sisters in a retreat from the Japanese; and vowed, after six months of caring for her dying mother, "I would never budget again."

Her personal narrative culminates in her meeting "the Old Man," General Claire Chennault, at the age of nineteen. A close friend of nationalist leader Chiang Kai-shek, the founder of the famed Flying Tigers had airlifted supplies and troops over the Hump from Burma to China during World War II. He quickly fell in love with Anna and married her in 1947. "Loving him, being loved by him," she writes in A Thousand Springs, "made me feel big and little at the same time." After her husband's death from lung cancer in 1958, Chennault moved to Washington, D.C., where she took up residence at the Watergate apartment complex, began to work in Republican politics, and became one of the city's leading hostesses.

"The Autumn Annals," devoted largely to the fall of 1968, begin with Chennault's first meeting with Richard Nixon in Taiwan during the mid-1950s. She remembers Nixon's letter of condolence after the general's death; "from then on we communicated periodically." In 1965 they met again in Taipei, where she called on him at the Grand Hotel. As Nixon followed her into the car, he cracked his forehead on the door. Blood began oozing out of the cut, Chennault reached for a handkerchief, Nixon mumbled an apology, and her dress ended up "conspicuously spattered with drops of blood."

In the spring of 1967, Nixon called Chennault and requested a meeting with her in New York. He asked her to serve as his adviser on Southeast Asian affairs, and told her he wanted to "end this war with a victory."

"At the height of the campaign," Chennault writes, "I was on the phone with Mitchell at least once a day." Following a request from the campaign—"I cannot now remember whether it was Nixon or Mitchell"—she arranged a July 12 meeting between Nixon and Bui Diem, the South Vietnamese ambassador to Washington. "Anna is my good friend," Nixon said to him, when they met in his New York apartment. The three talked for half an hour, and then Nixon, Mitchell, and Bui Diem went into Nixon's study for another conference.

Chennault had first met Nguyen Van Thieu a year earlier, in 1967, in Saigon. Spending a long evening with the president of South Vietnam and his wife, she delivered "a message from Nixon requesting that I be recognized as the conduit for any information that might flow between the two." As the campaign neared its climax, she had to listen to Thieu's "complaints about the steady pressure brought to bear on him by the Democrats to attend the Paris Peace Talks." Thieu told Chennault he "would much prefer to have the peace talks after your elections."

Toward the end of October, amidst talk of an unconditional bombing halt, Chennault reports, Thieu "was said to have agreed" to such a move by the Johnson administration, "provided his government were included in the negotiation and settlement process." Then, noting an apparent contradiction between what Thieu was said to have said, and what he eventually went on—publicly—to say, Chennault recalls Johnson's speech announcing the bombing halt and the cease-fire and the answer given by Thieu in Saigon on the following day. On Friday, Saigon time, four days before the U.S. presidential election, Thieu stood before the National Assembly and said: "The government of South Vietnam deeply regrets not to be able to participate in the present exploratory talks."

Chennault follows this paragraph with a series of rhetorical questions. "How could that be? How could Saigon have agreed and then reneged?" She then digresses for a page into a memory of a party given by the well-known Washington hostess Perle Mesta on the night of Johnson's address. Returning to her core narrative, she recalls receiving a phone call from Mitchell while she was finishing dessert. "As usual, he wanted me to call him back from another more 'anonymous' number. I jotted down his number: (914) WO7-0909." She then left the party with her escort, Tom Corcoran, drove to his apartment, and phoned Mitchell while Corcoran listened in.

"'Anna,' he said, 'I'm speaking on behalf of Mr. Nixon. It's very important that our Vietnamese friends understand our Republican position and I hope you have made that clear to them.'" Accustomed "to Mitchell's vagueness," she detected a "specific request behind the non-specific tone." Describing herself as tired, and not being "sure quite what it was I was to make clear to the South Vietnamese," she then proceeds to quote her response to Mitchell: "Look, John, all I've done is relay messages. If you're talking about direct influence, I have to tell you it isn't wise for us to try to influence the South Vietnamese. Their actions have to follow their own national interests, and I'm sure that is what will dictate Thieu's decisions." Sounding nervous, Mitchell responded: "Do you think they really have decided not to go to Paris?" "I don't think they'll go," she answered. "Thieu has told me over and over again that going to Paris would be walking into a smoke screen that has nothing to do with reality."

With this exchange, Chennault's narrative of the campaign ends. The chapter following describes her vigil at the Waldorf-Astoria on election night and culminates in one last, astonishing scene, a meeting with Mitchell on November 13. Telling her that the president and the president-elect have agreed to put out a joint statement on Vietnam policy, he adds, "We need to do something about our friends in Saigon."

"Do what about our friends in Saigon?" I asked, not yet understanding.

"Well, persuade them to go to Paris," he said.

"You must be joking," I said, flabbergasted. "Two weeks ago, Nixon and you were worried that they might succumb to pressure to go to Paris. What makes you change your mind all of a sudden?"

Mitchell just shook his head. "Anna, you're no newcomer to politics. This, whether you like it or not, is politics."

I gathered up my coat. "I don't play that kind of politics. You go and tell them yourself," I said, and left in a rage.

That evening Nixon aide Herb Klein called her and said,

"You must promise to say to the press that our friend does not know about our arrangement with President Thieu." (The friend in this case was Nixon. How I was beginning to hate their use and concept of that word.)

"What arrangement are you talking about," I said. "I know of no arrangement; I never made any arrangement."

As though he hadn't heard me, Klein said, "We know you're a good soldier; we just want to be sure our friend is protected."

"Why should your friend," I said, talking like them despite myself, "need protection?"

Months later, at a White House function, Nixon took Chennault aside and thanked her for her help in the election. "'I've certainly paid dearly for it,' I pointed out."

My reading of The Education of Anna gave me much of what I needed in order to recover the campaign strategy pursued by Nixon and his operatives. Her book, however, is no model of transparency. Like Nixon and Kissinger, Chennault writes out of her own unique blend of admission and omission. Finding herself "talking like them despite myself," she encodes her history in words like "information," "position," and "friend." At times her prose makes the displacements explicit, as when referring to Mitchell's "vagueness" or his "non-specific tone." At times she too hides behind a feigned cluelessness, repeating the word "arrangement" as if it had no specific meaning to her. If, as Walt Rostow claims, Chennault's writings on the October surprise can be taken "as gospel truth," it is a truth told slant, an act of self-defense which can be read, like RN and White House Years—neither one of which makes any mention of Anna Chennault—as an act of inadvertent self-exposure.

It was my reading of William Safire that first alerted me to the fact that "the great mystery of the 1968 campaign centers around Anna Chennault." In Before the Fall, however, he is also content to remain within the burthen of the mystery: "The question is: Did Anna Chennault act as an agent of candidate Nixon to urge South Vietnam's leaders to refuse to come to the Paris peace table under the terms offered by President Johnson just before Election Day? Dammit, the answer appears to be yes and no." Comments made by Chennault subsequent to the publication of her memoir, as well a close reading of books by Hersh, Catherine Forslund, William Bundy, Anthony Summers, Lloyd Garner, and Nguyen Tien Hung and Jerrold Schecter, have however made it clear to me that Safire's question can have only one answer.

The ever-increasing evidence shows that Nixon provided "the scheme," Kissinger "the information," and Chennault "the means." Or, as Forslund puts it, "With Kissinger exposing the peace talks' progress and Chennault reporting the [Vietnamese government's] reluctant attitude, Nixon was in a powerful position to manipulate the situation for his political advantage."

In reporting her conversations with Nixon and his people, Chennault represents her role as that of a mere messenger. The impression thereby created is, in a strict sense, accurate enough, since no evidence exists of her *generating* the messages she was to pass along. William Bundy deems Chennault's denials of direct influence a quibble: "She may have avoided direct appeals, but her message was hardly subtle or obscure." Moreover, as early as July 1968 she had abandoned any claim to the role of a passive conduit, since she engineered the meeting in New York between Nixon and Bui Diem, a turning point with which Bundy chooses to begin the story he tells in A Tangled Web (1998). As Clark Clifford argues in Counsel to the President, "the chain of events undeniably began in Richard Nixon's apartment in New York."

Read together, the five memoirs on which this chapter depends—books by Nixon, Kissinger, Chennault, Diem, and Haldeman—manage to reproduce the crisis of veracity each informant was living through in the summer and fall of 1968. In juxtaposing these performances, the art of omission finally collapses into the art of lying.

A phone call made three days before the election is one of the more artful omissions from The Education. On November 2, Chennault called Ambassador Bui Diem. The call to Diem was made in order to report to him about *another* call, one made to her by "her boss." By the time of the call to Bui Diem, Chennault had for some days been under surveillance by the National Security Agency, the CIA, and the FBI. An FBI file dated "11/2/68" and first published by Anthony Summers in 1999 reads:

On November two instant, an informant, who has furnished reliable information in the past, reported that Mrs. Anna Chennault contacted Vietnamese ambassador, Bui Diem, and advised him that she had received a message from her boss (not further identified), which her boss wanted her to give personally to the ambassador. She said the message was that the ambassador is to "Hold on, we are gonna win" and that her boss also said "Hold on, he understands all of it." She repeated that this is the only message. "He said please tell your boss to hold on." She advised that her boss had just called from New Mexico.

The boss in New Mexico was probably Spiro Agnew, then on a campaign swing through the state. Chennault had a habit of coding people as places; a wiretap made five days later records her telling Bui Diem's secretary that she has been "talking to Florida," where Nixon was vacationing.

In a 2000 interview, Chennault denied having spoken to Agnew while he was in Albuquerque. Later that November, Summers reports, "when things quieted down, Johnson would order the FBI to check all calls made by the Agnew party. He was unfortunately ill served. Director Hoover, a long-term Nixon supporter on cordial terms with Chennault, had already warned her that she was being surveilled. As much as possible, he told her, the bureau was merely 'making a show' of obeying Johnson's orders."

Lacking any hard evidence of a phone call to Chennault from "her boss," the White House nevertheless remained convinced that one had occurred. Ten days after the reference to "New Mexico," Rostow sent Johnson a memo referring to Anna Chennault as "the Lady" and to Agnew as "the gentleman in Albuquerque." Agnew only muddied these waters when, in *Go Quietly . . . or Else,* he wrote, "It is known now that Lyndon Johnson put me under surveillance in October 1968, when he thought I had been in contact with President Thieu through Anna Chennault."

As Catherine Forslund reports in *Anna Chennault: Informal Diplomacy and Asian Relations* (2002), "New material indicates that a call from Albuquerque did go to Anna Chennault, and that it could have been made by Agnew." She goes on to add however that it "seems implausible that Nixon would have shared his most dangerous secret" with Agnew, and that "late in the 1990s, Chennault wavered on these conversations while never faltering in her position that Nixon knew of and/or directed her actions." The wavering had to do with where the messenger was calling from. Chennault claimed that the FBI wiretap technicians had misunderstood her—she had in fact said "New Hampshire," not "New Mexico." John Mitchell happened to be in New Hampshire at the time of the purported phone call.

In *The Arrogance of Power* (2000), Summers returns to the heart of the matter, to the imperative "Tell your boss to hold on." Whoever the stateside boss might have been, it was clear that Thieu was the boss in Saigon. Thieu had to hold on because he had just given a speech announcing that the South Vietnamese would not be sitting down at the table in Paris, a speech in open defiance of the wishes of his powerful patron and ally. Chennault's later wavering about where the phone call originated did nothing to lessen the seriousness of the matter. Had the boss in fact been Mitchell rather than Agnew—New Hampshire rather than New Mexico—the link with Nixon would have only deepened. By her own later account, one that reinforces claims made by her in *The Education*, Chennault talked with Mitchell during the last week of the campaign "almost every day." In a 1985 interview with the authors of *The Palace File* (1986), she recalled joking with Mitchell about being wiretapped—"Who is listening on the other side?"—and that "Mitchell's message to her was always the same: 'Don't let him go.'"

The title of Bui Diem's memoir, In the Jaws of History (1987), indicates that he often felt caught between a rock and a hard place. In the Anna Chennault story he is a primary go-between on the Pacific side of the equation, just as Kissinger was for the Atlantic. Born into a mandarin North Vietnamese family in 1923, Diem was taught French history by Vo Nguyen Giap, later the hero of Dien Bien Phu. During the Japanese occupation he joined a nationalist cell, spending a year in hiding once the Viet Minh began their reign of terror. Believing that Vietnam could achieve a non-Communist nationalism, Diem came to see the 1954 division of his country as "a blessing," since without it there was "little hope of successfully opposing the Vietminh's drive for power." Deeply suspicious of President Ngo Dien Diem, he stayed out of official South Vietnamese politics until after the 1963 coup. He then quickly rose through the ranks, becoming minister of foreign affairs in Air Marshal Nguyen Cao Ky's cabinet, and then ambassador to the United States in 1966.

Clark Clifford called him "affable Bui Diem." He "was adept at playing difficult Americans against one another. He was small and wiry, with bright eyes and an ever-present pipe, which gave him an air of great Oriental wisdom." Diem sought out Chennault soon after his arrival in Washington. In early June 1968, she relayed the message that Nixon was eager to meet with him: "The Democrats, he said, had already contacted him with a similar request. 'Suddenly,' he told me, 'I have become very interesting. They tap my phone, they intercept my mail, they monitor messages I exchange with Saigon.' I wasn't sure if he was being serious. 'Why don't you complain?' I asked. 'I have,' he said, 'to the State Department. It's gotten me nowhere.'"

Near the end of *In the Jaws of History,* Diem admits that "the Anna Chennault affair had taught me that my cables were far from secure." Yet in his chapter about the affair, he writes as if unaware that anyone had begun, as he told Chennault in the summer of 1968, to monitor the messages he was exchanging with Saigon. This pretense lends the chapter a strange air of unreality, since Diem remains unable to grasp how his "statements led Johnson administration officials to presume the worst." The White House was in fact reading his cables, two of which caused particular concern: a cable sent on October 23, in which Bui Diem urged Saigon to "stand firm"; and a second sent on October 27 in which he assured Thieu that he was "regularly in touch with the Nixon entourage," by which he meant Senator John Tower, John Mitchell, and Anna Chennault.

"It was one night in June . . . that Anna suggested I get together with the Republican presidential candidate." The July 12 meeting in New York would duly occur, and Diem gives a diplomatically vague account of it, focusing largely on his anxieties about being seen as double-dealing by the Democrats. Diem was careful to inform the State Department of his impending visit to New York. Meanwhile, a member of Nixon's staff issued a memo arguing that the meeting "would have to be absolute top secret." "Should be," Nixon scrawled in response. For his part, Bui Diem suggests that the encounter in New York left no lasting mark; "in the rush of flying back and forth between Paris and Washington . . . I soon forgot the Nixon meeting."

The hot Washington summer continued, and "as the Democrats steered with all due haste away from the Indochinese involvement they had engineered, I was increasingly attracted to the Republican side." When it came to courting Republicans, "there were few places in Washington like Anna Chennault's penthouse apartment." Summer gave way to fall, and on October 15 Diem received word that the North Vietnamese had responded favorably to an American offer to stop the bombing above the 17th parallel. As a quid pro quo, they also agreed to include the South Vietnamese in the Paris talks along with the National Liberation Front, while maintaining their view that the NLF was "the sole legitimate" representative of the South Vietnamese people.

Thieu responded to the offer as nothing but a ploy. Knowing that the United States had already agreed to a "vague our-side, your-side" formula, he had hoped that the North would reject it. Neither Thieu nor Diem were in any way ready to accept the notion of NLF representation at the talks, a view forcefully conveyed to the American ambassador to South Vietnam, Ellsworth Bunker.

South Vietnam and the United States eventually agreed to issue a joint declaration backed up by an American pledge not to recognize the NLF as a separate entity and a guarantee that the North would engage in "direct talks" with the South. The declaration itself read: "Delegations of the Republic of Vietnam and the United States will attend that meeting."

The agreement to issue a joint resolution held for only a few days. On October 30, at 4 a.m., Diem received a phone call from Thieu's secretary, informing him that the United States was unable to force the North into direct talks with the South, and of Thieu's intention to withdraw his commitment to send a delegation to Paris. A few hours after receiving the phone call, Diem went to the State Department to meet with William Bundy, assistant secretary of state for East Asian and Pacific affairs.

There ensued a startling scene. As Diem narrates it, Bundy did not even invite him to sit down. "In a frigid tone I had never heard from him before, he informed me bluntly that the U.S. presidential election had nothing whatsoever to do with the negotiations in Paris." Bundy then stood up and turned his back to Diem, who could hear him mumbling words like "improper," "unethical," and "unacceptable." He also began making allusions to Diem's connections with the Nixon camp. Diem defended himself, maintaining "that I had done nothing that could be construed as detrimental to the good relations between our two countries." On the following day, Johnson "dropped his political bomb in a televised address," announcing a bombing halt and expanded talks. A day after that, on November 1, Thieu responded with a speech of his own, informing the world that "no South Vietnamese negotiating team would at present be going to Paris." With Thieu's announcement, Humphrey's hopes of winning the election were, effectively, over.

Diem manages to get a considerable distance into his story without quoting from any of his cables to Saigon. He can thus represent himself as an innocent bystander at the collapse of the agreement between Saigon and Washington and therefore as "dumbfounded" by Bundy's "performance." Only a call from a reporter from the *Christian Science Monitor* shakes him out of his chosen pose.

The correspondent confronts Diem with evidence that "the South Vietnamese had made a deal with Richard Nixon." Unwilling to deny or to confirm such allegations, Diem asks for time in which to review his cables to Saigon. It is only at this point—after his narrative has accomplished its goal of representing the collapse of the agreement as beyond his comprehension or control—that Diem begins "reviewing" the actual words of his cables. He find only "two relevant messages" sent back to Saigon. In one, "I had said, 'Many Republican friends have contacted me and encouraged us to stand firm.'" In the other, "I wrote, 'I am regularly in touch with the Nixon entourage.'" In putting the two cables together, Diem concludes, "I saw that they constituted circumstantial evidence for anybody ready to assume the worst."

Rumors of a bombing halt "came as no real surprise" to Richard Nixon. "I had known for several weeks," he writes in *RN*, "that plans were being made for such an action. . . . What I found difficult to accept was the timing. Announcing the halt so close to the election was utterly callous if politically calculated, and utterly naïve if sincere."

Nixon countered the rumors with a major act of occupatio. Deciding that "the only way to prevent Johnson from totally undercutting my candidacy at the eleventh hour was for me to make public the fact that a bombing halt was imminent," Nixon released a statement through spokesmen Herb Klein and Ron Ziegler on October 26:

> In the last thirty-six hours I have been advised of a flurry of meetings in the White House and elsewhere on Vietnam. I am told that top officials in the administration have been driving very hard for an agreement on a bombing halt, accompanied possibly by a cease-fire, in the immediate future. I have since learned these reports are true.
>
> I am . . . told that this spurt of activity is a cynical, last-minute attempt by President Johnson to salvage the candidacy of Mr. Humphrey.
>
> This I do not believe.

Nixon's "this I do not believe" was meant to be heard as meaning its exact opposite: "This is what I do believe." In *RN*, he even sets up such a reading of the sentence by preceding it with the claim that Johnson "had additional motives" other than "negotiating a peace" and that "everything he did was weighed a second time on a strictly political scale." Sensing the act of occupatio in Nixon's public disclaimer, a reporter present at the release of the statement replied, "I'm concerned that you're trying to get a rumor in the paper by denying it." Klein answered, "We don't participate in that sort of thing."

A week later, on *Meet the Press,* Nixon again indulged in "that sort of thing." NBC's Herb Kaplow conveyed his sense that some of Nixon's "close aides have been trying to spread the word that President Johnson timed the Vietnam bombing pause to help Vice-President Humphrey in Tuesday's election. Do you agree with them?" "No, I don't make that charge," Nixon answered. "I must say that many of my aides and many of the people supporting my candidacy around the country seem to share that view. They share it, I suppose, because the pause came at that time so late in the campaign. But President Johnson has been very candid with me throughout these discussions, and I do not make such a charge."

Born in 1924 and raised in the South in a Confucian household, Nguyen Van Thieu joined the Viet Minh near the end of World War II. After beginning to question Communist doctrine he found himself on an assassination list and fled to Saigon. Attending the Vietnamese Military Academy in Hué, Thieu earned a reputation for bravery in combat. He married into a prominent Catholic family in 1951 and was baptized in 1957. Never an ally of Ngo Dien Diem, he supported the coup against him and emerged thereafter as the leader of the group of younger military officers known as the Young Turks, becoming chief of state when Ky became prime minister. When Thieu ran for president in the September 1967 election, he was elevated to the presidency in a compromise move with the generals after receiving only 35 percent of the vote. Managing to cling to power until the bitter end, Thieu fled the country only five days before the fall of Saigon in 1975. It was his decision to furlough most of his army for the national holiday that left Saigon largely undefended during the Tet Offensive.

In 1967 Hubert Humphrey attended Thieu's inauguration as president of the Republic of Vietnam. The two men met in the Independence Palace after the ceremony. Using the phrase "time is running out," Humphrey expressed concern about the Americanization of South Vietnam's military. Replying that he understood, Thieu also insisted that "it will be necessary for you to remain here at present levels." In reply, Humphrey said that "several years more of the same aid levels, militarily and economically, are not in the cards." The authors of The Palace File conclude that at this moment "Thieu and Humphrey had become enemies." In a 1985 interview, Thieu maintained that he had believed "a Humphrey victory would mean a coalition government in six months; with Nixon at least there was a chance."

In mid-October, Ambassador Bunker cabled from South Vietnam that "Thieu was for the plan without reservations." The plan in question was Hanoi's agreement to direct talks with Saigon. Hanoi insisted as well on an NLF presence at the talks, with the tacit understanding that "each side should have its South Vietnamese representative, with neither accepting the asserted status of the rival." For the South, there could be no question of any official acknowledgment of the National Liberation Front; as General Ky said, "If we sit down with the NLF as equals, the whole *raison d'être* of this regime is finished." In late October 27, Rostow went so far as to draft a letter of reassurance from Johnson to Thieu: "I know the question of the NLF in the Paris talks is awkward for you. But you can feel sure that we shall make clear that no question of recognition by the U.S. is involved. . . . . Your people can also be sure that we have no intention of imposing a coalition government upon them." Additional private assurances to Thieu led him to say to Bunker, "I do not see how we can ask for anything more." A joint declaration was thereupon prepared for official release.

Johnson's habitual diffidence also led him to seek reassurance, this time from his military commander in Vietnam. Summoning General Creighton Abrams to Washington, he met with him and his advisers at 2:30 a.m. on Tuesday, October 28. Abrams told Johnson that halting the bombing was "the proper thing to do." Then, at five minutes past six, a message arrived from Bunker in Saigon: Thieu was stalling. "That's the old Nixon," Johnson muttered.

The comment reflected the president's sense that public diplomacy was being undermined by private back channels. He knew this because he had been bugging Bui Diem, Anna Chennault—and even Thieu's office in Saigon—for some time. As Thieu met with his security counsel, Johnson allowed himself a moment of empathy with his counterpart in Saigon. Referring to the complex situation in which the South Vietnamese president had been placed by the United States, he mused, "If I were Thieu, I wouldn't feel very kindly about it." After being put off by Thieu with various excuses, including the claim that Harriman had insulted Saigon's representative in Paris, Johnson cabled Bunker a message for Thieu: "If President Thieu keeps us from moving at this moment of opportunity, God help South Vietnam." Thieu responded, "All Vietnamese know our life depends on US support. But you cannot force us to do anything against our interest." Johnson then went on television to announce the bombing halt and the beginning of talks at which representatives of the government of South Vietnam "are free to participate." Thieu responded in a speech before the National Assembly the next day: "The government of South Vietnam deeply regrets not being able to participate in the present exploratory talks." The applause prompted by these words moved into a standing ovation. Thieu remembered looking at the U.S. ambassador: "I could see Bunker trying hard to control his emotions. He began to sweat. As I looked at his face I felt sorry for him, but there was nothing I could do." Next day's *Washington Post* headline read: "S. VIETNAM SPURNS NOV. 6 TALKS."

"This is treason!" Johnson exploded, after reading the cable from Bui Diem to Saigon intercepted on October 27. William Bundy was to refer to Diem's claim to be in regular touch with the Nixon entourage as "the smoking gun." By the time Thieu gave his speech to the National Assembly, Johnson had no need of gathered intelligence, his aide Joseph Califano remembers, to be "certain in his own mind, whatever the evidence he could uncover to prove it, that Nixon had betrayed his country and enlisted Thieu to torpedo the arrangement."

"We first became aware of these activities," Clark Clifford writes, "through the normal operations of the intelligence community in the weeks prior to the election." For Clifford, normal operations included tapping the phones of an American citizen, bugging the office of a head of state, and intercepting cables sent to and by his ambassador. Despite his gift for euphemism, Clifford's Counsel to the President nevertheless gives a compelling account of the twists and turns of the administration's thinking as the extent of these activities became known to it.

Once the "plot" had been discovered, "the President, Rusk, Rostow, and I discussed what to do about this attempt to thwart the negotiations." They found themselves facing "an extraordinary dilemma," since the positive evidence gathered about "the Little Flower" all came from "extremely sensitive" intelligence gathering operations. In a fateful decision, Johnson decided not to go public himself with what he knew. Clifford offers four reasons for this decision, none of them touching on the obvious point that in order to reveal what he knew Johnson would also have to reveal how he had come to know it—through "normal" intelligence operations that were also illegal. Johnson did offer Humphrey the information to use as a weapon against Nixon in the last days of the campaign, but Humphrey declined, saying it would be "terrible to do that sort of thing" when he was not absolutely sure of the facts.

Questioning the candor of Diem's memoir, Clifford maintains that "there were other messages" sent to Thieu than the two Diem admitted to sending and that in any case Chennault had another channel to Saigon through Thieu's brother, the Vietnamese ambassador to Taiwan. While admitting that what was conveyed to Thieu through the Chennault channel "may never be fully known," Clifford persists in calling it "decisive."

Once Thieu's delaying tactics began, Clifford found himself "furious" and "fed up with Saigon." "They are playing extraordinary games," he said about the South Vietnamese. "We must *force* them to Paris." At one point on October

30, Clifford broke into language he had never used before in the Cabinet Room: "Saigon's whole approach is delay. This latest message is thoroughly insulting. In fact, it is horseshit!" It was after this outburst that Johnson took over: "Tell Bunker we are ready to go tonight." The United States would go it alone if need be, stopping the bombing on the following day and scheduling the first plenary meeting in Paris for the day after the election, November 6. In the course of these deliberations, Johnson also made a prophecy that soon came true: "Nixon will double-cross them after November 5."

Johnson arranged a conference call with the three presidential candidates on the evening of his bombing halt speech. In comments directed expressly at Nixon, he indulged in a little occupatio of his own: "Some old China hands are going around and implying to some of the Embassies and some others that they might get a better deal out of somebody that was not involved in this. Now that's made it difficult and it's held up things a bit, and I know for sure than none of you candidates are aware of it or responsible for it." The president's "I know for sure that none of you" chimed nicely with Nixon's "This I do not believe." Extending the performance even into his memoirs, Johnson wrote of having reason to believe that the South Vietnamese had "been urged to delay going to the Paris meetings and promised they would get a better deal from a Nixon Administration than from Humphrey. I had no reason to think that Republican candidate Nixon was himself involved in this maneuvering."

The bluffing continued on Sunday, when Nixon called Johnson at his Texas ranch. Nixon called Johnson in order "to calm him down," he maintains in RN, after some comments on the timing of the bombing halt made by Nixon campaign aide Robert Finch. Nixon recounts the conversation as follows:

> "Who's this guy Fink?" Johnson asked. "Why is he taking out after me?"
>
> I said, "Mr. President, that's Finch, not Fink."
>
> He ignored my correction and continued to refer to Finch as "Fink."
>
> I pointed out that my public statements on the issue were responsible, but that I had to respond to developments as I saw them. He calmed down, and the rest of our conversation was relatively cordial.

According to Clifford, Nixon was worried not about Robert Finch but about Senator Everett Dirksen. Dirksen knew Nixon, Johnson, and Chennault, and, "in growing fury," Johnson had called Dirksen earlier that morning and told him that he knew all about Anna Chennault. A worried Dirksen then called Nixon.

Nixon's account of the call to Texas omits any mention of Dirksen or of the fact that during the conversation "Johnson quizzed Nixon about Chennault's activities." Assuring Johnson that Chennault was acting on her own, there was "absolutely no truth," he maintained, in any claims to the contrary. "This barefaced lie," Bundy concludes, "was his only tenable line of defense, and the word must have gone out to his top campaign people, accounting for the vehement denials [the journalist] Theodore White encountered at the Republican campaign offices on Monday." After Nixon hung up the phone, Robert Dallek reports, Nixon and his aides collapsed in laughter.

So Nixon won the election, and the talks became his. In the closing pages of White House Years, Kissinger provides an elegy for the peace talk process. It was a process Thieu resisted to the end, knowing, as Kissinger admits, that "peace involving American withdrawal was a traumatic event for the South Vietnamese." On January 16, 1973, Thieu received a letter from Nixon, one that could have been written by Johnson four years earlier: "I have therefore irrevocably decided to proceed to initial the Agreement on January 23, 1973 and to sign it on January 29, 1973 in Paris. I will do so, if necessary, alone. In that case I shall have to explain publicly that your Government obstructs peace. The result will be an inevitable and immediate termination of U.S. economical and military assistance."

Thieu came round on January 21, requesting only that the United States recognize "Saigon as the legal government of South Vietnam and that Hanoi had no right to maintain troops there." But of course the agreement Nixon was threatening to sign made no provision for the removal of North Vietnamese troops from the South. The agreement was duly signed, and Saigon fell twenty-seven months later. In the final paragraph of his chapter "Peace Is at Hand," Kissinger concludes: "We were determined to do our utmost to enable Saigon to grow in security and prosperity so that it could prevail in any political struggle. We sought not an interval before collapse, but lasting peace with honor. But for the collapse of executive authority as a result of Watergate, I believe we could have succeeded." The collapse of that authority was not an event without an agent, as Kissinger's prose might here seem to suggest, but rather one resulting from the ways in which Nixon and Kissinger sought to wage war.

Two months after the inauguration, the Nixon administration began bombing Cambodia. The goal was to take out NLF and North Vietnamese headquarters rumored to be situated somewhere just across the border with South Vietnam. The headquarters were never effectively located, but Cambodia, already suffering from coups and countercoups, was further destabilized. In the ensuing civil war, Pol Pot's Khmer Rouge came to power. By 1979, when the Vietnamese succeeded in ousting the Khmer Rouge, 1.7 million Cambodians had died in the killing fields.

The bombings were kept secret. General Earle Wheeler, chairman of the Joint Chiefs of Staff, cabled the American commander in Vietnam that U.S. spokesmen were to take a "no details" approach to any press questions about the bombing. Flight crews were instructed to burn "every scrap of paper with which the bombing had been plotted." Even the secretary of the Air Force was denied notice of the operations. For his part, Nixon attempted to keep the bombing secret in the very act of finally owning up to it. On April 30, 1970, he gave a televised speech in which he announced the beginning of "air and logistical support" for U.S. and South Vietnamese strikes against major enemy sanctuaries on the Cambodia–Vietnam border. The announcement was preceded by the claim that "for five years, neither the United States nor South Vietnam moved against those enemy sanctuaries." Nixon had inserted this sentence into a draft of the speech written by Patrick Buchanan. "He added a sentence," Kissinger writes, "as irrelevant to his central thesis as it was untrue, that we had heretofore not moved against the sanctuaries—overlooking the secret bombing." Kissinger's sentence, like Nixon's, had been "added" as well. After reading William Shawcross's *Sideshow* (1979), he had it inserted as "a last-minute acknowledgment" into the galleys of his forthcoming book.

When the *New York Times* had first broken the story of the secret bombing of Cambodia on May 9, 1969, it aroused "no public interest." The leak so alarmed Henry Kissinger, however, that he urged J. Edgar Hoover to "destroy whoever did this." In Haldeman's words, Watergate was an "offspring of Kissinger's attempt to control the leaks." Hoover began wiretapping Kissinger's aides, "the first of the domestic abuses of power," Shawcross claims, "known as Watergate."

As we have seen, however, any genealogy of abuse must begin almost a year earlier, in a July 1968 meeting in an apartment in New York. And the intrigues surrounding the bombing halt retained a strange fascination for the Nixon White House, as if their awareness of the abuse of power involved was so threatening to the ego-ideals of the participants as to require them to project it onto their political opponents. In *The Ends of Power* (1978), H. R. Haldeman reveals that soon after Nixon took office, he assigned his chief of staff a "long-term project," to look into "LBJ's bombing pause in late 1968, part of a last minute 'peace effort' by LBJ which had almost sunk Nixon." In an odd conflation of his own behavior with Johnson's, Nixon remained convinced that LBJ had "let politics enter into a war decision," he told his aide, "and I want the whole story on it."

A year and a half later, in June 1971, the search for the Bombing Halt file came up again, this time in connection with Daniel Ellsberg's release of the Pentagon Papers to the *New York Times.* On June 17, Nixon held a meeting attended by Kissinger, Haldeman, and Ehrlichman. In his memoir, Kissinger gives only a vague account of the meeting, acknowledging that he "supported" Nixon in his opposition to the release of the papers. Ellsberg's name never appears in *White House Years,* but the transcript of White House tape 525 on file at the Miller Center at the University of Virginia shows Kissinger dominating the June 17 conversation. He began by calling Ellsberg a "son of a bitch." Claiming to have taught Ellsberg at Harvard, Kissinger went on to describe him as "brilliant," "funny," and "unbalanced," a man who, when driving around Vietnam, would "shoot at peasants in the fields."

As the discussion of hitting back at the *Times* continued, Haldeman suddenly raised the issue of blackmail:

HALDEMAN: You can maybe blackmail Johnson on this stuff.

PRESIDENT NIXON: What?

HALDEMAN: You can blackmail Johnson on this stuff, and it might be worth doing.

PRESIDENT NIXON: How?

HALDEMAN: The Bombing Halt stuff is all in the same file. Or in some of the same hands.

PRESIDENT NIXON: Oh, how's that show—oh, I wondered, incidentally—

HALDEMAN: It isn't in this. It isn't in these papers, but the whole Bombing Halt file . . .

PRESIDENT NIXON: Do we have it? I've asked for it. You said you didn't have it, Henry.

HALDEMAN: We can't find—

KISSINGER: We have nothing here, Mr. President.

PRESIDENT NIXON: Damn it, I asked for that, because I need it.

KISSINGER: Yeah, but Bob and I have been trying to put the damn thing together for three years.

HALDEMAN: We have a basic history of it—constructed our own—but there is a file on it.

PRESIDENT NIXON: Where?

HALDEMAN: [White House aide Tom] Huston swears to God there's a file on it at Brookings.

Now believing that the Bombing Halt file has been deposited at the Brookings Institution, a Washington think tank, Nixon ordered a break-in: "I want it implemented on a thievery basis. Goddamn it, get in and get those files. Blow the safe and get it." The account in *RN* tones down this request. "I saw absolutely no reason for that report to be at Brookings," Nixon writes, "and I said I wanted it back right now—even if it meant having to get it surreptitiously." Nixon was now so committed to revenge that he proposed to steal and publicize documents that might result in his own incrimination, since this record contained a precise account of his dealings with Anna Chennault.

Haldeman's attempt in *The Ends of Power* to tell "the true story behind Watergate" abbreviates this meeting into a single undated encounter with the president. Having heard that "a man named Leslie Gelb had left his post at the Pentagon and transferred many pertinent files to a private organization, the Brookings Institution," Haldeman called the think tank and requested a look at the "document on the bombing halt." Informed by Brookings that the document "was, somehow, unavailable," he reported the situation to Nixon. The President slammed a pencil on his desk and said, "I want that Goddamn Gelb material and I don't care how you get it." Thinking "Good luck" to himself as he left the Oval Office, Haldeman adds in his memoir that "I knew of no way I could get my hands on the document we needed."

The "tap on the Dragon Lady" remained a recurring subject in the Nixon White House, as the president and his men continued to believe that the mere fact of having been bugged in 1968 might somehow trump all that the tapes were certain to reveal. "We have to hit the opposition with their activities," Nixon said, as he planned the "counterattack" over Watergate. As *The Haldeman Diaries* (1994) make clear, by "their activities," the president was referring to "the fact that Johnson bugged us in '68." On January 8, 1973, Haldeman reported White House counsel John Dean as saying "that if we can prove in any way by hard evidence that our plane was bugged in '68, he thinks that we could use that as a basis to say we're going to force Congress to go back and investigate '68 as well as '72, and thus turn them off." Discussion of the "everybody does it" defense culminated four days later, when Nixon proposed "going at LBJ" by exposing "the Johnson bugging process."

In response to this threat from the White House, Johnson met the threat with one of his own—to expose what the bugging had in fact revealed: that in 1968 the Nixon camp, in dealing with the South Vietnamese, "was asking that certain things be done." He did so in a telephone call to FBI agent Deke De Loach, the man who had overseen the bureau's original surveillance operation in 1968. Here is Haldeman: "LBJ got very hot and called Deke, and said to him that if the Nixon people are going to play with this, that he would release (*deleted material—national security*), saying that our side was asking that certain things be done. By our side, I assume he means the Nixon campaign organization. De Loach took this as a direct threat from Johnson. He says he'll bring his file in Monday for Mitchell to review. As he recalls it, bugging was requested on the planes, but was turned down, and all they did was check the phone calls, and put a tap on the Dragon Lady (*Mrs. Anna Chennault*)." After Johnson's threatening phone call, the Nixon people abandoned the plan to expose the 1968 bugging process.

But White House angst over leaks and bugging had already led to an outcome more consequential, the founding of the Plumbers unit in July 1971. Two months later, the Plumbers succeeded in breaking into the office of Daniel Ellsberg's psychiatrist. In June 1972 they committed a third-rate burglary in Washington, D.C. These attempts to protect or uncover secrets needed, in turn, to be kept secret, leading Nixon to issue the "smoking gun" order on June 23, 1972, in which he directed the CIA to obstruct the FBI's investigation of the Plumbers raid on the national Democratic campaign headquarters at the Watergate apartment complex.

As Haldeman was later to assert, "without the Vietnam War there would have been no Watergate." And, without Watergate, there might have been a far different end to the Vietnam War. Nixon and Kissinger had no intention of stopping all U.S. military involvement in the war once the peace accords were signed. "You can be sure that we stand with you," Nixon had said to Thieu on April 3, 1973, a month after the withdrawal of American forces from Vietnam was complete. "Throughout the remainder of 1973," George Herring writes, "the administration employed various subterfuges to sustain its military aid at a high level without overtly violating the terms of the Paris accords." It did not dismantle its bases; is simply transferred title to them to the South Vietnamese. Some nine thousand Americans were discharged from the military and converted into "civilian" advisers to Thieu's regime. "The only way we will keep North Vietnam under control is not to say that we are out forever," Kissinger said to the president's assembled speechwriters, as they pondered how to frame the announcement of the final agreement between Hanoi and Saigon.

But Watergate quickly undermined the administration's power to honor such secret promises. The scandal not only stripped Richard Nixon of his political power and finally drove him from office, it impelled Congress to reclaim its prerogative to declare war, one asserted in August 1973, when it voted to halt all U.S. bombing of Southeast Asia. The War Powers Act was passed in November, requiring the president to inform Congress within forty-eight hours of the deployment of U.S. forces. For Nixon and Kissinger, the addiction to secrets had come full circle, redounding back upon them with such force as to deny them the power to end the nation's involvement in Vietnam with either peace, or honor.

CHAPTER

12

Swift Boat

One may as well begin by quoting from President Nixon's Oval Office conversation with Charles Colson, on April 28, 1971:

COLSON: This fellow Kerry that they had on last week—
PRESIDENT: Yeah. Yeah.
COLSON: —hell, he turns out to be, uh, really quite a phony. We—
PRESIDENT: Yeah, I know.
COLSON: The story we're getting out, that—
PRESIDENT: Are ya?
COLSON: (Newspaper columnist Jerald) TerHorst is writing that for—
PRESIDENT: Good.
COLSON: —North American Newspaper Alliance.
PRESIDENT: Well, he is a sort of phony, isn't he? Is—
COLSON: Well, he stayed, when he was here—
PRESIDENT: Stayed out in Georgetown, yeah.
COLSON: He stayed in Georgetown with one of the old-line Washington socialites, Elsie Leiter, and was out at the best restaurants every night. And . . .
PRESIDENT: Sure.
COLSON: You know, he's just a complete opportunist.

PRESIDENT: A racket, sure.

COLSON: He was in Vietnam a total of four months. He's politically ambitious and just looking for an issue.

PRESIDENT: Yeah.

COLSON: He came back a hawk and became a dove when he saw the political opportunities.

PRESIDENT: Sure, well, anyway, keep the faith.

Nixon's White House tapes are being steadily transcribed and released on a website hosted by the Miller Center of Public Affairs at the University of Virginia. The actual audio tapes themselves are housed at the National Archives in College Park, Maryland. As the years pass, and as more tapes come out, the words spoken by the president and his men have lost none of their shocking power. The crude and deceptive indirection, the self-congratulatory echoing of something already said—like the word "phony"—the habitual projection of cynical motive, and the sheer violating nature of such subterfuge-in-language all point toward an emotional and political missed opportunity, since the listener is being asked to suffer in retrospect a knowledge willfully denied him at the time the words were spoken.

The man heard speaking to Nixon here, Charles Colson, served as special counsel to the president from 1969 to 1973. In his memoir *Born Again* (1976), Colson describes himself as "willing to blink at certain ethical standards, to be ruthless in getting things done." It was Colson who organized the break-in at the office of Daniel Ellsberg's psychiatrist, authored Nixon's "enemies list," and, a month prior to the conversation quoted above, authorized the Committee to Re-elect the President to spend $250,000 on intelligence gathering on the Democratic Party. When he speaks with Nixon about "this fellow Kerry," he is referring to the former Swift Boat commander's televised appearance before the Senate Committee on Foreign Relations during which he gave testimony about the experience of his fellow veterans in Vietnam and called the nation to a moment of "turning."

Colson was also reacting to conversations in the Oval Office that had begun on April 23, a day after Kerry gave his testimony. When Nixon asked about "this fellow . . . they put in the front row," Haldeman responded: "Kerry. He did a hell of a great job." Noting that his speechwriter Patrick Buchanan had found Kerry "extremely effective," Nixon went on to ask about Kerry's service in the war. Haldeman informed Nixon that Kerry had been a Navy lieutenant "on a gunboat" and was "over there for . . . four or five months." Nixon appeared confused about the medals pinned to Kerry's chest:

PRESIDENT: Bob, the Navy didn't have any casualties in Vietnam except in the air.

HALDEMAN: Well, this guy got a Purple Heart with two clusters and the Navy Star . . . He's got a hell of a bundle of lettuce up there.

The two men went on to agree that one day "you'll find Kerry running for political office."

Colson had anticipated the threat Kerry represented in an internal White House memo distributed earlier that year, "Plan to Combat Viet Nam Veterans Against the War." The memo was a response to the 1971 Winter Soldier Investigation held in Detroit, during which over one hundred veterans testified about their experiences in Vietnam. Dubbing them "pseudo-atrocity hearings," Colson advocated discrediting the Vietnam Veterans Against the War (VVAW) through the use of FBI wiretaps and surveillance.

Kerry had attended the Winter Soldier Investigation but had not spoken there. Shocked and moved by the extremity of what he had heard—"there was a lot of rough stuff out there, and it blew some of my images"—Kerry then suggested that the VVAW take its story to Washington. Less than four months later, he had moved to the forefront of the organization and had become its most visible spokesman.

"He forced us to create a counterfoil," Colson told the journalist Joe Klein in 2002. "We found a vet named John O'Neill and formed a group called Vietnam Veterans for a Just Peace. We had O'Neill meet the President and we did everything we could to boost his group." The boosting culminated in June 1971, in a televised debate between Kerry and O'Neill on *The Dick Cavett Show.*

O'Neill was an Annapolis graduate who served some fifteen months in minesweepers and Swift Boats off the coast and in the rivers of South Vietnam. He won two Bronze Stars during his time there. On returning from the war in 1971, and after Colson saw him speak at a press conference, the former Navy lieutenant "became the centerpiece of the Nixon White House plot to undermine Kerry."

O'Neill was the "perfect" counterfoil to Kerry in part because in Vietnam he had taken command of the *same boat* on which Kerry had served as a commander in 1969. Their fates were to continue to converge, since it was O'Neill who became one of the authors of *Unfit for Command* (2004) and a leader of the Swift Boat Veterans for Truth during the 2004 presidential campaign.

"My involvement had nothing to do with Nixon," O'Neill was later to claim. "I got involved because I was outraged with Kerry." Yet in surveying the surviving record, it becomes difficult to resist the sense that O'Neill materialized, like DeLillo's Oswald, in response to an emerging set of conspiratorial intentions. On June 2, 1971, for instance, Haldeman met with Nixon and mentioned "a Navy officer, just got out yesterday." Describing O'Neill as a "crew cut, real sharp looking guy," he added that "he's not as eloquent, he isn't the ham that Kerry is, but he's more believable." After telling Nixon that "Colson put this together," Haldeman assured the president that O'Neill is "gonna move on Kerry."

These conversations resulted in a meeting between O'Neill and Nixon in the Oval Office on June 16. The two men hit it off, and what was supposed to have been a brief grip-and-grin session turned into an hour-long conversation. Urging O'Neill to "reassure people that the few that come back—like Kerry and the rest—don't speak for all," Nixon added, "Give it to him—give it to him." Two weeks later O'Neill appeared on Dick Cavett and labeled Kerry "the type of person who lives and survives only on the war-weariness and fears of the American people."

In Book VI of *The Faerie Queene,* Edmund Spenser imagines a monster he calls the Blatant Beast. The subject of the book is the decline of "civility" in Elizabethan England and the rise of "vile tongue and venomous intent." The personification of this decline, the Beast has a big mouth and runs around saying bad things about people. Conceived by "three mightie ones"—their names might be Envy, Resentment, and Detraction—the Beast prefers to injure with words rather than with deeds, to "supplant by slight" rather than "by open might." The hero of Book VI defeats the Beast and puts him in chains, but given the irrepressible power of its parentage, as well as the enduring appeal of slander, the Beast eventually breaks his chains and "now he raungeth through the world again."

Colson put this together: Haldeman ran a tight ship and he rarely got such claims wrong. Yet the man who put it all together and who can be said to have invented Kerry's "counterfoil" in public life was to prove skeptical, in the long run, about the truth-claims of his efforts. In a 2003 interview Colson said, "I don't ever remember finding anything negative about Kerry or hearing anything negative about him. If we had found anything, I'm sure we would have used it to discredit him." By the time of Colson's admission he had however long since unloosed onto the world a Blatant Beast whose mouth, once opened, could not be quieted.

One of the more persistent rumors arising out of the Vietnam War was "the myth of the spat-upon Vietnam veteran." Jerry Lembcke's *The Spitting Image* (1998) makes a careful study of the birth and growth of the rumor.

"The outstanding fact," he argues, "is that stories of veterans being abused by anti-war activists only surfaced years after the abuses were alleged to have happened." Energy was given to the rumor by Bob Greene, a columnist for the *Chicago Tribune,* both in his column and in his 1989 book *Homecoming.* Greene used the leading question "Were you spat upon?" rather than a more open-ended question such as "What were your homecoming experiences?"; his book contains "sixty-three accounts of personal experience with spitting and sixty-one accounts of spit-free homecomings."

Lembcke attempts to situate the negative memories within the context of what he calls the "Nixon-Agnew counteroffensive" against "bad veterans" and argues as well for the power of war movies and recovered memory to reconfigure the past. Perhaps his most persuasive case is made, however, when he quotes Barry Romo, a former head of VVAW, who told Lembcke that "there is no news-source documentation (such as photographs) of any incidence of anti-war activists spitting on veterans." In the documentable cases of "veterans being treated abusively," it "was pro-war people who were the abusers." A 1969 *Life* magazine article supports this claim. At an antiwar rally held in October of that year, a Dallas realtor read out the names of men from Texas who had been killed in Vietnam. Hecklers yelled back: "Spit at those people, spit on 'em." "Hippies." "Dirty Commies." While the image of the spat-upon veteran might then have taken hold because of such an incident, how many "readers who saw the story," Lembcke asks, "remember that it was supporters of the war who would have been the perpetrators?" As he researched his book, Lembcke "found only one material representation of the spat-upon veteran image—in a 'GI Joe' comic book panel from the mid-1980s."

The headwaters of the Mekong River arise in the Tibetan Plateau and flow over 2,600 miles until they reach the South China Sea. As the waters enter South Vietnam they begin to divide into a vast branching network known to the Vietnamese as the River of the Nine Dragons. In 1965 the Mekong Delta had only one surfaced road; the movement of its peoples and goods depended on water. This was the rice bowl of Vietnam, and it was also a National Liberation Front (NLF) stronghold.

A force operating in such an area is known as a "brown water" navy. By both training and tradition, American sailors operate on blue water. As the Vietnam war intensified, and it became clear that the enemy was exploiting the delta's four thousand miles of waterways and using them to move supplies into and out of Cambodia, the Navy committed itself to a war of interdiction. As Thomas Cutler argues in *Brown Water, Black Berets*

(1988), this strategy faced "only two obstacles: the U.S. Navy had no river patrol craft to speak of, and no corporate knowledge of riverine warfare."

Admiral Elmo Zumwalt took command of U.S. naval forces in Vietnam in 1968. He quickly saw that "you have to make up riverine warfare as you go along." One of his ZWIs—"Zumwalt's Wild Ideas"—was to have the Navy shift from blue- to brown-water operations so as to begin "engaging the enemy" in the interior of the delta. A typical patrol carrying out the interdiction strategy involved a small craft making its way up a narrow canal lined with dense vegetation. In this effort, the Navy came to depend on the Patrol Craft Fast (PCF), also known as the Swift Boat.

Adapted from an all-welded aluminum craft used to ferry crews to drilling rigs in the Gulf of Mexico, the fifty-foot Swift Boat displaced nineteen tons with a shallow draft of 3.5 feet. Its two V-12 diesel engines could reach a top speed of twenty-five knots. Manned by a crew of six, the PCF was armed with an M-79 grenade launcher, three .50 caliber machine guns, a .60 caliber machine gun, and an arsenal of M-16s, antipersonnel and concussion grenades, .38 caliber revolvers, and a riot gun.

Lieutenant John Kerry reported for duty in Vietnam on November 17, 1968. Originally assigned to blue-water patrolling out of Cam Ranh Bay, he soon requested a transfer to brown-water duty. In early 1968, he had in fact written the chief of naval operations requesting assignment to a Swift Boat. As he recalled in *The Vietnam Experience: A War Remembered* (1986), he had believed at the time of the request that Swift Boats "had very little to do with the war. They were engaged in coastal patrolling and that's what I thought I was going to be doing. Although I wanted to go back and see for myself what was going on, I didn't really want to get involved in the war." By the time Kerry arrived in Vietnam, however, Zumwalt's wild idea had transformed "one of the safest assignments in the escalating conflict to one of the most dangerous." Persisting in his ambition nevertheless, Kerry was assigned command of PCF-44 and began river raiding in early December.

Three books about Kerry were published in the year he ran for president. They can be labeled the credulous, the skeptical, and the hostile. "Not meant to be a biography of John Kerry," Douglas Brinkley's *Tour of Duty* attempts instead to tell "the story of one young American's Vietnam War odyssey." Calling itself "The Complete Biography," *John F. Kerry,* written by three *Boston Globe* reporters, takes as its goal "nothing less than the definitive portrait." In the preface to *Unfit for Command: Swift Boat Veterans Speak Out against John Kerry,* authors John O'Neill and Jerome R. Corsi locate the origin of their project in a rebroadcast of Kerry's *Dick Cavett* appearance. After seeing it in 2004, Corsi "telephoned his old friend"; he and O'Neill had competed against each other in intercollegiate debate. "After reconnecting, they decided to work together to write this book. Both strongly oppose John Kerry's 2004 candidacy for president of the United States."

Despite Brinkley's disavowals, his book reads as a highly sympathetic campaign biography. Its narrative "is based largely on journals and correspondence Kerry kept while on his tours of duty." Many of the river action sequences in *Tour of Duty*, Brinkley acknowledges, "are, in fact, paraphrased from Kerry's unfinished book proposal." Brinkley clearly admires his subject and calls him "a genuine war hero." On the other hand, the authors of *John F. Kerry*—reporters Michael Kranish, Brian C. Mooney, and Nina J. Easton—begin by admitting that their relations with the Kerry campaign had "turned downright toxic by June 2003." As they prepared to go to press with a seven-part newspaper series, Kerry's campaign manager called the project "a seven day rip job." *John F. Kerry* went on to "significantly" expand the series of *Globe* articles, one which the authors maintain to have been "absolutely fair," a claim the Kerry campaign "would later acknowledge."

Kerry was to be awarded five medals during his four months of service in Vietnam: a Purple Heart on December 2, 1968; a second Purple Heart on February 20, 1969; the Silver Star on February 28, 1969; and a third Purple Heart and the Bronze Star on March 13, 1969. Three days after receiving his third Purple Heart, Kerry requested reassignment out of Vietnam.

O'Neill and Corsi focus on how Kerry won his medals. In claiming that Kerry deserved none of the medals awarded him, they also must take on the medal-issuing practices of the U.S. Navy. Any medal issued by the Navy is accompanied by a citation describing the action on which the award is based, and so it is against these careful wordings that O'Neill and Corsi must make their way.

They do so by engaging in attribution without supporting quotation, as in "Hoffmann recently expressed his contempt for Kerry as a liar, false warrior, and fraud." They rely on hearsay evidence, as in "I had heard that he wounded himself and others with M-79 rounds," a piece of gossip later taken up as fact and then used as the basis for claiming that Kerry gave himself "a self-inflicted" wound. They deploy misleading footnotes, as when they claim that "each of the officers who were requested by Kerry to defend him in 1996 also signed the May 4, 2004, letter, condemning his own many misrepresentations." Only by turning to footnote number 10 for chapter 5 would the reader discover that "each" of the original defenders of Kerry in 1996 did not, in fact, sign the 2004 letter. Admiral Elmo Zumwalt died in 1998 and it was Zumwalt's son, the footnote admits, who signed the 2004 "letter on his father's behalf." Finally, Corsi and O'Neill give credence to self-contradictory witnesses, like Kerry's former commanding officer, George Elliott. Elliott wrote the initial draft of Kerry's Silver Star citation. Years later, in a July 2004 affidavit, he stated that "when Kerry came back to the United States, he lied about what occurred in Vietnam." Then, in an attempt to recant his belated attack on Kerry, he later admitted to *Globe* reporter Michael Kranish, "It was a terrible mistake probably for me to sign the affidavit with those words."

The challenge in writing about *Unfit for Command* is to unpack its strategies and influence without dignifying its claims. Fortunately for the seeker after an adequate account of Kerry's story, we have Brinkley and the *Boston Globe*. By navigating between these two quite different accounts, it is possible to gain a working knowledge of how and why Kerry won his medals.

The rule regarding Purple Hearts in Vietnam was a simple one: if a sailor received a wound in combat, he received a Purple Heart. A few weeks before assuming command of his first Swift Boat, PCF-44, Kerry won his first Purple Heart on a covert mission out of Cam Ranh Bay. He and two other sailors were piloting a small "skimmer" craft upriver into a "free-fire" zone when "we got into a firefight." Kerry authorized return fire and subsequently was wounded with a piece of shrapnel. "I never saw where the piece of shrapnel had come from," he told Douglas Brinkley. In a 2004 interview, Kerry's commanding officer at that time, Grant Hibbard, recalled thinking that Kerry's wound had been slight. "He had a little scratch in his forearm, and he was holding a piece of shrapnel." As for Kerry's wound, "Obviously, he got it," Hibbard admitted. "I don't know how." A one-page document listing Kerry's medical treatment during his time in service notes that on "3 DEC 1968 . . . Shrapnel removed and appl. Bacitracin dressing." Later, the Navy Historical Center was unable to locate the original card recording the event, although "it verified that Kerry did receive the first Purple Heart."

Kerry was wounded again on a February mission up the Dan Doi River. Three months into his stint in Vietnam, Kerry was now in charge of his second Swift Boat, PCF-94. As the boats were cruising down the river, one of them began shooting at "targets of opportunity." Figures wearing black uniforms were spotted on the shore, and Kerry's boat came under automatic weapon and rocket fire. Kerry was hit by shrapnel in the left thigh and was treated for his injuries on an offshore ship.

The Silver Star came next. In an operation on the Dong Cung Canal, the Navy mounted an attack against an NLF encampment near a friendly village.

As a flotilla of three boats moved up the canal, Kerry, tired of being a sitting target, told his crew to be prepared to beach the boat. When one of the other two boats came under attack, its skipper beached it. Kerry's boat "was just behind," taking gunfire from the shore. A B-40 rocket narrowly missed it. "Beach the boat!" Kerry ordered. On the shore, a teenager in a loincloth held a grenade launcher. Kerry's forward gunner shot the NLF fighter in the leg, and Kerry then jumped off the boat and gave chase.

"Chased VC inland behind hootch and shot him while he fled," the after-action report reads. "The crewman with the best view of the action" was Fred Short. "That was a him-or-us thing," he was to say. "That was a loaded weapon with a shape charge on it. . . . It could pierce a tank." For this action Zumwalt wanted to give Kerry the Navy Cross, Brinkley reports, but that award took time to clear Navy bureaucracy and so the admiral settled instead for the Silver Star, "an 'impact' award, given shortly after an action to lift morale."

Kerry's last Purple Heart came along with the Bronze Star. The key figure in the story is James Rassmann, a twenty-one-year-old U.S. Army Special Forces lieutenant. On the morning of March 13, Rassmann found himself on a Swift Boat following PCF-94 up the Bai Hap River. Early on, a Chinese mercenary traveling with Rassmann had been "literally blown to pieces" in a rocket attack. As the boats proceeded up a narrow canal, a mine explosion threw Rassmann into the water. Rassmann was shot at "each of the five times he returned to the surface." He swam toward PCF-94, and "Kerry, who had been hit in the arm and was bleeding," reached down with his good arm and pulled Rassmann out of the canal. "He deserved the Silver," Rassmann was to say. In the event, he was awarded a Bronze and a Purple Heart. Part of the citation signed by Zumwalt read: "His arm bleeding and in pain and with disregard for his personal safety, he pulled the man aboard."

Naval Personnel Instruction no. 1300.39, then in effect, stated that any enlistee or officer wounded three times "will not be ordered to service in Vietnam." Kerry now had three Purple Hearts. He promptly applied for reassignment, and ended up as an admiral's aide in Brooklyn. Roy Hoffman, who oversaw command of Swift Boats in Vietnam, maintained that Kerry "simply bugged out," while Commodore Charles F. Horne, an administrative official in Kerry's squadron, was to say that "to get three Purple Hearts and not be killed is awesome."

By the time Kerry came home from the war, the doubts he had harbored had left him "upset about it and angry about it." These misgivings were nothing new; as early as his Yale commencement speech in 1966, he had predicted that supporters of the war were likely to claim, "if victory escapes us, it would not be the fault of those who led, but of the doubters who stabbed them in the back." While stationed on a guided-missile frigate in Oahu, in February 1968, he had written home with a looming question: "How one can oppose the war and still fight it."

First-hand knowledge only complicated such feelings. On arriving in country, Kerry quickly saw that "there was no love lost between the U.S. and South Vietnamese Navies. At times it seemed they were at war." After assuming his first command, he began to refine in his journal what he called "The Law of Increasing Excusable Casualties." To fellow crewman Mike Bernique he admitted, "Nobody has been able to tell me why we have to do what we're doing here." After his gunner's mate Stephen Garner was shot, Kerry pondered the "gap between the illusions of those who direct the war and the disillusionment of those who fight it." Remaining open to both doubt and faith, Kerry summed up in his journal his persistent sense of cognitive dissonance: "Everything was right and wrong at the same time."

Unfit for Command imagines no space in which to experience a conflicted will. "Given his extreme opposition to the Vietnam War," its authors write, "and his view that it was an immoral enterprise, Kerry's action has always puzzled most Swiftees." By "action" they mean Kerry's volunteering for Swift Boat duty. In remaining puzzled about how Kerry could have at once opposed the conduct of the war and yet still consented to fight in it, the authors turn away from the most instructive dimension of the Kerry story, the struggle between doubt and duty that left him torn between two conflicting goods.

Kerry's antiwar activities on his return to the United States could have come, to Kerry at least, as only a small surprise. The choice to "oppose" the war had been implicit in his thinking even before he had begun to "fight" in it. But the decision to speak out also came haltingly, since it finally expressed only one side of the conflict. This second Vietnam action was also to arouse fierce resistance in the men who became Kerry's political enemies and even, once he was called on in later years to acknowledge his complex fate, in Kerry himself.

Held in Detroit in January and February 1971, the Winter Soldier Investigation had its beginnings in the 1969 revelations about My Lai. As Gerald Nicosia reports in *Home to War* (2001), the claim by the Nixon administration that the massacre was an isolated incident "infuriated" a number of Vietnam veterans. The original organizers of the event were therefore "especially" interested in locating "veterans willing to testify that they themselves had committed 'war crimes' or seen them committed by others." When a rift in that leadership developed, Vietnam Veterans Against the War became the sole sponsors of the event.

Resistance by enlisted men to an American war in Vietnam was nothing new and can be traced as far back as 1945, when the crewmen of the U.S. Merchant Marine protested the use of their ships to transport French troops to Vietnam. "By early 1967 a network of deserters and civilian supporters had built an underground organization in Western Europe" and was instrumental in "building an antiwar infrastructure inside the army known as RITA (Resistance Inside the Army)." September 1968 witnessed the San Francisco GI–Veteran March for Peace. A group calling itself Citizens Commission of Inquiry also held "small war crimes hearings" throughout the country in 1970. Their work culminated in December in the first major war crimes tribunal, held in Washington, D.C., where Lieutenant Michael J. Uhls spoke of witnessing "electrical torture using the TA-312 field telephone" and Intelligence Specialist Kenneth Barton Osborne recalled seeing detainees being thrown from helicopters.

"Perhaps the most startling news to come out of Winter Soldier," Nicosia argues, "was the revelation of the U.S. invasion of Laos in February 1969, code-named Operation Dewey Canyon I." Five survivors of the operation testified that in order to protect its secrecy the military refused to medevac the American dead and the wounded. Only a few days before these accounts were made public, the Pentagon was still saying, "We have never had ground troops in Laos."

Shocking policy decisions were more than equaled by individual testimony about atrocities committed or seen. Steve Noetzel, who was attached to the 5th Special Forces Group, recalled prisoners locked in a room overnight with an eight-foot python. Marine Sergeant Scott Camil remembered a woman shot by a U.S. sniper who asked for water. Instead, her clothes were ripped off, she was stabbed in both breasts, and an entrenching tool was shoved "up her vagina."

Unfit for Command maintains that "Kerry's accusations of war crimes typically relied on impostors posing as veterans who concocted incidents that, when investigated, proved to be exaggerations or fabrications." This blanket accusation is directed at the testimony of the Winter Soldiers. The word "exaggeration" may refer to Al Hubbard, a leader in the VVAW who claimed to be an Air Force captain and who turned out to have been only a sergeant. The extent of his service in Vietnam also came into question. Hubbard and Kerry would eventually face off over these and other matters, but not before Hubbard's excessive claims had significantly undermined the credibility of the VVAW.

The VVAW did attempt to screen those testifying in Detroit. "All veterans participating in Winter Soldier were required to bring their discharge papers," Nicosia writes. In trying "to discredit the hearings by questioning the authenticity of the veterans who testified," the *Detroit News* discovered "not one fraudulent veteran." Dubious himself about some of what he heard in Detroit, Kerry admitted, "It was hard to understand what was believable and what wasn't. Was it all real? . . . There were enough bona fides in many of these people—you saw their DD-214s, you knew where they'd served, you could talk to them and see the anguish—you could cut through what was bull and what wasn't."

"I arrived in Detroit a student," Kerry later said. Like Mailer in the march on the Pentagon, he was "not central to the event." His friend George Butler recalled Kerry coming to watch, learn, and listen. He found much of the testimony "graphic and ugly," often feeling "numb and sickened" by what he heard. While he had come to Detroit "really concerned" about the war, none of the available evidence suggests that Kerry went there with the phrase "war crimes" ringing in his head.

In later years his association with these two words played a large part, however, in his political undoing. "I thought it would have been fair play to say the war was unwinnable," O'Neill said in 1971, "but the argument that there were large scale war crimes was a false charge." O'Neill's eventual attack on the validity of Kerry's medals was in fact a diversionary tactic away from a case much harder to make—that war crimes had not been committed on a large scale. Kerry too had resisted such terms, but by the time he arrived in Washington for Dewey Canyon III—the VVAW operation named after ill-fated incursions into Laos—he had come in any event to accept the words "war crimes" as applying to the case, and he was to use the phrase in the opening sentences of his statement before the Senate.

It was only "with the utmost consideration," Kerry was to admit on *The Dick Cavett Show,* "that we pose" the question "of war crimes." A man does not come back from Vietnam "to say" that he raped or burned or destroyed "for pleasure. I think he does it at the risk of certain kinds of punishment, at the risk of injuring his own character." Part of character, Kerry came to see, involved a careful choosing of the words one applied to experience. In this effort, the primacy of his own experience of Vietnam sometimes took second place to the stories he later heard from others. "I personally didn't see personal atrocities," Kerry maintained, although after issuing this proviso he went on to admit taking part in free-fire zones and in search and destroy missions that were contrary to the Hague and Geneva conventions. So he tried to be careful with words and was quick to affirm that "we are not trying to find war criminals." When the time came, and it was of "war crimes" that he spoke, he did so after engaging in a prolonged act of taking in new knowledge, of hearing "what everybody was saying." In the process he became, in the words of VVAW organizer Arthur Cramm, "a listening warrior."

One response made to his listening was to propose a follow-up event in the nation's capital. One of VVAW's founders, Jan Barry, remembered Kerry saying to him in Detroit, "Why don't we go to Washington and take the story right to Congress?" According to VVAW vice president Mike Oliver, the idea for such an action had been "growing in all their minds for months," and Winter Soldier "was simply the place where Dewey Canyon III was officially announced." Oliver soon moved to Washington while Kerry began a speaking tour in order to raise money for the operation.

John Prados begins his *Vietnam: The History of an Unwinnable War, 1945– 1975* (2009) with the story of the VVAW "incursion" into the capital city. The FBI now had the group under surveillance and set out to disrupt its plans by having the Penn Central Railroad tell veterans who attempted to rent a special train that "the railroad had no spare equipment." The administrator at Georgetown University who had promised the VVAW an encampment was suddenly fired. Spiro Agnew—as president pro tem of the Senate he controlled the capitol grounds—approved a rally at a Mall site but refused to approve the proposed medal return.

Meanwhile, Colson began rounding up the "Hard Hats," as Nixon called them, members of the construction industry opposed to the antiwar movement. Nixon also contacted the Veterans of Foreign Wars and asked them to issue a statement against the VVAW.

On Monday, April 19, 1971, the assembled veterans marched across Memorial Bridge to Arlington Cemetery, where the National Park Service closed the gates against them. The veterans then marched to the Capitol, where they were met by four congressmen. No permit for an overnight stay having been issued, they then established an illegal campsite nearby. When the Department of Justice sought a restraining order "prohibiting a camp on the Mall," the judiciary became caught up in a complex process of requests for injunctions and appeals leading all the way to the Supreme Court. When attorney general John Mitchell finally asked that the injunction be lifted, a furious chief justice responded that the courts had been "improperly used."

Dressed in green fatigues and wearing his Silver Star and Purple Heart ribbons, John Kerry addressed his remarks to the Senate Committee on Foreign Relations on April 22, 1971. He was there, in part, by chance, since the invitation to speak had been extended to him at a Georgetown party only a few nights before. Kerry had spoken that night about "what was in my heart and in my gut and on my mind," and, after hearing him, Senator William Fulbright invited Kerry to address his committee.

Brinkley calls Kerry's Senate testimony the "point of origin" of his public life. Kerry began by summing up what he had heard about "war crimes" in Detroit:

> They told stories that at times they had personally raped, cut off ears, cut off heads, taped wires from portable telephones to human genitals and turned up the power, cut off limbs, blown up bodies, randomly shot at civilians, razed villages in fashion reminiscent of Genghis Khan, shot cattle and dogs for fun, poisoned food stocks, and generally ravaged the countryside of South Vietnam in addition to the normal ravage of war and the normal and very particular ravaging which is done by the applied bombing power of this country.

He went on to talk about "the feelings these men carry with them after coming back from Vietnam." Attempting to "speak in very general terms" rather than about his individual case, he kept repeating and conjoining the first person plural with the word "feel"; "We feel . . . we feel . . . we feel . . . we feel . . . we feel." Most of the paragraphs that follow begin with the word "We."

Not all the veterans who listened, of course, felt included. While Kerry's boatmate Mike Bernique maintained "I would go up a river with that man any time," he also said, "I think there was a point in time when John was making it up fast and quick." James Wasser, second in command on PCF-44, "felt betrayed." "I thought it was sick," said Edward Peck, whose boat Kerry had inherited. "He looked ridiculous."

Despite the last-minute invitation by Fulbright, Kerry's speech was in no way an impromptu performance. It incorporated language from addresses given at the Valley Forge National Battlefield and at a high school in Massachusetts. "When I began it—in the previous summer—it was in the form of a letter," Kerry recalled. "Then it transitioned into a speech. It didn't quite work as a letter." The pace of things in Washington. D.C., "was ferocious that week," he continued. "I remember staying up much of the night, working on organizing my thoughts and collecting the testimonies of fellow veterans. I wrote directly from the heart, developed a collection of pages on yellow legal pads, and then joined them all together. The final product represented the best of my thinking, an emotional plea to Congress to stop funding the war."

He ended the speech with the word "turning":

> And so when 30 years from now our brothers go down the street without a leg, without an arm, or a face, and small boys ask why, we will be able to say "Vietnam" and not mean a desert, not a filthy obscene memory, but mean instead the place where America finally turned and where soldiers like us helped it in the turning.

While the turning imagined here can be understood as a physical act—a turning on one's heels and walking away—it operated at the time and in later years as a powerful metaphor for both Kerry's and the nation's fate. The "turning" he accomplished in April 1971 in no way resembled a "flip-flop," a charge that was to be leveled at him during the 2004 presidential campaign. This turning was not a move made against his Vietnam experience but a move made in light of it, an act that revised without repudiating. There was no attempt to renounce what had been done, only to see it and say it for what it was. Such turnings, made in public, are rare in American life, and they involve what William Blake calls a Last Judgment, the private activity of self-reckoning that continually befalls the thinking and feeling individual. That self here models something the nation also might accomplish, although the opportunity for such public turnings are only briefly offered to either a self or a nation. Writing near the end of World War II, Muriel Rukeyser anticipated Kerry's metaphor and extended it as well to a collective American "we": "In time of the crisis of the spirit, we are aware of our need, our need for each other and our need for ourselves. We call up, with all the strength of summoning we have, our fullness. And then we turn; for it is a turning that we have prepared; an act. The time of turning may be very long. It may hardly exist." While Kerry could prophesy and even briefly help to accomplish such a moment of turning, he could not foresee its ironic aftermath, in which both he and the nation would turn against the turning itself.

According to one observer, Kerry's speech evoked "*an atrocity-producing situation.*" The phrase comes from Robert J. Lifton's *Home from the War* (1973).

After studying the psychological aftereffects of the bombing of Hiroshima, Lifton turned to the men returning from Vietnam. He spoke to "about four hundred veterans" in the course of his researches and also participated in the Winter Soldier Investigation.

Home from the War provides one framework for understanding the intense rhetorics generated out of the Vietnam experience. Beyond the data gathered in his own interviews, Lifton based his conclusions on the work of Murray Polner's *No Victory Parades: The Return of the Vietnam Veteran* (1971). In talks with more than two hundred veterans, Polner had discovered that "not one of them—hawk, dove, or haunted—was entirely free of doubt about the nature of the war and the American role in it." Because of his doubt, a Vietnam veteran could no longer experience his war as a warrior quest achieving glory through suffering an ordeal. "In Vietnam," Lifton writes, "one undergoes the 'ordeal' or test without the possibility of that 'idea of glory' or 'decision of holy validity.' There is all of the pain but none of the form."

Part of the pain came from any thinking soldier's awareness of ways in which the war's official misinformation machines condemned the participants to a state of "false witness." Body counts were inflated. Massacres were rationalized. Entire operations were hidden from public view. "The murderous false witness of GIs in the Vietnamese countryside," Lifton argues, resulted not from the behavior of aberrant individuals but "directly from a more extensive false witness on a national scale."

"The atrocity issue" raised by the Winter Soldiers was to remain for over thirty years one of burning national consequence, with the most common defense against such testimony being simply to deny the truth of it. In September 1968, at a Veterans Administration hospital in Boston, Sarah Haley, a licensed social worker, interviewed a patient who told her he had killed women and children at a place called My Lai and that he had been warned by members of his platoon to say nothing about it. When she took the story to a staff meeting, "the staff told me that the patient was obviously delusional." The health professionals she worked with possessed only a minimal diagnostic framework for articulating "war-related trauma." In 1969, there simply were no words—not in the *DSM* at least—for the kinds of psychological wounds soldiers experienced as they were visited by memories of their time in Vietnam.

In the Civil War, the word for what later came to be called post-traumatic stress syndrome was "nostalgia." By World War I, soldiers were allowed to have "shell shock." In 1952, under the pressure of thousands of World

War II veterans showing major delayed symptoms, the first edition of the *Diagnostic and Statistical Manual of Mental Disorders,* known as *DSM-I,* listed a syndrome called "gross stress reaction." In 1968, the term was dropped from *DSM-II.* As Wilbur J. Scott reports in *The Politics of Readjustment* (1993), the editors of *DSM-II* then "suggested that psychiatrists might code symptoms previously associated with gross stress reaction under 'adjustment reaction to adult life.'"

During the next twelve years, Vietnam veterans and medical professionals battled to include words for the after-effects of combat in the *DSM.* In 1980, *DSM-III* listed for the first time a syndrome of illnesses "outside the range of such common experiences as bereavement, chronic illness, business losses, or marital conflict" in which "the characteristic symptoms involve reexperiencing the traumatic event." It was named post-traumatic stress disorder (PTSD). It was now seen "as 'normal' for the horrors of war to traumatize people," and a war neurosis, "or PTSD, occurs when this trauma is not recognized and is left untreated." Part of the cure, the official entry acknowledged, lay in the recognition that the injury had occurred.

Hemingway had written about war trauma denied recognition in his 1925 story "Soldier's Home." When Krebs returned from World War I to the Midwest, he "did not want to talk about the war at all. Later he felt the need to talk about it but no one wanted to hear it. His town had heard too many atrocity stories to be thrilled by actualities." These reassuring "atrocity stories"—always about the villainy of the enemy—function in the same way as do the "heroism stories" reporter Richard Boyle went in search of in Vietnam: they prevent "actualities" from registering. In order to be listened to, Krebs finds he has to lie. "In this way he lost everything." His war experience goes unrecognized, and, as his story unfolds, the repetition of sentences beginning with the words "He liked" or "He did not like" becomes Hemingway's stylistic marker for the ways in which Krebs registers the war's lasting and unacknowledged effects.

With Vietnam, the problem of belief extended even to the leaders of the VVAW. When Bill Crandall first heard of My Lai he said to himself, "'This is an apparition, this is shocking, this didn't happen.' You know, I mean, I believed the story but I thought this was way out of line. Nothing like this happened in my war." At the Winter Soldier Investigation, he began by resisting but ended up by identifying with the testifying veterans: "There were things that were very hard. . . . [S]ome of them had really done as well as seen some horrible things. . . . I had this sort of conflict between loving these guys and hating what they had been involved in. And I either had to put myself superior to them or share the guilt with them. And I chose the latter. And that was very hard. In a lot of ways, I took on some guilt that wasn't mine and became very depressed." One reason for Crandall's taking on of a guilt that was not his was because his country had not yet begun to acknowledge its part in creating the conditions its soldiers found themselves "involved in." As a result of their not being believed, returning veterans remained continually vulnerable to a reexperiencing of the traumatic event. With the story of their wounds unheard, they survived, as Chaim Shatan writes, in a state of "unconsummated grief."

The fight to validate PTSD and the medicalization of the Vietnam veterans' war burdens came at a cost, however. As Patrick Hagopian has shown, the *DSM-III* description of PTSD has a "basic problem: the designation of the condition as a single disorder, regardless of the type of stressor that causes the patient to develop symptoms." PTSD could be caused by war, certainly, but also by accidents and natural disasters. Moreover, guilt was glossed as "guilt about surviving when others have not, or about behavior required for survival." No distinction was made "between the trauma of perpetrators and victims." The result of a "narrowly conceived psychiatric approach to veteran's problems" was a failure "to engage with the historical, political, and ethical sources of veterans' pain and anger." The word "healing" came to dominate public statements about how to deal with the war. But "the cost of accepting 'healing' as a valid goal of commemoration was sidelining criticism of U.S. policies and actions in Vietnam." Hagopian's *The Vietnam War in American Memory* (2009) makes an eloquent plea against a rhetoric of healing that deprives individuals and nations of the opportunity to shoulder responsibility and to accept blame.

On August 5, 2004, a group calling itself Swift Boat Veterans for Truth released a 60-second ad in a few media markets. Titled "Any Questions?," the ad featured brief quotations from thirteen veterans who "claimed to have served with Kerry in Vietnam." George Elliott was quoted as saying: "John Kerry has not been honest about what happened in Vietnam." Kerry had "betrayed all his shipmates," Grant Hibbard said, "he lied before the Senate." By August 16, the National Annenberg Election Study discovered from its polling that a third of respondents had seen the ad and another 24 percent had heard something about it. The director of the survey, Kathleen Hall Jamieson, explained the remarkable payoff of the $550,000 spent on the ad to its "extensive coverage" in free media, especially on cable news and radio talk shows.

The Kerry campaign did not address the charges made in the ad for over two weeks. On August 20, the day after Kerry called on President Bush to "denounce" the ad, the Swifters released another 60-second spot. "Sellout" replayed part of Kerry's 1971 testimony before the Senate. "Because it used Kerry's own words, in his own voice," Paul Freedman writes, "the ad was most likely more believable and more effective in portraying Kerry as having betrayed his fellow soldiers after, if not during, the war."

As the ads made their way into the public mind, they demonstrated the brilliance of the decision by Bush's campaign manager, Karl Rove, to attack Kerry on his strongest point. "While largely acquiescing in that lie," Mark Crispin Miller writes, "the press ignored the president's own military record, although the White House kept flaunting its deceptive version of that history." As new information emerged about Bush's service in the Texas Air National Guard—including his failure to show up for a 1971 physical or to report for service as requested, as well as the fact of several missing documents from his official service file—much of it was "fastidiously overlooked by U.S. mainstream journalists." Meanwhile, CBS News anchor Dan Rather was drawn into a murky plot after deciding to air memos regarding Bush's military service that turned out, following public outcry and an internal CBS investigation, to be "highly suspect." But "what actually happened," Russ Baker argues in *Family of Secrets* (2009), "was that an accusation against Bush—probably an accurate one—was used to hang his accusers."

Kerry's acceptance speech at the Democratic National Convention had featured his fighting experience in Vietnam. Since "the basis of his candidacy was his biography—the Vietnam hero who came home and led the antiwar effort"—any undermining of that story posed a mortal threat to that candidacy. And Kerry was faced with a serious problem: the occurrence in his life of a pattern that had the look of a disturbing repetition. The pattern had to do with wars, and with having been both for and against them. With Iraq, Kerry had voted for the resolution authorizing the 2003 invasion and then against an appropriation bill to support it. While this shifting stance may have resulted from a serious rethinking—from judging the war in Iraq, belatedly, to have been, as he called the war in Vietnam, "a mistake"—the turning against his previous support of the Iraq venture involved none of the "agonizing reappraisal" of his turning on Vietnam. The two changes of mind and heart were in no way alike in terms of their existential weight, but they looked alike, and so cast Kerry to some as a flip-flopper.

The deeper problem was Kerry's own version of his story. It focused almost exclusively on his going to the war, not on his turning against it. Kerry never spoke up for the part of himself that had "led the antiwar effort." In failing to integrate the two parts of his story or to acknowledge how deeply conflicted a young veteran might have been, he allowed the narrative of his life to be captured and controlled by his enemies.

"What I seek is a Reckoning," David Harris wrote in 1996, in *Our War.* Describing this reckoning in a language worthy of Thoreau, Whitman, and Blake, Harris casts it as an experience in which "we stand outside our fears, revisit what we did so many years ago, and clear our souls of this perpetual shadow." In invoking "what we did," Harris directs us back toward the choices made in our youth. These choices matter—they are unassailably ours. And they were moral choices, actions or inactions reaching down to the deep heart's core. The big choices Harris made in his youth were to found The Resistance in 1967 and to refuse to report for military duty when called to do so in 1968, after which he was quickly indicted on felony charges and sent to prison.

What matters as much as our choices, Harris argues, is the act of *revisiting* them. This is a work of memory, and of words. Harris knows that action is always "existential," as he calls it in *Dreams Die Hard.* Its outcomes cannot be known. The act of reckoning, in contrast, is belated and retrospective, a re-owning and an acknowledging of the thing done. If it is true of life, as T. S. Eliot writes, that "we had the experience but missed the meaning," then the very possibility of life having meaning depends on such revisitings.

Harris has revisited the past in books I explore in detail in chapter 2. In *Our War,* he writes that "we were too young, and the choices were too hard." In the 1982 *Dreams Die Hard,* he does what he can to recover a decade now long gone but too important to ignore. In it, the young man who had been "comfortable making definitive statements" coexists with the writer who has become deeply skeptical of the retroactively imposed fiction, in the life of a man or a nation, of the "definitive 'break.'"

In a book titled *When America Turned,* it may appear counterintuitive to end with Harris's skepticism about our capacity to locate breaks and turnings. While the turning invoked in my title refers to something irrevocable, something happening in one momentous year, it also points toward the ongoing and always unfinished interplay between the act and the reckoning. This is the work of historical imagination without which there can be no usable past. The heartbreaking contrast between the ways in which David

Harris and John Kerry went about this work also marks a line of advance into a livable future.

In choosing so openly to resist the draft, Harris also knew he was choosing to go to prison. His became an exemplary act of self-sacrifice, one defining the limit at which civil disobedience would shift, as it did for Bill Ayers and Susan Stern, into self-destructive violence. Such acts can be subsumed under the heading of "resistance," a term that redirects attention toward another set of historical actors, onto those who prosecuted the war. What sets Harris apart from most of the resisters and the prosecutors is his willingness to pay a price.

Harris knew that he would have to pay for his antiwar activism: by the time he was arrested in 1969, he had "spent the last three years knowing prison was coming." While living with that expectation certainly exacted a price, being ripped from his life was to cost him even more. He was to spend twenty months in prison. The rupture led, in turn, to the loss of his marriage and of his standing as a central figure in American life.

In the same year Harris and his wife, Joan Baez, went on the road in an attempt to rouse their country's broken forces, Joan Didion published *Slouching Towards Bethlehem*. In it, she writes that "people with self-respect have the courage of their mistakes. They know the price of things." Her claim has special poignancy when applied to the life of David Harris. Harris did what he did, and then he had to live out the price. The self-respect driving the initial choice necessarily involved a refusal of regret. While I have immense admiration for the honesty and courage sending up the initial choice, it would have had and could have had no lasting value to the culture had Harris gone back on it. "We have two lives," Bernard Malamud writes in *The Natural*, "the life we learn with and the life we live with after that." If each of us lives these two lives, then the only way our one life can make any sense and have any integrity is for the second life to remain on nodding terms with the first. Harris might have turned away from his first life during his second one, since the discontinuities between the two lives had transformed him into a figure almost posthumous—but he did not. Instead, he kept turning toward it, enacting a painful work of self-reckoning. This, of course, is what John Kerry failed to do.

While Kerry lost the 2004 presidential election for many reasons, he could have won a significant moral victory had he risked teaching his country a much-needed lesson. "Vietnam is a lesson," he told the *Boston Globe* in

2003. "It is history to me. It can guide me but it doesn't run me. You have to move on and I moved on a long time ago. But the lessons are valuable. I love the lessons."

The lesson he had lived out and then seemed to forget in 2004 was the core lesson of his Vietnam story: his having had as a young man the courage to accept and display a divided self. In later suppressing his Winter Soldier, Kerry also distanced himself from an important work begun in Vietnam, from the "revolutionary revisions in the way combatants understood war, history, and the tradition of the soldier." Vietnam had produced a new kind of soldier, as the title of Kerry's first book was to maintain. In the epilogue to *The New Soldier* (1971), he wrote again about the need for America "to turn." The need was to turn away from the old "rhetoric" and toward the facing of an enduring gap between the actual and the ideal: "The New Soldier is trying to point out how there are two Americas—the one the speeches are about and the one we really are."

Kerry's life story falls into two distinct phases: what he did and said when he was young; and what he later said, or did not say, about things once said and done. The severity of the disparate elements the young Kerry sought to reconcile had given the emerging story a distinctly literary shape. It was honorable to fight in the war, and it was honorable to fight against it. His being caught up between two conflicting goods gave the story the dignity of a tragedy.

Then came the diffidence that faltered. "The diffidence that faltered" is Ezra Pound's phrase, and comes from the *Pisan Cantos,* where Pound offers up the phrase as a definition of the word "vanity." Vanity "is all in the not done/all in the diffidence that faltered." Finding himself compelled toward a moment in which he was called on to speak on behalf of both sides of his past, Kerry faltered, and tragedy declined into pathos. To use his own word, Kerry failed to look back and "say" Vietnam in a way that might have led to a binding up of the nation's wounds.

Even in his faltering, however, Kerry remained an emblematic figure. Not, any longer, of the warrior/antiwarrior, but of the *unhealed*. How many of us who continue to care about recovering a usable past—and by 'us' I mean Americans born between Pearl Harbor and Ike's election—can deny in him or herself a similar diffidence? The vanity, perhaps, lay in the expectation that experience would somehow speak for itself. But the past must be spoken for. Insofar as we have proven unable to connect our ever-advancing "now" with the consequential "then" of the late 1960s, we, too, have faltered, with the largest evidence for this claim resting on our continuing inability to narrate our past so as to establish it as a time seen as both serious and valuable by Americans who persist in reading that great and terrible time as a turning gone wrong.

It was time to "*rouse our broken forces and save the country,*" as Robert Lowell had written on November 6, 1968. Lincoln had made a similar call in 1862: "We must disenthrall ourselves, and then we shall save our country." As each man knew, the enthrallments created by war could only be undone by words. Finding the right ones, as Lowell did in "Election Night" and as Lincoln did in his Second Inaugural, was, truly, a work of saving the country. That Kerry could not find the words which might have helped to clear our souls of the "shadow" of 1968 is a failure perhaps more consequential than his losing the election.

In the preceding pages I have often invoked wavering and self-division as reasonable and perhaps even inevitable responses to the war in Vietnam. I have also characterized the war as an American tragedy insofar as it can be understood as a struggle between two conflicting goods. In watching an actual tragedy—a play like *Antigone*—the audience is invited to feel torn between the claims of each side. To be able to do so is the luxury provided by a work of art.

But the story that connects all the many stories I have been trying to tell in this book is, finally, a memory of choice. When it comes to being "people in history," as we all always are, the luxury of remaining in a state of negative capability is not afforded us. The phrase "people in history" comes from Graham Greene's *The Quiet American,* a novel that accurately predicts the defeat of American war aims by an American "innocence" embodied in Alden Pyle. Greene made his prediction in 1955, ten years before American ground troops arrived in Vietnam.

While it is useful to waver and to think against oneself and to attempt to see both sides of a complex situation, especially when contemplating it by way of a work of art, as people in history we are also confronted with the need to choose. The choices may come too young, as David Harris writes, or be too hard. But even Greene, after creating a fiction in which a reader can feel torn between feeling for the cynical British journalist Fowler and feeling for the young idealist Pyle, argues for the necessity of choice. And so Fowler consents to take his revenge. He becomes "as *engagé* as Pyle, and it seemed to me that no decision would ever be simple again." As Monsieur Heng says to him, "one has to take sides. If one is to remain human."

On the night Pyle is killed, Fowler asks himself, in his guilty musings, "Must I too have my foot thrust in the mess of life before I saw the pain?" Those of us of a certain age all chose, one way or another, in 1968. We can feel "sorry" about it, as Fowler does in the last sentence in Greene's novel, but we did what we did. A decent respect for the sides we took is the least we can ask of ourselves.

So let me attempt a version of what I have charged Kerry with not having done. Having asked my artists and public figures to "say" the past in such a way as to accomplish a necessary turning, and having attempted to do so myself on every one of the preceding pages, it may be fitting to end my book with a short speech I wrote on September 11, 2004, one written out of my frustration with a candidate who appeared unable to make a reckoning with his past. In the speech, I imagined a John Kerry speaking openly about a cultural divide that had become, by the time he returned from Vietnam, a divide in his own heart and mind.

It is a short speech; I allowed myself some eight hundred words. My friend John Auchard had contacts in the Democratic vice presidential campaign—he had written *Four Trials,* the John Edwards campaign biography—and for a few days in that fall I nourished the hope that he might be able to pass the speech through Edwards to Kerry. But I never sent John the speech, and of course Kerry never gave it.

I end, then, with these never-spoken but wished-for words:

> When I was a young man, I volunteered for the U.S. Navy. When he was a young man, President Bush volunteered for the Texas Air National Guard. I was sent to fight in Vietnam. The President did his military service in the United States. I believed then and I believe now that mine was an honorable choice. I believe the same thing about the President's choice.
>
> After four months in Vietnam, I returned to the United States. My experience in Vietnam, along with my serious study of the war, had led me to believe that it was a tragic mistake. I spoke out about my beliefs. My loyalty to the men in the field demanded this. It demanded an honest acknowledgment of the conditions on the ground in Vietnam, and an admission of our policy failures there. In my attempts to bring about a change of direction in Vietnam, I never condemned those fighting there, only the policies that had let them down.
>
> I fought in the war, and then I came to oppose the conduct of it. I experienced a change of mind and a change of heart. The change

I underwent—and it was a difficult and sometimes bitter, inward struggle—was the result of hard experience and careful thought. It was not a "flip-flop." This is a silly and a dismissive word, one my political opponents have sometimes applied to me. It is a word that willfully misses the point.

Vietnam came to divide my generation. In 1965, when ground troops were first sent to Vietnam, the great majority in my generation felt no opposition to the war. By 1969, when I returned from Vietnam, the opposition to the war among people of all ages was significant. Many people of good faith continued to support the war, as an increasing number of people of good faith came to oppose it. By 1969 it had become impossible to remain neutral on the question of the war. All knew that something had gone terribly wrong. We truly had become a house divided, perhaps as divided as at any time in our history since the Civil War.

The war brought to my generation an agony of choice: because of the draft, every young man had to face the question of when and whether he would go. I went to the war, chose for it. For equally good reasons, after I came home from the war I chose to join the resistance against it. I believed then, and I believe now, that every young man also had, in his own way, even if only in the privacy of his own heart, to make his own difficult choice.

F. Scott Fitzgerald makes the claim that the test of a first-rate intelligence is in its ability to hold two conflicting ideas in the mind at the same time. It would be nice to lay claim to such an intelligence; surely, it is the kind to be looked for in a president. I suppose, looking back, that there was time in which two conflicting ideas about Vietnam were at war in my mind. There was a time when I held in mind my love and admiration for my fellow soldiers and my anger and despair over the leadership that commanded them. But, at some point, I had to resolve the conflict in my mind. I had made one choice, to become a soldier. I had to make another one, a choice to fight for the lives and dignity of the fellows in arms I had left behind, upon returning from Vietnam. I regret neither choice; I am proud, in fact, of both. They were the product of my honest attempt to deal with my changing understanding of a complex time. And having lived through such an agony of choice, I have come to believe that the mark of leadership is not a foolish consistency, but an openness to evidence, and the courage to respond to it.

What each of us did during Vietnam is important. It is just as important to be clear about what we each did. And it is above all important to acknowledge that, as we lived through it, it was hard, at times, to know what to do. This is why it is important to stop trying to score points against people who went to the war, or against people who did not. We need to stop looking at Vietnam as a cynical game in which young men tried to second-guess the future. What unites all of us who lived through the Vietnam years is that we all went though them together. And we lived on, and learned to live together again. Like the Civil War, Vietnam is finally not about an experience of lasting division. It is about how Americans, through pain and struggle and deep disappointment, continue to find ways to come together again. Not in order to enjoy a perfect union. The promise is only of "a more perfect union," one that remains our always-unfinished and enduring project.

In Vietnam

On January 17, 2012, my wife, Ann, and I arrived in Hanoi. We were traveling with our friends Jay and Ann Hill and had come overland from northern Thailand to a port on the Mekong, down the river by slow boat to Luang Prabang, and then by prop plane to Noi Bai Airport. For the Hills, the trip had been a sentimental journey back to Chiang Mai, where they had worked and taught in the late seventies and again in the early nineties, but for Ann and myself it was our first trip to Southeast Asia and, for all of us, a first look at Vietnam.

"I wonder if it will be like *Blade Runner*," Jay said, as we climbed into a taxi. In the hour it took us to reach our hotel, his expectation was only party fulfilled. It was a chilly, drizzly night, obscured by what looked like a dense, low-lying fog. As we eased onto the main highway leading into town, we were suddenly enveloped by motor-scooters. They moved at a steady, inexorable thirty-mile-an-hour clip, weaving gracefully past and around the road's far fewer cars and trucks. The lights to be seen along the road were fluorescent, shining wanly down on figures gathered in makeshift restaurants. Here and there a corporate big box flared out a name in color like Canon, Samsung, Panasonic. These were factories, not outlet stores. Once in town, twinkle lights and illuminated paper lanterns began to relieve the gloom, and the driver wove skillfully through the narrowing streets and the ceaseless honking that signaled someone coming up from behind. "They move together, like a school of fish," Jay remarked. By the time we reached the Cinnamon Hotel, the fog, we had realized, was air pollution. But the most striking thing about the traffic, besides its density, was that every so often a scooter went by carrying a miniature orange tree.

"Oh, they're for Tet," our innkeeper told us, at breakfast. "It's a traditional gift." They were not orange trees, it turned out, but kumquats. Their bright shiny fruit, we were to learn, were meant to symbolize fertility and good luck; the more fruit, the luckier the family. Prominently on display as well were branches of peach in half-bloom, a blossom which, in North Vietnamese lore, had long been used to scare away devils.

Without meaning to we had come to Vietnam on the eve of its biggest national holiday. This year the Lunar New Year's celebration was to begin officially on January 22, the day after our scheduled departure. Judging from the lights and banners in the streets, however, the celebration had begun days before our arrival. And another anniversary had come round as well, one registered on the red and gold banners decorating many of the streets. Below the image of a hammer and sickle ran the dates 1930–2012. The meaning of the dates only became clear to me after visiting the Vietnam Military History Museum.

There, in a modest glass case, was a handwritten document of seventeen lines. "Political Thesis of the Indochina Communist Party in 1930," the caption read. This was the year, then, in which Ho Chi Minh had pulled together all the rival factions and announced the formation of the Dang Cong San Viet Nam. I thought of Michael Herr and of the difficulty of dating the doom, about when wars start and whether they ever fully end, and I realized that for all the true-blue Vietnamese Communists 1930 could be looked on as year zero.

The military museum was located in the buildings and grounds of a former French army barracks. Most of the story was told through photographs, documents, and remnant objects, like General De Castrie's captured electric fan. A do not miss, according to our guidebook, was the diorama of the battlefield at Dien Bien Phu, a huge and somewhat homey relief map reminiscent of the installations at Gettysburg.

It is odd to see American aircraft displayed in the museum of a foreign country, but there they were, a U.S. Air Force helicopter and two Skyraiders captured in Saigon in 1975. On entering the compound one is first met by a Soviet MiG with fourteen stars painted on its fuselage. "This fighter has been piloted by 9 men of Regiment 921–Air Division 371," the caption read, "who have downed in rotation 14 US aircraft." The five peach trees planted around the jet were beginning to bloom.

As for 1968, it was all there: from a photograph of Lyndon Johnson taken on March 31, when outlining his "four point statement," to Averell Harriman trudging past a limousine, the "US Delegation coming back to the Paris negotiation table for war ending discussion, 1968." I was able to locate only two images of the fighting during the Tet Offensive itself, one of "liberation troops" attacking the "Saigon General Staff Headquarters, Jan 31, 1968," and another of "keeping the main Western Gate of Hue City under control in 1968." A single image of the American peace movement was on display, a shot taken of demonstrators pulling at an American flag, accompanied by the caption: "The progressive Americans fight against the aggressive war in Viet Nam."

Captions like this, with their straining after a notation of the facts by way of an ideologically ordained vocabulary, made the museum a little awkward and even smile-inducing to read. As I tried and sometimes failed to decipher each encoded message, I thought again of how repeatedly we in the West have misread the text of Asian desires. Just what was the Vietnamese resistance to each and every colonizer meant to express? They had fought off the Chinese, the Mongols, the Japanese, the French, and, finally, the Americans, and yet somehow a number of those the Vietnamese managed to expel continued to have difficulty calling this centuries-long struggle a fight for national independence. Thinking that we could "read" the Vietnamese had been, perhaps, our crucial error, but we were not a people often content to rest in negative capability. It was no wonder that Michael Herr's *Dispatches,* my favorite book about America in Vietnam, begins with a man looking at a map of a country whose contours seem to fade continually back into earlier, ghostlier demarcations. We had been up against a history so shifting and complex that no one visual freeze-frame of its borders could ever hope to capture it, as Herr acknowledges: "It was late '67 now, even the most detailed maps didn't reveal much anymore; reading them was like trying to read the faces of the Vietnamese, and that was like trying to read the wind."

It so happened that a group of U.S. senators was visiting Hanoi during our time there, a delegation lead by John McCain. In its Friday, January 20, 2012, edition, the *Viet Nam News* reported the delegation as voicing support for improved "bilateral ties" and a willingness to "assist the country in overcoming the aftermath of the war."

One more war story then brought to mind, the story of a Navy pilot shot down while on a bombing run over North Vietnam in 1967. During his ejection from the plane and his descent into a rice paddy McCain had broken a leg and both arms. After being transferred to Hanoi's Hoa Lo Prison his injuries went untreated for several weeks. When the multiple fracture in his right arm was finally set, the doctors manipulated the bones without benefit of anesthetic. In March 1968, McCain began a two-year period of solitary confinement. A few months into it, the North Vietnamese offered to send him home, largely because his father, an admiral, had just been named commander of all U.S. forces in the Vietnam theater. McCain refused the offer and vowed to accept repatriation only if every man captured before him was to be released as well.

In August 1968, the month of the Democratic convention in Chicago, the Vietnamese began to subject McCain to a prolonged period of severe torture. Rope bindings were combined with painful beatings, sometimes at an interval of two hours. The unending abuse resulted in his "confession" of war crimes and "black criminal" activities. He was finally released from captivity two months after the Paris Peace Agreement, in March 1973.

That May, McCain published an account of his captivity in *U.S. News & World Report.* In its tone and substance, the article assumes that the war was one that the United States could have won. In spite of his war experience—or perhaps because of it—McCain continued to hold to the belief that France, and by extension the United States, had defeated itself. "As you may know," he writes, "back in 1954, the North Vietnamese had a big hand in toppling the French Government in Paris because the French voters had no more stomach for the Vietnam war their Government was waging at the time. That was the way the North Vietnamese won in 1954—they didn't win in Vietnam." Recycling an old argument that the Vietnamese were adept at defeating their enemies politically rather than militarily while implying at the same time that such a way of winning ought somehow not to count, McCain, writing in the spring of 1973, was clearly struggling to understand the recent American withdrawal from Vietnam in the context of his own prolonged sacrifice. Had America also been defeated not on the battlefield but, like France, through a similar failure of political will?

Reading McCain's words on the magazine's website, I think of the howitzer captured from the French on display in the museum grounds, a gun then trained by the North Vietnamese on the encampment at Dien Bien Phu. And I remember a long rope of braided hair also on display, one sent to Ho Chi Minh by Vietnamese women captured by the French as a token of their continuing commitment to the cause.

As early as 1964, Richard Nixon had written of Vietnam as a test of our "will to win." But the war in Vietnam, as Townsend Hoopes later observed, "was not a test of wills between two parties—Hanoi and Washington—with equal interests at stake." While "our attention was on our will itself," as if by invoking the word we could produce the effect, the Vietnamese simply went about fighting the war. "You can kill ten of my men for every one I kill of yours," Ho Chi Minh had told the French in the late 1940s, "but even at these odds, you will lose and I will win." The bravery of the North Vietnamese was to become legendary; one American general called them "the best enemy we have faced in our history."

There could have been no shame in losing to such an enemy: "the simple truth," as David Harris wrote in 1996, "is that we ran into a group of people who brought considerably more seriousness to this fight than we did." The endurance made possible by such seriousness was not without its human costs; it was not as if the Vietnamese did not also feel pain. In 1981, Stanley Karnow interviewed a war widow in a hamlet near Hanoi:

> I didn't receive a single letter from my husband after he went south. I wrote to him often, but I don't know whether he ever got my letters. Then, one day, I was suddenly handed an official notice saying that he had been killed, without any details about how he died. I was shattered by the news, and I've been miserable ever since. Sometimes I think I'm going out of my mind, as if my soul has departed from my body. I can't hear anything. I can't concentrate on anything. Yes, he died for the country, but it's been very painful for me, extremely painful.

In the same year, while talking with a prominent physician in Hanoi, Karnow "discerned a certain nostalgia for the war." The "extraordinary fervor" of those years had given way, the doctor observed, to worries "about food and housing shortages—complaints never heard during the war." So the Vietnamese, too, were subject to a certain romanticizing of the past. Only six short years after the final victory, the country found itself mired in the banalities of peace. Remembering this, on the streets of Hanoi, I thought of Don DeLillo's claim, one made in *White Noise*: "Nostalgia is a product of dissatisfaction and rage. It's a settling of grievances between the present and the past. The more powerful the nostalgia, the closer you come to violence. War is the form nostalgia takes when men are hard-pressed to say something good about their country."

Even during the war itself, however, Hanoi had been a city capable of producing nostalgia. As one of the founders of the National Liberation Front, Truong Nhu Tang spent most of his war fighting and hiding in the South. In 1974 the Provisional Revolutionary Government sent him to Hanoi. He had not seen the city for thirty years, since his student days. "Perhaps my nostalgia," he writes,

> magnified the dreariness and poverty of what I now saw around me. But there was no doubt that the city had suffered dreadfully

in the intervening years. Not only had it not been modernized or
beautified in any way; it seemed to have fallen apart. Through the
car windows I could see some bomb damage, but nothing seemed to
have been done to repair it. . . . The human landscape was equally
wrenching. People walking or biking in the streets shared a look of
grim preoccupation. They seemed poorer than they had been three
decades earlier. They walked slowly, as if resigned to their lives of
poverty and constant toil. Though the streets were crowded, there
was none of the bustle or vitality that Asian cities usually display. In
its place was an air of melancholy given off by people who seemed
to have aged prematurely. . . . A surge of pity came over me for what
Hanoi's citizens had gone through, for the sacrifices that the war
had demanded of them, not just for years but for a full generation.

The generation that had made such sacrifices was little in evidence on the
streets around me.

And so it was my own nostalgia, not any emotion discernable in the
Vietnamese, that I found myself confronting on every street corner in Hanoi.
Not for the war itself, an enterprise I had by 1968 come to hate, but for the
intensities the resistance to it had called up. Living through 1968 and the
years swirling around it had left many of us not with an experience to be
missed but an ordeal to be acknowledged, the last time a significant frac-
tion of my generation had pulled together and showed up to fight for real
social change. Once again, Michael Herr had found the articulating words:
"Vietnam was what we had instead of happy childhoods." And so, at the
age of fifty-eight, I had set about writing a book about the year in which
America began to turn against its own innocence, and about how some of
us had attempted to help it in the turning.

A year that meant so much to me appeared however to have far less force
for the Vietnamese. The launching of the Tet Offensive was, for them, only
the beginning of the end. In Vietnamese memory, as the military museum
clearly demonstrates, 1975 takes precedence over 1968. An entire room
was dedicated to the April 1975 conquest of Saigon. If the war "ended" for
the United States in January 1973, this display, centered around a captured
U.S. tank, was meant to remind an onlooker that the fighting continued
for the Vietnamese for the twenty-seven months it took for the National
Liberation Front and the North Vietnamese to complete their takeover of
the South. Sitting in front of a diorama of Saigon as it looked during that
fateful April, Ann said to me: "They're good at orchestrating. There's a grand
scheme, and they just keep at it."

What they had orchestrated was an American defeat. They had won the war, and they had moved on; the people visiting the museum's displays were American and European tourists, not Vietnamese. In wandering through this dusty, un-kept-up space, I realized once again how little I knew about Vietnam; I only knew something about what we had done *to* it, and what fighting the war had done to us.

Thirty-seven years into the aftermath referred to in the *Viet Nam News,* Vietnam did not look like a damaged culture. It looked like a young culture. Not only were almost all the motor-scooter riders under thirty, but, on our nightly forays through the city, it was the gathered young, sitting on tiny plastic stools around even tinier tables where they drank limeade and chewed sunflower seeds, who filled the streets. Clearly involved in a world of getting and spending, their black leather jackets and tight black jeans spoke a universal language, one bequeathed to them by us, the losers of the war.

But we, on the other hand, did not look or feel that young anymore. Instead our public life expressed the unease and exhaustion of a people haunted by unacknowledged ghosts. We had, truly, gone on to fulfill Robert Lowell's 1965 prediction, condemned to wishing

> peace to our children when they fall
> in small war on the heels of small
> war—until the end of time
> to police the earth, a ghost
> orbiting forever lost
> in our monotonous sublime.

If dead ground could come back to haunt you the way dead people do, as Herr had written in 1968, then by the year of my visit to Vietnam it had become clear that such hauntings had come to cast a continual shadow over the American heart. They spoke to us of something unfinished—not of a victory yet to be won, or reargued, but of a vast wrong turning still to be faced.

By the time Ann and I left the Vietnam Military History Museum, the streets were thick with rush-hour traffic. We turned left out the museum gate and headed south along one of the broad sidewalks lining Dien Bien Phu Street. A solid mass of scooters had gridlocked to a halt all the way back to the nearest intersection. Then, as if rising out of the ground, they suddenly filled the sidewalk, shooting straight past us. There was nowhere to walk, or hide. We stood frozen before them—there was a moment of panic—and then we walked on, having realized that they were not aiming at us but simply driving toward a bowl of noodles, or trying to get home.

Notes

PREFACE
Two Speeches

"the work we are in": Lincoln, "Second
Inaugural Address," in *Speeches and
Writings, 1859–1865*, 687.
"a clear mission": Obama, "Remarks by the
President Commemorating Memorial
Day."
"We will never again": Quoted in Shirley,
445.
"There is division": Johnson, "The
President's Address," 218.

INTRODUCTION
The Turning

"the sense of America": Mailer, *Armies of the
Night*, 113.
"mistake": Kerry, "Vietnam Veterans Against
the War Statement," 368.
"I had to explore": Laurence, 88.
"polemical cartoonization": von Bothmer, 3.
"revisionist historians and ideologues":
Wofford, 4.
"an era of magnificent": DeGroot, 448.
"Killing the Sixties": Morrison, 175–76.
"a fever of words": Quoted in Ambrose,
Nixon: The Triumph of a Politician, 244.
"what history says": Quoted in Hoff, 341.

"when 30 years from now": Kerry, "Vietnam
Veterans Against the War Statement," 372.
"It was a year": Ali and Watkins, 7.
"relations stop nowhere": James, preface to
Roderick Hudson, in *The Novels and Tales of
Henry James*, 1:213.
"Historians . . . undertake to arrange":
Adams, *Novels, Mont Saint Michel, The
Education*, 1068.
"It was a year": Zaroulis and Sullivan, 149.
"these weeks . . . a revolutionary time":
Kopkind, 3.
"form as proceeding": Coleridge, "On Poesy
or Art," in *Literary Remains*, 1:76.
"I am part of that": Fitzgerald, *The Great
Gatsby: The Authorized Text*, 184.
"the form which is its fiction": White, 89.
"*How it felt to*": Didion, *Slouching Towards
Bethlehem*, 134.
"Why not say what happened?": Lowell,
Collected Poems, 838.
"instrumental . . . expressive": Edward P.
Morgan, 8.
"there is something in": White, 89.
"With thinking we may": Thoreau, *Walden*,
in *A Week, Walden, Maine Woods, Cape
Cod*, 429.
"strange wavering": Berman, 332–33.
"the essence of 1968": Koning, 44.

"Some damn mistake had": Mailer, *Armies of the Night,* 29.

"the ability to think": Didion, *Slouching Towards Bethlehem,* 123.

"a Last Judgment passes": Blake, "A Vision of the Last Judgment" in *Poetry and Prose,* 562.

CHAPTER 1.
Tet

"Conventional journalism could": Herr, *Dispatches,* 218.

"to negotiate, not as victors": Cronkite, 215.

"a butcher shop in Eden": Quoted in Oberdorfer, 33.

"never able to enter": Quoted ibid., 35.

"complete failure": Quoted ibid., 167.

"achieved dramatic gains": Long, 89.

"too long in forward positions": Ibid., 89–90.

"the Vietnamese leadership": Ibid., 90.

"bloodiest ground action": Oberdorfer, 201.

"may well have been": Westmoreland, 400.

"the Americans pounded the Citadel": Quoted in Hoopes, 142.

"We took space back": Herr, *Dispatches,* 71.

"Like apples in a barrel": Acheson, 219.

"falling domino principle": Quoted in Patterson, 292.

"You have a row": Quoted ibid., 294.

"National status was explicitly *denied*": Prados, 36.

"had elections been held": Eisenhower, 372.

"predisposed to view": Hoopes, 15.

"with the most extreme version": Clifford, 414.

"the logic of metaphor": Crane, "A Letter to Harriet Monroe," in *Complete Poems & Selected Letters,* 163.

"last year's words": Eliot, "Little Gidding," in *The Complete Poems and Plays,* 141.

"an extraordinarily unfitting simile": Quoted in Goldstein, 138.

"represented the latest phase": Schulzinger, 3.

"the white man is finished": Quoted in Karnow, 153.

"Along the road": All quotes in this and the next paragraph are from Ellsberg, 134.

"most loyal followers": Quoted in Duiker, 100.

"two distinct countries": Quoted in Powers, 102.

"was never a country": Ball, 422.

"an American invention": Baritz, 116.

"It used to be": Quoted in Powers, 115.

"lying next to each": Mailer, *Why Are We in Vietnam?,* 201.

"unknown panic": Ibid., 203.

"go forth and kill": Ibid., 204.

"hard as a hammer": Ibid., 203.

"Tomorrow Tex and me": Ibid., 208.

"What I was saying": Schroeder, *Vietnam: We've All Been There,* 96.

"individual spontaneity": Schlesinger, *The Politics of Hope,* 301.

"conventional journalism": Herr, *Dispatches,* 218.

"straight history . . . something wasn't": Ibid., 49.

"we are living through": Gitlin, 337.

"insane with force": Mailer, *Why Are We in Vietnam,* 143.

"The guy who hits": Gitlin, 337.

"The difference was": Quoted in Small, *Covering Dissent,* 34.

"a nation in which": Hoganson, 1.

"manly resolve": Ibid., 9.

"U.S. aims": Sheehan et al., *The Pentagon Papers,* 432.

"that I was a coward": Quoted in Karnow, 485.

"During a private conversation": Dallek, *Flawed Giant,* 491.

"one full example of": Mailer, *Armies of the Night,* 72.

"a well-knit man": Ibid., 66.

"sentences had a non-poetic": Ibid., 71.

"an epiphany of manliness": Carroll, 240.

"to protest the war": Mailer, *Armies of the Night,* 31.

"to micturate": Ibid., 29.

"and taking a sip": Ibid., 31.

"to confess straight out": Ibid.

"from gap to gain": Ibid., 31.

"date the doom": Herr, *Dispatches,* 49.

"Fictions, whose ends are consonant": Kermode, 5.

"in the middest": Ibid., 17.

"the nicer knowledge of": Stevens, "The Pure Good of Theory," in *The Palm at the End of the Mind,* 268.

"The common run": Herr, *Dispatches,* 49.

"The war between North and South": Karnow, 106.

"a sense of Vietnamese": Ibid., 107.

"If any one date": Ibid., 149.

"Isn't it after all": Quoted in Ellsberg, 363.

"expectation in preference": Coleridge, "Shakspeare," in *Literary Remains,* 2:77.

"knew that a major enemy": Westmoreland, 390.

"beginning of a great defeat": Ibid., 381.

"suffered great casualties": "Saigon under Fire," 207.

"intelligence failure": Quoted in Karnow, 543.

"It finally became clear": Herr, "Hell Sucks," 61.

"a military defeat": Johnson, *The Vantage Point,* 383.

"His first phase . . .": Ibid., 385–86.

"the Tet Offensive was": Rostow, *The Diffusion of Power,* 464.

"the heart of Hanoi's": Ibid., 466.

"Losing" . . . "Standing still": Gallup polls quoted in Cohen, *Vietnam: Anthology and Guide,* 219.

"have left the ARVN": Rostow, 519.

"failure . . . forcing the end": Ibid., 520.

"the end begins": Quoted in Oberdorfer, 105.

"the war still offered": Herr, *Dispatches,* 206.

"the look that made": Ibid., 208.

"Their story was always there": Ibid., 31.

"A Marine came out": Ibid., 123.

"One of the Vietnamese": Ibid., 184.

"pity": Owen, Preface to *Collected Poems,* 31.

"We were people": Hayslip, xv.

"Talk about impersonating": Herr, *Dispatches,* 20.

"was the time and the place": Schroeder, 34.

"roughly one casualty": Herr, *Dispatches,* 80.

"Before the Tet Offensive": Quoted in DiGiacomo.

"Well, you're there": Schroeder, 33.

"the false love object": Herr, *Dispatches,* 106.

"were irresistible": Ibid., 100.

"was the worst place": Ibid., 88.

"a Dien Bien Phu": Quoted ibid., 163.

"A great many people": Ibid., 163.

"Mike Herr, who kept": Laurence, 486.

"some kind of massive collapse": Schroeder, 35.

"how to tell a true war": O'Brien, *The Things They Carried,* 73.

"It has finally become": Herr, "Hell Sucks," 66.

"Vietnam was a dark room": Herr, *Dispatches,* 71.

"a deuce-and-a-half": Ibid., 72.

"Way to pinpoint": Ibid., 74–75.

"snappish": Ibid., 82.

"But by then . . . the battle": Ibid., 83.

"thousands of NVA executions": Ibid., 72.

"true": Ibid., 85.

"over one thousand": Porter, "The 1968 'Hue Massacre,'" 4.

"academic dispute": Laderman, 88.

"were in fact victims": Porter, "The 1968 'Hue Massacre,'" 6.

"What happened in 1968": Laderman, 89.

"I went there behind": Herr, *Dispatches,* 20.

"Must be pretty hard": Ibid., 31.

"to perform a witness act": Ibid., 66.

"There is a map": Herr, "Hell Sucks," 66.

"*There was a map*": Herr, *Dispatches,* 3.

"straight history, auto-revised history": Ibid., 49–50.

"going out after one kind": Ibid., 65.

"Even when the picture": Ibid., 18.

"seeing . . . on real ground": Ibid., 19.

"another": Ibid., 259.

"personal style": Ibid., 134.

"dispersion . . . Vietnam Vietnam Vietnam": Ibid., 260.

CHAPTER 2.
The Movement and McCarthy

"probably had little or no": Quoted in Sandbrook, 216.

"moral seriousness": Powers, 287.

"the diffidence that faltered": Pound, *The Pisan Cantos,* 100.

"It was nothing like Saint Paul": Quoted in Herzog, 32.

"Although McCarthy was initially":
    Sandbrook, 165.
"called upon to make": Quoted ibid., 135.
"severe judgment": Quoted in Eisele, 272.
"Have you talked to": Quoted ibid., 278.
"by readily agreeing": Sandbrook, 167.
"continued to waver": Ibid.
"alleviate the sense of": Quoted in Eisele, 283.
"growing sense of alienation": Quoted ibid.,
    284.
"personalized presidency": Quoted ibid., 287.
"Instead of the language": Quoted in
    Herzog, 76.
"The anti-Vietnam War movement":
    Dellinger, 189.
"U.S.-armed French troops": Franklin, 50.
"neither consumed by misgivings":
    Hagopian, 36.
"They seem the most guilt-free":
    MacPherson, 382.
"refusing to go": Harris, Our War, 13.
"None of us should": Ibid., 51.
"the tool of a life": Quoted in Powers, xiii.
"I would have left": Harris, Dreams Die
    Hard, 2.
"So how did it": Ibid., 5.
"sought out and attracted": Ibid.
"given a safe pass": Ibid., 20.
"bridge": Ibid., 38.
"Lowenstein left his side": Ibid., 49.
"any explanation of him": Ibid., 50.
"politics was the most": Ibid.
"tremendous pressure": Ibid., 58.
"betrayed": Ibid., 75.
"Al has his way": Ibid., 76.
"Call off your dogs": Ibid., 302.
"was difficult for me": Ibid., 75.
"comfortable making definitive statements":
    Ibid., 5.
"What Dennis Sweeney eventually did":
    Ibid., 89.
"I still don't understand": Ibid., 81.
"nigger lover": Ibid., 84.
"As yet, I had no words": Ibid., 123.
"David Harris is the third": Ibid., 15.
"bull session": Ibid., 97.
"peaked on October 16": Ibid., 215.
"I was drawn to": Ibid., 4.
"An act of wonderment": Ibid., 148.

"spent the last three years": 269.
"It has to be": Ibid., 246.
"no more than a momentary pause": Ibid.,
    223.
"She got out of jail": Ibid., 224.
"the best speaker": Ibid., 234.
"Baez could barely get through": Howard
    Norman, interview by author, May 2011.
"Joan Baez and David Harris": Harris,
    Dreams Die Hard, 277.
"abandon": Ibid., 281.
"The rest amounted to aftermath": Ibid., 284.
"the work we are in": Lincoln, "Second
    Inaugural Address," in Speeches &
    Writings, 1859–1865, 687.
"soon became a ceremony": Mailer, Armies of
    the Night, 74.
"We are up, face this": Ibid., 38.
"activity like writing": Ibid., 28.
"ride the beast": Ibid., 88.
"the intimate truth": Ibid., 87.
"The clue to discovery": Ibid., 25.
"Now we may leave Time": Ibid., 4.
"a sharp searing love": Ibid., 113.
"liberties to dissent": Ibid., 114.
"we will look back": Lowell, Letters, 479.
"thousands of demonstrators": Small,
    Covering Dissent, 75–76.
"sometimes altered or refused": Ibid., 15.
"As many as 1,000 radicals": Small,
    Antiwarriors, 77.
"the real climax": Mailer, Armies of the Night,
    268.
"using excessive force": Small, Antiwarriors,
    78.
"a startling disproportion": Mailer, Armies of
    the Night, 271.
"Slowly the wedge began": Quoted ibid.,
    272–73.
"women beaten senseless and": Powers, 240.
"they beat the women": Mailer, Armies of the
    Night, 277.
"those who reported major": Small, Covering
    Dissent, 2.
"relied on the mainstream": Anderson, xxi.
"addiction to violence": Quoted in Small,
    Covering Dissent, 24.
"stepping neatly and decisively": Mailer,
    Armies of the Night, 129–31.

"a coarse, vulgar episode": DeBenedetti and Chatfield, 198.

"mob leader": Quoted in Small, *Covering Dissent*, 79.

"everyone is a loser": Quoted ibid., 76.

"Quiet Rally Turns Vicious": Quoted ibid., 77.

"scolded the press": Mailer, *Armies of the Night*, 79.

"a typically American reform": DeBenedetti and Chatfield, 390.

"had been obsessed with": Maraniss, 401.

"antiwar leaders and their": Ibid., 401–2.

"the feeling of siege": Ibid., 462.

"the first in a chain": Small, *Covering Dissent*, 70.

"The movement played": Wells, 11.

"The antiwar movement so effectively": Edward P. Morgan, 167.

"news junkie": Small, *Covering Dissent*, 27.

"prejudicing people": Quoted ibid., 29.

"a vested interest in defeat": Quoted ibid.

"changed our strategy": Westmoreland, 498–99.

"its major role": DeBenedetti and Chatfield, 407.

"the opposition to the war": Powers, xv.

"Why am I against": Mailer, *Armies of the Night*, 259.

"morally" . . . "militarily": Herr, "Hell Sucks," 109.

"the disparity between America's": McPherson, 395.

"dark patches": Whitman, "Crossing Brooklyn Ferry," in Hollander, *American Poetry: The Nineteenth Century*, 1:867.

"This also . . . has been": Conrad, 5.

"inscrutable intention": Ibid., 34.

"in cipher": Ibid., 38.

"Exterminate all the brutes!": Ibid., 50.

"had whispered to him": Ibid., 57–58.

"the most you can hope": Ibid., 69.

"the longest war": "Notes and Comments," *New Yorker*, May 5, 1975, reprinted in Cohen, *Vietnam: Anthology and Guide*, 419.

"All knew that this": Lincoln, "Second Inaugural Address," in *Speeches and Writings, 1859–1865*, 686.

"His trouble was innocence": Faulkner, *Absalom, Absalom!*, 182.

"infernal American innocence": Mailer, *Armies of the Night*, 169.

"The unquestioning conviction": Hagopian, 430.

"willing to open the box": Quoted in Witcover, *The Year the Dream Died*, 339.

"innocence, wanting not to know": Lee, 290.

"I guess I'm not": Quoted in Goodwin, *Remembering America*, 481.

"None": Quoted ibid., 488.

"aside the secret enemies": Ibid., 495.

"You, me, and this": Ibid., 489.

"There is no denying": Abigail McCarthy, 336.

"came to New Hampshire": Ibid., 337.

"a Trojan horse": Quoted in Abigail McCarthy, 337.

"at first seemed persuaded": Witcover, *The Year the Dream Died*, 49.

"not a particularly significant": Ibid., 50.

"live off the land": Quoted ibid., 61.

"the biggest and best": Goodwin, *Remembering America*, 495.

"There was plenty to do": Herzog, 7.

"immediate withdrawal or military victory": Stavis, 9.

"map man": Ibid., 10.

"her simple habit": Ibid., 12.

"innocent students": Ibid., 16.

"dignified and polite": Ibid., 17.

"core": Ibid., 34.

"which in a strange way": Ibid., 19.

"As I thought of that": Ibid., 20.

"would not push himself": Herzog, 87.

"The President and his circle": Oberdorfer, 281.

"our campaign was": Stavis, xi.

"People have remarked": Quoted in Goodwin, *Remembering America*, 513.

"It's all over": Quoted in Witcover, *The Year the Dream Died*, 258.

"He just kind of gave up": Quoted ibid., 269.

"a day of visiting": Quoted ibid., 466.

"politics of happiness . . . satisfaction": Ibid., 181.

"I'd rather win": Quoted ibid., 207.

"The seeking of me": Quoted ibid., 137.

"as a spontaneous happening": Stavis, 51.

"one cannot overrate": McCarthy, *Year of the People*, 249.

"If I go down": Quoted in Blum, 308.

"passive and self-absorbed": Larner, 124.

"a political *Portnoy's Complaint*": Quoted in Eisele, 340.

"a presidential campaign that": Eisele, 310.

"In the days after": Abigail McCarthy, 407.

"it seemed to Gene": Ibid., 414.

"You and I can": Quoted in Witcover, *The Year the Dream Died*, 148–49.

"The concentrated power": Quoted in Sandbrook, 194.

"balanced judgment": Larner, 29.

"should shun the devices": Quoted in Sandbrook, 182.

"to run *against* the Presidency": Quoted ibid., 194.

"again and again": Larner, 16–17.

"What reporters and others": Ibid., 30.

"some sort of inaccessible saint": Abigail McCarthy, 32.

"tightly clasped as if": Ibid., 41.

"He refused to use": Ibid., 4.

"loftiness . . . as distant as": Larner, 17.

"it was the great": Ibid., 15.

"style as the chief sign": Ibid., 149.

"Style can become substantive": McCarthy, *Up 'Til Now*, 153.

"Bobby's campaign is like": Quoted in Herzog, 128.

"America's moral mission": Quoted in Eisele, 317.

"bits," "fixed phrases": Larner, 49.

"The process is wrong": Quoted in Eisele, 317.

"American optimists at heart": Larner, 37.

"I don't want to talk": Quoted in Witcover, *The Year the Dream Died*, 244.

"Hardest to accept": Larner, 33.

"compelled to battle with": Goodwin, *Remembering America*, 491.

"my metaphors grow cold": McCarthy, *Other Things and the Aardvark*, 6.

"Who will swear you wouldn't": Lowell, *Collected Poems*, 572.

"learned how they might shape": Stavis, xi.

"rite of passage": Mailer, *Armies of the Night*, 280.

CHAPTER 3.
McNamara, Bombing, and the
Tuesday Lunch

"He is the first": Quoted in Kearns Goodwin, *Lyndon Johnson,* 177.

"performances formidable and scintillating": Ball, 174.

"I cannot find words": Quoted in Hendrickson, 294.

"heart": Quoted in McMaster, 88.

"made his most important": Ibid., 329.

"On February 27": Johnson, *The Vantage Point*, 388.

"three options": Ibid., 389.

"a fourth": Ibid., 390.

"I discussed, 'I listened": Ibid., 370.

"quivering": Califano, 58.

"pecker": Ibid., 110.

"his language became artificial": Kearns Goodwin, *Lyndon Johnson*, 354.

"bitterness seeping through memory": Quoted in McPherson, xxi.

"McNamara, who hadn't been": Hendrickson, 345.

"It was the most depressing": Califano, 263.

"I was physically shaken": Ibid., 264.

"talk and think in numbers": Shapley, *Promise and Power,* 13.

"objects, resources, and people": Ibid., 30.

"I was part of the mechanism": *The Fog of War.*

"no one knew what": Shapley, *Promise and Power,* 46.

"management control": Ibid., 21.

"a new way of assigning costs": Ibid., 22.

"numbers became the common": Ibid., 23.

"the monitoring of progress": McNamara, *In Retrospect,* 48.

"against the plan": Ibid., 24.

"I had no patience with": Ibid., 22.

"facade of consultation": McMaster, 84.

"the only professional military": Ibid., 26.

"the role of chief strategist": Ibid., 30.

"No one ever held": Clifford, 459.

"Johnson ruled out retaliation": Porter, *Perils of Dominance*, 193.

"thought they were being": Prados, 94.

"prevent further aggression": Herring, 122.

"agree . . . engagement was illusory": Prados, 95.

"well before the first": Porter, *Perils of Dominance*, 193–94.

"freak weather effects": Ibid., 194.

"a little doubt on": Ibid., 195.

"reference to the problem": Ibid., 196.

"limited and fitting": McMaster, 132.

"reprisal": Shapley, *Promise and Power*, 322.

"seduction, not rape": Kearns Goodwin, *Lyndon Johnson*, 264.

"a total assault on": Ibid., 265.

"the aim of force": McMaster, 62.

"not so much for": Quoted ibid., 187.

"signaling and bargaining among": Shapley, *Promise and Power*, 322.

"gradations of pain": Ibid., 323.

"Pressure for a bombing campaign": Powers, 40.

"cutting people down": Quoted ibid., 223.

"Flying in the North": Quoted in Appy, 222.

"We bombed *our* Vietnam": Salisbury, 4.

"actually stiffened North Vietnamese": McMaster, 157.

"An hour or so": Dellinger, 232.

"hurriedly through devastated towns": Ibid., 233.

"good coffee": Salisbury, 44.

"not impressed": Ibid., 61.

"Don't live near": Ibid., 63.

"incredibly vulnerable": Ibid., 87.

"all the consequential storage": Ibid., 90.

"human dimensions": Ibid., 95.

"The Americans think": Ibid., 102.

"an astonishing amount": Ibid., 124.

"himself approved every target": Ibid., 70.

"American planes": Ibid., 68.

"propaganda coup": Wolfe, 538.

"'It seemed as if'": Ibid., 539.

"a good hop": Ibid., 542.

"death . . . Pilots never mentioned": Ibid., 543.

"A yellow cylinder": Harris, *Dreams Die Hard*, 147.

"The original product": Quoted in Griffiths, 210.

"we alone possess": Gellhorn, 292.

""jets showed up": Wolff, 138.

"When I landed in": Quoted in Appy, 203.

"follow that particular story": Quoted ibid., 204.

"I have no wish": Schell, *The Real War*, 192–93.

"We're going to": Ibid., 77.

"as though, having once": Ibid., 188.

"fantastic fact that we": Ibid., 191.

"had been destroyed": Ibid., 199.

"many hamlets have been": Ibid., 205.

"Well, he walked real proud": Ibid., 293.

"Those villages are completely": Ibid., 330.

"I don't know what": Ibid., 301.

"a village could be": Ibid., 202–3.

"a good ten or fifteen": Ibid., 272.

"hostile civilians": Ibid., 127.

"was one of the": Ibid.

"no middle ground in": Ibid., 109.

"one hootch": Ibid., 358.

"That's not it": Ibid., 359.

"death from the sky": Ibid., 208.

"Everything looks so calm": Ibid., 325.

"adjust the gun's aiming": Ibid., 219.

"vast 'side-effects'": Ibid., 366.

"generation of writers": Hass, 170–71.

"leadership has been replaced": Baritz, 325.

"Approval from the supervisor": Ibid., 329.

"psychology of pleasing": Ibid., 332.

"a nation without citizens": Ibid., 335.

"we . . . it wrong on": McNamara, *In Retrospect*, xv.

"misplaced in retrospect": Ibid., 125.

"the lack of knowledge": Ibid., xvi.

"Vietnam was not": Clifford, 460.

"We failed to analyze": McNamara, *In Retrospect*, 33.

"an orderly, rational approach": Ibid., 277.

"quintessential advantage": Ball, 369–70.

"penchant for tactically useful": Shapley, *Promise and Power*, 85.

"unwinnable militarily": Ibid., 410.

"I believe that would": McNamara, *In Retrospect*, 314.

"McNamara, Robert": McMaster, 441.

"innocent": Shapley, *Promise and Power*, 40.

"assumptions . . . questions . . . analyses . . . problems": McNamara, *In Retrospect*, 203.

"jigsaw puzzle": Ibid., xvii.

"wishful thinking": Ibid., 48.

"a slippery slope": Ibid., 107.

"a serious breach": Ibid., 154.

"into quicksand": Ibid., 206.

"ambiguities": Ibid., 274.

"were motivated by": Ibid., 176.

"favorable settlement" . . . "such words": Graff, 247.

"Something is missing": Shapley, *Promise and Power,* 241.

"I want a man": Snow, *The Masters,* 51.

"Each of us is": Quoted in Garrow, 101.

"There was a real": Appy, 268.

"I think she died": Quoted in Shapley, *Promise and Power,* 581.

"'Bob has all the": Ibid., 425.

"to undermanage reality": McNamara, *The Essence of Security,* 109.

"scarred his mind": Karnow, 179.

"an abruptness and imperious": McMaster, 4.

"a field marshal psychosis": Westmoreland, 138.

"composed without any involvement": Goldstein, 23.

"The doves were right": Quoted ibid., 25.

"Gordon Goldstein's book": Moyar, "Disastrous Lessons."

"Intervention is a presidential": Goldstein, 241.

"activity savage enough to": Auchincloss, 247.

"'instant rationalization'": Hoopes, 21.

"Walt Rostow in particular": Quoted in Appy, 82.

"You know, the wonderful thing": Quoted ibid., 116.

"panglossian determination": McPherson, 258.

"The President remembered": Clifford, 465.

"my perceptions of the war": Ibid., 476.

"data and analysis showed": McNamara, *In Retrospect,* 114.

"leaned toward support of": Ibid., 170.

"I don't believe that": Ibid., 246.

"the inherent limitations of": Ibid., 286.

"completely illusory": Ibid., 290.

"North Vietnam's war-fighting": Clodfelter, 111.

"pressed to escalate the": Califano, 35.

"favored stepped-up bombing": Ibid.

"pressed for mining North": Clodfelter, 69.

"expanded military action against": McNamara, *In Retrospect,* 193.

"detailed notes, but in a sense": Hendrickson, 343.

"was the first time": Califano, 263.

"In my last official act": McNamara, *In Retrospect,* 315.

"He called the request": Califano, 263.

"This is unbelievable": Quoted in Clifford, 484.

"silent partner": Ibid., 485.

"They've dropped more bombs": Quoted in Hendrickson, 344.

"The goddamned Air Force": Witcover, *The Year the Dream Died,* 81.

"It's not just that": McPherson, 431.

"rage and grief": Shapley, *Promise and Power,* 444.

"We were all stunned": Clifford, 485.

"Rusk stared at his drink": McPherson, 431.

"I am not pushing": Quoted in Califano, 263.

"very weak . . . untenable": Quoted ibid.

"optimistic": Ibid., 263.

"How do we avoid": Quoted ibid., 263.

"I do not know": McNamara, *In Retrospect,* 311.

"loyalty to the republic": Quoted in Hendrickson, 294.

"Mr. President . . . I cannot": Quoted ibid.

"Dear Mr. President": McNamara, *In Retrospect,* 315.

"I cannot find words": Ibid.

"puzzle palace": Quoted in Shapley, "Robert McNamara: Success and Failure," 246.

"carrying his eloquent words": Hoopes, 166.

CHAPTER 4.
Thirty Days in March

"Momentum is *not*": Kearns Goodwin, *Lyndon Johnson,* 226.

"Johnson was the best": Quoted in Patterson, 546.

"We don't have a prayer": Quoted ibid., 516.

"taking a drink": Quoted in Schlesinger, *Robert Kennedy and His Times,* 705.

"not once did he": Rusk, 441.

"brilliantly controlled . . . toughness": Schlesinger, *A Thousand Days,* 841.

"Good evening, my fellow Americans": Johnson, "The President's Address to the Nation," 215.

"failed to achieve its": Ibid., 216.

"I believe that now": Ibid., 218.

"grand expectations": Taken from the title of Patterson's *Grand Expectations: The United States, 1945–1974.*

"A house divided against": Lincoln, *Speeches & Writings, 1832–1858,* 426.

"string of historical facts": Ibid., 430.

"such pain in his eyes": Lady Bird Johnson, *A White House Diary,* 642.

"educating": Douglass, 787.

"what we won": Johnson, "The President's Address to the Nation," 218.

"Accordingly": Ibid., 219.

"You just cannot resign": Quoted in Witcover, *The Year the Dream Died,* 140.

"I take my leave": Quoted in Middlekauf, 21.

"a remarkably taut time": Hoopes, 224.

"a President reaches": Johnson, *The Vantage Point,* 365.

"After long discussion": Ibid., 125.

"insulation from choice": Kearns Goodwin, *Lyndon Johnson,* 180.

"lifelong reluctance": Caro, *The Years of Lyndon Johnson: The Path to Power,* 137.

"the very small doses": Caro, *The Years of Lyndon Johnson: Master of the Senate,* 651.

"he'd always been too": Ibid., 653.

"entirely preoccupied": Quoted ibid., 343.

"view words as sticks": Kearns Goodwin, *Lyndon Johnson,* 355.

"the man who talked": Ibid., xiv.

"as if the spoken words": Ibid., 56.

"I was listening to": Ibid., xvii.

"lack . . . of any moral foundation": Caro, *The Years of Lyndon Johnson: The Path to Power,* 663.

"no solid core": Hoopes, 8.

"preoccupation with principle": Kearns Goodwin, *Lyndon Johnson,* 137.

"Quite obviously he believed": McPherson, 97–98.

"in the ambiguity": Ibid., 97.

"to compromise conflict": Kearns Goodwin, *Lyndon Johnson,* 283.

"anticipatory feedback": Ibid., 323.

"everyone agreeing with each other": Schandler, xv.

"That group never leaked": Kearns Goodwin, *Lyndon Johnson,* 320.

"You just came in": Quoted in Porter, *Perils of Dominance,* 202.

"Admiral Sharp . . . had no doubt": Johnson, *The Vantage Point,* 115.

"Johnson wanted the freedom": Dallek, *Flawed Giant,* 252.

"a difficult choice between war": McMaster, 84.

"The decision to finish": Johnson, *The Vantage Point,* 366.

"no President, at least": Ibid., 424.

"I could have unmade": Ibid.

"a dramatic change in": Ibid., 366.

"Any one of dozens": Ibid., 424.

"was all supposedly explained": Abigail McCarthy, 257.

"for the sake of an effect": Ibid., 258.

"The essence of ultimate": Sorensen, xxix.

"big decision": Lady Bird Johnson, *A White House Diary,* 566.

"I *like* writing": Ibid., viii.

"sampler": Ibid., ix.

"As far back as": Johnson, *The Vantage Point,* 427.

"with others . . . I doubt": Ibid., 366.

"coming down off the mountain": Lady Bird Johnson, *A White House Diary,* 549.

"I have thought that Lyndon": Ibid., 518.

"Lyndon must not make": Ibid., 519.

"Our decision, our hope": Ibid., 549–50.

"about Lyndon's big decision": Ibid., 566.

"roaring energy": Ibid., 567.

"John said, 'You ought'": Ibid., 612.

"What shall I do?": Ibid., 617.

"as he approached the end": Ibid., 619.

"a very beautifully written statement": Ibid., 643.

"Because so much": Dallek, *Flawed Giant,* 378.

"unrealistic optimism": Ibid., 461.

"entirely silent on": Hoopes, 177.

"The request has touched": Quoted in Oberdorfer, 269.

"had any suggestions": Witcover, *The Year the Dream Died,* 98.

"we can decide in": Quoted in Schlesinger, *Robert Kennedy and His Times,* 844.

"I do not know": McCarthy, *Up 'Til Now,* 187.

"would have preferred": Johnson, *The Vantage Point,* 537.

"The fact that I received": Ibid., 538.

"the Joint Chiefs of": Hoopes, 204.

"he told the President": Ibid., 205.

"rightful heir to the": Quoted in Kearns Goodwin, *Lyndon Johnson,* 200.

"He is not about to": Quoted ibid., 338.

"only hope for a settlement": Dallek, *Flawed Giant,* 510.

"We Shall Overcome draft": Hoopes, 209.

"the broad desire to make"; Ibid., 210.

"the general view": Ibid., 216.

"not seeking a military": Clifford, 517.

"a depreciation of all": James, "Henry James's First Interview."

"the glimpse he'd had": Herr, *Dispatches,* 259.

"a separate peace": Hemingway, *A Farewell to Arms,* 243.

"I was always embarrassed": Ibid., 184–85.

"No words are strong enough": Quoted in Blum, 135.

"outdated information": Johnson, *The Vantage Point,* 416.

"intelligent, experienced men": Ibid., 418.

"poised for a journey": Goodwin, *Remembering America,* 3.

"Not a theory at all": Goodwin, "Talk of the Town," 21.

"exhortation to remembrance": Goodwin, *Remembering America,* 10.

"a decisive turning point": Ibid., 9.

"saw his role as": McPherson, 327.

"Goodwin is like": Quoted in Schlesinger, *Robert Kennedy and His Times,* 870.

"A speech . . . is not": Goodwin, *Remembering America,* 327.

"put together a Johnson program": Ibid., 271.

"the Great Society": Ibid., 272.

"could fit a lot": Dallek, *Flawed Giant,* 81.

"every writer *creates*": Borges, "Kafka and His Precursors," in *Labyrinths,* 201.

"I had no intention": Goodwin, *Remembering America,* 276.

"where men are more": Ibid., 278.

"needs of the spirit": Ibid., 280.

"I wanted power to give": Quoted in Kearns Goodwin, *Lyndon Johnson,* 54.

"a generous and demanding": Ibid., ix.

"The giver decided what": Ibid., x.

"appreciated": Ibid., xi.

"resentment based, not on": Ibid., 220.

"We do not quite": Emerson, "Gifts," in *Essays and Lectures,* 536.

"Johnson believed that": Suri, 147.

"no one could make over": Ibid., 153.

"Washington's efforts produced devastation": Ibid., 162.

"the illiberal consequences": Ibid., 131.

"he needs a speech": Quoted in Goodwin, *Remembering America,* 326.

"the constraint of time": Ibid., 327.

"was pure Johnson": Ibid., 328.

"At times history": Ibid., 331.

"lay bare the secret": Ibid., 332.

"The last time a president": Ibid., 333.

"There was an instant": Ibid., 334.

"galloping distortions": Hoopes, 151.

"the McNamara men": Schandler, 123.

"seemed internally contradictory": Clifford, 476.

"office of President": Ibid., viii.

"slowly developing relationship": Quoted in Caro, *The Years of Lyndon Johnson: Means of Ascent,* 124.

"Give me the lesser": Johnson, *The Vantage Point,* 393.

"I was thrust into": Quoted in Schandler, 140.

"to write what we thought": Ibid., 150.

"modest recommendations": Ibid., 175.

"The scope and depth": Ibid., 200.

"It moved like wind": Quoted ibid., 201.

"churned up the whole": Quoted ibid., 202.

"we shouldn't have gone": Ibid., 211.

"thoughts coalesced": Ibid., 215.

"not only endless": Ibid., 216.

"Clifford approach": Ibid., 245.

"an extremely able, loyal": Ibid., 246.

"The president made a": Quoted ibid., 245.

"to ask what I": McPherson, 431.

"served the purpose": Schandler, 264.

"become a vast collective": Karnow, 563.

"when the President was": McPherson, 326.

"Madness": Quoted in Schandler, 272.

"possibility": Quoted ibid., 271.

"still essentially a defiant": Hoopes, 219.

"The Clifford manner": Ibid., 220.

"a hopeless bog": Quoted in McPherson, 434.

"brilliant and utterly courageous": Quoted in Hoopes, 220.

"winding it down": McPherson, 435.
"It was decided": Ibid., 436.
"left the State Department": Ibid., 437.
"What do you think": Quoted in Califano, 266.
"I speak to you": Clifford, 520.
"peace offer": Johnson, *The Vantage Point,* 420.
"painstakingly": McPherson, 437.
"what I planned to do": Johnson, *The Vantage Point,* 429.
"I thought I had": Ibid., 430.
"At the last minute": Dallek, *Flawed Giant,* 525.
"I was never more certain": Johnson, *The Vantage Point,* 432.
"I've got two endings": Quoted in Witcover, *The Year the Dream Died,* 140.
"sit down and write": Busby, 12.
"I want out of this cage": Quoted ibid., 194.
"what you wrote yesterday": Quoted ibid., 196.
"will not . . . would not": Ibid., 207.
"This is me": Quoted ibid., 212.
"would . . . will": Ibid., 222.
"and asked if I": McPherson, 439.
"I showed them the statement": Johnson, *The Vantage Point,* 434.
"You could have knocked": Quoted in Witcover, *The Year the Dream Died,* 141.
"what amounted to a retreat": Powers, 317.
"decisions made in March": Schandler, ix.

CHAPTER 5.
Fourteenth Street

"police considered this intersection": Gilbert, 13.
"go home": Ibid., 14.
"Get off the streets": Quoted ibid., 21.
"bumping it with her": Ibid., 22.
"White merchants scurried around": Ibid., 181.
"vengeful selectivity": Ibid., 180.
"The eastbound lanes": Busby, 239–40.
"smoke leaped into the sky": Ibid., 240.
"briefed him as clearly": Hayden, 270.
"It looked considerably more": Westmoreland, 440.
"the hardest hit was": Oates, 494.

"I felt so sad": Quoted in Schwartzman and Pierre, A10.
"always had the same question": Quoted ibid., A11.
"why we find it difficult": King, *A Testament of Hope,* 293.
"dramatic confrontations": Ling, 189.
"symbolic march": Ibid., 195.
"I'll try my best": Quoted ibid., 196.
"We will go back": Quoted in Branch, *At Canaan's Edge,* 77.
"Each of us is": Quoted in Garrow, 101.
"to both North and South": Lincoln, *Speeches and Writings, 1859–1865,* 687.
"fundamental and astounding result": Ibid., 686.
"the enemy's point of": King, *A Testament of Hope,* 237.
"a mighty walk": Ibid., 227.
"marching on": Ibid., 230.
"the politics of walking": Wofford, 201.
"standing before the forces": King, *A Testament of Hope,* 227.
"Put it in the center": Quoted in Branch, *At Canaan's Edge,* 226.
"long way": King, *A Testament of Hope,* 228.
"We are here": Ibid., 227.
"We are on the move": Ibid., 228.
"an address that will": Ibid., 228.
"the tiny community of": Ibid., 228.
"How long will it take?": Ibid., 230.
"How long? Not long": Quoted in Branch, *At Canaan's Edge,* 170.
"nationalized race": Ibid., 523.
"as a right and a theory": Quoted ibid., 232.
"a riot is the language": Quoted in Ling, 252.
"closer to . . . further from": Quoted in Horne, 184.
"a revolution of rising": Quoted in Garrow, 286.
"search for causes": Fogelson, 26.
"sleighrode from 35 per cent": Conot, 106.
"the Berlin Wall": Ibid., 206.
"Why Los Angeles?": Fogelson, 3.
"riffraff theory": Ibid., 118.
"A drive through": Cohen, 45.
"there was no clear": Patterson, 664.
"high level of discontent": Cohen, 247.
"Discontent increases": Ibid., 250.

"running into more and more": Quoted in Garrow, 273.

"bitter hatred develops toward": Branch, *At Canaan's Edge,* 555.

"scholarly friend": McPherson, 361.

"unwittingly teased and taunted": Ibid., 362.

"Why have law and order": Quoted ibid., 368.

"white society is deeply": Quoted in Witcover, *The Year the Dream Died,* 79.

"blames everybody for the riots": Quoted ibid., 91.

"You do not take a person": Quoted in Branch, *At Canaan's Edge,* 232.

"creative tension": King, *A Testament of Hope,* 291.

"The money to buy things": Quoted in Ling, 213.

"structural": Quoted in Garrow, 498.

"insensitive policing provoked": Ling, 228.

"I have to do this": Quoted in Garrow, 500.

"non-ghetto low rise": Ling, 232.

"the best housing": Ibid., 237.

"The Civil Rights Movement": Ibid., 209.

"The road of nonviolence": Lewis, 347.

"There were dark days": Quoted in Branch, *At Canaan's Edge,* 631.

"went to Detroit": Hersey, 31.

"were being fired upon": Ibid., 164.

"Army under heavy fire": Ibid., 244.

"news . . . Negro snipers": Ibid., 21.

"where most of this": Ibid., 15.

"At this point in the narrative": Ibid., 30.

"There is no such thing": Ibid., 34.

"At the outset I learned": Ibid., 31–32.

"*heard*": Smith, *Twilight,* xxiv.

"My reliance in this narrative": Hersey, 264.

"as much as possible": Ibid., 33.

"I was all too aware": Ibid., 33–34.

"There could be no": Ibid., 33.

"Why you got to": Quoted ibid., 271.

"Ain't you ashamed?": Quoted ibid., 272.

"was not even possible": Ibid., 226.

"sexual jealousy": Ibid., 288.

"scene of violence": Houston A. Baker, 38.

"Happen? What the hell": Faulkner, *Collected Stories,* 171–72.

"the Ogre": Cleaver, 19.

"I became a rapist": Ibid., 26.

"A black man growing up": Ibid., 23.

"displayed a better appreciation": Chester, Hodgson, and Page, 739.

"full enemy status": Branch, *Parting the Waters,* 692.

"the ghetto rebellions of the 1960s": McKnight, 8.

"tom cat": Branch, *Parting the Waters,* 861.

"obsessive degenerate sexual urges": McKnight, 5.

"sexual activity": Oates, 264.

"sex groans and party jokes": Branch, *Pillar of Fire,* 528.

"highlights": Garrow, 374.

"suicide package": Branch, *Pillar of Fire,* 529.

"Your end is approaching": Ibid., 528–29.

"the campaign against Martin": Young, *An Easy Burden,* 471.

"that he was so hurt": Ibid., 472.

"the greatest purveyor": King, *A Testament of Hope,* 233.

"*sting*": Lewis, 214.

"The war in Vietnam": Quoted in Branch, *At Canaan's Edge,* 23.

"to know them and hear": King, *A Testament of Hope,* 235.

"helpless and outcast children": Ibid., 234.

"broken and eviscerated": Ibid., 232.

"devastating the hopes": Ibid., 233.

"The whole structure": Quoted in Garrow, 564.

"We must be ready": King, *A Testament of Hope,* 239.

"vacillations": Garrow, 564.

"to break the betrayal": King, *A Testament of Hope,* 232.

"There is such a thing": Ibid., 243.

"plea to my beloved": Ibid., 232.

"distinct and separate": Quoted in Oates, 437.

"I've fought too long": Quoted ibid., 439.

"network of mutuality": King, *A Testament of Hope,* 290.

"the big nigger": Quoted in Oates, 455.

"spiritually exhausted": Garrow, 602.

"profound sadness": Ibid., 599.

"a conspicuous thread of": Branch, *At Canaan's Edge,* 686.

"This is what is going to happen": Quoted in Garrow, 307.

"Somehow he always felt": Quoted ibid., 232.

"everybody . . . to turn around": Branch, *At Canaan's Edge,* 732.

"the petty criminal class": McKnight, 58.

"What was supposed to": Young, 455.

"Maybe we just have to admit": Quoted in Branch, *At Canaan's Edge,* 734.

"The message is that": Quoted in Wyatt, 40.

"I want you to": Quoted in Branch, *At Canaan's Edge,* 766.

"Suddenly . . . we heard what sounded": Young, 464.

"standing up for the best": King, *A Testament of Hope,* 286.

"stand up for freedom": Ibid., 219.

"Martin Luther, stand up": Garrow, 58.

"I will die standing": Quoted ibid., 302.

"continuing story": King, *A Testament of Hope,* 619.

"The present . . . same story": Ibid., 619.

"I've been to the mountaintop": Quoted in Branch, *At Canaan's Edge,* 226.

"myth of time": King, *A Testament of Hope,* 296.

"If I were standing": Ibid., 279.

"If you allow me": Ibid., 280.

"been around": Ibid., 286.

"demented woman": Ibid., 285.

"It doesn't matter now": Ibid., 286.

"Fourteenth Street was our town": Quoted in Abigail McCarthy, 391.

CHAPTER 6.
RFK

"ranking official": Talbot, 6.

"telling him point blank": Ibid., 9.

"burden of knowledge": Wofford, 389.

"there was no way": Ibid., 415.

"Henry the Fourth": Quoted in Schlesinger, *Robert Kennedy and His Times,* 820.

"relations stop nowhere": James, *The Art of the Novel,* 5.

"the whole thing goes back": DeLillo, *Libra,* 170.

"the moonlit fixation": Ibid., 22.

"fucking the girlfriend": Ibid., 347.

"ripening . . . toughness and restraint": Schlesinger, *A Thousand Days,* 841.

"pacific ways": Wills, *The Kennedy Imprisonment,* 271.

"year after year": Ibid., 272.

"When Jack sent": DeLillo, *Libra,* 302.

"lay down fire": Ibid., 219.

"spectacular miss": Ibid., 51.

"to write the secret history": Ibid., 15.

"the conspiracy against": Ibid., 441.

"*might-have-been*": Faulkner, *Absalom, Absalom!,* 118.

"Some things are true": DeLillo, *Libra,* 382.

"This was the little surprise": Ibid., 53.

"I think you're fulfilling": Mailer, "Life and Letters: In the Ring," 62.

"the darker impulses": Witcover, *85 Days,* 116.

"It is not upon": Whitman, "Crossing Brooklyn Ferry," in Hollander, *American Poetry: The Nineteenth Century,* 2:867.

"Mr. Kennedy knows": Quoted in Schlesinger, *Robert Kennedy and His Times,* 189.

"charismatic protest": Wills, *The Kennedy Imprisonment,* 212.

"There is nothing stranger": Ibid., 210–11.

"the strong, stern faces": Kennedy, *The Enemy Within,* 261.

"human compassion": Quoted in Schlesinger, *Robert Kennedy and His Times,* 191.

"helped strengthen the instinct": Ibid.

"You know you fellows": Quoted ibid.

"a cooling off period": Palermo, 60.

"Do you know that": Quoted ibid., 47.

"the most attentive listener": Quoted in Schlesinger, *Robert Kennedy and His Times,* 434.

"willing to listen": Lewis, 213.

"Smith set the tone": Quoted in Schlesinger, *Robert Kennedy and His Times,* 331–32.

"When I pull the trigger": Quoted ibid., 332.

"that made everybody move": Quoted ibid., 332.

"primeval memory . . . our existence": Quoted ibid., 332.

"Look, if *you* can't": Quoted ibid., 332.

"Your family has been": Quoted ibid., 332–33.

"They seemed possessed": Quoted ibid., 333.

"He began . . . to grasp": Ibid., 335.

"The people, the young": Quoted in Lewis, 213.

"The violent youth": Quoted in Schlesinger, *Robert Kennedy and His Times*, 785.

"Let them show the": Quoted ibid., 798.

"I want to see": Quoted ibid., 794.

"My God, . . . I didn't": Quoted ibid., 795.

"I had the feeling": Quoted ibid., 349.

"influence . . . Now I know": Quoted in Newfield, 72.

"Troops saw us coming": Quoted in Schlesinger, *Robert Kennedy and His Times*, 877.

"People who have to live": Quoted in Witcover, *The Year the Dream Died*, 158.

"because I have such": Quoted in Witcover, *85 Days*, 87.

"the ability to respond": Quoted in Wofford, 177.

"he defined and created": Newfield, 18.

"small and difficult": Quoted in Schlesinger, *Robert Kennedy and His Times*, 773.

"cities and villages": Quoted ibid., 862.

"to visualize 'the horror'": Quoted ibid., 773.

"a new kind of courage": Wofford, 421.

"liquidation of leaders": Wills, *The Kennedy Imprisonment*, 252.

"to go to Viet Nam": Quoted in Schlesinger, *Robert Kennedy and His Times*, 728.

"it is not helpful": Quoted in Newfield, 120.

"air attacks by a government": Quoted ibid., 122.

"watershed decision": Ibid., 18.

"a share of power": Quoted ibid., 125.

"I can testify": Quoted ibid., 137.

"We are all participants": Quoted in Schlesinger, *Robert Kennedy and His Times*, 773.

"it's hard . . . to forgive": Quoted ibid., 897.

"I think he thought": Quoted ibid., 827.

"Gene will make himself": Ibid.

"Kennedy decided, in his own mind": Newfield, 211.

"So it is how": Quoted in Schlesinger, *Robert Kennedy and His Times*, 847.

"reassessing the possibility of": Quoted in Witcover, *85 Days*, 68.

"That night I decided": Quoted ibid., 80.

"council of war": Schlesinger, *Robert Kennedy and His Times*, 832.

"Bobby's future": Quoted ibid., 833.

"Bob's just about made up": Quoted in Witcover, *The Year the Dream Died*, 96.

"All of my sisters": Quoted in Vanden Heuvel and Gwirtzman, 297.

"But why, why are they": Abigail McCarthy, 368.

"In the mild chill": Goodwin, *Remembering America*, 481.

"Well, what do I do": Quoted ibid., 516–17.

"I'd like you to": Quoted ibid., 518.

"I'm sorry, Senator": Quoted ibid., 527.

"bitter interlude when Blair": Abigail McCarthy, 370.

"help . . . which have not": Ibid., 372–73.

"like the walrus": McCarthy, *Up 'Til Now*, 90.

"When they talked": Quoted in Witcover, *The Year the Dream Died*, 107.

"They never offer anything": Quoted in Abigail McCarthy, 374.

"How did it go?": Quoted in Vanden Heuvel and Gwirtzman, x.

"Depth had come to him": Wills, *The Kennedy Imprisonment*, 94.

"Bobby was the worst": Quoted in Schlesinger, *Robert Kennedy and His Times*, 127.

"Indian-er": Quoted ibid., 886.

"the sound of steel": Quoted ibid., 891.

"staccato . . . what comes through": Ibid., 886.

"imagining heart": Quoted ibid, 802.

"unskilled at hating on his own": Quoted ibid.

"a subtle sadness": Mailer, *Miami and the Siege of Chicago*, 200.

"psychic violence": Quoted in Schlesinger, *Robert Kennedy and His Times*, 804.

"an almost insolent fatalism": Ibid., 814.

"Unless you include the fact": Quoted ibid., 815.

"measure . . . against ancient tests": Newfield, 233.

"He knew the Greeks": Quoted in Schlesinger, *Robert Kennedy and His Times*, 619.

"If in this year": Quoted in Witcover, *The Year the Dream Died*, 116.

"to learn the harsh": Quoted ibid., 117.

"we have done . . . our": Quoted ibid., 116.

"I'm responsible and you're responsible": Quoted ibid., 117.

"How can you say": Quoted in Schlesinger, *Robert Kennedy and His Times,* 888.

"We want Kennedy": Quoted ibid., 882.

"Angry at the smugness": Halberstam, 120–21.

"I see you're for McCarthy": Quoted in Witcover, *The Year the Dream Died,* 202.

"I'm against the war": Quoted ibid., 203.

"had won in Indiana": Quoted ibid., 204.

"understood exactly what": Fallows, 382.

"having gotten away": Ibid., 383.

"white ethnics": Hayden, 286.

"We have to convince": Quoted ibid., 286.

"patient . . . some *sting*": Lewis, 214.

"entirely about the work": Ibid., 242.

"inactions . . . had dramatically changed": Ibid., 384.

"Near sunset . . . we were": Ibid., 385.

"I just stood there": Ibid., 386.

"I'm sorry . . . a leader": Ibid., 386.

"What should I say": Quoted in Boomhower, 64.

"Somebody has to speak": Lewis, 386.

"Kennedy broke down and": Ibid., 388.

"I'm only going to talk": All quotations from this speech are from Kennedy, "Remarks on the Assassination of Martin Luther King, Jr."

"He spoke simply": Lewis, 387.

"curiously withdrawn from the race": Goodwin, *Remembering America,* 532.

"I want to work": Quoted in Newfield, 20.

"Kids ran alongside the car": Witcover, *85 Days,* 175.

"Well, . . . I've done all": Quoted ibid., 177.

"To *love* the man": Lewis, 397.

"Oh my God!": Ibid., 395.

"'John,' he said": Ibid., 394.

"I dropped to my knees": Ibid., 395.

"That was the loneliest": Ibid., 396.

"started to cry hard": Hayden, 290.

"rode south . . . under": Schlesinger, *Robert Kennedy and His Times,* 915.

"We Love You, Bobby": Lewis, 396.

CHAPTER 7.
The Ditch

"at the bottom of": O'Brien, *In the Lake of the Woods,* 36.

"capable of being in uncertainties": Keats, *Selected Letters,* 60.

"there were no mitigating": O'Brien, "The Mystery of My Lai," 173.

"it's a mystery": Ibid., 177.

"There are seeds of evil": Ibid., 172.

"Evil is a mysterious thing": Ibid., 178.

"implacable otherness of others": O'Brien, *In the Lake of the Woods,* 103.

"we wish to penetrate by hypothesis": Ibid.

"Maybe she's still out there": Ibid., 58.

"All you had to do": Ibid., 206.

"when a man is": Keats, *Selected Letters,* 60.

"I know what happened": O'Brien, *In the Lake of the Woods,* 203.

"inconclusiveness": Ibid., 304.

"his secrets would remain": Ibid., 46.

"worse than the terrible thing": Ibid., 231.

"During the period 16–19 March": Peers, *The My Lai Inquiry,* 295.

"At every command level": Ibid., 297.

"noble acceptance of total": Fussell, 297.

"Vietnamese human beings": Belknap, 155.

"I'm the boss": Hersh, *My Lai 4,* 21.

"good and mad": Ibid., 35.

"to kill everything": Ibid., 40.

"You know what I want": Quoted ibid., 50.

"Push all those people": Quoted ibid., 63.

"only enemy person": Belknap, 74.

"heated discussion": Ibid., 75.

"We don't want Americans": Quoted in Hersh, *Cover-Up,* 148.

"machine gun confrontation problem": Quoted ibid., 163.

"We went in there": Quoted in Belknap, 101.

"Exactly what did, in": Quoted in Hersh, *My Lai 4,* 108.

"proper investigation": Belknap, 105.

"there was big trouble": Hersh, *Cover-Up,* 218.

"subsequent senior officers": Ibid., 221.

"Oriental human beings": Quoted in Belknap, 112.

"isolated incident": Quoted in Hersh, *Cover-Up,* 231.

"no knowledge": Quoted ibid., 251.

"that what had happened": Belknap, 167.

"commanded by somebody upstairs": Quoted ibid., 185.

"Calley Verdict: Who Else": Quoted in Hagopian, 59.

"engaged in a seven-month campaign": Ibid., 406.

"The My Lai massacre . . . was": Ibid.

"the exposure of My Lai": Turse, 247.

"corporate searching": Lang, 16.

"included more than 300": Turse, 14.

"The stunning scale": Ibid., 6.

"the scattered, fragmentary nature": Ibid., 22.

"a veritable system of suffering": Ibid., 23.

"massacre . . . tragedy of major": Belknap, 127.

"outclassed": Dallek, *Flawed Giant*, 270.

"We are continually chagrined": Sheehan, "Not a Dove," 302.

"the name 'government' ": Schell, *Observing the Nixon Years*, 4.

"of rank in that unhappy army": Wolff, 15.

"Good little fighters": Herr, "Hell Sucks," 67.

"father's memoir": Pham, 3.

"at three times the market": Ibid., 84.

"entrenched corruption, outrageous inefficiency": Ibid., 85.

"went to great lengths": Brigham, 3.

"one of the most maligned": Ibid., x.

"redefine the meaning": Ibid., xi.

"Even when the picture": Herr, *Dispatches*, 18.

"I didn't go through": Ibid., 256.

"no secrets about it": Ibid., 228.

"look away": Ibid., 208.

"coming back from the war": Hemingway, *A Moveable Feast*, 76.

"was omitted on my new theory": Ibid., 75.

"pictures were the first": Belknap, 112.

"the deep truth is imageless": Shelley, *Prometheus Unbound*, act II, scene IV, line 116.

"The story of the massacre": Oliver, 9.

"Five years ago . . . I began": Appy, xv.

"the actual victims of": Oliver, 9.

"on the wrong side": Cao, 27.

"the official moment": Ibid., 151.

"fabricating continuity": Ibid., 133.

"*is a Vietcong*": Ibid., 227.

"the military side . . . there was another side": Truong, xiii.

"like a physical blow": Ibid., 12.

"shabby incompetence": Ibid., 62.

"extralegal": Ibid., 66.

"largely nationalist": Ibid., 68.

"high level": Ibid., 73.

"Southern revolution . . . generated": Ibid., 68.

"the tangled feelings": Hunt, 59.

"Interviewee no. 135": Ibid., 33.

"the Destruction of the Oppression": Ibid., 34.

"Insurrection was in the air": Ibid., 35.

"When the revolution came": Ibid., 45.

"the line of Party control": Elliott, 158.

"there was a vast difference": Ibid., 331.

"the liberated zones lay": Hunt, 212.

"Only on the second day": Elliott, 301.

"in a state of semistarvation": Truong, 158.

"septic jungle": Ibid., 165.

"hiding and preparation": Ibid., 164.

"their victims senseless": Ibid., 167.

"one lost control": Ibid., 168.

"like uninvited guests": Ibid., 187.

"class deficiencies . . . the ideologues": Ibid., 189.

"locked in": Ibid., 191.

"a middle way": Ibid., 192.

"Practically the entire North": Ibid., 207.

"the true outlines of power": Ibid., 267.

"the last linkup": Ibid., 268.

"everyone had some family": Ibid., 278.

"more kidnappings than legal": Ibid., 279.

"the country where thirty years": Ibid., 309.

"the Vietnamese who fought": Ibid., xiv.

"Nixon and Kissinger suffered": Ibid., 209.

"You know, you never": Quoted ibid., 211.

"the enemy's internal contradictions": Ibid., 212.

"American leadership from its": Ibid., 213.

"ingrained distrust and ill will": Ibid., 212.

"effects . . . national psyche": Ibid., 213.

"For the first twelve years": Hayslip, ix.

"the beliefs we already had": Ibid., x.

"Because we had to appease": Ibid., xiv–xv.

"what we admired": Ibid., 33.

"extra people": Ibid., 39.

"the way one learns": Ibid., 44.

"Two thirds of my village": Ibid., 69.

"teeming mass": Ibid., 72.

"By giving my signal": Ibid., 73.

"It was just like": Ibid., 76.

"Nobody gets out of My Thi": Ibid., 86.
"Now I had no doubt": Ibid., 87.
"I no longer cared": Ibid., 97.
"a better 'killing zone'": Ibid., 195.
"see my mother again": Ibid., 24.
"I have not seen or spoken": Ibid.
"receiving money from the": Ibid., 233.
"For them, the war": Ibid., 218.
"bare feet stick out": Ibid., 242.
"like a bulletproof vest": Ibid., 243.
"Bay Ly's a capitalist": Ibid., 251.
"Central Vietnam—*Trung* land": Ibid., 252.
"for the first time": Ibid., 254.
"You've seen both sides": Ibid., 341.
"perfect . . . How are we": Ibid., 343.
"grown up to see": Ibid., 358.
"compliant fish": Lowell, *Collected Poems,*
    376.
"balloons": Ibid., 377.
"his bell-cheeked Negro": Ibid., 376.
"wanted no monument": Ibid., 377.
"the My Lai Theme Park": Michael Sullivan,
    reporting from Quang Ngai Province,
    National Public Radio, April 24, 2005.
"to give/each figure": Lowell, "Epilogue," in
    Collected Poems, 838.

CHAPTER 8.
Columbia

"Then Rudd did the thing": Kunen, 14.
"the April uprising started": Cox et al., 370.
"the universities, starting as": Coffin, 302.
"when the uprising began": Trilling, 77.
"Touch a university": Ibid., 80.
"not central to the event": Mailer, *Armies of
    the Night,* 53.
"the precise feel of": Ibid., 53.
"interpretative": McCaughey, xi.
"student misbehavior": Ibid., 423.
"first turned confrontational": Ibid., 429.
"shouting students": Ibid., 430.
"congested loneliness": Hayden, 26.
"Ultimately . . . you have to": Quoted ibid.,
    35.
"pattern of non-leadership": Ibid., 56.
"Where do we find ourselves?": Emerson,
    471.
"an intuitive alertness": Hayden, 82.
"had taken all political": Ibid., 75–76.

"politics should flow from": Ibid., 75.
"manifesto of hope": Ibid., 74.
"Few could understand": Ibid., 263.
"Hamlet-like vacillation": Ibid., 266.
"trying to get along": Ibid., 267.
"Why did we, who": Ibid., 503.
"I believe that as a nation": Ibid., 243.
"compared unfavorably with smoking":
    McCaughey, 433.
"All relevant elected officials": Ibid., 435.
"for some years now": Trilling, 85.
"the facilities of the building": Ibid., 88.
"getting arrested on behalf": Naison, 88.
"approached the fence": Ibid., 89.
"IDA thus became": Rudd, *Underground,* 47.
"an intentional mass violation": Ibid., 58.
"sure what to do": Ibid., 59.
"To the gym site!": Ibid., 60.
"Seize Hamilton!": Ibid., 63.
"Things were happening": Ibid., 65.
"I resign as chairman": Ibid., 75.
"liberated": Ibid., 57.
"sense of generous recollection": Beidler,
    124.
"vestige of idea": Trilling, 84.
"This book was written": Kunen, 6.
"Someone suggests we go": Ibid., 22.
"the blacks occupying Hamilton": Ibid., 23.
"one hundred seventy-three": Ibid., 24.
"I get up and": Ibid., 27.
"We get inside and": Ibid., 28.
"some black students": Hayden, 272.
"I had never seen": Ibid., 274.
"a nice, somewhat inarticulate": Ibid., 275.
"We arrived at a consensus": Ibid., 276.
"A secret committee": Ibid., 277.
"concerned with the breast": Kunen, 30.
"children of the new age": Ibid., 31.
"bullshit": Quoted in McCaughey, 450.
"something important . . .": Didion,
    Slouching Towards Bethlehem, 123–24.
"Parents were missing": Ibid., 84.
"the ambushes of family": Ibid., 167.
"give her *home*": Ibid., 168.
"Maybe we have stopped": Ibid., 123.
"child-rearing practices": Cavallo, 49.
"What distinguished the experiences": Ibid.,
    11.
"self-confidence nurtured": Ibid., 46.
"I am a mature woman": Trilling, 150.

"unseeing didacticism": Quoted ibid., 144.

"Columbia is my husband's": Ibid., 78.

"antiliberal in its lawlessness": Ibid., 127.

"With thinking we may": Thoreau, *Walden*, in *A Week, Walden, Maine Woods, Cape Cod*, 429.

"Our young people, in": Quoted in Hayden, 279.

"transitory birds": Quoted ibid., 272.

"Whether students vote yes": Quoted in Witcover, *The Year the Dream Died*, 187.

"inability to address the campus": Trilling, 103.

"the chief parental figures": Ibid., 121.

"first inclination was to call": McCaughey, 445.

"in all probability destroy": Quoted ibid., 446.

"was present, observably present": Trilling, 123.

"the very future of": Quoted in McCaughey, 456.

"I am skeptical of": Quoted in Taft, 87.

"I do not feel": Quoted ibid., 117.

"Frankly, you've got": Quoted ibid., 103.

"Above all . . . wanted to": Coffin, 302.

"Politically, the patrolling was": Dupee, 36.

"it was as if I were": Ibid., 38.

"instructor . . . those of us": Quoted in Michael Baker et al., 138.

"My God, how could": Quoted in Gitlin, 308.

"Only one totally lacking": Chomsky, 305.

"We are once and for all": Gitlin, 338.

"to keep on nodding terms": Didion, *Slouching Towards Bethlehem*, 139.

"Here at Columbia, we": Hofstadter, 385.

"community . . . a kind of": Ibid., 384.

"the realization of 1968": Readings, 145.

"beside myself with anger": Rudd, *Underground*, 88.

"a puny gesture": Ibid., 89.

"last building to fall": Hayden, 281.

"A girl comes up": Kunen, 33.

"they pull us apart": Ibid., 34.

"who was on the sixth": Ibid., 35.

"They tell us how": Ibid., 36.

"hit on the head": Quoted in Michael Baker et al., 61.

"falling or jumping on": McCaughey, 458.

"Ahab": Quoted ibid., 437.

"Okay, go ahead": Rudd, *Underground*, 110–11.

"visualizing" . . . "ruthless efficiency": Hayden, 281.

"I took leave of": Ibid., 282.

"Like the Lone Ranger": Kunen, 36.

"In any retelling": Rudd, *Underground*, 319.

"an uneasy experiment": Naison, 18.

"carried themselves very differently": Ibid., 19.

"lanky six footer": Ibid., 21.

"open to people of": Ibid., 14.

"none of my black": Ibid., 37.

"admirable people trapped": Ibid., 41.

"became romantically involved": Ibid., 50.

"social responsibility . . . as a": Ibid., 81.

"interracial DMZ": Ibid., 82.

"started working with several": Ibid., 68.

"describing the many unsuccessful": Ibid., 90.

"gym issue" . . . "manufactured": Quoted in Trilling, 102.

"race conscious": Naison, 17.

"I felt devastated": Ibid., 92.

"The racially bifurcated character": Ibid., 94.

"a separate deal": Ibid., 94.

"Separate treatment of blacks": Dupee, 26.

"multiracial settings": Naison, 98.

"guilt about whiteness": Ibid., 118.

"Machismo and physical aggressiveness": Ibid., 120.

"It was time for me": Ibid., 130.

"revolutionary anti-imperialism": Varon, 7.

"a fighting force": Ayers, 151.

"on fire": Ibid., 140.

"We meant to learn": Ibid., 146.

"A striking number of": Varon, 25.

"Weatherman grew directly": Rudd, "1968: Organizing vs. Activism."

"At the close of the sixties": Stern, 62,

"a body named Susan": Ibid., 154.

"The inexperience of": Ibid., 50.

"There seem to be": Hayden and King, 235.

"the way men looked": Clark, 79.

"the rewards are concentrated": Piercy, 424.

"house nigger" . . . "slow learner": Ibid., 429.

"fucking a staff": Ibid., 430.

"Only a woman willing": Ibid., 424.

"la Pasionaria": Quoted in Ayers, 168.

"She was not so": Stern, 47.

"individual": Ibid., 88.

"My lips were parted": Ibid., 96.

"an eight-foot tall nude": Ibid., 248.

"tall and blond, nude": Ibid., 249.

"I ran and I ran": Ayers, 172.

"I ran and ran": Stern, 142.

"Wait a minute": Ayers, 1.

"I am running for": Ibid., 3.

"swept us away completely": Ibid., 106–7.

"zinging" . . . "crystal chaos": Ibid., 170.

"thunderbolts": Ibid., 187.

"to hold on to": Ibid., 191.

"*There seems so little*": Ibid., 276.

"elusive moment": Ibid., 59.

"I cannot reproduce the": Ibid., 154.

"drug & alcohol ingestion": Stern, xxxvi.

"*helpful* figure" . . . "*machismo*": Naison, 152.

"growing hostility of Fordham's": Ibid., 175.

"tough new writing policy": Ibid., 176.

"a white island": Ibid., 205.

"who were risk-takers": Ibid., 223.

"battles" . . . "Black Studies programs": Patterson, 687.

"spoiled brats": Ibid., 688.

CHAPTER 9.

Nixon and Occupatio

"I was born in a house": Nixon, *RN*, 3.

"I graduated from Harvard": Quoted in Dallek, *Nixon and Kissinger*, 17.

"He really had no choice": Parmet, 6.

"It was not an easy time": Nixon, *RN*, 231.

"began to rise": Ibid., 1090.

"I am part of that": Fitzgerald, *The Great Gatsby: The Authorized Text*, 184.

"fighting against odds": Haldeman, *The Ends of Power*, 49.

"When I came back": Fitzgerald, *The Great Gatsby: The Authorized Text*, 6.

"the crisis of the self-made": From the subtitle of Wills's *Nixon Agonistes*.

"first home producers": Nicolaides, 4.

"Our life in Yorba Linda": Nixon, *RN*, 4.

"by the whistle of a train": Ibid., 3.

"My father had a deep belief": Ibid., 6.

"for those who were": Ibid., 5.

"On a warm night": Nicolaides, 1.

"riot area" . . . "wide and usually": Fogelson, 3.

"social experimentation": Quoted in Nicolaides, 295.

"a haven of the": Ibid., 181.

"to control the integrity": Ibid., 327.

"the secret frontiersmen": Didion, *The White Album*, 98.

"of domestic production": Nicolaides, 33.

"the center of gravity": Ibid., 2.

"against occupancy by non-Caucasians": Ibid., 19.

"self-reliance, independence": Ibid., 5.

"painfully conscious of slights": Wicker, 106.

"What starts the process": Quoted in Ambrose, *Nixon: The Education of a Politician*, 39.

"thrived on conflict": Kutler, xiv.

"vindictive": Quoted in Small, *The Presidency of Richard Nixon*, 13.

"all those . . . who have": Didion, *The White Album*, 95.

"the code phrase": Witcover, *The Resurrection of Richard Nixon*, 284.

"unprecedented lawlessness": Nixon, *RN*, 314–15.

"literally" . . . "learned that": Kissinger, 12.

"To deny that he": Ambrose, *Nixon: The Triumph of a Politician*, 19.

"I am . . . told that": Nixon, *RN*, 327.

"would argue against his": Safire, 83.

"if [John] Dean ever testified": Emery, 348.

"performance" . . . "decided that": Nixon, *RN*, 304.

"Bud Wilkinson acted": Ibid., 329.

"who then put them": Witcover, *The Year the Dream Died*, 431.

"standing up for what": Nixon, *RN*, 354.

"something unadmitted": Didion, *Slouching Towards Bethlehem*, 71.

"most political commentators missed": Small, *The Presidency of Richard Nixon*, 16.

"who shared their own": Morris, 844.

"there had been a gap": Mailer, *Miami and the Siege of Chicago*, 42.

"I see another child": Nixon, *RN*, 315.

"the grocer's son": Ibid., 341.

"I" . . . "the effort to": Ibid., 1004–5.

"you won't have Nixon": Ibid., 245.

"anarchists" . . . "a good crease": Quoted

in Witcover, *The Year the Dream Died,*
282–83.

"Very few people were": Quoted ibid., 475.

"the so-called civil rights": Quoted ibid., 77.

"I'm not going to be": Quoted in Blum, 310.

"vague unlocalized resentment": Wills, *Nixon
Agonistes,* 54.

"mockery": Ibid., 51.

"The desire for 'law and order'": Ibid., 51–52.

"that kids are screwing": Ibid., 52–53.

"Why *not* get away": Ibid., 53.

"cosmic spanking": Ibid., 50.

"bought": Blum, 311.

"I am not a candidate": Quoted in Witcover,
The Year the Dream Died, 120.

"the trick, for candidates": Carter, 347.

"get your guns": Quoted in Witcover, *The
Year the Dream Died,* 124.

"responded to demands for": Ibid., 125.

"strength": Ibid., 126.

"without sleep, walking streets": Wills, *Nixon
Agonistes,* 290.

"calling the city's war": Ibid., 286.

"Some of you here": Quoted ibid., 290.

"The Baltimore County": Cohen and
Witcover, 20–21.

"listing how much money": Ibid., 92.

"Say you gave at": Quoted ibid., 96.

"unhappy about something": Ambrose,
Nixon: The Triumph of a Politician, 178.

"those who": Ambrose, *Nixon: The Education
of a Politician,* 47.

"I kept on getting": Gaines, 137–38.

"exactly how the other side": Quoted in
Kutler, 617.

"double standard": Nixon, *RN,* 854.

"willful deviant from": Ibid., 872.

"My acceptance of contributions": Agnew,
16–17.

"left-wingers" . . . "to make": Ibid., 106–7.

"an indirect threat": Ibid., 186.

"the President has a lot": Ibid., 189.

"threats": Ibid., 192.

"I had to twist": Ibid., 193.

"stupid": Ibid., 125.

"striking unwillingness": Cohen and
Witcover, 23.

"enmity": Agnew, 65.

"confusion" . . . "sadness": Nixon, *RN,*
833–40.

"unwillingness to build": Wills, *Nixon
Agonistes,* 13.

"As soon as Dean's": Nixon, *RN,* 893.

"Nixon never had truly": Kimball, 7.

"spoiled brats who never": Quoted in
Witcover, *The Year the Dream Died,* 391.

"If you've seen one": Quoted ibid., 394.

"the fat Jap . . . He naively": Nixon, *RN,* 320.

"the bottom of a": Quoted in Witcover, *The
Year the Dream Died,* 457.

"positive polarization": Quoted in Parmet,
123.

"the most controlled": Witcover, *The Year the
Dream Died,* 351.

"to make that mistake": Witcover, *The
Resurrection of Richard Nixon,* 302.

"The candidate should take": Quoted in
Witcover, *The Year the Dream Died,* 230.

"the silent center": Quoted in Small, *The
Presidency of Richard Nixon,* 27.

"the silent Americans": Wills, *Nixon
Agonistes,* 311.

"the silent center, the millions": Quoted
in Ambrose, *Nixon: The Triumph of a
Politician,* 155.

"fairly frank language": Ibid., 11.

"plan for peace": Nixon, *RN,* 409.

"the biggest response ever": Ibid., 410.

"a man who had risen": Mailer, *Miami and
the Siege of Chicago,* 44.

"lovely looking": Ibid., 29.

"the remote possibility": Ibid., 30.

"What would have happened": Kissinger,
1476.

"suffocating . . . That world has": Ibid., 167.

"vertical yearning": Rodriguez, 81.

"I wore a black suit": Ibid., 82.

"fawning ambition": Ibid., 83.

"lukewarm cocktail": Ibid., 87.

"for all our professed": Ibid., 85.

"Gold-dusted and ghostwritten": Ibid., 88.

"Harvard College will always beat": Ibid.

"humbled enough by national": Ibid., 89.

"His pettiness showed": Ibid., 90.

"I thought I was the only one": Ibid., 93.

"the poor boy (he never": Haldeman, *The
Ends of Power,* 25.

"brown": Rodriguez, 94.

"In college, because of Lyndon": Ibid.

"after all that Richard": Ibid., 95.

"The deserving rise": Wills, *Nixon Agonistes*, 166.

"the saddest part of the story": Rodriguez, 95.

"Having betrayed his own": Ibid., 96.

"Republicanize": Ibid., 99.

"the Resting Place is": Ibid., 100.

"for the greater part": Ibid., 147.

"All serious daring . . . starts": Welty, *One Writer's Beginnings*, in *Stories, Essays, & Memoir*, 948.

"One can imagine a version": Rodriguez, 101.

"You do like California": Quoted in Price, 344.

"I liked and admired him": Ibid., 2.

"farewell": Ibid., 1.

"human side": Ibid., 14.

"intellectual range, the quickness": Ibid., 15.

"air of mystery": Ibid., 18.

"layer cake": Safire, 97.

"vertically, not horizontally": Price, 19.

"complexities": Ibid., 2.

"light side" . . . "dark side": Ibid., 29.

"instead of being embarrassed": Ibid., 34.

"the media": Ibid., 118.

"as almost aggressively square": Ibid., 119.

"At the heart of": Ibid., 73.

"eruption of resentment": Ibid., 129.

"mobs in the streets": Ibid., 117.

"orgies of mindless violence": Ibid., 128.

"violent protest was romanticized": Ibid., 72.

"Great universities" . . . "to their": Ibid., 71.

"mess": Ibid., 67.

"basic collaborator": Ibid., 42.

"a crisis of the spirit": Ibid., 378.

"strong spiritual emphasis": Ibid., 45.

"dark": Ibid., 382.

"under no circumstances": Quoted ibid., 158–59.

"To lower our voices": Ibid., 378–79.

"theme . . . most widely bannered": Ibid., 48.

"non-conservative initiatives": Quoted in Parmet, 105.

"successfully avoided the appearance": Ibid., 105.

"the fashionable liberal's": Price, 125.

"those with a monopoly": Ibid., 370.

"The arts, you know": Quoted in Kutler, 219.

"I no longer feel able": Price, 92.

"I care less about": Ibid., 88.

"There was no way": Ibid., 95.

"We need a resignation": Quoted ibid., 324.

"Profumo factor": Ibid., 327.

"worse than Haig had": Ibid., 329.

"disastrous mistake": Ibid., 330.

"the noblest possible interpretation": Wills, *Nixon Agonistes*, 143.

"what was best for the Nation": Quoted in Price, 382.

"The interests of the Nation": Quoted ibid., 384.

"speech proclaiming a guilt": Ibid., 339.

"Last week, in my review": Ibid., 330.

"voice of my conscience": Ibid., 101.

CHAPTER 10.
Chicago

"It was nearly dark": Hayden, 318.

"giant antiwar march": Ibid., 258.

"shoot to kill": *Rights in Conflict*, 3.

"Mayor Daley was pissed": Quoted in Kusch, 138.

"iron curtain": Hayden, 296.

"bitter evidence" . . . "America was": Ibid., 297.

"jurisdiction": Farber, *Chicago '68*, 249.

"to create a visual": Ibid., 250.

"the triumphant end-product": Styron, 11.

"My God, . . . there's nobody": Quoted in Kusch, 63.

"to make the arrest": *Rights in Conflict*, 110.

"We wanted to have legal": Quoted ibid., 63.

"the general media published": Ibid., 85.

"'hyper-potent' hippie males": Ibid., 86.

"turning delegates back into": Quoted ibid., 89.

"crud to throw": Quoted ibid., 88.

"cars and buildings will burn": Quoted ibid., 91.

"I realize at this time": Quoted in Farber, *Chicago '68*, 165.

"alternation of lawn": Mailer, *Miami and the Siege of Chicago*, 167.

"In Chicago, . . . there was": Ibid., 144.

"the fight was over space": Schultz, 78.

"quasi-demonstrator" . . . "experienced": Lane, 5.

"I was very afraid": Stein, 109.

"another fear" . . . "conservative": Mailer, *Miami and the Siege of Chicago,* 186.

"He had lived well": Ibid., 187.

"He liked his life": Ibid., 188.

"a description of the event": Ibid., 131.

"the Chicago cop, in": Schultz, 94.

"They simply stood there": Ibid., 2.

"Discovering that lines of escape": *Rights in Conflict,* 182.

"No one should know": Schultz, 180.

"a flagrant gift": Ibid., 14.

"clubbing, clubbing, clubbing": 173.

"made a mistake": Ibid., 80.

"here because I have found": Ibid., 9.

"winnowed out all": Ibid., 298.

"That no one was killed": Stavis, 193.

"is to shirk what happened": Schultz, 16.

"I think that this was planned": Quoted in Kusch, 136.

"There was no breakdown": Schultz, 193.

"the police isn't there": Quoted in Witcover, *The Year the Dream Died,* 353.

"This was white family war": Schultz, 19.

"sordid, parental self-protection": Hardwick, 6.

"That was the true menace": Wills, *Nixon Agonistes,* 334.

"events at the flagpole": Schultz, 175–76.

"an improbable shadow ambassador": James Miller, 287.

"uniting the mildest liberal critics": Ibid., 295.

"forced into a moral squeeze": Ibid., 299.

"they did not comprehend": Schultz, 96.

"I had learned at last": Ibid., 152.

"Have you met yours yet?": Hayden, 301.

"beefy, casually dressed man": Ibid., 300.

"to follow us": Ibid., 301.

"city police insist they'll bust": Quoted in *Rights in Conflict,* 136.

"When they approached": Ibid., 150.

"Hell no, we won't go": Ibid., 154.

"The thing about this crowd": Quoted in Kusch, 65.

"an incredible cacophony": *Rights in Conflict,* 156.

"balmy night air": Hayden, 302.

"I'm going to be arrested": Ibid., 304.

"There's a squad car": Quoted in *Rights in Conflict,* 175.

"Kill, kill, kill": Ibid., 176.

"invited" . . . "We don't want": Hayden, 306.

"I could not be me": Ibid., 307.

"Wednesday was the big day": James Miller, 302.

"forty years": Mailer, *Miami and the Siege of Chicago,* 223.

"many of the delegates": Hayden, 315.

"split open": Ibid., 316.

"avenge": Ibid., 317.

"Tom had walked": Dellinger, 331.

"The pictures and sound": Quoted in *Rights in Conflict,* 330.

"what 'the whole world' ": Ibid., 16.

"We had a feeling": Quoted ibid., 237.

"a little tear gas": Ibid., 239.

"Two blocks north": Ibid., 241.

"Just as we crossed": Stein, 117.

"Police officer needs help": *Rights in Conflict,* 250.

"forced the officers to": Quoted ibid., 252.

"To many other witnesses": Ibid., 253.

"Michigan Avenue looked": Stein, 119.

"reverse gears": *Rights in Conflict,* 253.

"There was no place": Quoted ibid., 254.

"calmly walked": Ibid., 259.

"The police were angry": Quoted ibid., 256.

"Then, as people started": Hayden, 319.

"a little old woman": Sayre, 11.

"against the building": Ibid., 24.

"The police continue to charge": Lane, 76–77.

"Half-blinded by the gas": Styron, 13.

"Now, the *inside*": Hayden, 320.

"in safety from the": Mailer, *Miami and the Siege of Chicago,* 172.

"The police attacked with": Ibid., 169.

"beautiful": Ibid., 172.

"Things are in the saddle": Emerson, "Ode, Inscribed to W. H. Channing," in Hollander, *American Poetry: The Nineteenth Century,* 1:284.

"It was as if the war": Mailer, *Miami and the Siege of Chicago,* 172.

"with George McGovern, we": Quoted in Kusch, 108.

"overwhelmingly supported the police": Ibid., 155.

"the true feelings of the people": Mailer, *Miami and the Siege of Chicago,* 150.

"inability to see the other": Farber, *Chicago '68,* 245.

"Almost every society seems": Powers, 200.

"the hardest part of writing": Farber, *Chicago '68,* ix.

"those who speak and those": Farber, *The Sixties,* 292.

"too mouthy": Ibid., 297.

"It was a piece": Quoted in Kusch, 121.

"And some of the guys": Quoted ibid., 124.

"Did the radicalism of Chicago": Hayden, 324.

"the principal force which broke": Phillips, 37.

"cleave along distinct ethnic": Ibid., 287–88.

"Nixon read the book": Isserman and Kazin, 272.

"for the majority of blacks": *Report of the Chicago Riot Study Committee,* 72.

"You don't know what": Quoted in Garrow, 455.

"hostile whites": Ibid., 500.

"white backlash": Ibid., 536.

"Nothing happened to them": Quoted in Kusch, 141.

"Chicago through his own soul": Bellow, *The Dean's December,* 263.

"So the sealed rooms": Bellow, *Collected Stories,* 177.

"cities were moods": Bellow, *The Dean's December,* 282.

"penitentiary": Ibid., 61.

"pleasure society": Ibid., 273.

"to find out what Chicago": Ibid., 282.

"broad-daylight rapes": Ibid., 160.

"the most controversial part": Ibid., 191.

"The victim was a": Ibid., 191–92.

"I'm trying to guess": Ibid., 193.

"the facts" . . . "what might": Ibid., 192.

"new version, wider in perspective": Ibid., 195.

"filled with a staggering passion": Ibid., 201.

"every man's *inner* inner city": Ibid., 204.

"whirling": Ibid., 158.

"The Mitchell case was": Ibid., 191.

"fewer than half": Walker, Spohn, and DeLone, 36.

"that most rapes": Mann, 49.

"reporting practices for certain": Ibid., 32.

"total crimes *known to police*": LaFree, 172.

"although few crimes are": Jacobs and Tope, 1460.

"are almost always intraracial": Ibid., 1465.

"Dr. William Wilbanks, a criminologist": Taylor, 93.

"differentially high offending rates": Walker, Spohn, and DeLone, 42.

"I became a rapist": Cleaver, 26.

"take stock": Ibid., 17.

"through reading": Ibid., 19.

"I, a black man, confronted": Ibid., 20.

"Get yourself a colored girl": Ibid., 21.

"a black man growing up": Ibid., 23.

"critique": Ibid., 24.

"ruthless attitude toward white": Ibid., 25.

"wrong" . . . "That is why": Ibid., 27.

"Through the bloody September": Faulkner, *Collected Stories,* 169.

"see at first hand": Bellow, *The Dean's December,* 159.

"the first requirement was": Ibid., 122.

"distortions of the atmosphere": Ibid., 308.

"theorizing": Ibid., 99.

"Corde felt": Ibid., 105.

"And he felt": Mailer, *Miami and the Siege of Chicago,* 203.

"These times we live in": Bellow, *The Dean's December,* 89.

"retrieve reality" . . . "the trash": Ibid., 122.

"Nothing true—really true": Ibid., 54.

"the right clearance": Ibid., 298.

"a bad profession": Ibid., 26.

"pity" . . . "love": Ibid., 165.

"stuff": Ibid., 166.

"tensions": Ibid., 308.

CHAPTER 11.
Kissinger and the Dragon Lady

"made history": Nixon, *RN,* 553.

"memory is fallible": Ibid., ix.

"you could omit anything": Hemingway, *A Moveable Feast,* 75.

"Each man . . . overwhelming detail": Ambrose, *Nixon: The Triumph of a Politician,* 232.

"convinced that consistent lying": Safire, 168.

"strong word": Dallek, *Flawed Giant,* 597.

"feeling of surprise": Kissinger, 3.

"The Phone Call": Ibid., 7.

"meet with his chief": Ibid., 8.

"screwed it up again": Quoted ibid., 14.

"I did not know": Ibid., 9.

"the grocer's son from Whittier": Nixon, *RN*, 341.

"not very orthodox Jew": Woodward and Bernstein, 423.

"Henry, please don't ever tell": Quoted ibid., 424.

"contribution to the American": Kissinger, 10.

"smile did not always": Ibid., 37.

"willing collaborator": Dallek, *Nixon and Kissinger*, 69.

"an open secret that": Hitchins, 6.

"Haldeman brought me": Nixon, *RN*, 323.

"a few weeks after": Hersh, *The Price of Power*, 12.

"I am through with": Quoted in Kimball, 58.

"something big was afoot": Nixon, *RN*, 323.

"important information": Hersh, *The Price of Power*, 20.

"a public telephone": Langguth, 523.

"Henry's information was basic": Quoted in Hersh, *The Price of Power*, 20.

"Kissinger's offer to report": Ibid., 14.

"I would never budget": Chennault, *The Education of Anna*, 40.

"Loving him, being loved": Chennault, *A Thousand Springs*, vii.

"from then on we communicated": Chennault, *The Education of Anna*, 164.

"conspicuously spattered with drops": Ibid., 170.

"At the height of": Ibid., 174.

"Anna is my good friend": Quoted ibid., 175.

"a message from Nixon": Ibid., 185.

"complaints about the steady": Ibid., 186.

"was said to have agreed": Ibid., 188.

"How could that be?": Ibid., 189.

"As usual, he wanted": Ibid., 190.

"Do you think they": Ibid., 191.

"We need to do something": Ibid., 193.

"You must promise to": Ibid., 193–94.

"I've certainly paid dearly": Ibid., 198.

"as gospel truth": Quoted in Forslund, 75.

"the great mystery of the 1968": Safire, 88.

"the scheme"..."the information": Parmet, 85.

"With Kissinger exposing": Forslund, 60.

"She may have avoided": Bundy, 41.

"the chain of events": Clifford, 584.

"On November two instant": Quoted in Summers, 303.

"talking to Florida": Quoted ibid., 304.

"when things quieted down": Ibid., 303.

"the Lady" . . . "the gentleman": Quoted ibid., 304.

"It is known now": Agnew, 106.

"New material indicates": Forslund, 70.

"late in the 1990s": Ibid., 71.

"almost every day": Quoted in Hung and Schecter, 23.

"Who is listening": Quoted ibid., 24.

"blessing": Diem, *In the Jaws of History*, 58.

"affable Bui Diem": Clifford, 581.

"was adept at playing": Ibid., 508.

"The Democrats, he said": Chennault, *The Education of Anna*, 175.

"the Anna Chennault affair": Diem, 298.

"statements led Johnson administration": Forslund, 64–65.

"stand firm": Ibid., 64.

"It was one night": Diem, 236.

"would have to be": Quoted in Summers, 299.

"in the rush of flying": Diem, 237.

"as the Democrats steered": Ibid., 238.

"the sole legitimate": Ibid., 239.

"direct talks": Ibid., 240.

"In a frigid tone": Ibid., 241.

"dropped his political bomb": Ibid., 242.

"dumbfounded" . . . "performance": Ibid., 241.

"the South Vietnamese had": Ibid., 243.

"two relevant messages": Ibid., 244.

"came as no real surprise": Nixon, *RN*, 323.

"the only way to prevent": Ibid., 327.

"I'm concerned that you're": Quoted in Witcover, *The Year the Dream Died*, 405.

"close aides have been": Quoted ibid., 422.

"time is running out": Quoted in Hung and Schecter, 21.

"Thieu and Humphrey had become": Ibid., 22.

"a Humphrey victory would": Quoted ibid., 21.

"Thieu was for the plan": Quoted in Bundy, 30.

"If we sit down": Quoted in Gardner, 498.

"I know the question": Quoted ibid., 502.

"I do not see": Quoted ibid., 503.

"the proper thing to do": Quoted ibid., 504.

"That's the old Nixon": Quoted ibid., 505.

"If I were Thieu": Quoted ibid., 507.

"If President Thieu keeps": Quoted ibid., 508.

"All Vietnamese know": Quoted ibid., 509.

"are free to participate": Quoted in Hung and Schecter, 26.

"The government of South Vietnam": Quoted ibid., 28.

"I could see Bunker trying hard": Quoted ibid.

"This is treason!": Quoted in Witcover, *The Year the Dream Died*, 410.

"the smoking gun": Quoted ibid., 409.

"certain in his own mind": Califano, 328.

"We first became aware": Clifford, 583.

"plot": Ibid., 581.

"an extraordinary dilemma": Ibid., 583.

"terrible to do that": Quoted in Califano, 328.

"there were other messages": Clifford, 582.

"furious" . . . "fed up": Ibid., 587.

"Saigon's whole approach": Ibid., 591.

"Nixon will double-cross them": Quoted ibid., 589.

"Some old China hands": Quoted ibid., 593.

"been urged to delay": Johnson, *The Vantage Point*, 517–18.

"calm him down": Nixon, *RN*, 329.

"in growing fury": Clifford, 594.

"Johnson quizzed Nixon": Forslund, 72.

"absolutely no truth": Quoted in Dallek, *Flawed Giant*, 590.

"This barefaced lie": Bundy, 43.

"peace involving American withdrawal": Kissinger, 1467.

"I have therefore irrevocably": Quoted ibid., 1469.

"Saigon as the legal government": Ibid., 1470.

"no details": Quoted in Shawcross, 22.

"every scrap of paper": Ibid., 31.

"kept in ignorance": Ibid., 29.

"air and logisitical support": Nixon, "Address by the President," 282.

"for five years, neither": Ibid., 281.

"He added a sentence": Kissinger, 505.

"a last-minute acknowledgement": Shawcross, 413.

"no public interest": Ibid., 34.

"destroy whoever did this": Ibid., 35.

"offspring of Kissinger's attempt": Haldeman, *The Ends of Power*, 118.

"long-term project": Ibid., 219.

"supported": Kissinger, 730.

"son of a bitch": White House Tape 525-001, Miller Center of Public Affairs website.

"I saw absolutely no reason": Nixon, *RN*, 512.

"the true story behind": Haldeman, *The Ends of Power*, xi.

"a man named Leslie Gelb": Ibid., 219.

"was, somehow, unavailable": Ibid., 220.

"tap on the Dragon Lady": Haldeman, *The Haldeman Diaries*, 567.

"We have to hit": Quoted ibid., 473.

"the fact that Johnson": Ibid., 504.

"that if we can prove": Quoted ibid., 563.

"going at LBJ": Ibid., 567.

"LBJ got very hot": Ibid.

"without the Vietnam War": Haldeman, *The Ends of Power*, 79.

"You can be sure": Quoted in Isaacs, 138.

"Throughout the remainder": Herring, 254.

"The only way we will keep": Quoted in Safire, 673.

CHAPTER 12.
Swift Boat

"Colson: This fellow Kerry": White House Tape 042-068, Miller Center of Public Affairs website.

"willing to blink at": Colson, 57.

"this fellow . . . they put in": White House Tape 487-001, Miller Center of Public Affairs website.

"Plan to Combat Vietnam Veterans": Quoted in Brinkley, 357.

"there was a lot": Quoted ibid., 351.

"He forced us to": Quoted in Klein, 72.

"became the centerpiece": Kranish, Mooney, and Easton, 133.

"My involvement had nothing": Quoted in Roth, A1.

"a Navy officer, just got out": White House Tape 508, Miller Center of Public Affairs website.

"reassure people that the few": White House Tape 535-5, Miller Center of Public Affairs website.

"the type of person": Quoted in Kranish, Mooney, and Easton, 134.

"civility": *The Faerie Queene,* book VI, canto XXIII.

"vile tongue and venomous": Ibid., book VI, canto VIII.

"three mightie ones": Ibid., book VI, canto XIII.

"now he raungeth through": Ibid., book VI, canto XL.

"I don't ever remember": Quoted in Kranish, Mooney, and Easton, 132.

"the myth of the": Lembcke, ix.

"The outstanding fact": Ibid., 81.

"Were you spat upon?": Ibid., 80.

"Nixon-Agnew counteroffensive": Ibid., 49.

"there is no news-source": Quoted ibid., 3.

"documentable cases": Ibid., 6.

"Spit at those people": Quoted ibid., 77–78.

"found only one material": Ibid., 141.

"only two obstacles": Cutler, 140.

"you have to make up": Zumwalt, 38.

"engaging the enemy": Kranish, Mooney, and Easton, 78.

"had very little to do": Kerry in Weiss et al., 113.

"one of the safest": Kranish, Mooney, and Easton, 77–78.

"Not meant to be": Brinkley, xiii.

"nothing less than the definitive": Kranish, Mooney, and Easton, ix.

"telephoned his old friend": O'Neill and Corsi, 2.

"is based largely on journals": Brinkley, xiii.

"are, in fact, paraphrased": Ibid., 520.

"a genuine war hero": Ibid., 2.

"turned downright toxic": Kranish, Mooney, and Easton, ix.

"significantly": Ibid., xv.

"absolutely fair" . . . "would later": Ibid., x.

"Hoffmann recently expressed": O'Neill and Corsi, 58.

"I had heard that": Ibid., 12.

"a self-inflicted": Ibid., 38.

"each of the officers": Ibid., 83.

"letter on his father's": Ibid., 204.

"when Kerry came back": "John Kerry Military Service Controversy," Wikipedia.

"It was a terrible mistake": Quoted in Kranish, "Veteran Retracts Criticism of Kerry."

"we got into a firefight": Quoted in Kranish, Mooney, and Easton, 71–72.

"I never saw where": Quoted ibid., 72.

"He had a little scratch": Quoted ibid., 73.

"Obviously, he got it": Quoted ibid., 74.

"3 DEC 1968": Quoted ibid., 75.

"it verified that Kerry": Ibid., 76.

"targets of opportunity": Ibid., 95.

"was just behind": Ibid., 100.

"Beach the boat!": Quoted ibid., 101.

"Chased VC inland": Quoted ibid., 102.

"That was a him-or-us": Quoted ibid., 102–3.

"an 'impact' award": Brinkley, 293.

"literally blown to pieces": Kranish, Mooney, and Easton, 105.

"each of the five times": Ibid., 106.

"His arm bleeding and in pain": Quoted in Brinkley, 317.

"will not be ordered": Quoted in Kranish, Mooney, and Easton, 107.

"simply bugged out": Quoted ibid., 108.

"to get three Purple Hearts": Quoted ibid., 107.

"upset about it and angry": Quoted ibid., 112.

"if victory escapes us": Quoted in Brinkley, 61.

"How can one oppose": Quoted ibid., 79.

"there was no love": Quoted ibid., 142.

"The Law of Increasing": Quoted ibid., 175.

"Nobody has been able": Quoted ibid., 182.

"gap between the illusions": Quoted ibid., 226.

"Everything was right": Quoted ibid., 180.

"Given his extreme opposition": O'Neill and Corsi, 25.

"infuriated": Nicosia, 74.

"especially" . . . "veterans willing to": Scott, 18.

"By early 1967 a network": Franklin, 60.

"small war crimes hearings": Nicosia, 62.

"electrical torture using": Quoted in Meyrowitz and Campbell, 131.

"Perhaps the most startling": Nicosia, 88.

"up her vagina": Quoted in Meyrowitz and Campbell, 134.

"Kerry's accusations of war": O'Neill and Corsi, 52.

"All veterans participating in": Nicosia, 87.

"It was hard to understand": Quoted ibid., 91.

"I arrived in Detroit": Quoted in Brinkley, 349.

"graphic and ugly": Quoted ibid., 354.

"really concerned": Kranish, Mooney, and Easton, 112.

"I thought it would": Quoted ibid., 133.

"with the utmost consideration": Quoted ibid., 135.

"what everybody was saying": Brinkley, 387.

"Why don't we go": Quoted in Stacewitz, 240.

"growing in all their minds": Nicosia, 98.

"the railroad had no": Prados, 3.

"prohibiting a camp on": Ibid., 8.

"improperly used": Ibid., 9.

"what was in my heart": Quoted in Nicosia, 124.

"point of origin": Brinkley, 1.

"They told stories that": Kerry, "Vietnam Veterans Against the War Statement," 367.

"speak in very general": Ibid., 366.

"I would go up": Quoted in Kranish, Mooney, and Easton, 125.

"When I began it": Quoted in Brinkley, 4.

"And so when 30 years": Kerry, "Vietnam Veterans Against the War Statement," 372.

"In time of the crisis": Rukeyser, xiv.

"*an atrocity-producing situation*": Lifton, 41.

"about four hundred veterans": Ibid., 18.

"not one of them": Ibid., 36.

"In Vietnam, . . . one undergoes": Ibid., 41.

"false witness": Ibid., 65.

"The atrocity issue": Scott, xviii.

"the staff told me": Quoted ibid., 5.

"nostalgia": Ibid., 29.

"gross stress reaction": Ibid., 32.

"suggested that psychiatrists might": Ibid., 33.

"outside the range of": Quoted ibid., 27.

"'normal' for the horrors": Ibid., 28.

"did not want": Hemingway, *In Our Time,* 69.

"heroism stories": Boyle, 29.

"In this way he lost": Hemingway, *In Our Time,* 70.

"He liked" . . . "He did not like": Ibid., 71.

"'This is an apparition'": Quoted in Scott, 12.

"There were things that": Quoted ibid., 19.

"unconsummated grief": Quoted ibid., 43.

"basic problem: the designation": Hagopian, 58.

"narrowly conceived psychiatric approach": Ibid., 77.

"the cost of accepting": Ibid., 402–3.

"Any Questions": Freedman, 169.

"John Kerry has not": Ibid., 177.

"extensive coverage": Quoted in Kenski and Kenski, 331.

"denounce": Freedman, 170.

"Because it used Kerry's": Ibid., 171.

"While largely acquiescing in": Mark Crispin Miller, 272.

"fastidiously overlooked": Ibid., 273.

"highly suspect": Williams, 249.

"what actually happened": Russ Baker, 452.

"the basis of his candidacy": Kranish, Mooney, and Easton, 360.

"a mistake": Kerry, "Vietnam Veterans Against the War Statement," 368.

"agonizing reappraisal": Lowell, "Memories of West Street and Lepke," *Collected Poems,* 188.

"What I seek is": Harris, *Our War,* 5.

"existential": Harris, *Dreams Die Hard,* 4.

"we had the experience": Eliot, "The Dry Salvages," in *The Complete Poems and Plays,* 133.

"we were too young": Harris, *Our War,* 50.

"comfortable making definitive statements": Harris, *Dreams Die Hard,* 5.

"'definitive 'break'": Ibid., 89.

"spent the last three years": Ibid., 269.

"people with self-respect": Didion, *Slouching Towards Bethlehem,* 145.

"We have two lives": Malamud, 158.

"Vietnam is a lesson": Quoted in Kranish, Mooney, and Easton, xxii.

"revolutionary revisions": Moser, 144.

"to turn": Kerry, *The New Soldier,* 158.

"The New Soldier is trying": Ibid., 160.

"The diffidence that faltered": Pound, 100.

"*rouse our broken forces*": Lowell, *Collected Poems,* 575.

"We must disenthrall ourselves": Lincoln, *Speeches and Writings, 1859–1865,* 415.

"people in history": Greene, 187.

"innocence": Ibid., 37.
"as *engagé* as Pyle": Ibid., 183.
"one has to take sides": Ibid., 174.
"Must I too have": Ibid., 185–86.

AFTERWORD
In Vietnam

"It was late '67 now": Herr, *Dispatches*, 3.
"As you may know": McCain, "John
   McCain, Prisoner of War."
"will to win": Quoted in Ambrose, *Nixon:
   The Triumph of a Politician*, 49.
"was not a test": Hoopes, 128.
"our attention was on": Schell, *The Real War*,
   23.

"You can kill ten": Quoted in Karnow, 17.
"the best enemy we": Quoted ibid., 18.
"the simple truth": Harris, *Our War*, 172.
"I didn't receive a": Quoted in Karnow,
   459–60.
"discerned a certain nostalgia": Ibid., 458.
"Nostalgia is a product": DeLillo, *White
   Noise*, 258.
"Perhaps my nostalgia magnified": Truong,
   243.
"Vietnam was what we": Herr, *Dispatches*,
   244.
"peace to our children": Lowell, "Waking
   Early Sunday Morning," *Collected Poems*,
   386.

Works Cited

Acheson, Dean. *Present at the Creation: My Years in the State Department*. New York: Norton, 1969.

Adams, Henry. *Henry Adams: Novels, Mont Saint Michel, The Education*. New York: Library of America, 1983.

Agnew, Spiro T. *Go Quietly . . . or Else*. New York: William Morrow, 1980.

Ali, Tariq, and Susan Watkins. *1968: Marching in the Streets*. London: The Free Press, 1998.

Ambrose, Stephen E. *Nixon: The Education of a Politician, 1913–1962*. New York: Simon & Schuster, 1987.

———. *Nixon: The Triumph of Politician, 1962–1972*. New York: Simon & Schuster, 1989.

Anderson, Terry H. *The Movement and the Sixties*. New York: Oxford, 1995.

Apocalypse Now (film). Dir. Francis Ford Coppola. United Artists. 1979.

Appy, Christian G. *Patriots: The Vietnam War Remembered from All Sides*. New York: Viking, 2003.

Auchincloss, Louis. *The Rector of Justin*. Boston: Houghton Mifflin, 1964.

Ayers, Bill. *Fugitive Days: A Memoir*. Boston: Beacon Press, 2001.

Baker, Houston A. "Scene . . . Not Heard." In *Reading Rodney King / Reading Urban Uprising*, edited by Robert Gooding-Williams, 38–48. New York: Routledge, 1993.

Michael Baker et al., eds. *Police on Campus: The Mass Police Action at Columbia University, Spring, 1968*. New York: Temco Press, 1969.

Baker, Russ. *Family of Secrets: The Bush Dynasty, the Powerful Forces That Put It in the White House, and What Their Influence Means for America*. New York: Bloomsbury Press, 2009.

Ball, George. *The Past Has Another Pattern: Memoirs*. New York: Norton, 1982.

Baritz, Loren. *Backfire: A History of How American Culture Led Us into Vietnam and Made Us Fight the Way We Did*. New York: Ballantine, 1985.

Beidler, Philip D. *Scriptures for a Generation: What We Were Reading in the 60's*. Athens: University of Georgia Press, 1994.

Belknap, Michal. *The Vietnam War on Trial: The Mai Lai Massacre and Court-Martial of Lieutenant Calley.* Lawrence: University Press of Kansas, 1999.

Bellow, Saul. *Collected Stories.* New York: Viking, 2001.

———. *The Dean's December.* New York: Harper & Row, 1982.

Berman, Paul. *A Tale of Two Utopias: The Political Journey of the Generation of 1968.* New York: Norton, 1997.

Blake, William. *The Poetry and Prose of William Blake.* Ed. David Erdman. Berkeley: University of California Press, 2008.

Blum, John Morton. *Years of Discord: American Politics and Society, 1961–1974.* New York: Norton, 1991.

Boomhower, Ray E. *Robert Kennedy and the 1968 Indiana Primary.* Bloomington: Indiana University Press, 2008.

Borges, Jorge Luis. *Labyrinths.* New York: New Directions, 1964.

Boyle, Richard. *Flower of the Dragon: The Breakdown of the U.S. Army in Vietnam.* San Francisco: Ramparts Press, 1972.

Branch, Taylor. *At Canaan's Edge: America in the King Years, 1965–68.* New York: Simon & Schuster, 2006.

———. *Parting the Waters: America in the King Years, 1954–63.* New York: Simon & Schuster, 1988.

———. *Pillar of Fire: America in the King Years, 1963–65.* New York: Simon & Schuster, 1998.

Brigham, Robert. *ARVN: Life and Death in the South Vietnamese Army.* Lawrence: University Press of Kansas, 2006.

Brinkley, Douglas. *Tour of Duty: John Kerry and the Vietnam War.* New York: William Morrow, 2004.

Bundy, William. *A Tangled Web: The Making of Foreign Policy in the Nixon Presidency.* New York: Hill & Wang, 1998.

Busby, Horace. *The Thirty-First of March: An Intimate Portrait of Lyndon Johnson's Final Days in Office.* New York: Farrar, Straus & Giroux, 2005.

Califano, Joseph A., Jr. *The Triumph and Tragedy of Lyndon Johnson: The White House Years.* New York: Simon & Schuster, 1991.

Cao, Lan. *Monkey Bridge.* New York: Penguin, 1997.

Caro, Robert A. *The Years of Lyndon Johnson: Master of the Senate.* New York: Knopf, 2003.

———. *The Years of Lyndon Johnson: Means of Ascent.* New York: Knopf, 1990.

———. *The Years of Lyndon Johnson: The Path to Power.* New York: Knopf, 1982.

Carroll, James. *An American Requiem: God, My Father, and the War That Came between Us.* Boston: Houghton Mifflin, 1996.

Carter, Dan T. *The Politics of Rage: George Wallace, the Origins of New Conservatism, and the Transformation of American Politics.* Baton Rouge: Louisiana State University Press, 1995 and 2000.

Cavallo, Dominick. *A Fiction of the Past: The Sixties in American History.* New York: St. Martin's Press, 1999.

Chennault, Anna. *The Education of Anna.* New York: Times Books, 1980.

———. *A Thousand Springs: The Biography of a Marriage.* New York: Paul S. Eriksson, 1962.

Chester, Lewis, Godfrey Hodgson, and Bruce Page. *An American Melodrama: The American Presidential Campaign of 1968.* New York: Viking, 1969.

Chomsky, Noam. *For Reasons of State.* New York: Pantheon, 2003.

Christiansen, Samantha, and Zachary Scarlett, eds. *The Third World in the Global 1960s.* New York: Berghahn, 2012.

Clark, Septima. *Ready from Within.* Trenton, N.J.: Africa World Press, 1986.

Cleaver, Eldridge. *Soul on Ice.* New York. McGraw Hill, 1968.

Clifford, Clark. *Counsel to the President.* New York: Random House, 1991.

Clodfelter, Mark. *The Limits of Air Power: The American Bombing of North Vietnam.* New York: Free Press, 1989.

Coffin, William Sloane. *Once to Every Man: A Memoir.* New York: Atheneum, 1977.

Cohen, Nathan. *The Los Angeles Riots: A Socio-Psychological Study.* New York: Praeger, 1970.

Cohen, Richard M., and Jules Witcover. *A Heartbeat Away: The Investigation and Resignation of Vice President Spiro T. Agnew.* New York: Viking, 1974.

Cohen, Steven, ed. *Vietnam: Anthology and Guide to "A Television History."* New York: Knopf, 1983.

Coleridge, Samuel Taylor. *Literary Remains of Samuel Taylor Coleridge.* 4 vols. (1836–1839). New York: AMS Press, 1967.

Colson, Charles W. *Born Again.* Grand Rapids: Chosen Books, 1976.

Conot, Robert. *Rivers of Blood, Years of Darkness.* New York: William Morrow, 1968.

Conrad, Joseph. *Heart of Darkness* (1899). New York: Norton, 2006.

Cox, Archibald, et al. *Crisis at Columbia* [The Cox Report] (1968). Excerpted in Smith and Bender, *American Higher Education Transformed,* 369–73.

Crane, Hart. *Crane: Complete Poems and Selected Letters.* New York: Library of America, 2006.

Cronkite, Walter. "Who, What, Where, When, Why: Report from Vietnam." Transcription of CBS news broadcast, February 27, 1968. In Cohen, *Vietnam: Anthology and Guide,* 214–15.

Cutler, Thomas J. *Brown Water, Black Berets: Coastal and Riverine Warfare in Vietnam.* Annapolis: Naval Institute Press, 1988.

Dallek, Robert. *Flawed Giant: Lyndon Johnson and His Times, 1961–1973.* New York: Oxford, 1998.

———. *Nixon and Kissinger: Partners in Power.* New York: HarperCollins, 2007.

DeBenedetti, Charles, and Charles Chatfield. *An American Ordeal: The Antiwar Movement of the Vietnam Era.* Syracuse: Syracuse University Press, 1990.

DeGroot, Gerard J. *The Sixties Unplugged: A Kaleidoscopic History of a Disorderly Decade.* Cambridge: Harvard University Press, 2008.

DeLillo, Don. *Libra.* New York: Penguin, 1988.

———. *White Noise.* New York: Penguin, 1985.

Dellinger, David. *From Yale to Jail: The Life Story of a Moral Dissenter.* New York: Pantheon, 1993.

Denton, Robert E., ed. *The 2004 Presidential Campaign: A Communication Perspective.* New York: Rowman & Littlefield, 2005.

Didion, Joan. *Slouching Towards Bethlehem.* New York: Farrar, Straus & Giroux, 1968.

———. *The White Album.* New York: Simon & Schuster, 1979.

Diem, Bui, with David Chanoff. *In the Jaws of History.* Boston: Houghton Mifflin, 1987.

DiGiacomo, Frank. "The *Esquire* Decade." *Vanity Fair,* Jan. 2007, www.vanityfair.com /culture/features/2007/01/esquire200701.

Douglass, Frederick. *Douglass: Autobiographies.* New York: Library of America, 1994.

Duiker, William J. *Sacred War: Nationalism and Revolution in a Divided Vietnam.* New York: McGraw-Hill, 1995.

Dupee, F. W. "The Uprising at Columbia" in *The New York Review of Books,* Sept. 26, 1968.

Eisele, Albert. *Almost to the Presidency: A Biography of Two American Politicians.* Blue Earth, Minn.: The Piper Company, 1972.

Eisenhower, Dwight D. *Mandate for Change, 1953–1956: The White House Years.* New York: Doubleday, 1963.

Eliot, T. S. *The Complete Poems and Plays, 1909–1950.* New York: Harcourt Brace Jovanovich, 1971.

Elliott, David W. P. *The Vietnamese War: Revolution and Social Change in the Mekong Delta, 1930–1975.* Concise Edition. New York: M. E. Sharpe, 2003 and 2007.

Ellsberg, Daniel. *Secrets: A Memoir of Vietnam and the Pentagon Papers.* New York: Viking, 2002.

Emerson, Ralph Waldo. *Essays and Lectures.* New York: Library of America, 1983.

Emery, Fred. *Watergate: The Corruption of American Politics and the Fall of Richard Nixon.* New York: Random House, 1994.

Fallows, James. "What Did You Do in the Class War, Daddy" (1975). In Cohen, *Vietnam: Anthology and Guide,* 381–85.

Farber, David. *Chicago '68.* Chicago: University of Chicago Press, 1988.

———, ed. *The Sixties: From Memory to History.* Chapel Hill: University of North Carolina Press, 1994.

Faulkner, William. *Absalom, Absalom!* (1936). In *Faulkner: Novels, 1936–1940,* 5–315. New York: Library of America, 1990.

———. *Collected Stories of William Faulkner.* New York: Random House, 1950.

Fitzgerald, Frances. *Fire in the Lake: The Vietnamese and the Americans in Vietnam.* New York: Random House, 1972.

Fitzgerald, F. Scott. *The Great Gatsby: The Authorized Text* (1925). New York: Scribner's, 1992.

The Fog of War: Eleven Lessons from the Life of Robert S. McNamara (film). Dir. Errol Morris. Sony Pictures Classics, 2003.

Fogelson, Robert M. *The Los Angeles Riots of 1965.* New York: Arno Press, 1969.

Forslund, Catherine. *Anna Chennault: Informal Diplomacy and Asian Relations.* Wilmington, Del.: Scholarly Resources Inc., 2002.

Franklin, H. Bruce. *Vietnam and Other American Fantasies.* Amherst: University of Massachusetts Press, 2000.

Freedman, Paul. "Swift Boats and Tax Hikes: Campaign Advertising in the 2004 Election." In *Divided States of America: The Slash and Burn Politics of the 2004 Presidential Election,* edited by Larry J. Sabato, 165–78. New York: Pearson Longman, 2006.

Fussell, Paul. *Wartime: Understanding and Behavior in the Second World War.* New York: Oxford, 1989.

Gaines, Ernest. *Bloodline.* New York: Random House, 1968.

Gardner, Lloyd C. *Pay Any Price: Lyndon Johnson and the Wars for Vietnam.* Chicago: Ivan R. Dee, 1995.

Garrow, David J. *Bearing the Cross: Martin Luther King, Jr. and the Southern Christian Leadership Conference.* New York: William Morrow, 1986.

Gellhorn, Martha. "Suffer the Little Children . . ." (1967). In *Reporting Vietnam: American Journalism 1959–1969, Volume One,* 281–97.

Gilbert, Ben W. *Ten Blocks from the White House: Anatomy of the Washington Riots of 1968.* New York: Praeger, 1968.

Gitlin, Todd. *The Sixties: Years of Hope, Days of Rage.* New York: Bantam, 1987.

Goldstein, Gordon M. *Lessons in Disaster: McGeorge Bundy and the Path to War in Vietnam.* New York: Henry Holt, 2008.

Goodwin, Doris Kearns. *Lyndon Johnson and the American Dream.* New York: St. Martin's Press, 1991.

———. *Team of Rivals: The Political Genius of Abraham Lincoln.* New York Simon & Schuster, 2005.

Goodwin, Richard. *Remembering America: A Voice from the Sixties.* Boston: Little, Brown, 1988.

———. "Talk of the Town" in *The New Yorker,* February 3, 1968.

Graff, Henry F. "Teach-In on Vietnam by . . . the President, the Secretary of State, the Secretary of Defense and the Under Secretary of State" (1966). In *Reporting Vietnam: American Journalism 1959–1969, Volume One,* 242–58.

The Green Berets (film). Dir. John Wayne and Ray Kellogg. Warner Brothers, 1968.

Greene, Graham. *The Quiet American.* (1955). New York: Penguin, 1977.

Griffiths, Philip Jones. *Vietnam Inc.* London: Phaidon, 1971.

Halberstam, David. *The Unfinished Odyssey of Robert F. Kennedy.* New York: Harcourt Brace Jovanovich, 1968.

Hagopian, Patrick. *The Vietnam War in American Memory: Veterans, Memorials, and the Politics of Healing.* Amherst: University of Massachusetts Press, 2009.

Haldeman, H. R. *The Ends of Power.* New York: Times Books, 1978.

———. *The Haldeman Diaries: Inside the Nixon White House.* New York: G. P. Putnam's Sons, 1994.

Hardwick, Elizabeth. "Chicago." *New York Review of Books,* 11, no. 5 (September 26, 1968): 5–7.

Harris, David. *Dreams Die Hard.* New York: St. Martin's, 1982.

———. *Our War: What We Did in Vietnam and What It Did to Us.* New York: Random House, 1996.

Harvey, Frank. *Air War—Vietnam.* New York: Bantam, 1967.

Hass, Robert. *Twentieth-Century Pleasures: Prose on Poetry.* New York: Ecco, 1984.

Hayden, Casey, and Mary King. "Sex and Caste" (1965). In *Personal Politics: The Roots of Women's Liberation in the Civil Rights Movement and the New Left,* edited by Sara Evans, 235–38. New York: Knopf, 1979.

Hayden, Tom. *Reunion: A Memoir.* New York: Random House, 1988.

Hayslip, Le Ly, with Jay Wurts. *When Heaven and Earth Changed Places.* New York: Penguin, 1989.

Hemingway, Ernest. *A Farewell to Arms.* New York: Scribner's, 1929.

———. *In Our Time.* New York: Scribner's, 1925 and 1930.

———. *A Moveable Feast.* New York: Scribner's, 1964.

Hendrickson, Paul. *The Living and the Dead: Robert McNamara and Five Lives of a Lost War.* New York: Knopf, 1996.

Herr, Michael. *Dispatches.* New York: Random House, 1977.

———. "Hells Sucks." *Esquire,* August 1968.

Herring, George C. *America's Longest War: The United States and Vietnam, 1950–1975.* New York: Wiley, 1979.

Hersey, John. *The Algiers Motel Incident.* New York: Knopf, 1968.

Hersh, Seymour. *Cover-Up: The Army's Secret Investigation of the Massacre at My Lai 4.* New York: Random House, 1972.

———. *My Lai 4: A Report on the Massacre and Its Aftermath*. New York: Random House, 1970.

———. *The Price of Power: Kissinger in the Nixon White House*. New York: Simon & Schuster, 1983.

Herzog, Arthur. *McCarthy for President*. New York: Viking, 1969.

Hitchins, Christopher. *The Trial of Henry Kissinger*. London: Verso, 2001.

Hoff, Joan. *Nixon Reconsidered*. New York: HarperCollins, 1994.

Hofstadter, Richard. "Columbia University Commencement Address" (1968). In Smith and Bender, *American Higher Education Transformed*, 383–86.

Hoganson, Kristin L. *Fighting for American Manhood: How Gender Politics Provoked The Spanish-American and Philippine-American Wars*. New Haven: Yale University Press, 1998.

Hollander, John, ed. *American Poetry: The Nineteenth Century*. 2 vols. New York: Library of America, 1993.

Hoopes, Townsend. *The Limits of Intervention*. New York: David McKay, 1969.

Horne, Gerald. *Fire This Time: The Watts Uprising and the 1960s*. Charlottesville: University of Virginia Press, 1995.

Hung, Nguyen Tien, and Jerrold L. Schecter. *The Palace File*. New York: Harper & Row, 1986.

Hunt, David. *Vietnam's Southern Revolution: From Peasant Insurrection to Total War*. Amherst: University of Massachusetts Press, 2008.

Interview with My Lai Veterans (film). Dir. Joseph Strick. Laser Films, 1970.

Isaacs, Arnold R. *Without Honor: Defeat in Vietnam and Cambodia*. Baltimore: Johns Hopkins University Press, 1983.

Isserman, Maurice, and Michael Kazin. *America Divided: The Civil War of the 1960s*. New York: Oxford University Press, 2000.

Jacobs, David, and Daniel Tope. "The Politics of Resentment in the Post-Civil Rights Era: Minority Threat, Homicide, and Ideological Voting in Congress." *American Journal of Sociology* 112, no. 5 (March 2007): 1458–94.

James, Henry. *The Art of the Novel*. Introduction by R. P. Blackmur. New York: Scribner's, 1934.

———. "Henry James's First Interview." *New York Times*, March 21, 1915.

———. *The Novels and Tales of Henry James*. Vol. 1. New York: Scribners, 1907.

"John Kerry Military Service Controversy." Wikipedia. http://en.wikipedia.org/wik1/John_Kerry_military_service_controversy. (accessed June 2, 2011).

Johnson, Lady Bird. *A White House Diary*. New York: Holt, Rinehart & Winston, 1970.

Johnson, Lyndon Baines. "The President's Address to the Nation." March 31, 1968. Reprinted in Cohen, *Vietnam: Anthology and Guide*, 215–19.

———. *The Vantage Point: Perspectives on the Presidency, 1963–1969*. New York: Holt, Rinehart & Winston, 1971.

Karnow, Stanley. *Vietnam: A History*. New York: Viking, 1983.

Keats, John. *Selected Letters of John Keats*. Ed. Grant F. Scott. Cambridge: Harvard University Press, 2002.

Kennedy, Robert F. *The Enemy Within: The McClellan Committee's Crusade against Jimmy Hoffa and Corrupt Labor Unions*. New York: HarperCollins, 1960.

———. "Remarks on the Assassination of Martin Luther King, Jr." www.americanrhetoric.com/speeches/rfk.

Kenski, Henry C., and Kate M. Kenski. "Explaining the Vote in a Divided Country: The Presidential Election of 2004." In Denton, *The 2004 Presidential Campaign: A Communication Perspective*, 301–42.

Kermode, Frank. *The Sense of an Ending: Studies in the Theory of Fiction.* New York: Oxford University Press, 1967.

Kerry, John. *The New Soldier.* New York: Macmillan, 1971.

———. "Vietnam Veterans Against the War Statement by John Kerry." April 23, 1971. In Cohen, *Vietnam: Anthology and Guide,* 366–72.

Kimball, Jeffrey. *Nixon's Vietnam War.* Lawrence: University Press of Kansas, 1998.

King, Martin Luther, Jr. *A Testament of Hope: The Essential Writings and Speeches of Martin Luther King, Jr.* Edited by James M. Washington. New York: HarperCollins, 1991.

Kissinger, Henry. *White House Years.* Boston: Little, Brown, 1979.

Klein, Joe. "The Long War of John Kerry." *New Yorker,* December, 2, 2002.

Koning, Hans. *Nineteen Sixty-Eight: A Personal Report.* New York: Norton, 1987.

Kopkind, Andrew. "The Thaw." *New York Review of Books,* April 25, 1968.

Kranish, Michael. "Veteran Retracts Criticism of Kerry." *Boston Globe,* August 6, 2004.

Kranish, Michael, Brian C. Mooney, and Nina J. Easton. *John F. Kerry: The Complete Biography by the* Boston Globe *Reporters Who Know Him Best.* New York: Perseus Books, 2004.

Kunen, James Simon. *The Strawberry Statement: Notes of a College Revolutionary.* New York: Random House, 1969.

Kusch, Frank. *Battleground Chicago: The Police and the 1968 Democratic Convention.* Westport, Conn.: Praeger, 2004.

Kutler, Stanley J. *The Wars of Watergate: The Last Crisis of Richard Nixon.* New York: Knopf, 1990.

Laderman, Scott. *Tours of Vietnam: War, Travel Guides, and Memory.* Durham: Duke University Press, 2009.

LaFree, Gary D. "Race and Crime Trends in the United States, 1946–1990." In *Ethnicity, Race, and Crime: Perspectives across Time and Place,* edited by Darnell F. Hawkins, 169–93. Albany: State University of New York Press, 1995.

Lane, Mark. *Chicago Eyewitness.* New York: Astor-Honor, 1968.

Lang, Daniel. *Casualties of War.* New York: McGraw-Hill, 1969.

Langguth, A. J. *Our Vietnam: The War, 1954–1975.* New York: Simon & Schuster, 2000.

Larner, Jeremy. *Nobody Knows: Reflections on the McCarthy Campaign of 1968.* New York: Macmillan, 1970.

Laurence, John. *The Cat from Hué.* New York: Perseus Books, 2002.

Lee, Chang-rae. *A Gesture Life.* New York: Penguin, 1999.

Lembcke, Jerry. *The Spitting Image: Myth, Memory, and the Legacy of Vietnam.* New York: NYU Press, 1998.

Lewis, John. *Walking with the Wind: A Memoir of the Movement.* New York: Simon & Schuster, 1998.

Lifton, Robert J. *Home from the War: Vietnam Veterans: Neither Victims nor Executioners.* New York: Simon & Schuster, 1973.

Lincoln, Abraham. *Lincoln: Speeches and Writings, 1832–1858.* New York: Library of America, 1989.

———. *Lincoln: Speeches and Writings, 1859–1865.* New York: Library of America, 1989.

Ling, Peter J. *Martin Luther King, Jr.* London: Routledge, 2002.

Long, Ngo Vinh. "The Tet Offensive and Its Aftermath." In *The Tet Offensive,* edited by Marc Jason Gilbert and William Head, 89–124. Westport, Conn.: Praeger, 1996.

Lowell, Robert. *Collected Poems.* New York: Farrar, Straus & Giroux, 2003.

————. *The Letters of Robert Lowell*. Ed. Saskia Hamilton. New York: Farrar, Straus & Giroux, 2005.

Lynd, Staughton, and Tom Hayden. *The Other Side*. Ithaca: Cornell University Press, 1969.

MacPherson, Myra. *Long Time Passing: Vietnam and the Haunted Generation*. Garden City, N.Y.: Doubleday, 1984.

Mailer, Norman. *The Armies of the Night: History as a Novel, the Novel as History*. New York: Viking, 1968.

————. "Life and Letters: In the Ring." *New Yorker,* October 6, 2008.

————. *Miami and the Siege of Chicago*. New York; Signet, 1968.

————. *Why Are We in Vietnam?* New York: Holt, Rinehart & Winston, 1967.

Malamud, Bernard. *The Natural*. New York: Farrar, Straus & Giroux, 1952.

Mann, Coramae Richey. *Unequal Justice: A Question of Color.* Bloomington: Indiana University Press, 1993.

Maraniss, David. *They Marched into Sunlight: War and Peace Vietnam and America, October 1967*. New York: Simon & Schuster, 2003.

McCain, John. "John McCain, Prisoner of War: A First-Person Account." *U.S. News & World Report,* May 14, 1973. Available at www.usnews.com/news/articles/2008/01/28/john-mccain-prisoner-of-war-a-first-person-account.

McCarthy, Abigail. *Private Faces/Public Places*. Garden City, N.Y.: Doubleday, 1972.

McCarthy, Eugene J. *Other Things and the Aardvark*. Rochester, Minn.: Lone Oak Press, 1997.

————. *Up 'Til Now: A Memoir*. New York: Harcourt Brace Jovanovich, 1987.

————. *The Year of the People*. Garden City, N.Y.: Doubleday, 1969.

McCaughey, Robert. *Stand, Columbia: A History of Columbia University in the City of New York, 1754–2004*. New York: Columbia University Press, 2003.

McKnight, Gerald D. *The Last Crusade: Martin Luther King, Jr., the FBI, and the PPC*. Boulder: Westview Press, 1998.

McMaster, H. R. *Dereliction of Duty: Lyndon Johnson, Robert McNamara, the Joint Chiefs of Staff, and the Lies That Led to Vietnam*. New York: HarperCollins, 1997.

McNamara, Robert S. *The Essence of Security: Reflections in Office*. New York: Harper & Row, 1968.

————. *In Retrospect: The Tragedy and Lessons of Vietnam*. New York: Random House, 1995.

McPherson, Harry. *A Political Education: A Washington Memoir.* Boston: Houghton Mifflin, 1988.

Meyrowitz, Elliot L., and Kenneth J. Campbell. "Vietnam Veterans and War Crimes Hearings." In *Give Peace a Chance: Exploring the Vietnam Antiwar Movement,* edited by Melvin Small and William D. Hoover, 129–40. Syracuse: Syracuse University Press, 1992.

Middlekauf, Robert. *The Glorious Cause: The American Revolution, 1763–1789*. New York: Oxford, 1982.

Miller, James D. *Democracy Is in the Streets: From Port Huron to the Siege of Chicago*. Cambridge: Harvard University Press, 1987.

Miller, Mark Crispin. *Fooled Again: How the Right Stole the 2004 Election and Why They'll Steal the Next One Too (Unless We Stop Them)*. New York: Basic Books, 2005.

Miller Center of Public Affairs. Presidential Recordings Program. millercenter.org/scripps/archive/presidentialrecordings.

Morgan, Edward P. *The 60s Experience: Hard Lessons about Modern America*. Philadelphia: Temple University Press, 1991.

Morris, Roger. *Richard Nixon: The Rise of an American Politician.* New York: Henry Holt, 1990.

Morrison, Toni. *What Moves at the Margins: Selected Nonfiction.* Ed. Carolyn C. Denard. Jackson: University of Mississippi Press, 2008.

Moser, Richard R. *The New Winter Soldiers: GI and Veteran Dissent during the Vietnam Era.* New Brunswick: Rutgers University Press, 1996.

Moyar, Mark. "Disastrous Lessons." *Foreign Policy* (online), October 19, 2009, www.foreignpolicy.com/node/64359.

Naison, Mark D. *White Boy: A Memoir.* Philadelphia: Temple University Press, 2002.

Newfield, Jack. *Robert Kennedy: A Memoir.* New York: Penguin, 1969.

Nicolaides, Becky M. *My Blue Heaven: Life and Politics in the Working-Class Suburbs of Los Angeles, 1920–1965.* Chicago: University of Chicago Press, 2002.

Nicosia, Gerald. *Home to War: A History of the Vietnam Veterans' Movement.* New York: Crown, 2001.

Nixon, Richard. "Address by the President on the Situation in Southeast Asia." April 30, 1970. In Cohen, *Vietnam: Anthology and Guide,* 280–85.

———. *RN: The Memoirs of Richard Nixon.* New York: Grosset & Dunlap, 1978.

Oates, Stephen B. *Let the Trumpet Sound: The Life of Martin Luther King, Jr.* New York: Harper & Row, 1982.

Obama, Barack. "Remarks by the President Commemorating Memorial Day." www.whitehouse.gov/the-press-office/2012/05/28/remarks-president-commemorating-memorial-day.

Oberdorfer, Don. *Tet!* New York: Doubleday & Company, 1971.

O'Brien, Tim. *In the Lake of the Woods.* New York: Penguin, 1994.

———. "The Mystery of My Lai." In *Facing My Lai: Moving beyond the Massacre,* edited by David L. Anderson, 171–78. Lawrence: University Press of Kansas, 1998.

———. *The Things They Carried.* Boston: Houghton Mifflin/Seymour Lawrence, 1990.

Oliver, Kendrick. *The My Lai Massacre in American History and Memory.* Manchester: Manchester University Press, 2006.

O'Neill, John E., and Jerome R. Corsi. *Unfit for Command: Swift Boat Veterans Speak Out against John Kerry.* Washington, D.C.: Regnery, 2004.

Owen, Wilfred. *The Collected Poems of Wilfred Owen.* New York: New Directions, 1963.

Palermo, Joseph A. *Robert F. Kennedy and the Death of American Idealism.* New York: Pearson Longman, 2007.

Parmet, Herbert S. *Richard M. Nixon: An American Enigma.* New York: Pearson Longman, 2008.

Path to War (film). Dir. John Frankenheimer. HBO Films, 2002.

Patterson, James T. *Grand Expectations: The United States, 1945–1974.* New York: Oxford, 1996.

Peers, William R. *The My Lai Inquiry.* New York: Norton, 1979.

Pham, Andrew. *The Eaves of Heaven: A Life in Three Wars.* New York: Random House, 2008.

Phillips, Kevin. *The Emerging Republican Majority.* New Rochelle, N.Y.: Arlington House, 1970.

Piercy, Marge. "The Grand Coolie Damn" (1969). In *Sisterhood Is Powerful: An Anthology of Writings from the Women's Liberation Movement,* edited by Robin Morgan, 421–38. New York: Random House, 1970.

Pike, Douglas. *Viet Cong: The Organization and Techniques of the National Liberation Front of South Vietnam.* Cambridge: MIT Press, 1966.

Polner, Murray. *No Victory Parades: The Return of the Vietnam Veteran.* New York: Holt, Rinehart & Winston, 1971.

Porter, D. Gareth. "The 1968 'Hue Massacre.'" *Indochina Chronicle*, no. 33 (June 24, 1974).
———. *Perils of Dominance: Imbalance of Power and the Road to War in Vietnam*. Berkeley: University of California Press, 2005.
Pound, Ezra. *The Pisan Cantos*. Ed. Richard Sieburth. New York: New Directions, 1948 and 2003.
Powers, Thomas. *The War at Home: Vietnam and the American People, 1964–1968*. New York: Grossman Publishers, 1973.
Prados, John. *Vietnam: The History of an Unwinnable War, 1945–1975*. Lawrence: University of Kansas Press, 2009.
Price, Raymond. *With Nixon*. New York: Viking, 1977.
Ranum, Orest. *Paris in the Age of Absolutism: An Essay*. New York: John Wiley & Sons, 1968.
Readings, Bill. *The University in Ruins*. Cambridge: Harvard University Press, 1996.
Report of the Chicago Riot Study Committee to the Honorable Richard J. Daley (1968).
Reporting Vietnam: American Journalism 1959–1969, Volume One. New York: Library of America, 1998.
Rights in Conflict: Convention Week in Chicago, August 25–29, 1968. Report submitted by Daniel Walker, director of the Chicago Study Team, to the National Commission on the Causes and Prevention of Violence. New York: E. P. Dutton, 1968.
Rodriguez, Richard. *Brown: The Last Discovery of America*. New York: Viking, 2002.
Rorty, Richard. *Achieving America: Leftist Thought in Twentieth-Century America*. Cambridge: Harvard University Press, 1998.
Rostow, W. W. *The Diffusion of Power*. New York: Macmillan, 1972.
Roth, Bennett. "An Old Kerry Foe, Houston Lawyer Back in Spotlight." *Houston Chronicle*, March 30, 2004, A1.
Rudd, Mark. "1968: Organizing vs. Activism." www.markrudd.com/?organizing-and -activism-now/1968-organizing-vs-activism.html.
———. *Underground: My Life with SDS and the Weathermen*. New York: William Morrow, 2009.
Rukeyser, Muriel. *The Life of Poetry*. New York: Current Books, 1949.
Rusk, Dean. *As I Saw It*. New York: Norton, 1990.
Safire, William. *Before the Fall: An Inside View of the Pre-Watergate White House*. New York: Doubleday, 1975.
"Saigon under Fire." Transcription of CBS News Special Report broadcast, January 31, 1968. In Cohen, *Vietnam: Anthology and Guide*, 205–8.
Salisbury, Harrison. *Behind the Lines—Hanoi: December 23, 1966–January 7, 1967*. New York: Harper & Row, 1967.
Sandbrook, Dominic. *Eugene McCarthy: The Rise and Fall of Postwar American Liberalism*. New York: Knopf, 2004.
Sayre, Nora. *Sixties Going on Seventies*. Rev. ed. New Brunswick, N.J.: Rutgers University Press, 1996.
Schandler, Herbert. *The Unmaking of a President: Lyndon Johnson and Vietnam*. Princeton: Princeton University Press, 1977.
Scheler, Max. *Ressentiment* (1912) Milwaukee: Marquette University Press, 1998.
Schell, Jonathan. *Observing the Nixon Years*. New York: Pantheon, 1989.
———. *The Real War: The Classic Reporting on the Vietnam War*. New York: Pantheon, 1987.
Schlesinger, Arthur M., Jr. *The Politics of Hope and The Bitter Heritage*. Princeton: Princeton University Press, 2008.

————. *Robert Kennedy and His Times.* Boston: Houghton Mifflin, 1978.

————. *A Thousand Days: John F. Kennedy in the White House.* Boston: Houghton Mifflin, 1965.

Schneir, Walter, ed. *Telling It Like It Was: The Chicago Riots.* New York: Signet, 1969.

Schroeder, E. J. *Vietnam: We've All Been There: Interviews with American Writers.* Westport, Conn.: Praeger, 1992.

Schultz, John. *No One Was Killed: Documentation and Meditation, Convention Week, Chicago, August 1968.* Chicago: Big Table Publishing Company, 1969.

Schulzinger, Robert D. *A Time for War: The United States and Vietnam, 1941–1975.* New York: Oxford, 1997.

Schwartzman, Paul, and Robert E. Pierre. "From Ruin to Rebirth in D.C." *Washington Post,* April 16, 2008.

Scott, Wilbur J. *The Politics of Readjustment: Vietnam Veterans Since the War.* Hawthorne, N.Y.: Aldine De Gruyter, 1993.

Shapley, Deborah. *Promise and Power: The Life and Times of Robert McNamara.* Boston: Little, Brown, 1993.

————. "Robert McNamara: Success and Failure." In *Leadership and Innovation: A Biographical Perspective on Entrepreneurship in Government,* edited by Jameson W. Doig and Erwin C. Hargrove, 246–69. Baltimore: Johns Hopkins University Press, 1987.

Shawcross, William. *Sideshow: Kissinger, Nixon, and the Destruction of Cambodia.* New York: Simon & Schuster, 1979.

Sheehan, Neil. *A Bright Shining Lie: John Paul Vann and America in Vietnam.* New York: Random House, 1988.

————. "Not a Dove, But No Longer a Hawk" (1966). In *Reporting Vietnam: American Journalism 1959–1969, Volume One,* 298–315.

Sheehan, Neil, Hedrick Smith, E. W. Kenworthy, and Fox Butterfield, eds. *The Pentagon Papers.* New York: Bantam, 1971.

Shelley, Percy Bysshe. *Shelley's Poetry and Prose.* Ed. Donald H. Reiman and Sharon B. Powers. New York: Norton, 1977.

Shirley, Craig. *Rendezvous with Destiny: Ronald Reagan and the Campaign That Changed America.* Wilmington, Del.: ISI Books, 2009.

Small, Melvin. *Antiwarriors: The Vietnam War and the Battle for America's Hearts and Minds.* Wilmington, Del.: S R Books, 2002.

————. *Covering Dissent: The Media and the Anti-Vietnam War Movement.* New Brunswick: Rutgers University Press, 1994.

————. *The Presidency of Richard Nixon.* Lawrence: University Press of Kansas, 1999.

Smith, Anna Deavere. *Twilight: Los Angeles, 1992.* New York: Doubleday, 1994.

Smith, Craig Allen, and Kathy B. Smith. *The White House Speaks: Presidential Leadership as Persuasion.* Westport, Conn.: Praeger, 1994.

Smith, Wilson, and Thomas Bender, eds. *American Higher Education Transformed, 1940–2005.* Baltimore: Johns Hopkins University Press, 2005.

Snow, C. P. *The Masters.* New York: Doubleday/Anchor, 1951.

Solberg, Carl. *Hubert Humphrey: A Biography.* New York: Norton, 1964.

Sorensen, Ted. *Counselor: A Life at the Edge of History.* New York: HarperCollins, 2008.

Stacewitz, Richard. *Winter Soldiers: An Oral History of the Vietnam Veterans Against the War.* New York: Twayne, 1997.

Stavis, Ben. *We Were the Campaign: New Hampshire to Chicago for McCarthy.* Boston: Beacon Press, 1969.

Stein, David Lewis. *Living the Revolution: The Yippies in Chicago.* Indianapolis: Bobbs-Merrill, 1969.

Stern, Susan. *With the Weathermen: The Personal Journal of a Revolutionary Woman.* New Brunswick: Rutgers University Press, 1975 and 2007.

Stevens, Wallace. *The Palm at the End of the Mind.* New York: Random House, 1972.

Styron, William. "In the Jungle." *New York Review of Books* 11, no. 5 (September 26, 1968): 11–13.

Summers. Anthony. *The Arrogance of Power: The Secret World of Richard Nixon.* New York: Viking, 2000.

Suri, Jeremi. *Power and Protest: Global Revolution and the Rise of Détente.* Cambridge: Harvard University Press, 2003.

Taft, John. *Mayday at Yale: A Case Study in Student Radicalism.* Boulder, Colo.: Westview Press, 1976.

Talbot, David. *Brothers: The Hidden History of the Kennedy Years.* New York: Free Press, 2007.

Taylor, Jared. *Paved with Good Intentions: The Failure of Race Relations in Contemporary America.* New York: Carroll & Graf Publishers, 1992.

Thoreau, Henry David. *Thoreau: A Week, Walden, Maine Woods, Cape Cod.* New York: Library of America, 1985.

Trilling, Diana. *We Must March My Darlings.* New York: Harcourt Brace Jovanovich, 1977.

Truong, Nhu Tang, with David Chanoff and Doan Van Toai. *A Viet Cong Memoir: An Inside Account of the Vietnam War and Its Aftermath.* New York: Random House, 1985.

Turse, Nick. *Kill Anything That Moves: The Real American War in Vietnam.* New York: Henry Holt, 2013.

Vanden Heuvel, William, and Milton Gwirtzman. *On His Own: Robert F. Kennedy, 1964–1968.* New York: Doubleday, 1970.

Varon, Jeremy. *Bringing the War Home: The Weather Underground, the Red Army Faction, and Revolutionary Violence in the Sixties and Seventies.* Berkeley: University of California Press, 2004.

von Bothmer, Bernard. *Framing the Sixties: The Use and Abuse of a Decade from Ronald Reagan to George W. Bush.* Amherst: University of Massachusetts Press, 2010.

Walker, Samuel, Cassia Spohn, and Miriam DeLone. *The Color of Justice: Race, Ethnicity, and Crime in America.* Belmont, Calif.: Wadsworth, 2000.

Weiss, Stephen, et al., eds. *The Vietnam Experience: A War Remembered.* Boston: Boston Publishing Company, 1986.

Wells, Tom. *The War Within: America's Battle over Vietnam.* Berkeley: University of California Press, 1994.

Welty, Eudora. *Stories, Essays, & Memoir.* New York: Library of America, 1998.

Westmoreland, William C. *A Soldier Reports.* Garden City, N.Y.: Doubleday, 1976.

White, Hayden. *Tropics of Discourse: Essays in Cultural Criticism.* Baltimore: Johns Hopkins University Press, 1978.

White House Tapes. Miller Center of Public Affairs, University of Virginia. http://millercenter.org/scripps/archive/presidentialrecordings/help.

Wicker, Tom. "Nixon Starts Over—Alone." *New York Times Magazine,* May 13, 1962.

Williams, Andrew Paul. "The Main Frame: Assessing the Role of the Internet in the

2004 U.S. Presidential Contest." In Denton, *The 2004 Presidential Campaign: A Communication Perspective,* 241–54.

Wills, Garry. *The Kennedy Imprisonment: A Meditation on Power.* Boston: Little, Brown, 1982.

———. *Nixon Agonistes: The Crisis of the Self-Made Man.* Boston: Houghton Mifflin, 1970.

Wilson, Edmund. *The Boys in the Backroom: Notes on California Novelists.* San Francisco: The Colt Press, 1941.

Witcover, Jules. *85 Days: The Last Campaign of Robert F. Kennedy.* New York: William Morrow, 1969.

———. *The Resurrection of Richard Nixon.* New York: G. P. Putnam's Sons, 1970.

———. *The Year the Dream Died: Revisiting 1968 in America.* New York: Warner Books: 1997.

Wofford, Harris. *Of Kennedys and Kings: Making Sense of the Sixties.* New York: Farrar, Straus & Giroux, 1980.

Wolfe, Tom. "The Truest Sport: Jousting with Sam and Charlie" (1975). In *Reporting Vietnam: American Journalism, 1959–1969, Volume One,* 525–56.

Wolff, Tobias. *In Pharaoh's Army: Memories of the Lost War.* New York: Random House, 1994.

Woodward, Bob, and Carl Bernstein. *The Final Days.* New York: Simon & Schuster, 1976.

Wyatt, David. *And the War Came: An Accidental Memoir.* Madison: University of Wisconsin Press, 2004.

Young, Andrew. *An Easy Burden: The Civil Rights Movement and the Transformation of America.* New York: HarperCollins, 1996.

Zaroulis, Nancy, and Gerald Sullivan. *Who Spoke Up? American Protest against the War in Vietnam, 1963–1975.* New York: Doubleday, 1984.

Zumwalt, Elmo. *On Watch: A Memoir.* New York: Quadrangle, 1976.

Index

DAVID WYATT was born in Lynwood, California, in 1948. He received a BA from Yale University in 1970 and a PhD from UC Berkeley in 1975. He is the author of two books on his native state, *The Fall into Eden* and *Five Fires,* and of a memoir about living through the fall of 2001 called *And the War Came.* In 2010 he published *Secret Histories: Reading Twentieth-Century American Literature.* He has taught at the University of Virginia and at Princeton University and is a member of the Department of English at the University of Maryland, where he is a Distinguished Scholar-Teacher. The father of three children, Luke, Courtenay, and Ian, he lives with his wife, Ann Porotti, in Charlottesville.